So Great Salvation

Sermon Outlines Given to His Men in Prison

by Bill Pierce

Go Soulwinning Ministries

All scripture quotations are taken from the *King James Version* (KJV) of the Holy Bible, unless otherwise indicated within the text.

All definitions of words mentioned to be defined in the texts of this book are explained from the *Noah Webster's First Edition of an American Dictionary of the English Language*, unless otherwise indicated within the text. Publisher information: Webster, Noah, and Rosalie J. Slater. *Noah Webster's First Edition of an American Dictionary of the English Language 1828.* San Francisco, California: Foundation for American Christian Education, 1995. Sixteenth Printing, 2004. C.J. Krehbiel Company, Cincinnati, Ohio, USA.

SO GREAT SALVATION
Sermon Outlines Given to His Men in Prison

Special thanks to Thomas C. Metcalf for designing the front cover.

ISBN-13: 9780615796925
ISBN-10: 0615796923
Printed in the United States of America

www.GoSoulwinning.com
www.GoSoulwinningPublishing.com

Contents

Dedication

This collection of Sermon Outlines for Bible Study is dedicated to "**the great God and our Saviour Jesus Christ**" (Titus 2:13), who, by his grace and mercy has saved a pitiful wretch like me, who is also "**not willing that any should perish, but that all should come to repentance**" (2 Peter 3:9).

I am grateful for the Father who "**so loved the world that he gave his only begotten Son**" (John 3:16); and to the Son, "**Who gave himself for us, that he might redeem us from all iniquity, and purify unto himself a peculiar people, zealous of good works**" (Titus 2:14); and for the Holy Ghost, who reproved me of my sin of unbelief (John 16:7-9), glorified the Saviour to my heart (John 16:14), abides with me for ever (John 14:16), sealed me unto the day of redemption (Ephesians 1:13), and who will raise me up together one day soon to ever be with the Lord (Romans 8:11; 1 Thessalonians 4:16-18).

I am grateful and amazed that the Lord has allowed me to preach "**the glorious gospel of Christ, who is the image of God**" (2 Corinthians 4:4), "**how that Christ died for our sins according to the scriptures; And that he was buried, and that he rose again the third day according to the scriptures**" (1 Corinthians 15:3-4) to so many men in prison over the past twenty-five years. "**Thanks *be* unto God for his unspeakable gift**" (2 Corinthians 9:15)!

I hope that you will not "**neglect so great salvation; which at the first began to be spoken by the Lord, and was confirmed unto us by them that heard *him***" (Hebrews 2:3), and that you will join me in the near future with the great cloud of redeemed sinners in heaven to worship and praise "**him who alone doeth great wonders**" (Psalm 136:4), "**Saying with a loud voice, Worthy is the Lamb that was slain to receive power, and riches, and wisdom, and strength, and honour, and glory, and blessing**" (Revelation 5:12).

Dedication

FORWARD

During our earthly journey we will come across only a few men who truly exemplify the word "Christian." Bill Pierce is one of those men. Like me, the first time you meet Bill you will sense the presence of the Holy Spirit. Then after getting to know him and wittiness his walk, you will see firsthand his strength in the Lord yet find a honest, kind, gentle, loving, compassionate man all displayed with a demeanor of humility.

As Proverbs 27:2 states, "*Let another man praise thee, and not thine own mouth; a stranger, and not thine own lips.*" I have never found Bill to be braggadocios or prideful in the good work God has allowed him to do. And he has had a very successful ministry as a volunteer Chaplin at the R.J. Donavan Prison for 25 years now. At the prison, God allowed him access into the reception center where 10,000 inmates were processed yearly. Thus far, over 9,000 inmates have received Christ as their Savior, 4,000 have been baptized, and he has helped disciple thousands of men by himself by personally sitting down with them or putting his Bible studies in their hands.

Bill is the last one to sing his own praises for he is well aware of the frail state of his humanity. All this is evidence of a man who has spent numerous hours in the Word of God and prayer communing with our Lord. He has been involved in preparing men and women for the Gospel Ministry as an instructor at the Lighthouse Bible Institute in Lemon Grove, California since 1988. His personal example and teaching have inspired many to a closer walk with the Lord Jesus Christ. Bill has consistently displayed this "Christ-like" spirit through the many years I have known him. There can be no greater compliment than that. After you have met Jesus, you need to meet Bill Pierce. Any Christ follower will be blessed and encouraged by using Bill's Bible Study Outlines in their quest to be "approved unto God." First Corinthians 4:2 says, "*Moreover it is required in stewards, that a man be found faithful.*"

Dr. Doug Jordan
Associate Pastor
Lighthouse Baptist Church, Lemon Grove, California

Introduction

Bill Pierce for several decades has faithfully devoted his service to the prison ministry. Bill has been serving the men at the R.J. Donovan Men's Correctional Facility quite longer than I have, however, for the past twenty-one years it has been my privilege to serve with him in this ministry.

This book contains just some of the hundreds of sermon outlines written by Bill over the many years. These outlines are written to contribute as Bible studies in the nurture and admonition of the Lord, and generously have been distributed primarily to inmates at the Donovan State Prison in southern California. Then over the years another opportunity arose for further distribution of the sermon outlines. As inmates have been transferred to other prisons, many have requested to be on Bill's mailing list to continue receiving them. What's more exciting is that these men then have sent the sermon outlines to their homes for their loved ones to study God's Word as well. Additionally, this then created a desire for more people requesting Bill to mail subsequent sermon outlines to them. Over the years he has done this with joy and thanksgiving to God.

The reason these sermon outlines came into being was that Bill desired for the inmates whom he serves to be given biblical literature which puts forth sound teaching from the Word of God. "*The entrance of thy words giveth light…*" (Psalm 119:130). I personally have witnessed that many men have been and continue to be greatly blessed as they study these sermon outlines. Many have come to know the Lord Jesus Christ as their Savior and have been given the opportunity for a fresh start on life. These sermon outlines over the years have encouraged the downtrodden, challenged the scornful to rethink and study their beliefs, and guided all to seek the Kingdom of God and believe on the Lord Jesus Christ.

I too have been greatly blessed by these sermon outlines, and I am confident others who have a desire and hunger for the Word of God will find this book to be a great asset to their studies. Bill has worked diligently in preparing his sermon outlines. Christians need to be rooted in God's truth (Colossians 2:7), which will enable us to combat the many false teachings that arise. I therefore urge God's people to read this book, study the subjects, and then share it with others.

Gerald Maynard
Fellow servant in Christ

Chapter 1

THE DOCTRINE OF CHRIST

We begin our studies with my favorite topic and the utmost important theme written and expounded about in God's holy word: the doctrine of Jesus Christ. Our scriptural texts that we shall base this sermon outline for are 2 John 1:9 and 1 John 2:23. As follows: Second John 1:9 says, "Whosoever transgresseth, and abideth not in <u>the doctrine of Christ</u>, hath not God. He that abideth in <u>the doctrine of Christ</u>, he hath both the Father and the Son." As well 1 John 2:23 tells us, "Whosoever denieth the Son, the same hath not the Father: *(but) he that acknowledgeth the Son hath the Father also*"

The Bible is, "**the record that God gave of his Son**," and clearly states that, "**he that believeth not God hath made him a liar**" (1 John 5:10). Do not let any man come along and deceive you with any thing that contradicts the Holy Bible (Colossians 2:8). The Apostle Peter says such men are unlearned and unstable, and that they wrest [twist, distort, pervert] the scriptures, "...**UNTO THEIR OWN DESTRUCTION**" (2 Peter 3:16)! God has written the Bible (2 Peter 1:21) in such a way that a man who is seeking only to rebel against the clear teachings of God will only end up condemning himself (Isaiah 28:9-13). The heretic who will not be corrected or admonished, "**is subverted, and sinneth, <u>being condemned of himself</u>**" (Titus 3:10-11)! Such a man has believed a lie told by another man. The LORD said this man is cursed (Jeremiah 17:5)!

In this sermon, we are going to do a little searching and comparing of scripture concerning *The Doctrine of Christ*. Proverbs 25:2 says, "It is the glory of God to conceal a thing: but the honour of kings is to search out a matter."

If you do not believe what the Bible says about Jesus Christ, then you do not abide [rest and trust] in the doctrine of Christ, and you are believing a lie. You are also calling God a liar (Romans 3:3-4): in short, you are an unbeliever. To such I would encourage you to read and meditate on Revelation 21:8.

Proverbs 21:30 says, "There is no wisdom nor understanding nor counsel against the LORD."

I. THE SON OF GOD BEFORE HIS BIRTH

A. HE CREATED ALL THINGS

Genesis 1:1 says, "In the beginning God created the heaven and the earth."

In the gospel of John we are given "Word" as another name for Jesus Christ, and in the very first verse of that gospel we discover that, "**the Word was God. The same was in the beginning with God. All things were made by him; and without him was not any thing made that was made**" (John 1:1-3). This glorious truth is repeated in more detail by the Apostle Paul in Colossians and by John again in the book of Revelation:

Colossians 1:16-17 says, "For by him [the Son of God (Colossians 1:13)] were all things created, that are in heaven, and that are in earth, visible and invisible, whether they be thrones, or dominions, or principalities, or powers: all things were created by him, and for him: And he is before all things, and by him [the Son of God] all things consist."

Revelation 4:11 says, "Thou art worthy, O Lord, to receive glory and honour and power: for thou hast created all things, and for thy pleasure they are and were created."

B. HE IS ETERNAL

Micah 5:2 speaks of Christ and the verse says, "But thou, Bethlehem Ephratah, though thou be little among the thousands of Judah, yet out of thee shall he come forth unto me that is to be ruler in Israel; whose goings forth have been from of old, from everlasting."

C. HE IS GOD

Psalm 90:2 says, "Before the mountains were brought forth, or ever thou hadst formed the earth and the world, even from everlasting to everlasting, thou art God."

Hebrews 3:3-4 says, "For this man [Jesus Christ] was counted worthy of more glory than Moses, inasmuch as he who hath builded the house hath more honour than the house. For every house is builded by some man; but he that built all things [Jesus Christ] is God."

The Lord Jesus Christ is not another God, but "**God himself that formed the earth and made it**" (Isaiah 45:18).

D. HE IS THE SAVIOUR BEFORE THE CREATION

First Peter 1:20 says, "Who verily was foreordained before the foundation of the world, but was manifest in these last times for you."

Second Timothy 1:9 says, "Who hath saved us, and called us with an holy calling, not according to our works, but according to his own purpose and grace, which was given us in Christ Jesus before the world began."

E. HE APPEARED TO MEN

Abram: Genesis 17:1 says, "And when Abram was ninety years old and nine, **the LORD appeared to Abram**, and said unto him, I am the Almighty God; walk before me, and be thou perfect."

Isaac: Genesis 26:2 says, "**And the LORD appeared unto him**, and said, Go not down into Egypt; dwell in the land which I shall tell thee of."

Jacob: Genesis 32:30 says, "And Jacob called the name of the place Peniel: **for I have seen God face to face**, and my life is preserved."

Moses: Exodus 33:11 says, "**And the LORD spake unto Moses face to face**, as a man speaketh unto his friend…"

Moses and the seventy elders of Israel: Exodus 24:9-11 says, "Then went up Moses, and Aaron, Nadab, and Abihu, and seventy of the elders of Israel: **And they saw the God of Israel**: and there was under his feet as it were a paved work of a sapphire stone, and as it were the body of heaven in his clearness. And upon the nobles of the children of Israel he laid not his hand: **also they saw God**, and did eat and drink."

Gideon: Judges 6:12-17 says, "And **the angel of the LORD appeared unto him**, and said unto him, The LORD *is* with thee, thou mighty man of valour. And Gideon said unto him, Oh my Lord, if the LORD be with us, why then is all this befallen us? and where *be* all his miracles which our fathers told us of, saying, Did not the LORD bring us up from Egypt? but now the LORD hath forsaken us, and delivered us into the hands of the Midianites. And **the LORD looked upon him, and said**, Go in this thy might, and thou shalt save Israel from the hand of the Midianites: have not I sent thee? **And he said unto him**, Oh my Lord, wherewith shall I save Israel? behold, my family *is* poor in Manasseh, and I *am* the least in my father's house. **And the LORD said unto him**, Surely I will be with thee, and thou shalt smite the Midianites as one man."

Micaiah: 1 Kings 22:19 says, "And he said, Hear thou therefore the word of the LORD: **I saw the LORD sitting on his throne**, and all the host of heaven standing by him on his right hand and on his left."

Isaiah: Isaiah 6:1,5 say, "In the year that king Uzziah died **I saw also the Lord sitting upon a throne**, high and lifted up, and his train filled the temple... Then said I, Woe is me! for I am undone; because I am a man of unclean lips, and I dwell in the midst of a people of unclean lips: **for mine eyes have seen the King, the LORD of hosts**."

Ezekiel: Ezekiel 1:26 says, "And above the firmament that was over their heads was the likeness of a throne, as the appearance of a sapphire stone: and upon the likeness of the throne was **the likeness as the appearance of a man above upon it**."

Amos: Amos 9:1 says, "**I saw the Lord standing upon the altar**: and he said, Smite the lintel of the door, that the posts may shake: and cut them in the head, all of them; and I will slay the last of them with the sword: he that fleeth of them shall not flee away, and he that escapeth of them shall not be delivered."

You may well ask about John 1:18 which says, "**No man hath seen God at any time; the only begotten Son, which is in the bosom of the Father, he hath declared him**." Also see 1 John 4:12. This is an example of how the

UNBELIEVER will deceive himself, because he refuses to study all of the Bible. Remember, the Bible always interprets the Bible. The biblical interpretation is that John 1:18 is plainly a reference to God the <u>Father</u>, who "**is a Spirit**" (John 4:24), and who is "**invisible**" (Colossians 1:15); for Jesus Christ said in John 6:46, "**Not that any man hath seen <u>the Father</u>, save he which is of God, he hath seen the Father**."

Therefore these accounts of men seeing God in the Old Testament are clearly a reference to the Son of God, for he is "**the image of the invisible God**" (Colossians 1:15). God records for us the declaration of king Nebuchadnezzar when he looked into the burning fiery furnace after throwing the three Hebrew children into it:

"**He answered and said, Lo, I see four men loose, walking in the midst of the fire, and they have no hurt; and the form of <u>the fourth is like the Son of God</u>**" (Daniel 3:25).

II. THE SON OF GOD AFTER HIS BIRTH

A. HIS VIRGIN BIRTH

1. Prophesies given:

Isaiah 7:14 says, "Therefore the Lord himself shall give you a sign; Behold, a virgin shall conceive, and bear a son, and shall call his name Immanuel [which means, 'God with us' (Matthew 1:23)]."

Jeremiah 31:22 says, "How long wilt thou go about, O thou backsliding daughter? for the LORD hath created a new thing in the earth, A woman shall compass a man [a woman shall conceive by the Holy Ghost]."

Isaiah 9:6 says, "For unto us a child is born [made of a woman], unto us a son is given [the eternal Son of God] and the government shall be upon his shoulder: and his name shall be called Wonderful, Counsellor, The mighty God, The everlasting Father, The Prince of Peace."

2. Prophecy fulfilled:

Luke 2:11 says, "For unto you is born this day in the city of David a Saviour, which is Christ the Lord."

First Timothy 3:16 says, "And without controversy great is the mystery of godliness: God was manifest in the flesh, justified in the Spirit, seen of angels, preached unto the Gentiles, believed on in the world, received up into glory."

B. THE SAVIOUR OF THE WORLD

First John 4:14 tell us that "[the] Father sent the Son to be THE SAVIOUR OF THE WORLD."

Hebrews 7:26 says, "For such an high priest became us, who is holy, harmless, undefiled, separate from sinners, and MADE HIGHER THAN THE HEAVENS."

C. THE SON CAME AS AN HUMBLE SERVANT

Philippians 2:6-8 says, "Who, being in the form of God, thought it not robbery to be EQUAL WITH GOD: But made himself of no reputation, and took upon him the form of a servant, and was made in the likeness of men: And being found in fashion as a man, he humbled himself, and became obedient unto death, even the death of the cross."

Hebrews 2:9 says, "But we see Jesus, who was MADE A LITTLE LOWER THAN THE ANGELS FOR THE SUFFERING OF DEATH, crowned with glory and honour; that he by the grace of God should taste death for every man."

Jesus had to suffer as the "Lamb of God" before he entered BACK into his glory (compare Genesis 22:8 with John 1:29).

John 17:5 depicts Jesus' prayer to God the Father, saying, "And now, O Father, glorify thou me with thine own self with the glory which I had with thee before the world was."

Luke 24:26 says, "Ought not Christ to have suffered these things, and to enter into his glory?" See also John 7:37-39 and Isaiah 53:2.

D. HE MADE HIMSELF EQUAL WITH GOD

John 5:18 says, "Therefore the Jews sought the more to kill him, because he not only had broken the sabbath, but said also that God was his Father, making himself equal with God." SEE ALSO John 10:29-33 and 1 John 5:7.

Through envy and pride Lucifer wanted to be equal with God. He is the king over all the children of pride (Job 41:34). These are men who will not submit themselves to God and who are going to hell with Lucifer, unless they repent of their unbelief and their rejection of Jesus Christ. Lucifer said in his heart, "...I will ascend into heaven, I will exalt my throne above the stars of God: I will sit also upon the mount of the congregation, in the sides of the north: I will ascend above the heights of the clouds; **I will be like the most High. Yet thou shalt be brought down to hell, to the sides of the pit**" (Isaiah 14:13-15).

E. JESUS CHRIST IS THE ETERNAL "I AM"

Some unbelievers attempt to subvert and overthrow the word of God by saying that Jesus himself never said, "I am God." Therefore, they say, Jesus was not God. How ignorant and foolish! Although the Lord Jesus used different words, he did indeed claim to be God! God revealed his name, "I AM" to Moses:

"And God said unto Moses, I AM THAT I AM: and he said, Thus shalt thou say unto the children of Israel, I AM hath sent me unto you" (Exodus 3:14).

The Lord Jesus Christ "**said unto them** [the Jews], **Verily, verily, I say unto you, Before Abraham was, I am**" (John 8:58). Jesus identified himself, "I am," as the God that spoke to Moses out of the burning bush!

Again Jesus said that anyone who saw him had also seen the Father, such as in John 14:7-9: **"If ye had known me, ye should have known my Father also: and from henceforth ye know him, and have seen him.** Philip saith unto him, Lord, show us the Father, and it sufficeth us. Jesus saith unto him, Have I been so long time with you, and yet hast thou not known me, Philip? **he that hath seen me hath seen the Father;** and how sayest thou then, Show us the Father?"

F. HE WAS GLORIFIED BEFORE PETER, JAMES, AND JOHN

Matthew 17:1-2 says, "And after six days Jesus taketh Peter, James, and John his brother, and bringeth them up into an high mountain apart, And was transfigured before them: and his face did shine as the sun, and his raiment was white as the light."

G. "WHOSE SON IS HE?"

JESUS was called "the son of David" by blind men (Matthew 9:27; 20:30), a Canaanite woman (Matthew 15:22), and by the people (Matthew 12:23; 21:9,

15). Matthew 22:41-46 says, "**While** the Pharisees were gathered together, Jesus asked them, Saying, **What think ye of Christ? whose son is he?** They say unto him, The son of David. He saith unto them, How then doth David in spirit call him Lord, saying, The LORD said unto my Lord, Sit thou on my right hand, till I make thine enemies thy footstool? **If David then call him Lord, how is he his son?** And no man was able to answer him a word, neither durst any man from that day forth ask him any more questions."

THE EXPLANATION

Jesus is called "**her seed**" in Genesis 3:15. This is a reference to Mary who gave birth to the only begotten Son of God without "**knowing**" a man (Luke 1:34-35). Mary's virgin born Son was conceived by the Holy Ghost (Matthew 1:20). Mary is a direct descendent of Abraham and David (Luke 3:23-38).

Hebrews 2:16-17 says, "For verily he took not on him the nature of angels; but **he took on him the seed of Abraham.** Wherefore in all things it behoved him to be made like unto his brethren, that he might be a merciful and faithful high priest in things pertaining to God, to make reconciliation for the sins of the people."

Jesus Christ was "made of a woman" (Galatians 4:4):

Romans 1:3-4 says, "Concerning his Son Jesus Christ our Lord, which was made of the seed of David according to the flesh; And declared to be the Son of God with power, according to the spirit of holiness, by the resurrection from the dead." SEE ALSO Romans 8:3; John 1:1, 14; 1 Corinthians 15:47.

III. THE SON AFTER HIS RESURRECTION

A. THE FATHER HAS GLORIFIED THE SON

God clearly said in Isaiah 42:8, "I am the LORD: that is my name: and **my glory will I not give to another**, neither my praise to graven images." God also promised in Ezekiel 39:21: "And I will set my glory among the heathen, and all the heathen shall see my judgment that I have executed, and my hand that I have laid upon them."

Philippians 2:9-11 says, "**Wherefore God also hath highly exalted him, and given him a name which is above every name**…"

Hebrews 1:8 says, "**But unto the Son he** [God the Father] **saith, Thy throne, O God**, is for ever and ever: a sceptre of righteousness is the sceptre of thy kingdom."

Jesus Christ is the KING OF KINGS because Psalm 95:3 informs us that "**For the LORD is a great God, and a great King above all gods**." In addition, Psalm 83:17-18 says, "...**JEHOVAH, art the most high over all the earth**." I encourage you also to see Jeremiah 10:10. Revelation 19:16 says, "**And he** [the Lord Jesus Christ] **hath on his vesture and on his thigh a name written, KING OF KINGS, AND LORD OF LORDS**."

Matthew 19:28 says, "And Jesus said unto them, Verily I say unto you, That ye which have followed me, in the regeneration when **the Son of man shall sit in the throne of his glory**, ye also shall sit upon twelve thrones, judging the twelve tribes of Israel." SEE ALSO Matthew 16:27; James 2:1; Hebrews 1:3; 1 Pet. 4:11; Matthew 28:18; Daniel 7:13-14.

B. THOMAS CALLED HIM GOD

John 20:28-29 says, "And Thomas answered and said unto him, **My Lord and my God**. Jesus saith unto him, Thomas, because thou hast seen me, thou hast believed: blessed are they that have not seen, and yet have believed." See also John 1:1; 1 Timothy 3:16.

C. THE HOLY GHOST GLORIFIES HIM

John 16:14 says, "**He** [the Spirit of truth (John 16:13)] **shall glorify me**: for he shall receive of mine, and shall show it unto you."

D. THE KNOWLEDGE OF GOD'S GLORY IS IN HIS FACE

Second Corinthians 4:6 says, "For God, who commanded the light to shine out of darkness, hath shined in our hearts, to give **the light of the knowledge of the glory of God in the face of Jesus Christ**."

E. JOHN SAW HIM ON PATMOS

John wrote in Revelation 1:12-18, saying, "And I turned to see the voice that spake with me. And being turned, I saw seven golden candlesticks; And in the midst of the seven candlesticks *one* like unto the Son of man, clothed with a garment down to the foot, and girt about the paps with a golden girdle. His head and *his* hairs *were* white like wool, as white as snow; and his eyes *were* as a flame of fire; And his feet like unto fine brass, as if they burned in a furnace; and his voice as the sound of many waters. And he had in his right hand seven stars: and out of his mouth went a sharp twoedged sword: and his countenance *was* as the sun shineth in his strength. And when I saw him, I fell at his feet as dead. And he laid his right hand upon me, saying unto me, Fear not; I am the first and the last: I *am* he that liveth, and was dead; and, behold, I am alive for evermore, Amen; and have the keys of hell and of death."

CONCLUSION

The Bible clearly and undeniably declares the Lord Jesus Christ to be "**the express image of his** [God's] **person**" (Hebrews 1:3), and that he is indeed God manifest in the flesh (1 Timothy 3:16). The redeemed in heaven will praise the Lord Jesus Christ saying, "Great and marvellous are thy works, **Lord God Almighty**; just and true are thy ways, thou King of saints. **Who shall not fear thee, O Lord, and glorify thy name? for thou only art holy**: for all nations shall come and worship before thee; for thy judgments are made manifest" (Revelation 15:3-4).

If you will be saved, you must believe the doctrine of Jesus Christ, otherwise the Bible calls you "a deceiver and an antichrist" (2 John 1:7-11) who will die in your sins (John 8:21, 24). There is no salvation outside of Jesus Christ. His name is above all other names. Acts 4:12 tell us, "Neither is there salvation in any other: for there is none other name under heaven given among men, whereby we must be saved."

If you find that you do not believe the doctrine of Christ, then you are an "unbeliever" who will, unless you repent of your unbelief, be cast into the lake of fire at the "great white throne" judgment (Revelation 20:11-15)! If I were you, I would ask God to give me repentance to acknowledge the truth of the gospel (2 Timothy 2:24-26)! I would ask God to take away any ill-conceived challenges against the word of God that I might have believed, and replace this deception by faith in his holy word, that I might believe the gospel. The gospel is "[H]ow that Christ died for our sins according to the scriptures; And that he was buried, and that he rose again the third day according to the scriptures" (1 Corinthians 15:3-4).

This gospel is, "[**the**] **power of God unto salvation to EVERY ONE THAT BELIEVETH**" (Romans 1:16). If I were an unbeliever, I would get a

New Testament and read the gospel of John, for John's gospel was written for the purpose of giving the unbeliever faith (John 20:30-31).

Second John 1:9 says, "Whosoever **transgresseth, and abideth not in the doctrine of Christ, hath not God**. He that abideth in the doctrine of Christ, he hath both the Father and the Son. First John 5:12 says, "He that hath the Son hath life; and **he that hath not the Son of God hath not life**."

We have studied, "*The Doctrine of Christ*" from, "**the record that God gave of his Son**" (1 John 5:10). The Holy Bible is a book of many prophecies, each of which has come to pass at the time appointed, without error or failure of any kind! If you do not believe the record that God gave of his Son, then you are calling the Almighty God a liar. That's a very foolish thing for you to do! May God be merciful to you!

Therefore, take heed and do according to Acts 16:31: "**Believe on the Lord Jesus Christ, and thou shalt be saved**..."

Chapter 2

CRUCIFIXION

THE FEAR OF MAN

The gospel of John 19:12-14 tells us, "And from thenceforth Pilate sought to release him [Jesus]: but the Jews cried out, saying, If thou let this man go, thou art not Caesar's friend: whosoever maketh himself a king speaketh against Caesar. When Pilate therefore heard that saying, he brought Jesus forth, and sat down in the judgment seat in a place that is called the Pavement, but in the Hebrew, Gabbatha. And it was the preparation of the passover, and about the sixth hour: and he saith unto the Jews, Behold your King!"

At this time Pilate was the Roman governor over Judea (Luke 3:1), and he wanted to release the Lord Jesus, for he knew that he had done nothing worthy of death. We learn from the scriptures that three times Pilate had declared to the Jews that he found no fault in Jesus (John 18:38; 19:4, 6)! Nevertheless, when these malicious blood thirsty Jews said that he would be no friend of Caesar by letting Jesus go, Pilate feared for his own well being. He knew that if he let Jesus go he could be reported to Caesar under the charge of conspiracy and treason; and he could lose the governorship and his head as well! Pilate had to choose between Christ and his own well-being. He could either do what was right and release the Lord, and face the consequences; or he could go against his own conscience and against doing the right thing, and have the Lord crucified! The Jews had saved their strongest argument for the last. Being hypocrites themselves, they saw that Pilate was also a hypocrite who could be persuaded to accomplish their demands should he be threatened with acting in such a way as to displease the Emperor! The Jews were correct in their assessment of Pilate, who caved in to their threat. Proverbs 29:25 is correct in stating, "The fear of man [always] bringeth a snare…"

When Pilate was sat down in the judgment seat he made one more feeble attempt to have Jesus released. He [Pilate] "**saith unto the Jews, Behold your King!**" However, this only stirred up the Jews the more!

Next, John 19:15 begins by saying, "But they cried out, Away with *him*, away with *him*, crucify him. Pilate saith unto them, Shall I crucify your King?" Yes, they wanted him crucified! Nothing but the blood of Jesus would satisfy these murderous Jews! Even so it is the blood of Jesus Christ that washes us from our sins (Revelation 1:5)! Jesus Christ must die. God had foreordained it (1 Peter 1:17-21): these Jews demanded it! God meant his death for the good of all the world, for Jesus Christ did "taste death for every man" (Hebrews 2:9)! Although the Jews meant his death for evil and their aim was barbarous cruelty to him who is sinless, the design of God was mercy for all sinners. The rejection of their Messiah was prophesied Isaiah 49:7. In addition, Isaiah 53:3 prophesied: "**He is despised and rejected of men; a man of sorrows, and acquainted with grief: and we hid as it were *our* faces from him; he was despised, and we esteemed him not**."

Moreover the rest of John 19:15 continues to explain, "…The chief priests answered, We have no king but Caesar."

This was not the first time the Jews had rejected God as their king! When the Jews demanded a king to rule over them a little over a thousand years before (1 Samuel 8:5), the LORD told the Prophet Samuel: "Hearken unto the voice of the people in all that they say unto thee: for they have not rejected thee, but they have rejected me, that I should not reign over them" (1 Samuel 8:7). While Jesus was on this earth, he knew the Jews would reject their God and King. He many times would directly rebuke them. Then other times he would rebuke them through a parable, such as the parable of the ten pounds in Luke 19:11-27. I would encourage you to open up your Bible and read it. The nobleman in this parable represents the Lord Jesus Christ, who commissioned his servants and commanded them, "Occupy till I come" (Luke 19:13). Then at the very end of the parable, the Lord gives the judgment of the chief priests, who rejected him, saying: "But those mine enemies, which would not that I should reign over them, bring hither, and slay *them* before me" (Luke 19:27).

Even though the Lord has very patiently watched and allowed men out of their own free will to choose to reject Him, one day the Lord Jesus Christ will reign as King over all things for ever (Revelation 11:15). However, the Jews did not recognize their Messiah. Theirs is an example of man's religion, which will eventually enthrone a world political leader, known as the antichrist—"that man of sin" (2 Thessalonians 2:3). As a consequence of their fatal decision, Israel has been "many days without a king, and without a prince, and without a sacrifice, and without an image, and without an ephod, and *without* teraphim" (Hosea 3:4). The Jewish religion is now an empty shell. They refuse to come to God now by the new and living way, through the veil of the flesh of the Lord Jesus Christ (Hebrews 10:20), as do all unbelievers!

At this point in time, Matthew records: "When Pilate saw that he could prevail nothing, but *that* rather a tumult was made, he took water, and washed *his* hands before the multitude, saying, I am innocent of the blood of this just person: see ye *to it*. Then answered all the people, and said, His blood *be* on us, and on our children" (Matthew 27:24-25). By washing his hands, Pilate was intending to cast the entire responsibility of Christ's crucifixion upon the Jews. However, Luke writes, "And Pilate gave sentence that it should be as they required. And he released unto them him that for sedition and murder was cast into prison, whom they had desired; but he delivered Jesus to their will" (Luke 23:24-25). Pilate released a murderer to the Jews, and ordered his Roman soldiers to crucify Jesus as the Jews demanded! Pilate was *not* innocent! He ordered the death of Christ!

Let us not forget that behind the governor of Judea, who *delivered* the Lord Jesus unto the Jews, was the Governor of the universe, who "spared not his own Son, but delivered him up for us all…" (Romans 8:32); "Who was delivered for our offences, and was raised again for our justification" (Romans 4:25)! God was behind it all.

John 19:16 brings enlightenment concerning the fulfillment of ancient prophecy, saying, "Then delivered he him therefore unto them to be crucified. And they took Jesus, and led *him* away." As the prophecy had so long ago foretold: "he is brought as a lamb to the slaughter" (Isaiah 53:7). As a sheep he was "led," not dragged or driven. He made no resistance to their leading him to the cross, for "Christ Jesus came into the world to save sinners" (1 Timothy 1:15).

Then John 19:17 further explains, "And he bearing his cross went forth into a place called *the place* of a skull, which is called in the Hebrew Golgotha." These cruel bloodthirsty haters of Jesus lost no time in bringing about the Lord's crucifixion. They did not offer him any alone time with family and friends, as normal criminals were given. No, instead he was taken immediately from Gabbatha to Golgotha—from judgment to execution! The Saviour bearing his cross was typified when "Abraham took the wood of the burnt offering, and laid *it* upon Isaac his son" (Genesis 22:6). I would encourage you to study Genesis chapter 22 and familiarize yourself with a wonderful similitude of the Father's sacrifice of his Son.

They took Jesus just outside the gates of Jerusalem: "Wherefore Jesus also, that he might sanctify the people with his own blood, suffered without [outside] the gate" (Hebrews 13:12). After leaving the judgment hall bearing his cross, Matthew gives us a further detail: "And as they came out, they found a man of Cyrene, Simon by name: him they compelled to bear his cross" (Matthew 27:32). Most commentators say that Simon was compelled to carry the Lord's cross, because Jesus was not able to carry it. There is not a word in the Bible that suggests this. In fact, everything we read about the Lord's complete composure and alertness on the cross conflicts with this idea. The Bible does show, however, there was not one in that entire crowd with sufficient compassion and courage to volunteer to carry it for him!

Once at the top of Golgotha John 19:18 explains the carrying out of Jesus' execution, saying, "Where they crucified him, and two other with him, on either side one, and Jesus in the midst." This one verse records the fulfillment of at least two Old Testament prophecies. First, the manner of his death would be by crucifixion: "they pierced my hands and my feet" (Psalm 22:16). Second, Isaiah had declared, "he was numbered with the transgressors" (Isaiah 53:12). He who had done no wrong was not only being punished for wrong, additionally, he was being punished in the worst governmental execution style available to men with the worst of the worst criminals. Prophecy was being fulfilled to the jot!

LINE UPON LINE

John 19:19 says, "And Pilate wrote a title, and put *it* on the cross. And the writing was, JESUS OF NAZARETH THE KING OF THE JEWS." Adversaries of the truth will be quick to jump at the *apparent* contradiction between the words of the title that Pilate placed on the cross. Nevertheless, there is no real contradiction: only a tremendous opportunity and example to reveal how that the entire word of God is written as a man who speaks "with stammering lips and another tongue" (Isaiah 28:11). When the word of God is read by a foolish and insincere mocker, one who is trying to discredit and find error, the scriptures will seem like babbling to him. God has written his word in this manner to show that, "For precept *must be* upon precept, precept upon precept; line upon line, line upon line; here a little, *and* there a little" (Isaiah 28:10). Therefore, if we add the four *lines* of scripture given by Matthew, Mark, Luke, and John, we can find out all of the words that were on the *title* written by Pilate. See the following tabulation:

THIS IS JESUS THE KING OF THE JEWS (Matthew 27:37)
THE KING OF THE JEWS (Mark 15:26)
THIS IS THE KING OF THE JEWS (Luke 23:38)
<u>JESUS OF NAZARETH THE KING OF THE JEWS</u> (John 19:_19)

THIS IS JESUS OF NAZARETH THE KING OF THE JEWS [complete title]

Before Christ was born, the angel announced to Mary that, "of his kingdom there shall be no end" (Luke 1:32-33). In his infancy, wise men from the east heralded him as "King of the Jews" (Matthew 2:2). At the beginning of the week, the multitudes had cried, "Blessed is the King of Israel" (John 12:13). Before Pilate, the Lord himself bore witness to his "kingdom" (John 18:36-37). And now his royal title was fixed to his cross!

In the future, how appropriate it will be when we see "on *his* vesture and on his thigh a name written, KING OF KINGS, AND LORD OF LORDS" (Revelation 19:16).

John 19:20 goes on to explain, "This title then read many of the Jews: for the place where Jesus was crucified was nigh to the city: and it was written in Hebrew, *and* Greek, *and* Latin."

Hebrew was the language of *religion;* Greek of *science, culture* and *philosophy;* Latin of *law.* In each of these realms, Christ is "king." In the *religious*, he is the final revelation of "the true God" (1 John 5:20; John 14:9; Hebrews 1:1-8). In *science*, he is the *power* behind all things, for "he is before all things, and by him all things consist" (Colossians 1:17). He is "upholding all things by the word of his power" (Hebrews 1:3); "In whom are hid all the treasures of wisdom and knowledge" (Colossians 2:3). You can safely toss all your philosophy to the wind (Colossians 2:8), and confidently embrace "the holy scriptures, which are able to make thee wise unto salvation through faith which is in Christ Jesus" (2 Timothy 3:15)! In *law*, he is the "one lawgiver, who is able to save and to destroy" (James 4:12): "For the LORD *is* our judge, the LORD *is* our lawgiver, the LORD *is* our king; he will save us" (Isaiah 33:22). "For the Father judgeth no man, but hath committed all judgment unto the Son" (John 5:22).

IT IS WRITTEN

John 19:21-22 tell us, "Then said the chief priests of the Jews to Pilate, Write not, The King of the Jews; but that he said, I am King of the Jews. Pilate answered, What I have written I have written." Pilate had written the truth, and he was not going to change it! Could it be that this was the cause for the thief on the cross to repent and believe on the Lord? We cannot be sure, but we do know that "faith cometh by hearing, and hearing by the word of God" (Romans 10:17)!

John 19:23-24 further explains how ancient prophecy was once being fulfilled during the crucifixion of Jesus Christ, saying, "Then the soldiers, when they had crucified Jesus, took his garments, and made four parts, to every soldier a part; and also *his* coat: now the coat was without seam, woven from the top throughout. They said therefore among themselves, Let us not rend it, but cast lots for it, whose it shall be: that the scripture might be fulfilled, which saith, They parted my raiment among them, and for my vesture they did cast lots. These things therefore the soldiers did."

The soldiers did not do these things in order that the scriptures might be fulfilled! The soldiers did not even know what the scriptures said! They did not even know what they were doing (Luke 23:34)! They fulfilled the scriptures, because God knew from the foundation of the world what they would do, and wrote it down beforehand in the scriptures. All scripture is given by inspiration of God (2 Timothy 3:16); therefore the Spirit of Christ spoke through the psalmist and wrote: "They part my garments among them, and cast lots upon my vesture" (Psalm 22:18). All scripture will be fulfilled, whether by unbelievers who do not have a clue as to what they are doing, or by the Lord who knows all things! You can count on it! The Lord Jesus Christ said, "[T]he scriptures must be fulfilled" (Mark 14:49; Matthew 5:17-18); and, "[T]he scripture cannot be broken" (John 10:35).

COMPASSION FROM THE CROSS

John 19:25-27 tells us, "Now there stood by the cross of Jesus his mother, and his mother's sister, Mary the *wife* of Cleophas, and Mary Magdalene. When Jesus therefore saw his mother, and the disciple standing by, whom he loved, he saith unto his mother, Woman, behold thy son! Then saith he to the disciple, Behold thy mother! And from that hour that disciple took her unto his own *home*."

The Lord spoke seven times while he was upon the cross:

1. The word of *forgiveness* for his enemies (Luke 23:34).
2. The word of *salvation* to the dying thief (Luke 23:42-43).
3. The word of *affection* to his mother (John 19:25-26).
4. The word of *anguish* to God (Matthew 27:46).
5. The word of *thirsting* to the spectators (John 19:28).
6. The word of *victory* to his people (John 19:30).
7. The word of *commendation* to the Father (Luke 23:46).

"The disciple standing by, whom he loved," is John's way of identifying himself (John 13:23; 20:2; 21:7, 20). John was to take care of Jesus' mother, Mary. Evidently Mary's husband Joseph had already passed away, and the Lord did not consider his unbelieving brethren, his half brothers (John 7:5; Psalm 69:8), worthy of this responsibility. This illustrates how spiritual bonds take preference over natural ones.

IT IS FINISHED

John 19:28-30 says, "After this, Jesus knowing that all things were now accomplished, that the scripture might be fulfilled, saith, I thirst. Now there was set a vessel full of vinegar: and they filled a spunge with vinegar, and put *it* upon hyssop, and put *it* to his mouth. When Jesus therefore had received the vinegar, he said, It is finished…"

The act of the Lord receiving the vinegar here is not the same as when "They gave him vinegar to drink mingled with gall: and when he had tasted *thereof*, he would not drink" (Matthew 27:34). The first drink of vinegar and gall, commonly given to criminals to deaden their pains, the Lord refused. He took upon himself all sin and endured all of its brutal agonizing pains. But, according to God's will, at the end of his crucifixion he did receive the unmixed vinegar here. The same is recorded in Matthew 27:48: "And straightway one of them ran, and took a spunge, and filled *it* with vinegar, and put *it* on a reed, and gave him to drink."

Early in his earthly ministry, at Jacob's well, the Lord told his disciples, "My meat is to do the will of him that sent me, and to finish his work" (John 4:34)! Now the work is finished! By the Lord Jesus saying, "It is finished," meant that all things had been done which the law of God required; all things established which God had foreordained through prophecy; all things brought to pass which the *types* foreshadowed; all things accomplished which the Father had given him to do; all things performed which were needed for our redemption. Nothing was left to do! Nothing more remained for him to do or say; nothing more awaited its fulfillment. His work on earth was completed.

He had executed the great designs of the Father. He had satisfied the demands of his justice. He had suffered the utmost malice of his enemies; and now the way to the holy of holies is made manifest "through his blood" (Ephesians 1:7; Colossians 1:14). It was an awful, yet a glorious finish. Through his tragic death, God is reconciled to man, and the kingdom of heaven opened to every believing soul. In his sinless and perfect life, the law was fulfilled as never before, nor since, when the Lord Jesus was "obedient unto death, even the death of the cross" (Philippians 2:8).

HE LAID DOWN HIS LIFE

John 19:30 continues with the words, "...and he bowed his head, and gave up the ghost." His head had been held erect up to this point. His head did not fall forward, but he consciously, calmly, and reverently *bowed* his head. *Then* he "gave up the ghost." Jesus was "obedient unto death, even the death of the cross" (Philippians 2:8). Earlier the Lord had declared: "Therefore doth my Father love me, because **I lay down my life, that I might take it again. No man taketh it from me, but I lay it down of myself. I have power to lay it down, and I have power to take it again. This commandment have I received of my Father**" (John 10:17-18). When Stephen, the first Christian martyr, was dying from stoning, he prayed, saying, "Lord Jesus, receive my spirit. And he kneeled down, and cried with a loud voice, Lord, lay not this sin to their charge. And when he had said this, he fell asleep" (Act 7:59-60). Stephen's spirit was *taken* from him, but the Lord Jesus *gave up* his Spirit.

NO BROKEN BONES

John 19:31 says, "The Jews therefore, because it was the preparation, that the bodies should not remain upon the cross on the sabbath day, (for that sabbath day was an high day,) besought Pilate that their legs might be broken, and *that* they might be taken away."

According to the law, "In the fourteenth *day* of the first month at even *is* the LORD'S passover. And on the fifteenth day of the same month *is* the feast of unleavened bread unto the LORD: seven days ye must eat unleavened bread" (Leviticus 23:5-6). We know that the Lord ate the passover meal with his disciples in "the fourteenth *day* of the first month at even," because the Lord always obeyed the scriptures, fulfilling "all righteousness" (Matthew 3:15). It is important to understand that the day of the Lord's crucifixion was on the *same day*—the passover; for the Jewish *day* begins and ends at sundown! The day after the passover was the first day of the *feast* of unleavened bread, called "the sabbath day, (for that sabbath day was an high day)." The seventh day (Exodus 35:2) was not the only day called a *sabbath day.* Other holy days were also designated as *sabbath days* (Leviticus 16:29-31; 23:24-39). The passover day is referred to here as "the preparation of the passover," the day when the passover sacrifice was killed, prepared, and eaten (2 Chronicles 35:6; Ezekiel 43:25). On the day of the passover, the Jews also prepared for the first day of unleavened bread by removing all leaven from their houses (Exodus 12:15-19).

It is understood that Jesus and his disciples were together at the passover meal until late that night. After the meal, "Then he came out, and went, as he was wont, to the mount of Olives; [unto a place called Gethsemane (Matthew 26:36)] and his disciples also followed him (Luke 22:39). After Jesus' time in prayer, a multitude came and arrested Christ, and then the numerous trials during the night and early day proceeded with him being executed by crucifixion.

John 19:32-37 continues to explain the events after his death, saying, "Then came the soldiers, and brake the legs of the first, and of the other which was crucified with him. But when they came to Jesus, and saw that he was dead already, they brake not his legs: But one of the soldiers with a spear pierced his side, and forthwith came there out blood and water. And he that saw *it* bare record, and his record is true: and he knoweth that he saith true, that ye might believe. For these things were done, that the scripture should be fulfilled, A bone of him shall not be broken. And again another scripture saith, They shall look on him whom they pierced."

The Lord Jesus Christ is "the Lamb of God, which taketh away the sin of the world" (John 1:29). He is "Christ our passover" (1 Corinthians 5:7)! All of the passover lambs before him only typified [pictured] his final sacrifice. Although his bones were "out of joint" (Psalm 22:14), none of his bones were "broken," in agreement with the scriptures (Exodus 12:46; Numbers 9:12; Psalm 34:20). The LORD prophesied through Zechariah, declaring: "And I will pour upon the house of David, and upon the inhabitants of Jerusalem, the spirit of grace and of supplications: **and they shall look upon me whom they have pierced**, and they shall mourn for him, as one mourneth for *his* only *son*, and shall be in bitterness for him, as one that is in bitterness for *his* firstborn" (Zechariah 12:10). After his resurrection, the Lord told Thomas, "Reach hither thy finger, and behold my hands; and reach hither thy hand, and thrust *it* into my side: and be not faithless, but believing" (John 20:27). Furthermore, one day all will see him: "Behold, he cometh with clouds; and every eye shall see him, and they *also* which pierced him: and all kindreds of the earth shall wail because of him. Even so, Amen" (Revelation 1:7).

HE WAS BURIED

John 19:38-42 provides the remainder of prophetic details which occurred surrounding the crucifixion of Christ, saying, "And after this Joseph of Arimathaea, being a disciple of Jesus, but secretly for fear of the Jews, besought Pilate that he might take away the body of Jesus: and Pilate gave *him* leave. He came therefore, and took the body of Jesus. And there came also Nicodemus, which at the first came to Jesus by night, and brought a mixture of myrrh and aloes, about an hundred pound *weight*. Then took they the body of Jesus, and wound it in linen clothes with the spices, as the manner of the Jews is to bury. Now in the place where he was crucified there was a garden; and in the garden a new sepulchre, wherein was never man yet laid. There laid they Jesus therefore because of the Jews' preparation *day*; for the sepulchre was nigh at hand."

Joseph of Arimathaea was "a rich man" (Matthew 27:57), who laid the body of Jesus "in his own new tomb, which he had hewn out in the rock: and he rolled a great stone to the door of the sepulchre, and departed" (Matthew 27:60). Therefore the prophecy that the Lord would make his grave "with the rich in his death; because he had done no violence, neither *was any* deceit in his mouth" (Isaiah 53:9), was fulfilled. Luke 23:50-51 tells us, "Joseph was "a counsellor; *and he was* a good man, and a just: (The same had not consented to the counsel and deed of them;) *he was* of Arimathaea, a city of the Jews: who also himself waited for the kingdom of God." However, Joseph was a secret disciple, and probably among those who “believed on him; but because of the Pharisees they did not confess *him*, lest they should be put out of the synagogue: For they loved the praise of men more than the praise of God” (John 12:42-43).

According to Mark’s gospel, when Joseph asked Pilate for the body of Jesus, “Pilate marvelled if he were already dead: and calling *unto him* the centurion, he asked him whether he had been any while dead” (Mark 15:44). Pilate wanted to make sure that Jesus had died. Evidently breaking the legs of a man being crucified caused him to die more quickly, but did not cause his death immediately.

It was in a garden where the first Adam sowed the seed of sin, which resulted in death (Romans 5:12). Likewise, it was in a garden where the “seed” of the woman (Genesis 3:15) was sown, which would bear much fruit unto eternal life (John 12:24). It was in a garden where John chapter 19 ends with the burial of the body of Jesus Christ. But that was not the end of him! And it was in a garden that the “glorious gospel of Christ, who is the image of God” (2 Corinthians 4:4) occurred (John 19:41 and Matthew 28:6); the glorious gospel which is “how that Christ died for our sins according to the scriptures; And that he was buried, and that he rose again the third day according to the scriptures” (1 Corinthians 15:3-4)!

After his glorious resurrection, the Lord Jesus said: “I *am* he that liveth, and was dead; and, behold, I am alive for evermore, Amen; and have the keys of hell and of death” (Revelation 1:18). Are you thirsty for truth in this “present evil world” (Galatians 1:4)? The Lord Jesus Christ is “alive for evermore” (Revelation 1:18)! He is “able also to save them to the uttermost that come unto God by him, seeing he ever liveth to make intercession for them” (Hebrews 7:25). “And the Spirit and the bride say, Come. And let him that heareth say, Come. And let him that is athirst come. And whosoever will, let him take the water of life freely” (Revelation 22:17). It is as simple as believing within your heart: “**Believe on the Lord Jesus Christ, and thou shalt be saved**” (Acts 16:31).

Chapter 3

ETERNAL REDEMPTION

In the Holy Bible, which was written when "holy men of God spake *as they were* moved by the Holy Ghost" (2 Peter 1:21), we read in Colossians 1:14, "In whom [Jesus Christ] we have redemption through his blood, *even* the forgiveness of sins." Either someone will choose to believe or not to believe the Holy Bible. I do not know about you, but I choose to believe the words which are written for our learning (Romans 15:4) and admonition (1 Corinthians 10:11). The words in this particular scriptural text are very precious indeed. And these are the words which we shall use as a foundation and build upon the wonderful truth of our redemption in Christ Jesus.

INTRODUCTION

In his 1828 dictionary, Noah Webster defines REDEMPTION as "the repurchase of captured goods, prisoners, or lands; the act of procuring the deliverance of persons or things from the possession and power of captors by the payment of an equivalent; ransom; release; as the redemption of prisoners taken in war; the redemption of a ship and cargo." The first mention of the word *redemption* in the Holy Bible is found in Leviticus 25:24, where the LORD is commanding Israel: "**And in all the land of your possession ye shall grant a**

redemption for the land" (Leviticus 25:24). The land was divided and given as an inheritance to all the tribes of Israel, with the exception of Levi, for: "The LORD God of Israel was their inheritance" (Deuteronomy 18:1-8; Joshua 13:14, 33). The LORD gave commandments to the children of Israel regarding their possession of the land of promise: Then the Lord gave instructions, regarding redemption, to insure that their inheritance would remain in the possession of the tribe to which he had originally given it (Leviticus 25:25-28).

In theology, redemption is the purchase of God's favor by the death and sufferings of Christ; the ransom or deliverance of sinners from the bondage of sin and the penalties of God's violated law by the atonement of Christ. As the LORD redeemed Israel from Egyptian bondage "**with a stretched out arm, and with great judgments**" (Exodus 6:6), so God also made possible the redemption of fallen and sinful men from the bondage and eternal penalty of sin by his stretched out arm, when they nailed Jesus Christ to the cross, where he "**died for our sins according to the scriptures; And…was buried, and…rose again the third day according to the scriptures**" (1 Corinthians 15:3-4)! According to the words of Abraham to Isaac: "**My son, God will provide himself a lamb for a burnt offering**" (Genesis 22:8); it was on the cross where God "**his own self bare our sins in his own body on the tree** [the wooden cross]**, that we, being dead to sins, should live unto righteousness: by whose stripes ye were healed**" (1 Peter 2:24).

After all of the firstborn of the Egyptians were destroyed, God claimed all the firstborn of Israel for his own. Then he commanded Moses: "**Take the Levites instead of all the firstborn among the children of Israel**…" (Numbers 3:45). The LORD claimed all the firstborn of Israel as his own, for he had bought them with the blood of the sacrificed lamb, whose blood had been placed upon the door posts of their houses (Exodus 12:1-13). They had been *redeemed* by the blood of the lamb! In like manner, God now claims for his own those who have been "**purchased with his own blood**" (Acts 20:28), by the precious blood of the Lamb of God, the Lord Jesus Christ (1 Peter 1:18-19).

WHO IS THE REDEEMER?

God himself alone must be man's redeemer, for the psalmist wrote in Psalm 49:6-9: "They that trust in their wealth, and boast themselves in the multitude of their riches; **None *of them* can by any means redeem his brother, nor give to God a ransom for him**: **(For the redemption of their soul *is* precious, and it ceaseth for ever**:**) That he should still live for ever, *and* not see corruption**."

All attempts by man to redeem his own or another's soul from eternal destruction is entirely worthless and vain. Speaking through Isaiah the prophet to the nation of Israel, over seven hundred years before the birth of the Lord Jesus Christ, the LORD [Jehovah (Exodus 6:3)] said: "Fear not...**For thy Maker *is* thine husband; the LORD of hosts *is* his name; and thy Redeemer the Holy One of Israel; The God of the whole earth shall he be called**" (Isaiah 54:4-5; 9:6). Earlier, the LORD told Israel that the time will come when "**all flesh shall know that I the LORD *am* thy Saviour and thy Redeemer, the mighty One of Jacob**" (Isaiah 49:25-26).

One night while alone and fearful about meeting his brother Esau on the following day, Jacob wrestled with a mysterious "man" who would not make known his name to Jacob (Genesis 32:24-29). In due course of the night, Jacob realized who he had been wrestling with, "**And Jacob called the name of the place Peniel: for I have seen God face to face, and my life is preserved**" (Genesis 32:30). Later the Prophet Hosea recorded Jacob's encounter, saying, "**by his strength he had power with God: Yea, he had power over the angel, and prevailed: he wept, and made supplication unto him: he found him *in* Bethel, and there he spake with us; Even the LORD God of hosts; the LORD *is* his memorial**" (Hosea 12:2-5). In his last days, Jacob identified his redeemer as *God*, when he "blessed Joseph, and said, **God, before whom my fathers Abraham and Isaac did walk, the God which fed me all my life long unto this day, [t]he Angel which redeemed me from all evil**, bless the lads; and let my name be named on them, and the name of my fathers Abraham and Isaac; and let them grow into a multitude in the midst of the earth" (Genesis 48:15-16).

In the midst of a terrible storm at sea, the Apostle Paul was visited by the angel of the Lord. Then Paul gave an encouraging message to the others on the ship, saying: "And now I exhort you to be of good cheer: for there shall be no loss of *any man's* life among you, but of the ship. **For there stood by me this night the angel of God, whose I am, and whom I serve, Saying, Fear not, Paul; thou must be brought before Caesar: and, lo, God hath given thee all them that sail with thee**" (Acts 27:22-24). Later Paul identifies the "**angel of God, *even* as Christ Jesus**" (Galatians 4:14).

All of the recorded appearances of God to men in the entire Holy Bible are appearances of the Son of God, either before or after he was made flesh. Even though John 1:18 and 1 John 4:12 both declare: "**No man hath seen God at any time,**" the Lord Jesus Christ himself clears up any confusion, saying: "**Not that any man hath seen the Father, save he which is of God, he hath seen**

the Father" (John 6:46). Therefore the biblical interpretation is that John 1:18 is plainly a reference to God *the Father*, who "**is a Spirit**" (John 4:24), and who is "**invisible**" (Colossians 1:15)! When "**Philip saith unto him** [Jesus], **Lord, shew us the Father, and it sufficeth us. Jesus saith unto him, Have I been so long time with you, and yet hast thou not known me, Philip? he that hath seen me hath seen the Father; and how sayest thou *then*, Shew us the Father?**" (John 14:8-9). In the Lord Jesus Christ "**dwelleth all the fulness of the Godhead bodily**" (Colossians 2:9). And the "**Godhead**" (Acts 17:29; Romans 1:20; Colossians 2:9) is defined by the following scripture: "**For there are three that bear record in heaven, the Father, the Word, and the Holy Ghost: and these three are one**" (1 John 5:7).

When Nebuchadnezzar looked into the burning fiery furnace, after throwing the three Hebrew children into it: "He answered and said, Lo, I see four men loose, walking in the midst of the fire, and they have no hurt; and **the form of the fourth is like the Son of God**" (Daniel 3:25)! The scriptures plainly declare that men saw "**the LORD**," "**God**," "**the God of Israel**," or "**the LORD of hosts**." The following verses record these appearances: Genesis 17:1; 26:2; 32:30; Exodus 33:11; 24:9-11; 1 Kings 22:19; Isaiah 6:1, 5; and Ezekiel 1:26.

The Holy Scriptures make it abundantly clear that the LORD God is the Saviour and Redeemer (Isaiah 49:25-26). "**And without controversy great is the mystery of godliness: God was manifest in the flesh**…" (1 Timothy 3:16). Therefore the Lord Jesus Christ is God "**made flesh**" (John 1:1, 14), who came into the world to redeem men by his sacrificial death on the cross, and by the shedding of his blood.

REDEMPTION IS AVAILABLE FOR ALL MEN

To repeat our sermon's main text, Colossians 1:14, the beginning of it states, "In whom [Jesus] we have redemption through his blood…" Redemption is necessary for all men. Because of Adam's sin, all men are born into captivity and slavery of sin (Romans 5:12). All sinners are in bondage to sin, to the law, and to Satan. Without God's redemption, all sinners, except for children who die having not the knowledge of good and evil (Deuteronomy 1:39; Isaiah 7:15-16; Romans 7:9), will die and go to the eternal torments of the damned in the lake of fire (Revelation 20:14-15).

Before the foundation of the world, God devised a way for all men to be delivered from this captivity (2 Samuel 14:14) and from the eternal consequences of sin. Sinners have a sin nature, which is inherited by all of the descendants of Adam (Romans 5:12). All men therefore come into the world as sinners (Psalms 51:5; 58:3; Proverbs 22:15; Romans 3:23; 1 Kings 8:46; Isaiah 53:6; Psalm 130:3; Romans 3:19, 23; Galatians 3:22). Sinners are "**sold under sin**" (Romans 7:14). They are sold to work wickedness (1 Kings 21:20, 25; 2 Kings 17:17; Isaiah 50:1; 52:1-12). They are the servants of sin (Romans 6:17). They are the servants of the flesh (Romans 7:5), which cannot please God (Romans 8:8; Galatians 5:17): captives to a body of flesh and ruled by the lust of the flesh (Romans 6:6; James 1:14-15) and the law of sin which works in the flesh (Romans 7:23-24; Psalm 119:25). Sinners are servants of corruption (2 Peter 2:19); they walk in darkness; they are blind, ignorant, and alienated from the life of God (Ephesians 4:18-19). Sinners are all as an unclean thing whose iniquities have taken them away (Isaiah 64:6). Sinners are *spiritually* "**dead in trespasses and sins**" (Ephesians 2:1; 1 John 3:14). Sinners are under the yoke of transgressions [sins] (Lamentations 1:14). They are held captive by the cords of their sins, and will die without instruction (Proverbs 5:22-23). Sinners are also under the yoke of bondage of the law (Acts 15:5-11; Galatians 5:1). They are under the curse of the law (Galatians 3:13). They are all guilty and condemned already under God's "law" (Romans 3:19).

Sinners are taken captive by the devil at his will (2 Timothy 2:26). Sinners are under the "power of darkness," "the power of Satan" (Colossians 1:13; Acts 26:18). The spirit of the devil works in all of the children of disobedience (Ephesians 2:2-3). According to the Lord Jesus Christ, the devil is the "father" of all unbelievers (John 8:44). All unbelievers have been blinded by the lies of the devil (2 Corinthians 4:3-4), who is a liar and the father of it (John 8:44).

Not only is redemption necessary for all men, because all have sinned and are under the power of darkness, but redemption is also necessary for all men in order to satisfy God's holiness and to demonstrate his great merciful *will* to show mercy and lovingkindness to all sinners (Jeremiah 9:24). Since all things were created for God's pleasure (Revelation 4:11), and God has "**no pleasure in the death of the wicked**" (Ezekiel 18:32; 33:11), then it is only reasonable (Isaiah 1:18) to conclude that God's plan of redemption and salvation most certainly includes the redemption of all men (John 1:29; 3:16-17; 6:33; 2 Corinthians 5:18-20; 1 Timothy 2:3-6; 4:10; 2 Peter 3:9; Hebrews 2:9; 2 Corinthians 5:14-15; 1 John 2:2; 1 Peter 2:7-8). The disobedient, "which stumble at the word," were "also" appointed to receive eternal life through faith in the redeeming blood of the Lamb of God. However, they, of their own free will, were disobedient to the gospel and rejected the Lord (1 Peter 2:7-8).

The Redeemer must be a "kinsman." Under the law a Hebrew, who had sold himself to a stranger, could be redeemed by one of his brethren (Leviticus 25:48-49). However, no man has the power or the wealth to redeem his own or anyone else's *soul* (Psalm 49:6-9)! Even if a man could accumulate all the wealth of the world and gain the power to rule over the whole world, this would still not be sufficient to redeem his soul back to God (Matthew 16:26). The Lord Jesus Christ qualifies to be our kinsman Redeemer, because he was made flesh (Romans 1:3; 2 Timothy 2:8; John 1:14; 1 Timothy 3:16) when he took upon him the seed of Abraham (Hebrews 2:14-15). The Lord Jesus Christ was "**made of a woman, made under the law, TO REDEEM them that were under the law, that we might receive the adoption of sons**" (Galatians 4:4-5). According to the determinate counsel and foreknowledge of God (Acts 2:23), eternal life for man would be purchased by God himself (Genesis 22:8) and offered to all fallen and sinful men as a free gift (Romans 5:15-18; 6:23). God's plan to redeem man included the preparation of a body for his eternal Son (Hebrews 10:5) that he might send him into this world in the likeness of sinful flesh (Romans 8:3) to become the innocent sacrifice and sin bearer for all sinners.

The Redeemer must have power to redeem (Ruth 4:4-6; John 10:11, 18, Jeremiah 50:34). The Lord Jesus Christ said, "I am the good shepherd: the good shepherd giveth his life for the sheep; no man taketh it from me, but I lay it down of myself. **I have power to lay it down, and I have power to take it again. This commandment have I received of my Father**" (John 10:11, 18). There is no other "man" besides the Lord Jesus Christ who is able to redeem men's souls (Psalm 142:4; Isaiah 59:16; Hebrews 7:25)!

He must be willing to redeem. The Lord Jesus Christ clearly demonstrated his willingness always to do that which his Father commanded. He "**made himself of no reputation, and took upon him the form of a servant, and was made in the likeness of men: And being found in fashion as a man, he humbled himself, and became obedient unto death, even the death of the cross**" (Philippians 2:7-8).

The Lord Jesus Christ has no need of redemption himself! He is our great Redeemer, our great high priest who "**became us, who is holy, harmless, undefiled, separate from sinners, and made higher than the heavens**" (Hebrews 7:26). God his Father "**made him to be sin for us, who knew no sin; that we might be made the righteousness of God in him**" (2 Corinthians 5:21). Jesus Christ paid the sin debt in full (1 Peter 1:18-19; Ephesians 1.7, Acts 20:28; Galatians 3:13). Under the Old Testament law, God gave sinners the blood of bulls and goats upon the altar of sacrifice to make an atonement for their sins (Leviticus 17:11). This was only a "type" or figure of the true atoning blood of the Lamb of God which taketh away the sin of the world, the Lord Jesus Christ (John 1:29).

REDEEMING BLOOD

The blood of Adam's offspring (all natural men) is cursed with the penalty of sin, which is death (Genesis 2:17; Hebrews 9:27). Only the blood of a sinless man can possibly redeem men's souls, and only the blood of Jesus Christ can meet that qualification. It is a known scientific fact that the blood of a child is produced by the "seed" of the father. Although the baby receives food from the mother's body through the placenta, under normal conditions there is never a transfer of blood from the mother to the child. The Lord Jesus Christ's Father is God; therefore, the blood of Jesus Christ is God's blood: "Take heed therefore unto yourselves, and to all the flock, over the which the Holy Ghost hath made you overseers, to feed the church of **God, which he hath purchased with his own blood**" (Acts 20:28). Redemption is by "**the precious blood of Christ**, as of a lamb without blemish and without spot" (1 Peter 1:18): "In whom we have **redemption through his blood**" (Ephesians 1:7). There would be no hope for this world at all without the Redeemer! The Lord Jesus Christ has already bought both his people and the field (world) where they live (Matthew 13:38, 44-46; Hebrews 12:2; 1 Corinthians 6:20; 7:23). He has redeemed his people from the awful curse of eternal death in the lake of fire!

It was necessary that the ransom price be paid to God, against whom our sin has been committed (1 Timothy 2:5-6). The ransom price offered to God had to be sufficient to satisfy him. This satisfactory payment, which brings forgiveness and peace between the sinner and God, is called "**propitiation**" (1 John 2:2; 4:10). Propitiation is the atonement or atoning sacrifice offered to God to assuage [to reduce to perfect peace or ease] his wrath and render him propitious [disposed to be gracious or merciful; ready to forgive sins and bestow blessings] to sinners. The only possible ransom price and sacrifice acceptable to God is the sacrifice of his own precious, and only begotten Son, the Lord Jesus Christ. The ransom price is the blood of the Lord Jesus Christ, who "**also hath loved us, and hath given himself for us an offering and a sacrifice to God for a sweetsmelling savour**" (Ephesians 5:2; Revelation 5:9; Matthew 20:28).

God the Father foreordained, before the foundation of the world, that his eternal Son Jesus Christ should come into the world as a man and die for sinful men, paying the awful penalty of their sins Himself (John 3:16-17; 1 Peter 1:18-21; 1 Timothy 1:5). "**Yet it pleased the LORD to bruise him; he hath put *him* to grief: when thou shalt make his soul an offering for sin, he shall see *his* seed, he shall prolong *his* days, and the pleasure of the LORD shall prosper in his hand**" (Isaiah 53:10). "**For he hath made him *to be* sin for us, who knew no sin; that we might be made the righteousness of God in him**" (2 Corinthians 5:21).

Just after Jesus' resurrection, and before anyone touched his resurrected body (John 20:17), as our "**great high priest**" (Hebrews 4:14), the Lord Jesus Christ, ascended to heaven where he offered his own blood in the holy place to make an atonement for our sins (Leviticus 17:11). We who have been saved by grace through faith have "**eternal redemption**," which was obtained for us by the Lord Jesus Christ through his own blood: "**Neither by the blood of goats and calves, but by his own blood he entered in once into the holy place, having obtained eternal redemption *for us***" (Hebrews 9:12).

God has redeemed his blood washed children with an "**eternal redemption**" (Hebrews 9:12), a "**plenteous redemption**" (Psalm 130:7) "**from all iniquity**" (Titus 2:14; Psalm 130:8), "**from all evil**" (Genesis 48:16), "**out of all distress**" (1 Kings 1:28-29). God has redeemed his children's lives from everlasting destruction (Psalm 103:4; 2 Thessalonians 1:9)! There is only one Redeemer. God is the Redeemer. "**The Word was God**" (John 1:1), "**And the Word was made flesh**" (John 1:14), and his name is the Lord Jesus Christ! He is the eternal God (1 John 5:20) who provided "**himself a lamb for a burnt offering**" (Genesis 22:8).

THE FREEWILL OF MAN

God has made man with a free will. Man can choose to *reject* his Creator (John 12:48), or he can choose to fear the Lord (Proverbs 1:29) and believe the word of God and *receive* the Lord Jesus Christ into his heart (John 1:12-13). Man will suffer eternal consequences for his conscious and willful decision to reject God's Son. On the other hand, if the sinner humbles himself as a little child (Luke 18:17), repents (Luke 13:3; 2 Corinthians 7:10), and receives Jesus Christ as his personal Saviour (John 1:12-13), he will enjoy the eternal pleasures of the Lord (Psalm 16:11) in his everlasting kingdom.

No man can modify or alter God's plan to redeem the lost by faith in the blood of Jesus Christ (Isaiah 43:12-13; Deuteronomy 32:39; Isaiah 46:9-11;

Proverbs 21:30; Daniel 4:35; Ecclesiastics 7:12-14). However, even though no man can disannul God's eternal plan, God has given to every man the power to exercise his birthright to *receive* or to *reject* God's pardon for his sins. Any man can refuse to receive the gift of God which is eternal life through Jesus Christ our Lord (Romans 6:23)!

Only after men first close their own eyes and ears to "the truth of the gospel" (Colossians 1:5) does God then turn them over to a reprobate (evil) mind (Romans 1:28). Paul told the Christ-rejecting-Jews in Rome the prophecy that was written concerning them by Isaiah, saying: "Well spake the Holy Ghost by Esaias the prophet unto our fathers, Saying, Go unto this people, and say, Hearing ye shall hear, and shall not understand; and seeing ye shall see, and not perceive: For the heart of this people is waxed gross, and their ears are dull of hearing, and **their eyes have they closed; lest they should see with *their* eyes, and hear with *their* ears, and understand with *their* heart, and should be converted, and I should heal them**" (Acts 28:25-27).

God calls men by the gospel (2 Thessalonians 2:13-14; Ephesians 4:4-5), "**how that Christ died for our sins according to the scriptures; And that he was buried, and that he rose again the third day according to the scriptures**" (1 Corinthians 15:3-4), and he commands them to believe it (1 John 3:23) so that he might have mercy upon their souls and redeem them from the eternal punishment of the damned in the lake of fire. Nonetheless, if men refuse to obey God's call, then they seal their own eternal destiny (Proverbs 1:23-33)! Only after men close their own eyes and ears to the truth of God does God blind their eyes (John 12:39-40).

It is within the power of the free will of each individual to resist the Holy Ghost and go against God's will to redeem him personally (Acts 7:51), even limiting the work that God desires to do on his behalf (Psalm 78:41)! It is not God's will that "**ANY should perish, but that ALL should come to repentance**" (Acts 17:30; 1 John 3:23; 2 Peter 3:9). Moreover, God never overrides man's free will. If a man is still determined to continue in wickedness, after he receives a knowledge of the truth, and after God calls him by the gospel (2 Thessalonians 2:13-14; Ephesians 4:4-5), this man will remain lost and under the wrath and condemnation of God (John 3:18-19, 36). If he dies in unbelief, he will have his "**part in the lake which burneth with fire and brimstone: which is the second death**" (Revelation 21:8).

Our first father Adam sold himself, and all his offspring, under sin to the devil. The "last Adam"—Jesus Christ (1 Corinthians 15:45)—came to redeem the lost offspring of the first Adam, who cannot redeem themselves. He paid the ultimate price for your soul through his death on the cross and by his blood. **But in order for you to be redeemed, you must want to be redeemed!** You must willfully repent of your wicked ways and receive the Lord Jesus Christ into your heart by faith (Isaiah 55:6-7; John 1:12-14). In the last invitation given to sinners in the Bible, God offers the water of life freely to "**whosoever will**" (Revelation 22:17): "And the Spirit and the bride say, Come. And let him that heareth say, Come. And let him that is athirst come. **And whosoever will, let him take the water of life freely**."

The devil will do whatever he can to keep you distracted while you are in "**this present evil world**" (Galatians 1:4). He is "**the god of this world**" who blinds "**the minds of them which believe not, lest the light of the glorious gospel of Christ, who is the image of God, should shine unto them**" (2 Corinthians 4:4). The devil offers fame and riches to those who will serve him (Matthew 4:8-9). If you are an unsaved and unregenerate man, you are in great need of God's redemption. God commands you to repent (Acts 17:30) and to believe on his Son the Lord Jesus Christ (1 John 3:23). God does not want you to perish (suffer in the lake of fire forever), but you cannot escape the damnation of hell (Matthew 23:33), or the eternal torments of the lake of fire, if you neglect this great salvation which is made possible through the redeeming blood of the Lord Jesus Christ. Therefore, I would humbly and strongly encourage you to, "**Believe on the Lord Jesus Christ, and thou shalt be saved**" (Acts 16:31).

Chapter 4

WHAT IS A CHRISTIAN?

In today's sermon outline we shall examine the question, "What is a Christian?" Just what really is a Christian? Does being a Christian merely mean believing in Jesus Christ? Or is there more to it? We shall find the answer to these questions based on our scriptural text of Romans 6:17-20, which says, "But God be thanked, that ye were the servants of sin, but ye have obeyed from the heart that form of doctrine which was delivered you. Being then made free from sin, ye became the servants of righteousness. I speak after the manner of men because of the infirmity of your flesh: for as ye have yielded your members servants to uncleanness and to iniquity unto iniquity; even so now yield your members servants to righteousness unto holiness. For when ye were the servants of sin, ye were free from righteousness."

I. THE GREAT CHANGE

A Christian is a person who has undergone a great change. It is a change which affects his whole personality. Verse 17 says, "**Ye have obeyed**"—there is your *will*. You have of your own free *will* obeyed the gospel. You were not forced to obey it. The last invitation in the Bible says, "**Come. And let him that heareth say, Come. And let him that is athirst come. *And whosoever***

***will*, let him take the water of life freely**" (Revelation 22:17). If you *will* come, then you may come to the Lord and **believe on the Lord Jesus Christ and thou shalt be saved** (Acts 16:31). Verse 17 goes on to say, "Ye have obeyed **from the heart**"—there is your *emotion*. We read in Ephesians 6:6, "**Not with eyeservice, as menpleasers; but as the servants of Christ, doing the will of God *from the heart*.**" What have you obeyed from the heart? Ye have obeyed from the heart **that form of doctrine which was delivered you**. Doctrine is understood by the *mind*. So the change a man undergoes to be a Christian is a change which affects him in his *will,* in his *heart,* and in his *mind*—in his entire personality.

CHANGE OF PERSONALITY

This great change involves the Christian's whole personality. It is not simply an emotional change. Some who profess to be Christians seem to be caught up in emotionalism. When they are questioned about their doctrine they will say that doctrine is divisive, and that all that matters to them is "Jesus." Their Jesus must not be the Jesus of the Bible, who prayed, "**Sanctify them through thy truth: thy word is truth**" (John 17:17)! Doctrine is the truth of the word of God. How can it not be important to them? I wonder what "Jesus" they are talking about! These are **deceitful workers** (2 Corinthians 11:13) who preach **another Jesus, whom we have not preached** (2 Corinthians 11:4). Those who are caught up in emotionalism often put their feelings and their experiences ahead of the word of God in importance. In so doing they are greatly deceived. In order for one to be a Christian there must also be doctrine which is obeyed from the heart! If our *minds,* and *wills,* and *hearts* are not all engaged in the **obedience of faith** (Romans 16:26) then we are not true Christians.

I like what D.M. Lloyd-Jones once wrote. He stated, "You cannot be converted in your *mind* only, you cannot be converted in your *heart* only, you cannot be converted in you *will* only; if you are truly converted and born again, the three are involved, the whole man is involved."[1]

A Christian is a person who was a servant of sin in the past but has been made a servant of righteousness (Romans 6:17-18). Before their salvation, the Bible says of all men: "**ye were the servants of sin** (Romans 6:17, 20); **ye were without Christ…having no hope, and without God in the world** (Ephesians 2:12); **ye were sometimes darkness** (Ephesians 5:8); **ye were as sheep going astray**" (1 Peter 2:25).

A CHANGE OF OWNERSHIP

A Christian is a person who has had a change of masters! All men are servants of sin by nature (Ephesians 2:3). They are **shapen in iniquity** and conceived in sin (Psalm 51:5), and held captive and servants of sin until the Lord Jesus Christ makes them free from that terrible bondage (John 8:36). The real proof that all of mankind are servants of sin is not so much in what they do, but in what they do not do! They are in bondage to so many lies that the truth seems beyond their comprehension. When men hear the truth of the glorious gospel of Christ, then why do they not readily receive the Lord Jesus Christ and believe on him? The gospel is by far the greatest news this old wicked world has ever heard! The truth as to why lost people do not believe the gospel is that their master does not allow them to believe. Sinners are held captive by sin by their master who keeps their minds blinded to **the light of the glorious gospel of Christ, who is the image of God** (2 Corinthians 4:3-4). Whenever they hear the word of God, Satan comes immediately and takes **away the word that was sown in their hearts** (Mark 4:15). Many of them are not violent or openly wicked sinners, but they are nevertheless servants of sin. Their master will not allow them to believe in God's Son and in his glorious gospel. They are blinded by him. They are in a terrible situation. **There is none righteous, no, not one** (Romans 3:10).

Satan uses many devices to keep his servants captive to the darkness of unbelief. Science and religion take the two leading positions in the devil's fight against the truth. The false and unbiblical theory of evolution—**science falsely so called** (1 Timothy 6:20)—has become a world "religion." This false theory is taught as science in the government schools, by books and magazine articles, and by the news media. It is not science, and it is certainly not truth. But the devil's greatest weapon of deception is religion. He is, with the exception of true faith in the Bible, the author of all of the world's religions, because he is the spiritual **god of this world** (2 Corinthians 4:3-4). God only knows how many different religions there are in the world. Everyone of these false religions are simply tools of the devil to keep his blinded servants on the broad way that leads to destruction in hell (Matthew 7:13-14). The way of salvation and eternal life is in the Lord Jesus Christ alone. Sinners are saved by God's grace through faith in Jesus Christ. And they are saved one by one, as individuals. You must come as you are in repentance and faith to the Lord Jesus, and he will save you (John 6:37).

Man is always a servant. Man is never free; he is either a servant of sin and Satan or he is a servant of God and of the Lord Jesus Christ. At his physical birth, he comes into the world a servant of sin. By the spiritual birth, he becomes the servant of Jesus Christ. Paul refers to himself as, "**Paul, a servant of Jesus Christ**" in Romans 1:1. Likewise Paul reminds the Corinthians, "What? know ye not that your body is the temple of the Holy Ghost which is in you, which ye have of God, and **ye are not your own**? **For ye are bought with a price**: therefore glorify God in your body, and in your spirit, which are God's" (1 Corinthians 6:19-20).

Usually it is fairly obvious whether a man is a real Christian or not. The master of a servant insists upon a certain kind of conduct; therefore if you look at a servant's conduct you can tell who his master is (Romans 6:16). Jesus Christ said, "**Ye shall know them by their fruits**" (Matthew 7:16).

Romans 6:16 reminds us, "Know ye not, that to whom ye yield yourselves servants to obey, his servants ye are to whom ye obey; whether of sin unto death, or of obedience unto righteousness?"

Obviously a man who has been born again has made Jesus Christ his master by his own free will, and he has believed and obeyed the gospel with his whole heart. He knows to whom he belongs, and who is his master, and in whose kingdom he lives and acts. Can you say that you were the servant of sin, but now you are a servant of Jesus Christ? That is what makes us Christian, nothing less than that. It is the most profound and greatest change that is possible in a human life. Unfortunately there are those who **profess that they know God; but in works they deny him, being abominable, and disobedient, and unto every good work reprobate** (Titus 1:16). These have believed with their mind, but they have not **obeyed from the heart that form of doctrine which was delivered** them (Romans 6:17). They profess they are Christians. They think that they are Christians. But they are not Christians! They are still on the broad way that leadeth to destruction (Matthew 7:13-14)! They are still bound in sin, blinded by the devil, and on their way to hell. They have **believed in vain** (1 Corinthians 15:2). Their faith is dead and without works (James 2:26). God is not working in them to will and to do of his good pleasure (Philippians 2:13; Ephesians 3:20)! Likewise, the question to you is, "Are you a real born again believer?"

Therefore, take heed to the exhortation of 2 Corinthians 13:5, "**Examine yourselves, whether ye be in the faith; prove your own selves. Know ye not your own selves, how that Jesus Christ is in you, except ye be reprobates?**"

II. THE AUTHOR

THE WORD OF GOD

The Lord Jesus Christ has given his great commission to Christians in the world. He has commanded us: "**Go ye into all the world, and preach the gospel to every creature**" (Mark 16:15). For the gospel **is the power of God unto salvation to everyone that believeth** (Romans 1:16); and the Lord **is not willing that any should perish, but that all should come to repentance** (2 Peter. 3:9). The gospel is **how that Christ died for our sins according to the scriptures; And that he was buried, and that he rose again the third day according to the scriptures** (1 Corinthians 15:3-4). We are to get the gospel out to every creature in the world. That is the commission given to living Christians in the world.

Therefore, the first cause of the great change from sinner to saint of God is the **word of God**. This is what Paul calls **that form of doctrine** (Romans 6:17). Peter wrote, "**Being born again, not of corruptible seed, but of incorruptible, by the word of God, which liveth and abideth for ever**" (1 Peter 1:23). But what is this **form of doctrine** that is to be used to affect so great a change in the servants of sin?

The **form of doctrine** is not only a message of forgiveness, although it certainly includes forgiveness of sins. Some people think that forgiveness is the only message to be given. They say, "Come to Christ; come to Jesus, decide for him. If you want forgiveness, here it is." This teaching is dangerous and unscriptural. There is not enough to it. The **form of doctrine** delivered to the Roman believers was the full doctrine that Paul had been writing to them in his letter—nothing less.

The correct message of the gospel starts with man in sin under the wrath of a holy God (John 3:36). Paul started with that subject back in Romans chapter 1 in verses 16 through 18. The doctrine of sin and God's holy wrath against sin is a vital part of the gospel message. Before we can see the need of salvation we must all see ourselves as **condemned already** (John 3:18), bound for hell, hopeless and helpless in sin. We must see the terrifying and awful nature of such a condition, its slavery to sin and Satan, and the terrible end to which this condition will inevitably lead.

Then the **form of doctrine** must explain to the sinner that there is utter hopelessness to obtain favour with God through any and all human works.

Paul used the first three chapters of Romans to explain this part of the doctrine. For example, the Gentiles cannot deliver themselves through their philosophy. Neither can the Jews deliver themselves by keeping the law. Paul then concludes his argument by saying, "**for there is no difference: For all have sinned, and come short of the glory of God**" (Romans 3:22-23). The entire human race is in the same condition before they are individually saved by the grace of God. Man cannot save himself. It does not matter how good and moral and excellent and religious he may be. That counts for nothing with God. Neither circumcision, nor baptism, nor church membership, nor faithful church attendance, nor any work on man's part can save him.

This **form of doctrine** then goes on to tell the sinner that God has provided a way for him to escape the hopelessness, helplessness, and despair of his condition. After declaring, "**For all have sinned, and come short of the glory of God**" (Romans 6:23), Paul goes on to tell the sinner that he may be justified freely by God's grace through faith in the blood of Jesus Christ:

Romans 3:24-26 gloriously states, "**Being justified freely by his grace through the redemption that is in Christ Jesus: Whom God hath set forth to be a propitiation through faith in his blood, to declare his righteousness for the remission of sins that are past, through the forbearance of God; To declare, I say, at this time his righteousness: that he might be just, and the justifier of him which believeth in Jesus.**"

THE HOLY GHOST

Certainly, the **form of doctrine** is found in the written word of God, but how does God cause his word to affect a change in the lost man, who is **dead in trespasses and sins** (Ephesians 2:1)? How can God cause the natural man, **who receiveth not the things of the Spirit of God** (1 Corinthians 2:14) to hear the gospel? How can he cause the lost man to understand and see the **light of the glorious gospel of Christ** (2 Corinthians 4:4)? The answer is that the Spirit of God must visit the lost man and reveal **that form of doctrine** to him! And that is exactly what God has been doing throughout the past almost two thousand years since the resurrection of the Lord Jesus Christ from the dead! The Lord Jesus told his disciples in John 16:7-11, "**Nevertheless I tell you the truth; It is expedient for you that I go away: for if I go not away, the Comforter will not come unto you; but if I depart, I will send him unto you. And when he is come, he will reprove the world of sin, and of righteousness, and of judgment: Of sin, because they believe not on me; Of righteousness, because**

I go to my Father, and ye see me no more; Of judgment, because the prince of this world is judged."

The Holy Ghost visits men at times of his own choosing (John 3:8) to illuminate their hearts with the truth (Hebrews 10:32). **The wind bloweth where it listeth** (John 3:8), that is, the Holy Ghost moves when and where he desires or chooses. He enlightens men intellectually with knowledge and grace, and by the word of God, he reproves men of sin, of righteousness, and of judgment. To reprove means "to convince of a fault, or to make it manifest," according to Noah Webster 1828 Dictionary. By his Holy Spirit God is now **visiting the Gentiles, to take out of them a people for his name** (Acts 15:14). He calls men **by our gospel, to the obtaining of the glory of our Lord Jesus Christ** (2 Thessalonians 2:14). When the Lord Jesus breathed on his apostles and said unto them, "**Receive ye the Holy Ghost**" (John 20:22), **[t]hen opened he their understanding, that they might understand the scriptures** (Luke 24:45).

On the glorious day when the Holy Ghost visited this poor wretched sinner [ME!], I had already read the gospels of Matthew, Mark, and Luke. However, it was not until I began to read John's gospel that the Holy Ghost opened my understanding and called me by the gospel. Praise God! **God be thanked** (Romans 6:17)! **Thanks be unto God for his unspeakable gift** (2 Corinthians 9:15)! **Salvation is of the LORD** (Jonah 2:9).

Colossians 1:12-14 says, "**Giving thanks unto the Father, which hath made us meet to be partakers of the inheritance of the saints in light: Who hath delivered us from the power of darkness, and hath translated us into the kingdom of his dear Son: In whom we have redemption through his blood, even the forgiveness of sins.**"

III. THE EVIDENCE

If you were tried in a court of law for being a Christian, would there be enough evidence to convict you? What is the evidence that the great change of being born again has taken place in a man's heart? We find the answer in one of our text verses:

Romans 6:17—"But God be thanked, that ye were the servants of sin, but **ye have obeyed from the heart** that form of doctrine which was delivered you."

To say that a man obeys from his heart is the same as saying that he believes with all his heart (Romans 10:16). The faith that saves is not a vain faith, but an obedient faith. He believes and obeys from his heart not just the part of the gospel that he likes, but the entire truth of the gospel, **that form of doctrine which was delivered**. In the first chapter of Romans, Paul says that he had received **grace and apostleship, for OBEDIENCE to the faith among all nations** (Romans 1:5). Later in chapter two of Romans he writes of the contrast between the obedient Christian and the disobedient rebels. The Christian seeks for glory and honour by patient continuance in well doing (Romans 2:7); meanwhile the contentious **do not OBEY the truth, but OBEY unrighteousness** (Romans 2:8). In the final chapter of Romans, Paul writes that the gospel is **made known to all nations for the OBEDIENCE of faith** (Romans 16:26). The Lord Jesus Christ is **the author of eternal salvation unto all them that OBEY him** (Hebrews 5:9). Nevertheless, the Lord Jesus Christ is also the destroyer of those **that OBEY NOT the gospel of our Lord Jesus Christ: Who shall be punished with everlasting destruction from the presence of the Lord, and from the glory of his power** (2 Thessalonians 1:8-9)! God is commanding all men everywhere to repent (Acts 17:31). Jesus Christ said, "**Except ye repent, ye shall all likewise perish**" (Luke 13:3, 5). Likewise, my question to you is, "Have you **obeyed the gospel**?"

Obedience to the faith begins immediately at salvation: "**For the grace of God that bringeth salvation hath appeared to all men, Teaching us that, denying ungodliness and worldly lusts, we should live soberly, righteously, and godly, in this present world**" (Titus 2:11-12). The very reality of sin is disobedience of God, his word, and his way; therefore the very reality of faith is obedience to God. A Christian man is one who obeys God. He obeys everything that God has said in his word. He rejoices in the word of God (Psalm 119:162) which makes him free (John 8:31-32). He has undergone a profound change. The Christian is a willing servant of God, a happy servant who has the desire to live his life to the praise and glory of God and his dear Son who **came into the world to save sinners** (1 Timothy 1:15).

Faith is obedience, and any so-called faith that does not put its emphasis on obedience is unworthy of the term. Furthermore, the Christian not only obeys, he obeys **from the heart** (Romans 6:17)! He does not grudge or feel that the Christian life is too narrow. He does not try to live as close as he can to the world and to that old life of sin. That is not Christianity! A man that feels like that is a man who is not saved.

Therefore, are you a Christian? Have you obeyed from the heart that form of doctrine which was delivered to you? If you have not, I pray that you will before it is too late for you to **repent...and believe the gospel** (Mark 1:15). The books of John and Romans in the Holy Bible are a good place for you to start. I would encourage you to then open them up and start reading and meditating on their words.

Chapter 5

Self Examination

God gives an emphatic command to individuals who claim to be a Christian. If God commands it then it is wise to take heed and do what he says. In 2 Corinthians 13:5 God says, "**Examine yourselves, whether ye be in the faith; prove your own selves. Know ye not your own selves, how that Jesus Christ is in you, except ye be reprobates?**" Therefore, in this sermon we will examine ourselves using the scriptures.

The verse above contains a clear command for us to examine ourselves and make sure that we are indeed "in the faith," that is, that we are in "the faith of Jesus Christ" (Galatians 2:16), "the faith which was once delivered unto the saints" (Jude 1:3). We are commanded to examine ourselves. No one in the world is capable of examining you to determine whether you are saved or not. It is a tragic and damning tradition, that there are certain churches with men who confirm people in the faith. I studied the catechism of a certain church when I was a young boy and successfully answered the questions asked by the minister. On the following Sunday I received a white New Testament and was admitted to the membership of the church. Man's confirmation confused me, because I was no more saved than a dog! Thirty some years later, while alone in my house reading the Bible for the first time in my life, God opened my eyes to the truth, convicted me that I was a lost, hell-bound sinner, gave me repentance to acknowledge the truth of my condition and faith to believe the glorious gospel of Jesus Christ. I received the Lord Jesus Christ into my heart and was born again by the Spirit of God. Now I KNOW that I am saved; not because of any man's confirmation but because God's Spirit bears witness with my spirit that I am a child of God (Romans 8:16). Not only that, but God's word agrees and confirms to my heart that I am his.

The Bible teaches that the born again believer is, "in Christ," and has "the mind of Christ," and has been given a new heart and spirit by the Lord. "**Therefore if any man *be* in Christ, *he is* a new creature: old things are passed away; behold, all things are become new**" (2 Corinthians 5:17). God promises to born again believers in Ezekiel 36:26, "**A new heart also will I give you, and a new spirit will I put within you: and I will take away the stony heart out of your flesh, and I will give you an heart of flesh.**"

The new spiritual birth (John 3:3-7) takes place when a man repents of his unbelief and turns to Jesus Christ in faith. This "**new creature**" is said to be God's workmanship which has been "**created in Christ Jesus unto good works**" (Ephesians 2:10). Jesus said that his children shall be known by the "fruit" of their lives (Matthew 12:33; 7:15-20).

The fruitful life of the Christian is the outworking of the indwelling Holy Spirit of God. "**For it is God which worketh in you both to will and to do of *his* good pleasure**" (Philippians 2:13).

In direct opposition to the work of the Holy Spirit, the wickedness in the life of a lost man is the outworking of the spirit of the devil which works in him. "**And you *hath he quickened*, who were dead in trespasses and sins; Wherein in time past ye walked according to the course of this world, according to the prince of the power of the air** [Satan], **the spirit that now worketh in the children of disobedience**" (Ephesians 2:1-2).

The Bible also says that you can tell what is in a man's heart by his actions, "**For as he thinketh in his heart, so is he...**" (Proverbs 23:7). Therefore, "**Keep thy heart with all diligence; for out of it *are* the issues of life**" (Proverbs 4:23). In addition, Jesus said, "**But those things which proceed out of the mouth come forth from the heart; and they defile the man. For out of the heart proceed evil thoughts, murders, adulteries, fornications, thefts, false witness, blasphemies: These are *the things* which defile a man: but to eat with unwashen hands defileth not a man**" (Matthew 15:18-20).

Therefore, a man who constantly curses, steals, lies, gluts, commits fornication, or is constantly drunk or high on drugs, and does these things habitually without any conviction and punishment from God, gives evidence that he still has a wicked heart and that he must not have ever received a new heart from God!

Please hear and realize I am not your judge, but I have already judged myself by the same Bible that will judge you (John 12:48; 1 Corinthians 11:31). I know that by the grace of God my life changed dramatically and very noticeably since the day I met and received the Lord Jesus Christ. Please look with me at a few passages of scripture that were written "**that ye may know that ye have eternal life**" (1 John 5:13)! The book of 1 John gives us many statements by which we can individually judge ourselves concerning salvation. I hope that you will judge yourself and be honest about the results. They will be between you and the Lord. This self-examination is not given to condemn you, but to make you aware of your true condition and that, if need be, you might get things right with God and be saved by his grace.

I. DO YOU KEEP GOD'S WORD?

God lets us know in 1 John 2:3-5, "**And hereby we do know that we know him, if we keep his commandments. He that saith, I know him, and keepeth not his commandments, is a liar, and the truth is not in him. But whoso keepeth his word, in him verily is the love of God perfected: hereby know we that we are in him.**"

I do not know how many times men have said to me, "Well, you know, nobody's perfect, preacher!" Of course I know that, but that is a lame excuse for living like the devil, for living in willful rebellion against the word of God! If you are going "on unto perfection" (Hebrews 6:1), then your life should be getting more and more like Jesus as time moves on. Proverbs 4:18 explains, "**the path of the just *is* as the shining light, that shineth more and more unto the perfect day.**"

Do you find yourself back in the mire of sin? Have you ever considered that you should by faith be gaining the victory over the lust of the flesh and the lust of the eyes and the pride of life [the world] (1 John 5:4)? Perhaps you did not believe the gospel "from the heart" (Romans 6:17-18). Perhaps you only believed it in vain in your head (1 Corinthians 15:2). Examine yourselves by reflecting on these scriptures.

"For this is the love of God, that we keep his commandments: and his commandments are not grievous [burdensome]" (1 John 5:3).

Jesus said, "**If ye love me, keep my commandments**" (John 14:15).

Please do not go around telling people how much you love the Lord, when your life itself proves you to be a hypocrite. Your "lip service" amounts to nothing but hot air. You might say, "Well, I know that I love the Lord in my heart!" If you really did, then you would keep his words. Or will you call Jesus Christ a liar? He said plainly, "**If a man love me, he WILL KEEP MY WORDS**" (John 14:23).

The Lord Jesus said that there were those who profess to know him, but he does not know them! "**They profess that they know God; but in works they deny *him*, being abominable, and disobedient, and unto every good work reprobate**" (Titus 1:16).

Jesus wants us to realize this so much that he provided us to see into the future. Jesus spoke about the Day of Judgment, saying, "**Not every one that saith unto me, Lord, Lord, shall enter into the kingdom of heaven; but he that doeth the will of my Father which is in heaven. Many will say to me in that day, Lord, Lord, have we not prophesied in thy name? and in thy name have cast out devils? and in thy name done many wonderful works? And then will I profess unto them, I never knew you: depart from me, ye that work iniquity**" (Matthew 7:21-23).

"**Nevertheless the foundation of God standeth sure, having this seal, The Lord knoweth them that are his. And, Let every one that nameth the name of Christ depart from iniquity** [sin]" (2 Timothy 2:19).

One day Jesus was speaking to a great crowd, someone called out that Christ's biological family was wanting him. Jesus looked around "**[a]nd he answered and said unto them, My mother and my brethren are these which hear the word of God, and do it**" (Luke 8:21).

II. DO YOU HATE YOUR BROTHER?

God lets us know through the writing of the Apostle John in 1 John 2:9, "**He that saith he is in the light, and hateth his brother, is in darkness even until now.**" In the next chapter, God repeats, "**Whosoever hateth his brother is a murderer: and ye know that no murderer hath eternal life abiding in**

him" (1 John 3:15). Yet another time, in 1 John 4:20-21, God reiterates, "**If a man say, I love God, and hateth his brother, he is a liar: for he that loveth not his brother whom he hath seen, how can he love God whom he hath not seen? And this commandment have we from him, [t]hat he who loveth God love his brother also.**" Why do you think God would repeat three times something so important to us? Should God have to repeat himself? Not really. But God patiently understands that when he speaks, yes, even twice, that man still perceiveth it not (Job 33:14). Therefore, God repeats himself for our safety (Philippians 3:1). Therefore the question is, "Can you hear what God is saying to you through these three verses?"

I once knew a man who had been a pretty rough gang member and he got saved by the grace of God. Soon after his salvation, he received orders from the gang's "shot caller" to do violence to another man. Being a *real* Christian he refused to obey the shot caller. As a result of his disobedience he was rewarded by his former "friends" by being attacked and stabbed by another member of his former gang. When I visited him in "the hole" at the prison I minister in, I found that he was not bitter nor planning to take vengeance on the man who hurt him. Instead, he was rather praying for him! His faith had been severely tested, and he passed the test. He followed the example of his Saviour who prayed for his own executioners just after they had nailed him to the cross (Luke 23:34). This inmate was obeying the Lord's commandment. He showed that he truly loved the Lord, and that he was not simply giving "lip service" to the truth of the gospel.

Praise God for the commandment from God, "**Bless them that curse you, and pray for them which despitefully use you**" (Luke 6:28).

III. DO YOU LOVE THE WORLD?

The Bible speaks of "**this present evil world**" (Galatians 1:4), and proclaims that "**the whole world lieth in wickedness**" (1 John 5:19).

Do you enjoy watching prime time television? Does it bother you to see that wickedness and evil are rapidly increasing in our country and in the world? Do you enjoy the latest worldly music? Believers are commanded: "**Love not the world, neither the things *that are* in the world. If any man love the world, the love of the Father is not in him**" (1 John 2:15).

Do you love drugs? Would you rather get high on drugs than to fellowship with other born again believers in a good church? Do you love the newspaper or magazines more than the Bible? Is it relaxing or entertaining to read these periodicals but a boredom to read the Bible? Be honest with yourself. Be completely honest with God, because he is the only one who can search your heart (Jeremiah 17:10). You must have a new heart from God if you will escape hell fire!

If you honestly answer, "Yes" to any of these questions, than are you a lover of pleasure more than a lover of truth? Is the love of the Father in you? You fit the description of those poor lost souls who will perish forever in the lake of fire. You may be one of them. If God calls you by the gospel, and you do not repent before the Lord gathers his church up to meet him in the air, you will not have another opportunity. "**And for this cause God shall send them strong delusion, that they should believe a lie: That they all might be damned who believed not the truth, but had pleasure in unrighteousness**" (2 Thessalonians 2:11-12).

Do you often find yourself saying, "Well, it is just too hard to serve God"? That's simply not true. It is a blessing to serve him. It is a blessing to have the great privilege to know and walk with the Lord Jesus Christ through this wicked world. I love the Lord! I love his word! I love the truth! I love his people! He has delivered me from a GREAT DEATH, the second death, the eternal torments of the lake of fire (2 Corinthians 1:10; Revelation 21:14-15)!

This rotten world stinks! Why would I want to turn my back on my Lord and Saviour Jesus Christ for the garbage of this sin cursed world? By his grace I have been given victory over the world!

"**But thanks *be* to God, which giveth us the victory through our Lord Jesus Christ**" (1 Corinthians 15:57). "**For whatsoever is born of God overcometh the world: and this is the victory that overcometh the world, *even* our faith. Who is he that overcometh the world, but he that believeth that Jesus is the Son of God?**" (1 John 5:4-5).

IV. ARE YOU PURIFYING YOURSELF?

Finally, let's look at what God commands his children to do for their own good and for the good of others.

"**Behold, what manner of love the Father hath bestowed upon us, that we should be called the sons of God: therefore the world knoweth us not, because it knew him not. Beloved, now are we the sons of God, and it doth**

not yet appear what we shall be: but we know that, when he shall appear, we shall be like him; for we shall see him as he is. <u>And every man that hath this hope in him purifieth himself, even as he is pure</u>" (1 John 3:1-3).

The hope in the Christian is Jesus Christ himself! That gets us back to our text: "**Examine yourselves, whether ye be in the faith; prove your own selves. Know ye not your own selves, how that Jesus Christ is in you, except ye be reprobates?**" (2 Corinthians 13:5).

I have spoken to many men who have a very wrong attitude toward God. They think that the Lord makes puppets out of men when he saves them, and that after they are saved, God is responsible for all of their behavior. When they leave prison and go back to the same sins, they say, "Well, it must have been God's will," or, "God works in mysterious ways!" What a wicked thing it would be for you to blame God for the sins that you commit! Let it be known that God is not responsible for your sins that you commit against his will, you are! The only things in your life that God is the author of are the good works and godly thinking and living that he works in you.

"**For it is God which worketh in you both to will and to do of *his* good pleasure**" (Philippians 2:13).

"**Now unto him that is able to do exceeding abundantly above all that we ask or think, according to the power that worketh in us**" (Ephesians 3:20).

"**But by the grace of God I am what I am: and his grace which *was bestowed* upon me was not in vain; but I laboured more abundantly than they all: yet not I, but the grace of God which was with me**" (1 Corinthians 15:10).

I hope you do not use Paul's example of the pitiful state he was in as a lost man before he was saved (Romans 7), when he said that the law of sin in his members kept him from doing what he wanted to do. If you have been born again, you need to study and discover that the "old man," who had that law of sin in his members, has been crucified (Romans 6:6) and buried (Romans 6:4). Furthermore, the body of the new man in Christ Jesus is a member of "**his body, of his flesh, and of his bones**" (Ephesians 5:30). Therefore, "**the law of the Spirit of life in Christ Jesus hath made me free from the law of sin and death** [that used to work in the members of the "old man"]" (Romans 8:2)!

CONCLUSION

Have you examined yourself by these few scriptures from the word of God? Do you know—without a shadow of doubt—that if you were to die at this moment that you would go to be with the Lord (2 Corinthians 5:6-8)? If the answer is, "No," then perhaps all you have is "jail house religion," or perhaps you have never even thought about receiving Jesus Christ as your Saviour. There is nothing in the world more important than the eternal destiny of your soul! The Lord Jesus asked: "**For what is a man profited, if he shall gain the whole world, and lose his own soul? or what shall a man give in exchange for his soul?**" (Matthew 16:26).

The Lord Jesus Christ has made it very clear that unless a man repents of his unbelief and receives the Lord into his heart that he will perish (Luke 13:3-5). This message is not to condemn you, but to give you one more opportunity to hear the gospel, "**how that Christ died for our sins according to the scriptures; And that he was buried, and that he rose again the third day according to the scriptures**" (1 Corinthians 15:3-4). If you have examined yourself and found that Jesus Christ is not truly in you, then you can repent and be saved today.

"**And the servant of the Lord must not strive; but be gentle unto all *men*, apt to teach, patient, In meekness instructing those that oppose themselves; if God peradventure will give them repentance to the acknowledging of the truth; And *that* they may recover themselves out of the snare of the devil, who are taken captive by him at his will**" (2 Timothy 2:24-26).

Time is quickly running out! The Lord is coming soon! Today is the day of salvation (2 Corinthians 6:2)! Tomorrow may be too late! God does not want you to perish, but commands you now to repent (Acts 17:30).

"Seek **ye the LORD while he may be found, call ye upon him while he is near: Let the wicked forsake his way, and the unrighteous man his thoughts: and let him return unto the LORD, and he will have mercy upon him; and to our God, for he will abundantly pardon**" (Isaiah 55:6-7).

Chapter 6

CRUCIFIED WITH HIM

God said, "My people are destroyed for lack of knowledge" (Hosea 4:6). If the people of God today do not continue in the word of God, they also will be destroyed for lack of knowledge (Romans 8:13; 1 Corinthians 3:16-17)! The born again child of God can never lose the gift of eternal life, but he will never live the abundant and victorious life without the knowledge that God has so graciously given us in his precious word. Faith comes by understanding the word of God (Romans 10:17), and faith is the victory that overcomes the world (1 John 5:4). The "world" refers to "the lust of the flesh, and the lust of the eyes, and the pride of life" (1 John 2:16).

As you read this sermon, my prayer is that you will be quick to hear the word of God, and that you will also be quick to discard any false assumptions and understandings that you may have in disagreement with the word of God. The Lord Jesus promised the believing Jews, "If ye continue in my word, *then* are ye my disciples indeed; And ye shall know the truth, and the truth shall make you free" (John 8:31-32).

TWO GREAT MYSTERIES OF THE CROSS

According to the Noah Webster 1828 Dictionary, a mystery is a truth "which is beyond human comprehension until explained." Two mysterious operations of God (Colossians 2:10-13) were accomplished by Jesus Christ on the cross: the death of Christ for our sins, and the death of the believer in Christ.

I. SALVATION

"**Christ died for our sins according to the scriptures**" (1 Corinthians 15:3). It was on the cross that God "made him to be sin for us, who knew no sin; that we might be made the righteousness of God in him" (2 Corinthians 5:21): "Even the righteousness of God which is by faith of Jesus Christ" (Romans 3:22).

On the day of my salvation I had only read Matthew, Mark, Luke, and a small part of the gospel of John. I have no doubt whatsoever that on that rainy June afternoon alone in my house in Tennessee I was born again! The word of God had given me faith to believe on the Lord Jesus Christ, and the Holy Ghost had reproved me for my sin of unbelief (John 16:7-9). But I really didn't know very much at all about the Bible doctrines of salvation. I don't think I would have even used the term, "born again," because I hadn't yet read John chapter 3. I remember the difficulty I had telling my wife what had happened to me when she returned from work that afternoon. I told her that something wonderful had happened to me, that I believe that Jesus Christ is God! I had read John 1:1-14, and I believed it!

According to the scriptures, which I would later read, so many things happened to me that afternoon, of which I had no knowledge. It has taken me many years of reading and studying the Bible everyday to learn and understand most of the wonderful doctrines of the faith. Of course, I'm still learning. Some of my learning was misdirected by Bible teachers who meant well, but were only repeating what they had been taught and not understanding the accuracy of Bible doctrines. As a babe in Christ, I received their teaching as the truth. As I continued in God's word I have been gradually made free of these misunderstandings (John 8:31-32).

Of all the precious doctrines that I have learned concerning my security in Christ and the permanent indwelling of the Holy Ghost, I knew none of them at the time when I was born of the Spirit! I learned them later as I continued in God's word. Although I did not know or understand these things at the first, nevertheless they were true and applied to my life regardless of my knowledge of them. If I had stopped reading the Bible on the day of my salvation, only God knows what could have become of me. I would certainly be going to heaven, but my life could have been a real mess! I could have ended up in a false cult teaching false doctrines of men. I did attend two false churches after my salvation, but God's word showed me their errors and made me free. Thank God for his word! It is the only certain antidote for confusion.

II. SANCTIFICATION

"**And now, brethren, I commend you to God, and to the word of his grace, which is able to build you up, and to give you an inheritance among all them which are sanctified**" (Acts 20:32). God's word is able "[t]o open [people's] eyes, *and* to turn *them* from darkness to light, and *from* the power of Satan unto God, **that they may receive forgiveness of sins, and inheritance among <u>them which are sanctified by faith that is in me</u>**" (Acts 26:18).

There are many who teach the doctrine of sanctification in error. Because of my own belief of this erroneous teaching I wrote a sermon many years ago, which I called, *Two Men in One Body.* Now that I look back on that, I regret that I taught it to so many men. I believed it to be true at the time. I have taught through the book of Romans many times, and each time I missed this very important doctrine in chapters 6 through 8! I now encourage you to open up your Bible and read those three important chapters; meanwhile I comment on them.

I hope that you will read the following scriptures, along with a few comments, and that these truths will make you to become a more fruitful and bountiful Christian to the glory of God. May the Lord Jesus Christ and his perfect doctrine and plan be glorified! Some so-called charismatics make the scriptures of none effect by their "experience." Let us not disbelieve the scriptures for our lack of "experience." Some of God's truths are referred to as mysteries. We simply do not experience them in physical reality, nevertheless they are true.

"**For we walk by faith, not by sight**" (2 Corinthians 5:7).

The Lord Jesus Christ prayed to the Father: "**Sanctify them through thy truth: thy word is truth**" (John 17:17).

May the following truths give you a more perfect walk with your Saviour.

OUR OLD MAN IS CRUCIFIED

Be sure to please read Romans 6.

My Comments on Romans 6:1-11

Paul is speaking to born again believers, who have been baptized by Jesus Christ "**with** [into] **the Holy Ghost**" (Matthew 3:11-12) and into the body of Jesus Christ by the Spirit (1 Corinthians 12:13). When the believer was baptized with the Holy Ghost, he was joined unto the Lord's Spirit and is now "**one spirit**" with the Lord (1 Corinthians 6:17). By being baptized into the body of Christ, the believer becomes a member "**of his** [Christ's] **body, of his flesh, and of his bones**" (Ephesians 5:30). Therefore we who have been born again are one with the Lord in spirit and body—"one new man" (Ephesians 2:15).

The "old man" has miraculously and mysteriously been crucified with Christ and has become "one new man" in Christ (Ephesians 2:15)! You say, I don't feel it! I don't see it! But do you believe it? The Bible clearly declares, "**Therefore if any man *be* in Christ, *he is* a new creature: old things are passed away; behold, all things are become new**" (2 Corinthians 5:17). The Lord Jesus essentially repeated the following parable three times (Matthew 9:17; Mark 2:22; Luke 5:36-38), saying: "And he [Jesus] spake also a parable unto them; **No man putteth a piece of a new garment upon an old; if otherwise, then both the new maketh a rent, and the piece that was *taken* out of the new agreeth not with the old. And no man putteth new wine into old bottles; else the new wine will burst the bottles, and be spilled, and the bottles shall perish. But new wine must be put into new bottles; and both are preserved**." (Luke 5:36-38)

God does not join "the new man" to "the old man." The "old man" must first die and then rise as a "new creature," "one new man" (Ephesians 2:15) in Christ. God does not put the Holy Ghost into the "old man." "The old man" must first be crucified and then raised in newness of life in Christ Jesus.

"[O]ld things are passed away; behold, all things are become new" (2 Corinthians 5:17). The "old man" is passed away. He was **buried with him by baptism** [the baptism by the Holy Ghost (1 Corinthians 12:13)] **into death** (Romans 6:3-4; Colossians 2:12-13)].

According to the apostle we should know, **<u>that our old man is crucified with *him*</u>, that the body of sin might be destroyed, that henceforth we**

should not serve sin (Romans 6:6). The "old man" is called here, "**the body of sin**." This is **the body of this death** (Romans 7:24) spoken of by Paul as he expounded on his condition before salvation (Romans 7:9-25). This is the "old man" which had "the law of sin" in his members, the law which kept Paul from obeying the law of God. The law of sin overcame and ruled over the inward desire Paul had to serve God. The "old man" is a "wretched man" who cannot do the things he desires to do, for he is under the dominion of sin working in his members! The "law of sin" works in the members of the "old man," but not in the members of the body of Christ! **For he that is dead is freed from sin. Now if we be dead with Christ, we believe that we shall also live with him** (Romans 6:7-8).

RECKON GOD'S WORD IS TRUE

After telling us that we are dead to sin, baptized into the death of Christ, and risen with him in the likeness of his resurrection, we read the commandment, "**Likewise reckon ye also yourselves to be dead indeed unto sin, but alive unto God through Jesus Christ our Lord**" (Romans 6:1-11). According to the Noah Webster 1828 Dictionary, to reckon means "to reason with one's self and conclude from arguments" that what God has told us in his word is so! Do you believe that "**with God all things are possible**" (Matthew 19:26)? I believe I was crucified with Christ, buried with him, and have been raised together with him. I believe that God has "**quickened** [made alive] **us** [all born again believers] **together with Christ, (by grace ye are saved;) And hath raised *us* up together, and made *us* sit together in heavenly *places* in Christ Jesus**" (Ephesians 2:5-6). And God did all this for me without my knowledge or experience. Nevertheless, it is true, because that is what God said!

If you have been "born of the Spirit" (John 3:6), it is my hope and prayer that you will trust the word of God and believe that the "**old man is crucified with him**" (Romans 6:6). He is dead now and forever. He does not come back to life and commit sins in the believer's body! He is dead! Trust what God has said, and do not continue under a curse because you believe and trust what man has said!

"**Trust in the LORD with all thine heart; and lean not unto thine own understanding. In all thy ways acknowledge him, and he shall direct thy paths**" (Proverbs 3:5-6).

"Thus saith the LORD; Cursed *be* the man that trusteth in man, and maketh flesh his arm, and whose heart departeth from the LORD" (Jeremiahs 17:5).

"Blessed *is* the man that trusteth in the LORD, and whose hope the LORD is" (Jeremiah 17:7).

THE OLD MAN IS DEAD

Be sure to please Read Romans 7.

<u>My Comments on Romans 7:1-6</u>

Like a woman married to a wretched husband, she is loosed from the law of marriage at the death of her husband and is thereby made free to marry another man, so the born again believer is free to be married to Christ after the "old man" has been crucified with Christ. We **are become dead to the law** which worked in the members of our "old man"! **"That being dead wherein we were held"** (Romans 7:6) speaks of the "old man" wherein we were held in "captivity to the law of sin" (Romans 7:23), which worked in his members! **"For the law of the Spirit of life in Christ Jesus hath made me free from the law of sin and death"** (Romans 8:2). The law of sin worked in the members of the old man who is now dead! Through his great work on the cross, the Lord Jesus Christ has not only made us free from the penalty of the law, but from the power of sin! We are no longer compelled to sin by the law of sin in our members, because those "members" are now dead! The Lord Jesus has not only saved us from the penalty of our sins, but he has saved us from the power of sin!

"And she shall bring forth a son, and **thou shalt call his name JESUS: for he shall save his people from their sins"** (Matthew 1:21).

CRUCIFIED WITH CHRIST

The Apostle Paul wrote: **"I am crucified with Christ: nevertheless I live**; yet not I, but Christ liveth in me: and the life which I now live in the flesh I live by the faith of the Son of God, who loved me, and gave himself for me" (Galatians 2:20). Paul's crucifixion with Christ took place when Christ was crucified! It is the same with all of God's children. When Paul said, "I die daily," the context was the physical death that he faced daily as he served the Lord (1 Corinthians 15:31-32). He was certainly not speaking of himself having to be crucified daily with Christ. For this to be true, Christ would also have to be crucified daily! The Lord Jesus Christ died only once for sins for ever (Hebrews 7:27; 9:28)!

DEAD WITH CHRIST

Many times we read that God's children are dead, that is, the old man is dead!

"Wherefore if ye be **dead with Christ** from the rudiments of the world, why, as though living in the world, are ye subject to ordinances" (Colossians 2:20).

"If ye then be **risen with Christ**, seek those things which are above, where Christ sitteth on the right hand of God. Set your affection on things above, not on things on the earth. **For ye are dead**, and your life is hid with Christ in God. When Christ, *who is* our life, shall appear, then shall ye also appear with him in glory" (Colossians 3:1-4).

"*It is* a faithful saying: For if we be **dead with *him***, we shall also live with *him*" (2 Timothy 2:11).

"Who his own self bare our sins in his own body on the tree, that **we, being dead to sins, should live unto righteousness: by whose stripes ye were healed**" (1 Peter 2:24).

THE OLD MAN WAS PUT OFF AT SALVATION

The following scripture, Ephesians 4:20-25, has been taken out of context and misunderstood to mean that the saint of God is to participate in putting off the old man and in putting on the new man. How this is to be accomplished has been the subject of many books on the spiritual life. According to the foregoing scriptures, we discovered that "our old man is crucified with him" (Romans 6:6). Then for what reason would we believe that we must have a part in putting off the old man again? Read the following verses:

"But ye have not so learned Christ; If so be that ye have heard him, and have been taught by him, as the truth is in Jesus: **That ye put off concerning the former conversation the old man**, which is corrupt according to the deceitful lusts; And be renewed in the spirit of your mind; **And that ye put on the new man, which after God is created in righteousness and true holiness**. Wherefore [for which reason] putting away lying, speak every man truth with his neighbour: for we are members one of another" (Ephesians 4:20-25).

These verses do not command the saint to put off the old man and to put on the new man! These verses declare to the saint what the operation of God has already done to and for him. Put in other words, they say that if you have heard Christ and have been taught by him, then you have learned, that ye [have] put off concerning the former conversation the old man...And that ye [have] put on the new man (verses 20-24). Then in light of this truth we are commanded to put away lying (verse 25).

Colossians 3:1-11 proves that this is a correct interpretation of Ephesians 4:20-25. Open up your Bible and read this passage of scripture. In the first three verses we find that we are risen with Christ, and that we are dead to sin. Certainly there can be no doubt that all born again believers "**are risen with him through the faith of the operation of God, who hath raised him from the dead**" (Colossians 2:12). **For ye are dead, and your life is hid with Christ in God** (Colossians 3:3). "God forbid. How shall we, that **are dead to sin**, live any longer therein?" (Romans 6:2). It could not be put any plainer than this!

Then, in light of these great truths, we read, "**Mortify therefore your members which are upon the earth**" (Colossians 3:5). To mortify does not mean, put to death! A mortician does not put bodies to death, he prepares and disposes of bodies that are already dead! In like manner therefore the born again child of God is to reckon himself to be dead indeed unto sin (Romans 6:11). The born again child of God is to dispose of the sinful habits and desires that the past experiences of the old man have left in his conscious mind: things like, "fornication, uncleanness, inordinate affection, evil concupiscence, and covetousness, which is idolatry" (Colossians 3:5). The "old man" was incapable of bringing his body under subjection (1 Corinthians 9:27). He had the law of sin working in his members (Romans 7:23). The new man is a member of Christ's body (Ephesians 5:30) and is empowered by the Holy Ghost (John 1:12) to become a son of God. Because of what God has done for him, he is now able to put away all the deeds of the old man and walk in newness of life (Romans 6:4).

Child of God, there was a time when you walked and lived in these sins, but this was in the past (Colossians 3:7). Now you are "dead indeed unto sin" (Romans 6:11). Now you have been "made free from sin" (Romans 6:18). Therefore we read, "Lie not one to another, seeing that **ye have put off the old man with his deeds**; **And have put on the new *man*, which is renewed in knowledge after the image of him that created him**: Where there is neither Greek nor Jew, circumcision nor uncircumcision, Barbarian, Scythian, bond *nor* free: but Christ *is* all, and in all" (Colossians 3:9-11). The "old man" was crucified with Christ, and the "new man" was created by God!

CONCLUSION

The Lord Jesus Christ died on the cross to save us, and we were crucified with him to sanctify us. I hope some of you will stop justifying your sins by blaming "the old man," for he is dead! The Christian still has a free will. He can choose to sin or to obey God, but he is no longer compelled to sin by the "law of sin" which did work in the members of the "old man," or by some so-called "sin nature," which term is not to be found anywhere in the scriptures. When a Christian sins he sins "wilfully" (Hebrews 10:26).

In the light of the great truths revealed in Romans chapters 6 through 8, Paul wrote, "I beseech you therefore, brethren, by the mercies of God, that ye present your bodies a living sacrifice, holy, acceptable unto God, *which is* your reasonable service. And be not conformed to this world: but be ye transformed by the renewing of your mind, that ye may prove what *is* that good, and acceptable, and perfect, will of God" (Romans 12:1-2).

"What? know ye not that your body is the temple of the Holy Ghost *which is* in you, which ye have of God, and ye are not your own? For ye are bought with a price: therefore glorify God in your body, and in your spirit, which are God's" (1 Corinthians 6:19-20).

If you are not saved, I hope this sermon will draw you to Christ. Being saved and knowing that you are going to heaven is wonderful. But it is also very wonderful to live and have fellowship with the Lord daily, to live a victorious life through faith in the word of God. In the Bible, the gospel of John was written to give the unbeliever faith in Christ so that he could be saved. Christ died for your sins. When you receive him a new life begins (John 1:12-13).

Chapter 7

The Believer's Hope

Today sermon outline is based on 1 Thessalonians 4:13-18, which says, "But I would not have you to be ignorant, brethren, concerning them which are asleep, that ye sorrow not, even as others which have no hope. For if we believe that Jesus died and rose again, even so them also which sleep in Jesus will God bring with him. For this we say unto you by the word of the Lord, that we which are alive *and* remain unto the coming of the Lord shall not prevent them which are asleep. For the Lord himself shall descend from heaven with a shout, with the voice of the archangel, and with the trump of God: and the dead in Christ shall rise first: Then we which are alive *and* remain shall be caught up together with them in the clouds, to meet the Lord in the air: and so shall we ever be with the Lord. Wherefore comfort one another with these words."

It is my desire that you might not be ignorant concerning the blessed glorious hope that we have in Christ, but that you might be filled with the knowledge of the believer's hope in all wisdom and spiritual understanding. Therefore, let's get right into our sermon.

IGNORANT BRETHREN

The beginning of this passages begins with an important point. First Thessalonians 4:13 starts by stating, "But I would not have you to be ignorant, brethren…"

God does not want his children to be ignorant of the truth of his word. Several things are mentioned in the following scriptures of the passage of our text that we should *not* be ignorant of:

1. God's righteousness is not obtained by the works of the law (Romans 10:3-4), but only "by faith of Jesus Christ" (Romans 3:22).
2. Israel's spiritual blindness is only "in part" for the present time, and one day "all Israel shall be saved" (Romans 11:25-26).
3. The Rock out of which the water came for the children of Israel in the wilderness, represented the Lord Jesus Christ (1 Corinthians 10:1-4), from which now comes the Holy Ghost to all them that believe on him (John 7:37-39).
4. Many spiritual gifts come from God (1 Corinthians 12:1).
5. The devices of Satan (2 Corinthians 2:11).
6. The present state and position of those who "sleep in Jesus" (1 Thessalonians 4:13-14).
7. That "one day *is* with the Lord as a thousand years, and a thousand years as one day" (2 Peter 3:8).

All of the above scriptures are found in books of the Holy Bible which were written by the Apostle Paul. And concerning these scriptures, Paul wrote in 1 Corinthians 14:37-38: **"If any man think himself to be a prophet, or spiritual, let him acknowledge that the things that I write unto you are the commandments of the Lord. But if any man be ignorant, let him be ignorant.**" In other words, if you deny that the scriptures written by Paul are "in truth, the word of God" (1 Thessalonians 2:13), then you are willingly ignorant (2 Peter 3:5, 15-16)!

SLEEP IN JESUS

First Thessalonians 4:13 continues to say, "…concerning them which are asleep…"

In the context here, "sleep" is a reference to the death of the physical body. See the following supporting references:

1. When Jesus heard the news that the daughter of the ruler of the synagogue was dead, he said, "Fear not: believe only, and she shall be made whole" (Luke 8:50). And when he came to the house, "all wept, and bewailed her: but he said, Weep not; **she is not dead, but sleepeth**. And they laughed him to scorn, knowing that **she was dead**. And he put them all out, and took her by the hand, and called, saying, Maid, arise. **And her spirit came again**, and she arose straightway: and he commanded to give her meat. And her parents were astonished: but he charged them that they should tell no man what was done" (Luke 8:52-56).
2. The Lord Jesus referred to Lazarus' death as sleep: "These things said he: and after that he saith unto them, **Our friend Lazarus sleepeth; but I go, that I may awake him out of sleep**. Then said his disciples, Lord, if he sleep, he shall do well. **Howbeit Jesus spake of his death**: but they thought that he had spoken of taking of rest in sleep. Then said Jesus unto them plainly, **Lazarus is dead**" (John 11:11-14).
3. When Stephen was stoned to death by the Jews, the scripture said that: "**he fell asleep**" (Acts 7:60).
4. After the resurrection of Jesus Christ from the dead, we read: "And the graves were opened; and **many bodies of the saints which slept arose**" (Matthew 27:52).
5. Whether the believer's body is alive [awake] or dead [asleep], the believer's soul lives together with the Lord, "Who died for us, that, **whether we wake or sleep, we should live together with him**" (1 Thessalonians 5:10).

The Holy Bible does NOT teach so called "soul sleep." At death the soul and spirit of the believer go to be with the Lord in heaven: "Therefore *we are* always confident, knowing that, whilst we are at home in the body, we are absent from the Lord: (For we walk by faith, not by sight:) **We are confident, *I say*, and willing rather to be absent from the body, and to be present with the Lord**" (2 Corinthians 5:6-8). The Apostle Paul had a desire to leave his body and be with the Lord. He wrote: "For to me to live *is* Christ, and **to die *is* gain**. But if I live in the flesh, this *is* the fruit of my labour: yet what I shall choose I wot not. For I am in a strait betwixt two, **having a desire to depart, and to be with Christ; which is far better**" (Philippians 1:21-23).

When a lost man dies, his soul and spirit go to hell: "And it came to pass, that the beggar died, and was carried by the angels into Abraham's bosom: **the rich man also died, and was buried** [his body was asleep in the grave]; **And in hell he lift up his eyes, being in torments, and seeth Abraham afar off, and Lazarus in his bosom**" (Luke 16:22-23). The early Christians called their burial ground a "cemetery." The word cemetery comes from the Greek word "koimētḗrion." The Greek word means dormitory, sleeping chamber, or a sleeping place. (koimē- is the variant stem of koimân—to put to sleep, and –tērion is the suffix, meaning of locality.) Isaiah and Daniel both speak of the resurrection of the dead as the dead being awakened: "Thy dead men shall live, together with my dead body shall they arise. Awake and sing, ye that dwell in dust: for thy dew *is as* the dew of herbs, and the earth shall cast out the dead" (Isaiah 26:19). "**And many of them that sleep in the dust of the earth shall awake**, some to everlasting life, and some to shame *and* everlasting contempt" (Daniel 12:2).

Next, the end of 1 Thessalonians 4:13 says, "…that ye sorrow not, even as others which have no hope."

The "others which have no hope" are called "aliens from the commonwealth of Israel, and strangers from the covenants of promise, **having no hope, and without God in the world**" (Ephesians 2:12).

The believer's "HOPE" is the Lord Jesus Christ himself:

1. "To whom God would make known what *is* the riches of the glory of this mystery among the Gentiles; which is **Christ in you, the hope of glory**" (Colossians 1:27).
2. "And every man that hath **this hope in him** purifieth himself, even as he is pure" (1 John 3:3; 2 Corinthians 5:17).
3. "Paul, an apostle of Jesus Christ by the commandment of God our Saviour, and **Lord Jesus Christ, *which is* our hope**" (1 Timothy 1:1).
4. "**Looking for that blessed hope, and the glorious appearing of the great God and our Saviour Jesus Christ**" (Titus 2:13).
5. "The LORD also shall roar out of Zion, and utter his voice from Jerusalem; and the heavens and the earth shall shake: but **the LORD *will be* the hope of his people**, and the strength of the children of Israel" (Joel 3:16).
6. "Blessed *is* the man that trusteth in the LORD, and **whose hope the LORD is**" (Jeremiah 17:7).
7. "**Which *hope* we have as an anchor of the soul**, both sure and stedfast, and which entereth into that within the veil; Whither the forerunner is for us entered, ***even* Jesus**, made an high priest for ever after the order of Melchisedec" (Hebrews 6:19-20). "**And every man that hath this hope in him purifieth himself, even as he is pure**" (1 John 3:3).

First Thessalonians 4:14 says, "For if we believe that Jesus died and rose again, even so them also which sleep in Jesus will God bring with him."

The souls and spirits of the "dead in Christ," those whose bodies are in the grave, and "sleep in Jesus," are with the Lord now. When the Lord descends from heaven (1 Thessalonians 4:16), he will bring these souls "with him." At that time they will be given their new, glorified bodies. These new bodies shall rise from their sleep in the earth. God will give every soul "**a body as it hath pleased him, and to every seed his own body**" (1 Corinthians 15:38). They were "**sown** [buried] **in corruption**," but they will be "**raised in incorruption**" (1 Corinthians 15:42). The old body "**is sown in dishonour; it is raised in glory: it is sown in weakness; it is raised in power**: **It is sown a natural body; it is raised a spiritual body. There is a natural body, and there is a spiritual body**" (1 Corinthians 15:43-44).

The scriptures make it clear that the soul and spirit depart the body at death:

1. When the Lord Jesus raised the daughter of the ruler of the synagogue from death, we read: "**And her spirit came again, and she arose straightway**: and he commanded to give her meat" (Luke 8:55).
2. Speaking of Rachel's death at the birth of Benjamin, we read: "And it came to pass, **as her soul was in departing, (for she died)** that she called his name Benoni: but his father called him Benjamin" (Genesis 35:18).
3. At death the soul will be "**absent from the body, and...present with the Lord**" (2 Corinthians 5:6-8).
4. Paul knew that his soul would depart his body at death (2 Timothy 4:6).
5. Elijah prayed for the LORD to restore the life of a dead child, "And the LORD heard the voice of Elijah; and **the soul of the child came into him again, and he revived**" (1 Kings 17:22).
6. Paul wrote: "For to me to live *is* Christ, and **to die *is* gain**. But if I live in the flesh, this *is* the fruit of my labour: yet what I shall choose I wot not. For I am in a strait betwixt two, **having a desire to depart, and to be with Christ**; which is far better" (Philippians 1:21-23).
7. Since the soul and spirit of the saved person go to be with the Lord at the time of their physical death, we can therefore understand why the scripture declares: "**Precious in the sight of the LORD *is* the death of his saints**" (Psalm 116:15)!

First Thessalonians 4:15 says, "For this we say unto you by the word of the Lord, that we which are alive *and* remain unto the coming of the Lord shall not prevent them which are asleep."

According to the Noah Webster 1828 Dictionary, "prevent" means to go before; to precede. David wrote: "**The God of my mercy shall prevent** [go before] **me**: God shall let me see *my desire* upon mine enemies" (Psalm 59:10). So verse 15 is saying that living Christians will not "prevent [go before]" those who are asleep in Jesus. This is confirmed by the very next verse.

The beginning of 1 Thessalonians 4:16 says, "For the Lord himself..."

"The Lord himself" will personally come to catch his church up to meet him in the air. When the Lord comes for his church, he will fulfill the promise he made to his apostles, saying: "**In my Father's house are many mansions: if *it were* not *so*, I would have told you. I go to prepare a place for you. And if I go and prepare a place for you, I will come again, and receive you unto myself; that where I am, *there* ye may be also**" (John 14:2-3). This is remarkably similar to what a traditional Jewish groom would say to his bride. The groom would then leave her in her own house to build an addition onto his father's house before returning to get his bride. Then he would return for his bride in the middle of the night, "as a thief" (1 Thessalonians 5:2), at an hour she might not think (Matthew 24:44), with a loud cry, and a procession of trumpet blast, and his friends saying: "Behold, the bridegroom cometh; go ye out to meet him" (Matthew. 25:6).

Several Old Testament prophets seemed to prophesy of the seven year period during which the church will be in heaven while the earth experiences the seven year long tribulation period. Isaiah wrote: "**Thy dead *men* shall live, *together with* my dead body shall they arise. Awake and sing, ye that dwell in dust: for thy dew *is as* the dew of herbs, and the earth shall cast out the dead. Come, my people, enter thou into thy chambers, and shut thy doors about thee: hide thyself as it were for a little moment, until the indignation be overpast**. For, behold, the LORD cometh out of his place to punish the inhabitants of the earth for their iniquity: the earth also shall disclose her blood, and shall no more cover her slain" (Isaiah 26:19-21). David also wrote: "**For in the time of trouble he shall hide me in his pavilion: in the secret of his tabernacle shall he hide me**; he shall set me up upon a rock" (Psalm 27:5). This "**time of trouble**" is specifically called "**the time of Jacob's trouble**" (Jeremiah 30:7). This is the seven year period, the last week of Daniel's seventy week prophecy (Daniel 9:27), during which time, according to the Lord Jesus Christ, the world will suffer "**great tribulation, such as was not since the beginning of the world to this time, no, nor ever shall be**" (Matthew 24:21). Zephaniah wrote: "Seek ye the LORD, all ye meek of the earth, which have wrought his judgment; seek righteousness, seek meekness: **it may be ye shall be hid in the day of the LORD'S anger**" (Zephaniah 2:3). The Lord promised the church in Philadelphia: "**Because thou hast kept the word of my patience, I also will keep thee from the hour of temptation, which shall come upon all the world, to try them that dwell upon the earth**" (Revelation 3:10).

The Lord himself will gather the church up to meet him in the air *before* the tribulation period (1 Thessalonians 4:16). Then later there will be an entirely different gathering together of different believers *after* the tribulation period. The Lord prophesied of this gathering, when he said: "**Immediately after the tribulation of those days…he shall send his angels with a great sound of a trumpet, and they shall gather together his elect from the four winds, from one end of heaven to the other**" (Matthew 24:29-31). It is important to notice that "the Lord himself" will gather the church to meet him in the air, while the Lord will "send his angels" to gather the tribulation believers together after the tribulation period. Many have confused these two events, and have wrongly been led to believe that the church will go through the tribulation period.

But the Church *must* be taken out of the way *before* the antichrist can be revealed. After writing about "the man of sin…the son of perdition" who shall be revealed, the man "[w]ho opposeth and exalteth himself above all that is called God, or that is worshipped; so that he as God sitteth in the temple of God, shewing himself that he is God" (2 Thessalonians 2:3-4), Paul then writes: "And now ye know what withholdeth that he might be revealed in his time. For the mystery of iniquity doth already work: only he who now letteth [restrains or withholdeth] *will let* [restrain or withhold], until he be taken out of the way. And then shall that Wicked be revealed, whom the Lord shall consume with the spirit of his mouth, and shall destroy with the brightness of his coming" (2 Thessalonians 2:6-8). At this present time, and ever since the Lord Jesus Christ ascended and sent the Holy Ghost into the world on the day of Pentecost (Acts 2:1-4), the Holy Ghost has been indwelling all true born again believers, which are "members" of "the body of Christ" (1 Corinthians 12:12). Before that time, and before the death, burial, and resurrection of Jesus Christ, the Spirit of God came upon (Judges 6:34; 1 Samuel 10:10; 2 Chronicles 24:20) and was in believers (1 Peter 1:10-11), but he also left them (Psalm 51:11). But now, after the resurrection of the Lord Jesus Christ, all born again believers have God's promise: "**I will never leave thee, nor forsake thee**" (Hebrews 13:5). Believers are commanded: "**And grieve not the holy Spirit of God, whereby ye are sealed unto the day of redemption**" (Ephesians 4:30), which speaks of "**the redemption of our body**" (Romans 8:23).

The very presence of the Holy Ghost in the world *withholds* the revealing of "that man of sin…the son of perdition" (2 Thessalonians 2:3), also known as the "antichrist" (1 John 2:18). But when the Holy Ghost is "taken out of the way…then shall that Wicked be revealed" (2 Thessalonians 2:7-8). When the Holy Ghost leaves this world, he will also take all of the born again believers up with him to meet the Lord Jesus in the air! Likewise, a beautiful "similitude [likeness; similar account]" (Hosea 12:10) of this great, soon coming event is given in the historical account recorded in Genesis chapter 24. As Abraham sent his servant to a far country to get a bride for his son Isaac, so God the Father has sent the Holy Ghost into the world to get a bride [the church (John 3:29)] for his Son Jesus Christ. After hearing about Isaac from the servant Rebekah, of her own free will, she decided to go with the servant to marry Isaac. Then she traveled with the servant to meet and to marry Isaac.

One rainy day I was reading a Bible, when the Holy Ghost spoke to me through "the word of the gospel" (Acts 15:7), and told me about God's only begotten Son Jesus Christ. I was invited, sight unseen, to come to him and receive him by faith as my Saviour. Of my own free will, I did believe on the Lord Jesus Christ and was saved by his grace through faith in him (Ephesians 2:8-9; Acts 16:31)! Now, over thirty years later, the Holy Ghost is still with me! And one day soon, the Lord Jesus Christ will descend from heaven, and I will be changed and caught up by the power of the Holy Ghost to meet the Lord in the air: and so shall I ever be with the Lord! Now I am eagerly: "**Looking for that blessed hope, and the glorious appearing of the great God and our Saviour Jesus Christ**" (Titus 2:13).

COME UP HITHER

The middle section of 1 Thessalonians 4:16 continues expounding about this glorious truth, and says, "…shall descend from heaven with a shout, with the voice of the archangel, and with the trump of God…"

Shouting and the sound of trumpets are together associated with great victories (Joshua 6:5-20; Psalm 47:5-9) and celebrations (2 Samuel 6:15; 1 Chronicles 15:28; 2 Chronicles 15:14). What a great victory celebration there will be when all the church of God is gathered up to meet the Lord in the air! The command, "**Come up hither**," is found three times in the scriptures. These represent three stages of the first resurrection: "the firstfruits" (Revelation 14:4), the main harvest (Matthew 9:38), and the "gleanings," the fruit that is left after the main harvest.

The first command is found in Proverbs: "For better *it is* that it be said unto thee, **Come up hither**; than that thou shouldest be put lower in the presence of **the prince whom thine eyes have seen**" (Proverbs 25:7). Some of the Old Testament saints saw the Lord (Genesis 17:1; 26:2; 32:30; Exodus 33:11; 24:9; 1 Kings 22:19; Isaiah 6:1; Ezekiel 1:26); therefore this first command to "Come up hither" would signify the gathering of the Old Testament believers which were translated to heaven from "paradise" (Luke 23:43) after the resurrection of Jesus Christ (2 Corinthians 12:1-4; Ephesians 4:8). Some of them rose again from the dead and were seen in the holy city, after the resurrection of Jesus Christ (Matthew 27:52-53). This group of believers are the firstfruits.

The second command is found in Revelation, where the Apostle John was caught up into heaven and shown the future. John is also a "similitude" for the church. John wrote: "After this I looked, and, behold, a door *was* opened in heaven: and **the first voice which I heard *was* as it were of a trumpet talking with me**; which said, **Come up hither**, and I will shew thee things which must be hereafter" (Revelation 4:1).

After his translation to heaven, John saw the redeemed church *already* in heaven praising God (Revelation 5:8-10). *After* that John saw the Lamb open the seals, which reveal the events of the tribulation. At the opening of the first seal the antichrist will come on a white horse to deceive many with a false peace (Revelation 6:1-2; Daniel 8:25; 1 Thessalonians 5:3). This is additional verification that the church will leave the earth to meet the Lord in the air *before* the "son of perdition" is revealed!

The sudden catching away of the church is also spoken of in Paul's letter to the Corinthians, where he writes: "**Behold, I shew you a mystery; We shall not all sleep** [die physically]**, but we shall all be changed, In a moment, in the twinkling of an eye, at the last trump: for the trumpet shall sound, and the dead shall be raised incorruptible, and we shall be changed. For this corruptible must put on incorruption, and this mortal *must* put on immortality**" (1 Corinthians 15:51-53). And another great scripture says, "**For our conversation is in heaven; from whence also we look for the Saviour, the Lord Jesus Christ: Who shall change our vile body, that it may be fashioned like unto his glorious body, according to the working whereby he is able even to subdue all things unto himself**" (Philippians 3:20-21).

The final and third command to "Come up hither" is found in Revelation 11:12, where the two witnesses during the tribulation are raised from the dead:

"And they heard a great voice from heaven saying unto them, Come up hither. And they ascended up to heaven in a cloud; and their enemies beheld them" (Revelation 11:12). These two witnesses are a "similitude" for the tribulation saints. It appears that they will be caught up to heaven "out of great tribulation" (Revelation 7:14) at the same time.

The last part of 1 Thessalonians 4:16 says, "...and the dead in Christ shall rise first."

This simply means that the dead in Christ, the physical bodies which "sleep in Jesus" (1 Thessalonians 4:14), will arise in glorious, incorruptible bodies (Philippians 3:20-21) to clothe the souls of those that return from heaven with the Lord Jesus. This will take place before the bodies of the living saints are changed from corruptible to incorruptible, and from mortal to immortal.

First Thessalonians 4:17 says, "Then we which are alive *and* remain shall be caught up together with them in the clouds, to meet the Lord in the air: and so shall we ever be with the Lord."

Both groups, the dead in Christ, and those who are alive and remain until the coming of the Lord for his church, will meet the Lord in the air, and will be with the Lord for ever!

Our study of this wonderful passage ends with 1 Thessalonians 4:18, which gloriously states, "Wherefore comfort one another with these words."

All truly saved, born again, children of God greatly rejoice and are greatly comforted by the promises of God regarding our eternal life with him! David wrote: "Thou wilt shew me the path of life: **in thy presence *is* fulness of joy; at thy right hand *there are* pleasures for evermore**" (Psalm 16:11). As God's word was a lamp to David's feet, and a light to his path (Psalm 119:105), so also is God's word the light in which his children may remain in spiritual communion and fellowship with Jesus Christ today (1 John 1:7). "**Surely the righteous shall give thanks unto thy name: the upright shall dwell in thy presence**" (Psalm 140:13). Read also 2 Corinthians 4:17-18; Psalm 17:15; 1 Corinthians 13:12; 1 John 3:2; Jude 1:24; and Revelation 22:5.

ARE YOU READY FOR THE LORD TO COME?

The "**glorious gospel of Christ**" (2 Corinthians 4:4), "**how that Christ died for our sins according to the scriptures; And that he was buried, and that he rose again the third day according to the scriptures**" (1 Corinthians 15:3-4) "**is the power of God unto salvation to every one that believeth**" (Romans 1:16). If you have never been saved, I pray that you will trust Jesus Christ to save you today, for the scripture says: "**behold, now *is* the accepted time; behold, now *is* the day of salvation**" (2 Corinthians 6:2)!

"**Believe on the Lord Jesus Christ, and thou shalt be saved**" (Acts 16:31).

Chapter 8

The Believer's Walk

Our sermon outline begins with the scriptural text of 1 Thessalonians 4:1-12, which says, "Furthermore then we beseech you, brethren, and exhort *you* by the Lord Jesus, that as ye have received of us how ye ought to walk and to please God, *so* ye would abound more and more. For ye know what commandments we gave you by the Lord Jesus. For this is the will of God, *even* your sanctification, that ye should abstain from fornication: That every one of you should know how to possess his vessel in sanctification and honour; Not in the lust of concupiscence, even as the Gentiles which know not God: That no *man* go beyond and defraud his brother in *any* matter: because that the Lord *is* the avenger of all such, as we also have forewarned you and testified. For God hath not called us unto uncleanness, but unto holiness. He therefore that despiseth, despiseth not man, but God, who hath also given unto us his holy Spirit. But as touching brotherly love ye need not that I write unto you: for ye yourselves are taught of God to love one another. And indeed ye do it toward all the brethren which are in all Macedonia: but we beseech you, brethren, that ye increase more and more; And that ye study to be quiet, and to do your own business, and to work with your own hands, as we commanded you; That ye may walk honestly toward them that are without, and *that* ye may have lack of nothing."

WALK TO PLEASE GOD

The text begins in 1 Thessalonians 4:1 by saying, "Furthermore then we beseech you, brethren, and exhort *you* by the Lord Jesus, that as ye have received of us how ye ought to walk and to please God, *so* ye would abound more and more."

This passage begins with Paul exhorting the believers "**to walk and to please God**," and ends in verse twelve instructing these same believers to "**walk honestly toward them that are without**"—that is, those who are still lost, who are "**without Christ, being aliens from the commonwealth of Israel, and strangers from the covenants of promise, having no hope, and without God in the world**" (Ephesians 2:12). If we walk to please God, by presenting our "bodies a living sacrifice, holy, acceptable unto God" which is our reasonable service (Romans 12:2), then we will certainly have a walk that is *honest* toward the unbelievers, who themselves, being "in the flesh cannot please God" (Romans 8:8). We are "ambassadors for Christ" (2 Corinthians 5:20). The Lord Jesus commanded his disciples: "**Let your light so shine before men, that they may see your good works, and glorify your Father which is in heaven**" (Matthew 5:16).

Paul wrote to the Colossian believers: "**That ye might walk worthy of the Lord unto all pleasing, being fruitful in every good work, and increasing in the knowledge of God**" (Colossians 1:10). Believers are commanded in 2 Peter 3:18 to "**grow in grace, and *in* the knowledge of our Lord and Saviour Jesus Christ**." We are told in 1 Peter 2:2 to be as newborn babes, and "**desire the sincere milk of the word**," so that we "**may grow thereby**." Hebrews 13:16 instructs us that we are "to do good and to communicate forget not: for with such sacrifices God is well pleased." Pleasing God will result in answered prayers: "**And whatsoever we ask, we receive of him, because we keep his commandments, and do those things that are pleasing in his sight**" (1 John 3:22).

Notice that God instructs us in 1 Thessalonians "to walk," that is to handle your life in such a way that is pleasing to God. If we do this, God explains to us the outcome of a walk that pleases him. God says at the end of 1 Thessalonians 4:1 "*so* ye would abound more and more." The walk of the born again believer should be ever increasing in love, understanding, good works, and faith, for God's purpose is to conform all believers "**to the image of his Son**" (Romans 8:29). And it is God which works in the believer "**both to will and to do of *his* good pleasure**" (Philippians 2:13). Therefore, our path should grow greater in good works and praise to our God: "**But the path of the just *is* as the shining light, that shineth more and more unto the perfect day**" (Proverbs 4:18). Paul wrote to the church of Philippi, and in his epistle Philippians 1:9-11 he said, "And this I pray, that your love may abound yet more and more in knowledge and *in* all judgment; That ye may approve things that are excellent; that ye may be sincere and without offence till the day of Christ; Being filled with the fruits of righteousness, which are by Jesus Christ, unto the glory and praise of God." May it be said of us too.

First Thessalonians 4:2 says, "For ye know what commandments we gave you by the Lord Jesus."

As "the apostle of the Gentiles" (Romans 11:13), Paul delivered the infallible word of God through preaching and by writing inspired scripture. Paul told the Corinthians: "If any man think himself to be a prophet, or spiritual, let him acknowledge that **the things that I write unto you are the commandments of the Lord**" (1 Corinthians 14:37). Paul gave commandment to the believers "**in the name of our Lord Jesus Christ**" (2 Thessalonians 3:6). Peter warned the believers to "be mindful of the words which were spoken before by the holy prophets, **and of the commandment of us the apostles of the Lord and Saviour**" (2 Peter 3:2). Jude also wrote in Jude 1:17: "**But, beloved, remember ye the words which were spoken before of the apostles of our Lord Jesus Christ**." In Hebrews, we read: "How shall we escape, if we neglect so great salvation; which at the first began to be spoken by the Lord, and was **confirmed unto us by them that heard *him*** [the apostles]; God also bearing *them* witness, both with signs and wonders, and with divers miracles, and gifts of the Holy Ghost, according to his own will?" (Hebrews 2:3-4).

All scripture is "**the word of God**" (1 Thessalonians 2:13), for "**All scripture *is* given by inspiration of God**, and *is* profitable for doctrine, for reproof, for correction, for instruction in righteousness: That the man of God may be perfect, throughly furnished unto all good works" (2 Timothy 3:16-17). God inspired holy men to write his word: "**Knowing this first, that no prophecy of the scripture is of any private interpretation. For the prophecy came not in old time by the will of man: but holy men of God** [apostles and prophets] **spake *as they were* moved by the Holy Ghost**" (2 Peter 1:20-21). Paul wrote that the Lord had made known to him the mystery of Christ, "**Which in other ages was not made known unto the sons of men, as it is now revealed unto his holy apostles and prophets by the Spirit**" (Ephesians 3:5).

THE SIN THAT SETS APART

First Thessalonians 4:3 says, "For this is the will of God, *even* your sanctification, that ye should abstain from fornication."

God's will for his children is very clearly stated here. They are commanded to abstain [hold back or voluntarily refrain] from fornication. *Fornication* may be simply defined as ANY sexual activity outside of the marriage bed: "**Marriage *is* honourable in all, and the bed undefiled: but whoremongers and adulterers God will judge**" (Hebrews 13:4). This includes indulgence in pornography of all sorts, for the Lord Jesus said: "**That whosoever <u>looketh</u> on a woman to lust after her hath committed adultery with her already in his heart**" (Matthew 5:28). This is the reason the LORD commanded the children of Israel to destroy all the *pictures* of the heathen in the land of Canaan (Numbers 33:52). Today, pornography is displayed openly even on the cover of magazines located at the grocery store check out lanes, on billboards, and continuously on television, not to mention all of the filthy pornographic magazines and websites on the internet! And there is no lack of loose women today who walk around dressed like prostitutes, who tempt men to commit adultery with them in their hearts (Matthew 5:28). The scriptures also teach that masturbation is *fornication*, for we read that: "**The wife hath not power of her own body, but the husband: and likewise also the husband hath not power of his own body, but the wife**" (1 Corinthians 7:4).

MINIMUM REQUIREMENT FOR GENTILES

When some of the sect of the Pharisees which believed declared that the Gentiles had to keep the law of Moses to be saved, the apostles, in agreement with the Holy Ghost, wrote a letter to the Gentiles giving them four minimum requirements: "That ye **abstain** from meats offered to idols, and from blood, and from things strangled, and **from fornication**: from which if ye keep yourselves, ye shall do well. Fare ye well" (Acts 15:29). Abstinence from fornication was the only one of the requirements that came from the ten commandments (Exodus 20:14). Therefore *fornication*—the unnatural and unlawful engagement in sexual activity, is a very serious sin in the sight of God.

A SIN AGAINST CHRIST'S BODY

The born again believer is a member of Christ's body (1 Corinthians 12:27): "**For we are members of his body, of his flesh, and of his bones**" (Ephesians 5:30).

The following scripture needs no explanation: "Meats for the belly, and the belly for meats: but God shall destroy both it and them. **Now the body *is* not for fornication, but for the Lord; and the Lord for the body**. And God hath both raised up the Lord, and will also raise up us by his own power. **Know ye not that your bodies are the members of Christ? shall I then take the members of Christ, and make *them* the members of an harlot? God forbid. What? know ye not that he which is joined to an harlot is one body? for two, saith he, shall be one flesh. But he that is joined unto the Lord is one spirit. Flee fornication. Every sin that a man doeth is without the body; but he that committeth fornication sinneth against his own body. What? know ye not that your body is the temple of the Holy Ghost *which is* in you, which ye have of God, and ye are not your own? For ye are bought with a price: therefore glorify God in your body, and in your spirit, which are God's**" (1 Corinthians 6:13-20).

THE DEPTHS OF SATAN

The Lord Jesus Christ spoke to the church at Thyatira concerning a woman named Jezebel, who was seducing God's children to commit fornication. This is the same "doctrine" [teaching] as that of Balaam, "**who taught Balac to cast a stumblingblock before the children of Israel, to eat things sacrificed unto idols, and to commit fornication**" (Revelation 2:14). The Lord refers to this doctrine as "**the depths of Satan**" (Revelation 2:24)!

GOD'S JUDGMENT AGAINST FORNICATION

There had been a man in the church at Corinth who committed fornication with his father's wife, and the Apostle Paul judged that it was right, "**To deliver such an one unto Satan for the destruction of the flesh, that the spirit may be saved in the day of the Lord Jesus**" (1 Corinthians 5:1-5)! Considering God's hatred for this sin, this was NOT a harsh judgment! God's law to Moses demanded the death penalty for fornication (Leviticus 20:10). Men committing sodomy were judged in like manner: "**If a man also lie with mankind, as he lieth with a woman, both of them have committed an abomination: they shall surely be put to death; their blood *shall be* upon them**" (Leviticus 20:13).

God killed 23,000 of the children of Israel in one day because of fornication (1 Corinthians 10:8). God's hatred of this sin has not changed! As he promised to send plagues, sicknesses, and diseases to those of the children of Israel who did not obey his law (Deuteronomy 28:58-61), so the Lord is still sending plagues, sicknesses, and diseases to the transgressors of his law. There are special plagues that come upon fornicators and sodomites, and Romans 1:26-27 says, "For this cause God gave them up unto vile affections: for even their women did change the natural use into that which is against nature: And likewise also the men, leaving the natural use of the woman, burned in their lust one toward another; men with men working that which is unseemly, **and receiving in themselves that recompence of their error which was meet**." In other words, those who commit such acts receive the consequences of their sins from God, consequences that are suited to their sin. There are many diseases associated with sexual sins, such as bacterial vaginosis, chlamydia, gonorrhea, viral hepatitis, genital herpes, HIV/AIDS, human papillomavirus, pelvic inflammatory disease, syphilis, trichomoniasis, and other STDs! A recent review of life expectancy information "indicates that on average, even apart from AIDS, homosexual persons will probably not live past their 40's, an appalling loss of about 30 years, or nearly 40% of normal American lifespan!"[2]

God still sends judgment upon sin. He chastens his own children, sometimes with sickness, and sometimes with death (Hebrews 12:6-8; 1 Corinthians 11:30-32). King David lost four sons to an untimely grave, because of his fornication with another man's wife (2 Samuel 12:9-10). The Lord Jesus Christ warned those in the church in Thyatira [those whom Jezebel had seduced to commit fornication] with great tribulation and death, unless they repented of their deeds: "**Behold, I will cast her into a bed, and them that commit adultery with her into great tribulation, except they repent of their deeds. And I will kill her children with death; and all the churches shall know that I am he which searcheth the reins and hearts: and I will give unto every one of you according to your works**" (Revelation 2:22-23).

HOW TO AVOID FORNICATION

The scriptures make it clear how a man is to avoid fornication: "Now concerning the things whereof ye wrote unto me: *It is* good for a man not to touch a woman. **Nevertheless, *to avoid* fornication, let every man have his own wife, and let every woman have her own husband**" (1 Corinthians 7:1-2). God established marriage between a man and a woman from the beginning; and God expects the man and the woman to be faithful to the marriage until death: "**But from the beginning of the creation God made them male and female. For this cause shall a man leave his father and mother, and cleave to his wife; And they twain shall be one flesh: so then they are no more twain, but one flesh. What therefore God hath joined together, let not man put asunder**" (Mark 10:6-9).

There are only three scriptural grounds for divorce: 1) Death (Romans 7:2); 2) Desertion of the unbelieving spouse (1 Corinthians 7:15); and 3) Fornication (Matthew 19:9). Although God will permit one of his children to divorce because their spouse committed fornication, the Lord hates divorce (Malachi 2:16), and would rather see the husband and wife forgive each other and remain together in marriage. Fornication is a very serious sin! It is the only sin committed by God's children, the cause of which God permits them to divorce the offending spouse! God also hates murder, but he does not allow one of his children to put away their wife because she murdered someone!

Marriage is used as an example of the Lord's relationship to his "**body, the church**" (Colossians 1:18): "**Husbands, love your wives, even as Christ also loved the church, and gave himself for it; That he might sanctify and cleanse it with the washing of water by the word, That he might present it to himself a glorious church, not having spot, or wrinkle, or any such thing; but that it should be holy and without blemish**. So ought men to love their wives as their own bodies. He that loveth his wife loveth himself. **For no man ever yet hated his own flesh; but nourisheth and cherisheth it, even as the Lord the church**: **For we are members of his body, of his flesh, and of his bones. For this cause shall a man leave his father and mother, and shall be joined unto his wife, and they two shall be one flesh. This is a great mystery: but I speak concerning Christ and the church**" (Ephesians 5:25-32). The Apostle Paul wrote to the Corinthian church: "**For I am jealous over you with godly jealousy: for I have espoused you to one husband, that I may present *you as* a chaste virgin to Christ**" (2 Corinthians 11:2).

THE CONSEQUENCES OF FORNICATION

Unwanted pregnancies are often the results of fornication between men and women. The "heathen" used to take care of that "problem" by casting their infants into the sea, or river, or into the arms of one of their false gods. Ezekiel wrote: "**That they have committed adultery, and blood *is* in their hands, and with their idols have they committed adultery, and have also caused their sons, whom they bare unto me, to pass for them through *the fire*, to devour *them***" (Ezekiel 23:37). Jeremiah wrote: "**They have built also the high places of Baal, to burn their sons with fire *for* burnt offerings unto Baal**, which I commanded not, nor spake *it*, neither came *it* into my mind" (Jeremiah 19:5). The writer of the book of 2 Kings wrote: "**And they caused their sons and their daughters to pass through the fire**, and used divination and enchantments, and sold themselves to do evil **in the sight of the LORD, to provoke him to anger**"

(2 Kings 17:17). Please make note that God was well aware of their evil deeds and they provoked him to anger.

Today the heathen take care of the "problem" by murdering their babies while they are still in their mother's womb! Since the infamous Roe vs. Wade Supreme Court decision in 1973 up to 2005 there were over fifty million babies aborted [murdered]! That's just in U.S. history. Just think of the untold millions if not billions of babies which have been aborted all over the world. Lifenews.com reports that 1 to 2 billion babies have been aborted worldwide in the last fifty years.[3]

Four thousand years ago, God set forth an example for all men to observe, to warn them of his intense hatred of the sin of fornication, and his eternal judgment upon those who give themselves over to fornication. We read: "**Even as Sodom and Gomorrha, and the cities about them in like manner, giving themselves over to fornication, and going after strange flesh, are set forth for an example, suffering the vengeance of eternal fire**" (Jude 1:7)! I pray that you will not allow the pursuit of this pleasure of "**sin for a season**" (Hebrews 11:25) to result in your eternal damnation! The heathen are given over to fornication like dogs. They commit fornication not to obtain children, but only for the pleasure they derive from this sin. Be forewarned that many men are burning in hell this very moment because of a strange and adulterous woman. They did not realize that "**Her house is the way to hell, going down to the chambers of death**" (Proverbs 7:27), and that the guests of the foolish woman "**are in the depths of hell**" (Proverbs 9:18)!

After naming the specific sin of fornication, the apostle continues in 1 Thessalonians 4:4: "That every one of you should know how to possess his vessel in sanctification and honour."

His "vessel" is a reference to his physical body in which the believer has the treasure (2 Corinthians 4:7) of "the Spirit of Christ" (Romans 8:9), "that the excellency of the power may be of God, and not of us" (2 Corinthians 4:7). Our bodies are to be kept under the dominion of the Spirit and brought into subjection (1 Corinthians 9:27).

First Thessalonians 4:5 says, "Not in the lust of concupiscence, even as the Gentiles which know not God."

CONCUPISCENCE according to the Noah Webster 1828 Dictionary is the unlawful or irregular desire of sexual pleasure. In a more general sense, it is the coveting of carnal things, or an irregular appetite for worldly goods; an inclination for unlawful enjoyments. Paul reminded the believers at Ephesus that they had been "**in time past Gentiles in the flesh**" (Ephesians 2:11), and "**That at that time ye were without Christ, being aliens from the commonwealth of Israel, and strangers from the covenants of promise, having no hope, and without God in the world: But now in Christ Jesus ye who sometimes were far off are made nigh by the blood of Christ**" (Ephesians 2:12-13). He wrote to the believing Corinthians: "**Know ye not that the unrighteous shall not inherit the kingdom of God? Be not deceived: neither fornicators, nor idolaters, nor adulterers, nor effeminate, nor abusers of themselves with mankind, Nor thieves, nor covetous, nor drunkards, nor revilers, nor extortioners, shall inherit the kingdom of God. And such were some of you: but ye are washed, but ye are sanctified, but ye are justified in the name of the Lord Jesus, and by the Spirit of our God**" (1 Corinthians 6:9-11). Jude wrote that those who are sensual, and separate themselves from the true believers with their own lusts, have "**not the Spirit**" (Jude 1:16-19). If you are still walking after your own lusts, in the same manner as you were before you made a profession of salvation, then perhaps you are deceived, and not saved at all!

First Thessalonians 4:6 says, "That no *man* go beyond and defraud his brother in *any* matter: because that the Lord *is* the avenger of all such, as we also have forewarned you and testified."

Christians are commanded not to take vengeance upon any one: "**Dearly beloved, avenge not yourselves, but *rather* give place unto wrath: for it is written, Vengeance *is* mine; I will repay, saith the Lord**" (Romans 12:19). This is totally opposite to the way of the worldly man who is constantly seeking ways to get back at someone. What a blessing and great peace it is for a child of God to pray for his enemies (Matthew 5:44), and to let his heavenly Father take care of them!

First Thessalonians 4:7-8 says, "For God hath not called us unto uncleanness, but unto holiness. He therefore that despiseth, despiseth not man, but God, who hath also given unto us his holy Spirit."

If you hate these words, then you are despising God's word! "For this is the love of God, that we keep his commandments: and his commandments are **not grievous** [oppressive or burdensome]" (1 John 5:3). David wrote: "**O how love I thy law! it *is* my meditation all the day**" (Psalm 119:97), and "**Great peace have they which love thy law: and nothing shall offend them**" (Psalm 119:165).

First Thessalonians 4:9-10 says, "But as touching brotherly love ye need not that I write unto you: for ye yourselves are taught of God to love one another. And indeed ye do it toward all the brethren which are in all Macedonia: but we beseech you, brethren, that ye increase more and more."

Speaking to his disciples, the Lord Jesus said: "**A new commandment I give unto you, That ye love one another; as I have loved you, that ye also love one another**" [(John 13:34) see also John 15:12, 17; Romans 13:8; 1 Peter 1:22; 1 John 3:11, 33; 1 John 4:7, 11-12; 2 John 1:5)]. After being born of the Spirit, "**the love of God is shed abroad in our hearts by the Holy Ghost which is given unto us**" (Romans 5:5). And this love of God will "increase more and more" in the believer who is growing in grace (2 Peter 3:18).

First Thessalonians 4:11-12 says, "And that ye study to be quiet, and to do your own business, and to work with your own hands, as we commanded you; That ye may walk honestly toward them that are without, and *that* ye may have lack of nothing."

Paul exhorted Timothy to pray for all men, "and *for* all that are in authority; **that we may lead a quiet and peaceable life in all godliness and honesty**" (1 Timothy 2:1-2). Paul worked for a living as an example to the other believers (2 Thessalonians 3:7-11; 1 Thessalonians 2:9). Paul told the Ephesians' elders: "**I have coveted no man's silver, or gold, or apparel. Yea, ye yourselves know, that these hands have ministered unto my necessities, and to them that were with me. I have shewed you all things, how that so labouring ye ought to support the weak, and to remember the words of the Lord Jesus, how he said, It is more blessed to give than to receive**" (Acts 20:33-35). Paul also wrote to the church in Ephesus: "**Let him that stole steal no more: but rather let him labour, working with *his* hands the thing which is good, that he may have to give to him that needeth**" (Ephesians 4:28). Generally, diligent workers are quiet, honest, and "have lack of nothing" (1 Thessalonians 4:12). In his next letter to them, Paul would write: "For even when we were with you, this we commanded you, **that if any would not work, neither should he eat. For we hear that there are some which walk among you disorderly, working not at all, but are busybodies. Now them that are such we command and exhort by our Lord Jesus Christ, that with quietness they work, and eat their own bread**" (2 Thessalonians 3:10-12). All other things being equal, the true born again believer should be the very best worker on the job! "**Whether therefore ye eat, or drink, or whatsoever ye do, do all to the glory of God**" (1 Corinthians 10:31).

CONCLUSION

Peter and Jude both wrote of fornicators who were in the visible local church, but not saved (2 Peter 2:13-17; Jude 1:17-19). A man who is not ashamed of the sin of fornication or sodomy is said to be: "**sensual, having not the Spirit**" (Jude 1:19). He separates himself from the true believers by his sin, and because he has "**not the Spirit of Christ, he is none of his**" (Romans 8:9)! He is deceived. Had he truly repented of this ungodly sin, he would have forsaken it (Proverbs 8:13)! If he does not repent, he will perish (Luke 13:3, 5).

If you are not saved, do you seek forgiveness and a pardon from God? The LORD said that he would look to a man who trembled at his word, who was of a sorrowful heart, a man who feared him, a man who would turn from and leave his wicked ways (Isaiah 66:2; Psalm 34:18). Isaiah 55:6-7 warns to, "**Seek ye the LORD while he may be found, call ye upon him while he is near: Let the wicked forsake his way, and the unrighteous man his thoughts: and let him return unto the LORD, and he will have mercy upon him; and to our God, for he will abundantly pardon.**"

"**Believe on the Lord Jesus Christ, and thou shalt be saved**" (Acts 16:31).

Chapter 9

BUILT ON THE **ROCK**

Jesus, with the following parable, taught an important principal concerning what foundation a believer should build his life upon. In Matthew 7:21-29 Jesus said, "Not every one that saith unto me, Lord, Lord, shall enter into the kingdom of heaven; but he that doeth the will of my Father which is in heaven. Many will say to me in that day, Lord, Lord, have we not prophesied in thy name? and in thy name have cast out devils? and in thy name done many wonderful works? And then will I profess unto them, I never knew you: depart from me, ye that work iniquity. Therefore whosoever heareth these sayings of mine, and doeth them, I will liken him unto a wise man, which built his house upon a rock: And the rain descended, and the floods came, and the winds blew, and beat upon that house; and it fell not: for it was founded upon a rock. And every one that heareth these sayings of mine, and doeth them not, shall be likened unto a foolish man, which built his house upon the sand: And the rain descended, and the floods came, and the winds blew, and beat upon that house; and it fell: and great was the fall of it. And it came to pass, when Jesus had ended these sayings, the people were astonished at his doctrine: For he taught them as *one* having authority, and not as the scribes."

Only a very foolish man would build a house on the sand! And yet the vast majority of men build their faith on the wisdom of men, which is "**foolishness with**

God" (1 Corinthians 3:19). Men trust the leaders of their churches rather than the words of the living God. The blinding influence of the devil is so great in these "**perilous times**" (2 Timothy 3:1) that many are preaching the name of Jesus Christ, but even they themselves believe in "**another Jesus**" (2 Corinthians 11:4), and are not the children of God by faith in Jesus Christ (Matthew 7:21-23; Galatians 3:26).

Instead of trusting the pure, true, and preserved word of God, men trust in other men. They leave their eternal souls in great jeopardy, because they leave their knowledge of God entirely in the hands of fallible men. But we are warned, "**Thus saith the LORD; Cursed *be* the man that trusteth in man, and maketh flesh his arm, and whose heart departeth from the LORD**" (Jeremiah 17:5). Even, "**He that trusteth in his own heart is a fool: but whoso walketh wisely, he shall be delivered**" (Proverbs 28:26).

It is my hope that this message will leave no doubt as to the identity of the true and living Lord Jesus Christ, and that you might put all your trust in him! By trusting Jesus Christ, I mean that you believe in his holy and unchanging word. He will never change or shift like the shifting sands of science, philosophy, and religions of men. Therefore, he may be trusted completely for the eternal salvation of your soul!

I. THE ROCK

According to the scriptures, there are two "rocks." One is the true Rock, the Lord Jesus Christ, who is God manifest in the flesh (John 1:1, 14; 1 Timothy 3:16). The other rock represents Satan, who is the foundation for all false religions.

"**Of the Rock *that* begat thee thou art unmindful, and hast forgotten God that formed thee**" (Deuteronomy 32:18).

"**For their rock *is* not as our Rock, even our enemies themselves *being* judges**" (Deuteronomy 32:31).

Any church that has a man as their foundation is built upon the sand. The Lord Jesus Christ said that he would build his church upon himself:

"**He saith unto them, But whom say ye that I am? And Simon Peter answered and said, Thou art the Christ, the Son of the living God. And Jesus answered and said unto him, Blessed art thou, Simon Barjona: for flesh and blood hath not revealed *it* unto thee, but my Father which is in heaven. And I say also unto thee, That thou art Peter, and upon this rock** ["the Christ, the

Son of the living God"] **I will build my church; and the gates of hell shall not prevail against it**" (Matthew 16:15-18).

Some have made the error of teaching that Jesus said he would build his church on Peter. That's a very strange teaching. Certainly the Lord would not build his church upon a sinful man, much less upon the man Peter, a man he soon after addressed as Satan (Matthew 16:23)! The Lord was telling Peter that he would build his church upon himself, the Christ of Peter's confession. The Lord used similar wording to speak of himself in the third person another time. First, the Lord identified himself as the bread of life:

"**And Jesus said unto them, <u>I am the bread of life</u>: he that cometh to me shall never hunger; and he that believeth on me shall never thirst**" (John 6:35).

Then Jesus said, "**<u>This is the bread which cometh down from heaven</u>, that a man may eat thereof, and not die**" (John 6:50).

If you believe the Bible, then there can be no doubt who the Rock really is:

"**And did all drink the same spiritual drink: for they drank of that spiritual Rock that followed them: and <u>that Rock was Christ</u>**" (1 Corinthians 10:4).

II. THE FOUNDATION

The foundation and corner stone upon which the Lord is building his church had to be sent down from heaven, for the Lord Jesus Christ is "**not of this world**" (John 8:23).

"**Therefore thus saith the Lord GOD, Behold, I lay in Zion for a foundation a stone, a tried stone, a precious corner *stone*, a sure foundation: he that believeth shall not make haste**" (Isaiah 28:16).

"**For other foundation can no man lay than that is laid, which is Jesus Christ**" (1 Corinthians 3:11).

III. THE CHIEF CORNERSTONE

Not only is the Lord Jesus Christ the Rock and the foundation of the church, but he is the chief cornerstone, the head stone of the corner.

"And are built upon the foundation of the apostles and prophets, Jesus Christ himself being the chief corner *stone*" (Ephesians 2:20).

"The stone *which* the builders refused is become the head *stone* of the corner" (Psalm 118:22).

The Lord Jesus Christ is a stone of stumbling to everyone who stumbles at the word of God, to everyone who does not believe it.

"Unto you therefore which believe *he is* precious: but unto them which be disobedient, the stone which the builders disallowed, the same is made the head of the corner, And a stone of stumbling, and a rock of offence, *even to them* which stumble at the word, being disobedient: whereunto also they were appointed" (1 Peter 2:7-8).

IV. APOSTLES AND PROPHETS

The church is also built upon the foundation of the apostles and prophets. This means that it is built upon the word of God spoken and written by the apostles and prophets.

"And are built upon the foundation of the apostles and prophets, Jesus Christ himself being the chief corner *stone*" (Ephesians 2:20).

"For the prophecy came not in old time by the will of man: but holy men of God spake *as they were* moved by the Holy Ghost" (2 Peter 1:21).

V. THE CHURCH BUILT UPON THE ROCK

Now that the "Rock," the "foundation," the "chief cornerstone," and the "foundation of the apostles and prophets" have all been established by the word of God to be the foundation of the church, we can get to the main point of this message. God has made salvation, "**…of faith, that *it might be* by grace; to the end the promise might be sure to all the seed; not to that only which is of the law, but to that also which is of the faith of Abraham; who is the father of us all"** (Romans 4:16). Since salvation is sure to all the seed, those who have been born again by the incorruptible seed of the word of God (1 Peter 1:23), there never should arise any doubt about their eternal salvation in Christ in the minds of God's children!

"For all the promises of God in him *are* yea, and in him Amen, unto the glory of God by us" (2 Corinthians 1:20).

1. Jesus Christ

What did Jesus Christ mean when he said that he would build his church on the Rock, which is Christ? It means that men would be saved by believing the testimony of Jesus, "**for the testimony of Jesus is the spirit of prophecy**" (Revelation 19:10). It means that the solid and unmovable and unchangeable Rock can be trusted in every word (Hebrews 13:8), for Jesus Christ is "**the way, the TRUTH, and the life**" (John 14:6). According to Jesus Christ, those who believe on him have everlasting life. Jesus said, "**Verily, verily, I say unto you, He that believeth on me hath everlasting life**" (John 6:47).

Beware of the fact that there are two kinds of "believing" spoken of in the Bible: (1) true faith, which is delivered to the repentant sinner who turns away from sin unto God, and (2) vain [empty, worthless] faith (1 Corinthians 15:2), which professes an acknowledgement of the truth, but does not include true "**repentance from dead works, and of faith toward God**" (Hebrews 6:1; 2 Corinthians 7:10; Psalms 34:18; 51:17).

Jesus Christ promised that his saints would not come into condemnation [they would never be condemned eternally], because they have already passed from death unto life.

"**Verily, verily, I say unto you, He that heareth my word, and believeth on him that sent me, hath everlasting life, and shall not come into condemnation; but is passed from death unto life**" (John 5:24).

Jesus Christ promised to never cast out his saints.

"**All that the Father giveth me shall come to me; and him that cometh to me I will in no wise cast out**" (John 6:37).

Jesus Christ promised that his saints would never perish—never go to hell.

"**My sheep hear my voice, and I know them, and they follow me: And I give unto them eternal life; and they shall never perish, neither shall any *man* pluck them out of my hand**" (John 10:27-28).

Jesus Christ promised that his saints would never die [the second death].

"**Jesus said unto her, I am the resurrection, and the life: he that believeth in me, though he were dead, yet shall he live: And whosoever**

liveth and believeth in me shall never die. Believest thou this?" (John 11:25-26).

Do you really believe these promises that Jesus Christ, who is "the TRUTH," said? If you begin to add to the word of God by adding exceptions to his words, then you are NOT a Bible believer. You are a Bible corrector!

Are you trusting in the LORD with all your heart (Proverbs 3:5-6)? Then why is there all this confusion about doing good works or getting baptized by a man in order to be saved? And why is there so much confusion about losing salvation once you are saved? Where does all this error and confusion come from? It certainly does not come from the lips of the Saviour! It certainly does not come from the word of God, "**For God is not *the author* of confusion, but of peace, as in all churches of the saints**" (1 Corinthians 14:33).

2. The Prophets

By saying that the church is built upon the foundation of the prophets also means that the word of God spoken by his prophets may be trusted, because every word of God is pure (Proverbs 30:5-6). These were holy men of God who spoke as they were moved by the Holy Ghost (2 Peter 1:21). The Holy Ghost speaking through David said: "**Also I will make him *my* firstborn, higher than the kings of the earth. My mercy will I keep for him for evermore, and my covenant shall stand fast with him. His seed also will I make *to endure* for ever, and his throne as the days of heaven**" (Psalm 89:27-29).

God's word can be trusted. There is nothing that can reverse it. There are no conditions added to it. God said that everything that came out of his lips would stand for ever.

"**My covenant will I not break, nor alter the thing that is gone out of my lips**" (Psalm 89:34).

"**Search the scriptures; for in them ye think ye have eternal life: and they are they which testify of me**" (John 5:39).

"**Then he said unto them, O fools, and slow of heart to believe all that the prophets have spoken: Ought not Christ to have suffered these things, and to enter into his glory?**"(Luke 24:25-26).

"He that believeth on the Son hath everlasting life: and he that believeth not the Son shall not see life; but the wrath of God abideth on him" (John 3:36).

The scriptures of the prophets (Romans 16:25-26) teach that the believer has eternal life, and that God will make them to endure for ever!

3. The Apostles

The following are a few scriptures that establish the testimony of the apostles regarding eternal life and the eternal security of the believer.

The Apostle Paul was persuaded that nothing could separate him or any other true believer from the love of God, which is in Christ Jesus our Lord.

"For I am persuaded, that neither death, nor life, nor angels, nor principalities, nor powers, nor things present, nor things to come, Nor height, nor depth, nor any other creature, shall be able to separate us from the love of God, which is in Christ Jesus our Lord" (Romans 8:38-39).

Paul also wrote that God, that cannot lie, promised eternal life before the world began.

"Paul, a servant of God, and an apostle of Jesus Christ, according to the faith of God's elect, and the acknowledging of the truth which is after godliness; In hope of <u>eternal life, which God, that cannot lie, promised before the world began</u>" (Titus 1:1-2).

The Apostle John wrote all those promises made by the Lord Jesus Christ that we might KNOW that we have eternal life.

"These things have I written unto you that believe on the name of the Son of God; that ye may know that ye have eternal life, and that ye may believe on the name of the Son of God" (1 John 5:13).

So, what is the problem? A saved man who does not know that he has eternal life, and that he will always have eternal life—no matter what—is either still very ignorant of the scriptures and trusting in the word of man, or he is simply living in UNBELIEF! This is the same sin committed by the children of Israel after they had been delivered from the hand of Pharaoh. They got into the wilderness and failed to believe that God would bring them into the promised land. Because of their unbelief God would not allow them to enter into rest; that is, he would not allow them to enter into the promised land (Hebrews 3:19). They were still saved, but God was so provoked by them that he forced them to wander in the wilderness for forty years rather than to allow them to go into the promised land! This represents the same kind of a wasted life the devil desires for God's true but doubtful children to suffer.

The writer of the book of Hebrews warned those believers not to follow the example of Israel in the wilderness and fail, because of unbelief. He warned them to enter into the rest of knowing the perfect salvation obtained for us through the blood of Jesus Christ (Hebrews 9:12). The word of God plainly tells the believer that the Lord Jesus Christ has by one offering, "**perfected for ever them that are sanctified**" (Hebrews 10:14). Their sanctification was by faith in Jesus Christ (Acts 26:18), and not by any good works on their part. Perfect love cast out all fear of judgment and gives the saint complete rest in this life, knowing that he has eternal life, and that there is no way for him to lose it!

"**Herein is our love made perfect, that we may have boldness in the day of judgment: because as he is, so are we in this world. There is no fear in love; but perfect love casteth out fear: because fear hath torment. He that feareth is not made perfect in love**" (1 John 4:17-18).

The eternal salvation of God by grace through faith alone (Ephesians 2:8-9) is not a debatable subject. It is the clear teaching of a great number of plain, easy to be understood scriptures. You do not have to be a theologian to understand the foundational or first principles of salvation and eternal life (Hebrews 5:12). Even a little child cannot understand the deep things of God, but he can understand the gospel! The Lord Jesus said: "**Verily I say unto you, Whosoever shall not receive the kingdom of God as a little child shall in no wise enter therein**" (Luke 18:17).

And yet foolish and ignorant men allow false teachers and unlearned and unstable men to wrest (twist) the scriptures to their own destruction (2 Peter 3:16)! God does not want his children to be ignorant or to walk in unbelief, but many of God's people "**are destroyed for lack of knowledge**" (Hosea 4:6). They do not perish and go to the lake of fire, but because of their lack of knowledge, their lives are destroyed and made of none effect for the Lord's work on earth. Satan has gained the advantage over them. For example, men who are ignorant of the scriptures may be deceived into believing that they lost their salvation when they sinned. If they believe that they have lost their salvation, some of them will give up ever trying to fight the good fight of faith. They may get mad at God and become discouraged with themselves. They may give up on the Bible and church altogether. They may come to the conclusion that they must not have been saved in the first place or that there is no way they can keep it anyway. By this lack of faith in the foundation, the devil deceives God's own blood bought children into living a God dishonoring life! Their lives are destroyed, and any reward they may have received at the judgment seat of Christ will be lost! Yet they themselves will still be saved (1 Corinthians 3:15) if they were ever "**born of the Spirit**" (John 3:6, 8) in the first place!

Men who teach that a born again child of God can lose salvation are teaching heresy. If a child of God could lose salvation, then he would lose it because of sin. What sin would cause him to lose it? According to the scriptures, any sin would do the job.

"**For whosoever shall keep the whole law, and yet offend in one *point*, he is guilty of all**" (James 2:10).

Therefore, according to this heresy, the man who keeps his salvation must live a life without any sin! But, according to the scriptures, a man who claims to be a Christian and says that he has no sin calls God a liar!

"**If we say that we have no sin, we deceive ourselves, and the truth is not in us. If we confess our sins, he is faithful and just to forgive us *our* sins, and to cleanse us from all unrighteousness. If we say that we have not sinned, we make him a liar, and his word is not in us**" (1 John 1:8-10).

Furthermore, according to this heresy, a man is therefore responsible for keeping his salvation by doing "good works." He is completely ignoring the plain teaching of the scriptures that eternal life is the "**GIFT of God**" (Romans 6:23), and this "**gift**" is a "**FREE GIFT**" (Romans 5:15-16, 18), "**not of works, lest any man should boast**" (Ephesians 2:8-9)! "**For the gifts and calling of God *are* without repentance**" (Romans 11:29), meaning that God will never repent [change his mind] regarding his gift of eternal life to the believer. "**Thanks be unto God for his unspeakable gift**" (2 Corinthians 9:15)!

CONCLUSION

Several passages in the scriptures may be misunderstood to teach against the eternal security of the believer, such as: Matthew 12:43-45; 2 Peter 2:19-22;

Hebrews 6:1-12; and Hebrews 10:26-31. But none of these scriptures actually teach against eternal security. According to the solid rock foundation of Jesus Christ, the Prophets, and the Apostles, salvation could never be gained by good works, and salvation can never be lost by bad works! God's word guarantees that his children are saved for ever, because their "**Salvation is of the Lord**" (Jonah 2:9), and "**I know that, whatsoever God doeth, it shall be for ever: nothing can be put to it, nor any thing taken from it: and God doeth *it*, that *men* should fear before him**" (Ecclesiastes 3:14).

"**Lift up your eyes to the heavens, and look upon the earth beneath: for the heavens shall vanish away like smoke, and the earth shall wax old like a garment, and they that dwell therein shall die in like manner: but my salvation shall be for ever, and my righteousness shall not be abolished. Hearken unto me, ye that know righteousness, the people in whose heart *is* my law; fear ye not the reproach of men, neither be ye afraid of their revilings. For the moth shall eat them up like a garment, and the worm shall eat them like wool: but my righteousness shall be for ever, and my salvation from generation to generation**" (Isaiah 51:6-8).

If you have been truly saved by grace through faith, then you are God's "**workmanship, created in Christ Jesus unto good works, which God hath before ordained that we should walk in them**" (Eph. 2:10). How are you doing?

If you are not saved, I recommend that you read the gospel according to John [the fourth book in the New Testament]. John wrote his book, "**that ye might believe that Jesus is the Christ, the Son of God; and that believing ye might have life** [everlasting life] **through his name**" (John 20:30-31).

Chapter 10

Created for His Pleasure

Today's sermon outline will be based on the glorious prophetic words written by the Apostle John when he was exiled to the island of Patmos. In Revelation 4:11 John wrote, "**Thou art worthy, O Lord, to receive glory and honour and power: for thou hast created all things, and for thy pleasure they are and were created.**"

THE CREATOR

The Bible states very clearly that, "**All things were made by him** [the Word: the Son of God who was made flesh (John 1:14; 1 Timothy 3:16)]" (John 1:1-3); "**For by him** [the Son] **were all things created, that are in heaven, and that are in earth, visible and invisible, whether *they be* thrones, or dominions, or principalities, or powers: all things were created by him, and for him: And he is before all things, and by him all things consist**" (Colossians 1:12-17). See also Hebrews 1:1-8 and Genesis 1:1.

Therefore we can say that the Son of God made all things for his pleasure! Before the foundation of the world he knew that he would have to be made a man to go to the cross to die for the sins of men (1 Peter 1:18-20).

And yet he still made Adam in his own image and breathed into him the breath of life (Genesis 1:26-27; 2:7). It was because of the joy that was set before him [his glorious eternal kingdom inhabited by men redeemed by his precious blood] that he endured the cross, despising the shame, and is set down on the right hand of the throne of God (Hebrews 12:2). And it pleased the Father to bruise him, that all men might be saved through Jesus Christ the Saviour of the world (Isaiah 53:10; John 3:16-17). The Lord Jesus knew that one glorious day he would stand in the midst of his church of blood-bought saints and rejoice with them and sing praise to the Father (Hebrews 2:10-12)!

Every thing the Lord Jesus Christ did was pleasing to his Father! Jesus himself testified: "**And he that sent me is with me: the Father hath not left me alone; for I do always those things that please him**" (John 8:29).

God spoke of the Lord Jesus Christ through the prophet Isaiah, saying: "**Behold my servant, whom I have chosen; my beloved, in whom my soul is well pleased: I will put my spirit upon him, and he shall shew judgment to the Gentiles**" (Matthew 12:18; see also Isaiah 42:1)

"**The LORD is well pleased for his righteousness' sake; he will magnify the law, and make *it* honourable**" (Isaiah 42:21).

God the Father witnessed of his Son from heaven at his baptism: "**And lo a voice from heaven, saying, This is my beloved Son, in whom I am well pleased**" (Matthew 3:17).

God the Father spoke out of the cloud of Jesus Christ in the presence of Peter, James, John, Moses, and Elias on the mountain where he was transfigured before them: "**While he yet spake, behold, a bright cloud overshadowed them: and behold a voice out of the cloud, which said, This is my beloved Son, in whom I am well pleased; hear ye him**" (Matthew 17:5; see also 2 Peter 1:17).

The Holy Ghost records the words of the Son of God to the Father concerning his coming into the world to do the Father's will: "**In burnt offerings and *sacrifices* for sin thou hast had no pleasure** [see Isaiah 1:11]**. Then said I, Lo, I come (in the volume of the book it is written of me,) to do thy will, O God**. Above (Hebrews 10:6) when he said, Sacrifice and offering and burnt offerings and *offering* for sin thou wouldest not, neither hadst pleasure *therein*; which are offered by the law; **Then said he, Lo, I come to do thy will, O God**.

He taketh away the first, that he may establish the second. **By the which will we are sanctified through the offering of the body of Jesus Christ once *for all*"** (Hebrews 10:6-10).

The sacrifice of the Lord Jesus Christ on the cross for our sins was the only offering and sacrifice to God for our sins that was "**for a sweetsmelling savour**" (Ephesians 5:2). This sacrifice "**perfected for ever them that are sanctified**" (Hebrews 10:12-14) by faith that is in Jesus Christ (Acts 26:18).

The Spirit of Christ spoke through David: "**I delight to do thy will, O my God: yea, thy law *is* within my heart**" (Psalm 40:8).

Therefore we see that God was well pleased with his Son, because he always did the will of the Father. This is how all born again believers, who follow in his steps, can please God (1 Peter 2:21-24).

PLEASING GOD BRINGS BLESSINGS

"**But without faith *it is* impossible to please *him*: for he that cometh to God must believe that he is, and *that* he is a rewarder of them that diligently seek him**" (Hebrews 11:6).

God will repay [recompense or reward] to every man that which he has coming to him! No one escapes God's watchful eye, and no one escapes the results of the law of sowing and reaping (Galatians 6:7-8)! David wrote, "**The LORD rewarded me according to my righteousness; according to the cleanness of my hands hath he recompensed me. For I have kept the ways of the LORD, and have not wickedly departed from my God. For all his judgments *were* before me, and I did not put away his statutes from me. I was also upright before him, and I kept myself from mine iniquity. Therefore hath the LORD recompensed me according to my righteousness, according to the cleanness of my hands in his eyesight. With the merciful thou wilt shew thyself merciful; with an upright man thou wilt shew thyself upright; With the pure thou wilt shew thyself pure; and with the froward thou wilt shew thyself froward**" (Psalm 18:20-26).

In other words, if you desire mercy from the LORD, you must yourself be merciful. If you are froward [froward means: Perverse, that is, turning from, with aversion or reluctance; not willing to yield or comply with what is required; unyielding; ungovernable; refractory; disobedient; peevish; as a froward child, according to Noah Webster 1828 Dictionary], then God will see to it that you get the same kind of treatment in this world! Our prisons are full of froward men who do not know the mercies and goodness and uprightness and pureness of God, because they are out and deliberate rebels against God! If you have acted like a froward man, then have you noticed that God has surrounded you with froward men? You're reaping what you've sown. Why not begin today to walk uprightly with the Lord, showing mercy to others, and having a pure thought life? The Lord is watching. He will reward your actions.

God hears the prayers of the righteous. "**The eyes of the LORD *are* upon the righteous, and his ears *are open* unto their cry**" (Psalm 34:15; see also 1 Peter 3:8-12).

God can make your enemies to be at peace with you. "**When a man's ways please the LORD, he maketh even his enemies to be at peace with him**" (Proverbs 16:7).

God examines all the goings of men, "beholding the evil and the good" (Proverbs 5:21; 15:3).

"**The eyes of the LORD preserve knowledge, and he overthroweth the words of the transgressor**" (Proverbs 22:12).

"**For the word of God *is* quick, and powerful, and sharper than any twoedged sword, piercing even to the dividing asunder of soul and spirit, and of the joints and marrow, and *is* a discerner of the thoughts and intents of the heart. Neither is there any creature that is not manifest in his sight: but all things *are* naked and opened unto the eyes of him with whom we have to do**" (Hebrews 4:12-13).

OLD TESTAMENT EXAMPLES

The Lord recorded many examples in the Old Testament for our learning and admonition (Romans 15:4; 1 Corinthians 10:6-11; Hebrews 4:11; James 5:10; Jude 1:7). In these examples, we find that when the LORD was pleased with men's faith and obedience to his commandments, he blessed them. But when men turned away from their trust in the LORD and relied on other men, or disobeyed God's commandments, the LORD was displeased and removed his blessing. See the examples below.

Walk in obedience to the light of God's word:

"**And Samuel said, Hath the LORD** ***as great*** **delight in burnt offerings and sacrifices, as in obeying the voice of the LORD? Behold, to obey** ***is*** **better than sacrifice,** ***and*** **to hearken than the fat of rams**" (1 Samuel 15:22).

VICTORY OVER A'I—When Joshua obeyed the word of the LORD and his plan to conquer the city of A'i, the LORD gave them the victory (Joshua 9:1-29).

VICTORY OVER JERICHO—Because Joshua and Israel obeyed the word of the LORD and his plan to conquer the city of Jericho, even though God's plan may have seemed very strange to them, God gave them the victory (Joshua 6:1-27).

VICTORY OVER JEROBOAM AND ISRAEL—Although Judah was outnumbered two to one, because king Abijah and Judah kept the charge of the LORD according to his law, and they relied upon the LORD, he gave Judah a great victory over Jeroboam and Israel (2 Chronicles 13:1-20).

Through prayer and faith in God:

KING ASA'S TRUST AND DISTRUST—Asa the king of Judah began his kingdom doing the will of God. He took away the altars of the strange gods and "**he took away the sodomites out of the land, and removed all the idols that his fathers had made**" (1 Kings 15:12) and commanded Judah to seek the LORD and keep his commandments. And God gave his kingdom rest (2 Chronicles 14:1-6). When Asa came against Zerah the Ethiopian and his million man army, "**Asa cried unto the LORD his God, and said, LORD, it is nothing with thee to help, whether with many, or with them that have no power: help us, O LORD our God; for we rest on thee, and in thy name we go against this multitude,**" and the LORD fought against the Egyptians for Asa and gave him a great victory (2 Chronicles 14:8-15).

But later, when Baasha king of Israel came up against Judah, Asa took silver and gold out of the treasures of the house of the LORD and gave the money to Ben-hadad king of Syria to help him defeat Baasha king of Israel. After the conflict was over we read in 2 Chronicles 16:1-9, "And at that time Hanani the seer came to Asa king of Judah, and said unto him, Because thou hast relied on the king of Syria, and not relied on the LORD thy God, therefore is the host of the king of Syria escaped out of thine hand. Were not the Ethiopians and the Lubims a huge host, with very many chariots and horsemen? yet, because thou didst rely on the LORD, he delivered them into thine hand. **For the eyes of the LORD run to and fro throughout the whole earth, to shew himself strong in the behalf of *them* whose heart *is* perfect toward him. Herein thou hast done foolishly: therefore from henceforth thou shalt have wars**."

King Asa pleased the LORD by doing his will, and God blessed him and his people with rest from war. When Asa turned to men for help, not trusting on the LORD his God, then the LORD allowed wars to return to his kingdom.

ONE ANGEL KILLS 185,000 MEN—The king of Assyria sent three ambassadors with a great host against Jerusalem. The three ambassadors stood outside the wall of the city and threatened the men of Hezekiah and boasted themselves against the LORD (1 Kings 18:17-37). When Hezekiah heard their threats, he humbled himself and went into the house of the LORD, after sending men to tell the prophet Isaiah. Isaiah told them that God would take care of the Assyrians and send them back to their own land. Then Hezekiah received a threatening letter from Rabshakeh of Assyria. The king took the letter into the house of the LORD and spread it before the LORD. There he prayed for God's deliverance out of the hand of the Assyrians. He then received a message from Isaiah promising God's deliverance (2 Kings 19:8-34). Then we read:

"**And it came to pass that night, that the angel of the LORD went out, and smote in the camp of the Assyrians an hundred fourscore and five thousand: and when they arose early in the morning, behold, they *were* all dead corpses. So Sennacherib king of Assyria departed, and went and returned, and dwelt at Nineveh. And it came to pass, as he was worshipping in the house of Nisroch his god, that Adrammelech and Sharezer his sons smote him with the sword: and they escaped into the land of Armenia. And Esarhaddon his son reigned in his stead**" (2 Kings 19:35-37).

THREE ENEMY NATIONS DESTROY EACH OTHER—When threatened by Moab and Ammon and the inhabitants of mount Seir, king Jehoshaphat declared a fast throughout all Judah and prayed to the LORD to help them. Jehoshaphat humbled himself and praised God. God answered him through Jaziel the prophet, saying, "**Be not afraid nor dismayed by reason of this great multitude; for the battle is not yours, but God's**" (2 Chronicles 20:15). Then the prophet instructed Jehoshaphat and Israel to go out against their enemies on the next day, for "**the LORD will be with you**" (2 Chronicles 20:17). Then Jehoshaphat and Judah worshipped the LORD. And the Levites praised the

LORD God of Israel with a loud voice. Early the next morning Jehoshaphat sent singers to go in front of the army to praise the LORD.

"And when they began to sing and to praise, the LORD set ambushments against the children of Ammon, Moab, and mount Seir, which were come against Judah; and they were smitten. For the children of Ammon and Moab stood up against the inhabitants of mount Seir, utterly to slay and destroy *them*: and when they had made an end of the inhabitants of Seir, every one helped to destroy another. And when Judah came toward the watch tower in the wilderness, they looked unto the multitude, and, behold, they *were* dead bodies fallen to the earth, and none escaped" (2 Chronicles 20:22-24).

GOLIATH AND THE PHILISTINES DEFEATED—When David went out against the giant Goliath, he was trusting in the LORD to deliver him. David declared to Saul the king, **"The LORD that delivered me out of the paw of the lion, and out of the paw of the bear, he will deliver me out of the hand of this Philistine"** (1 Samuel 17:37). David killed the giant with a stone from his sling. Then he cut off the giant's head with his own sword.

"...And when the Philistines saw their champion was dead, they fled. And the men of Israel and of Judah arose, and shouted, and pursued the Philistines, until thou come to the valley, and to the gates of Ekron. And the wounded of the Philistines fell down by the way to Shaaraim, even unto Gath, and unto Ekron" (1 Samuel 17:51-52).

THE ENEMY MELTED AWAY—When Jonathan and his armourbearer went out against the Philistines trusting in the LORD to deliver them into their hands, God worked a great victory.

"And Jonathan climbed up upon his hands and upon his feet, and his armourbearer after him: and they fell before Jonathan; and his armourbearer slew after him. And that first slaughter, which Jonathan and his armourbearer made, was about twenty men, within as it were an half acre of land, *which* a yoke *of oxen might plow*. **And there was trembling in the host, in the field, and among all the people: the garrison, and the spoilers, they also trembled, and the earth quaked: so it was a very great trembling. And the watchmen of Saul in Gibeah of Benjamin looked; and, behold, the multitude melted away, and they went on beating down *one another*"** (1 Samuel 14:13-16).

THE BATTLE OF BELIEVERS TODAY

OUR WARFARE—In the Old Testament times God's people were fighting enemies in physical warfare with swords and spears, bows and arrows, and slings. Their victories through God are given to us for examples. In the New Testament times believers are not engaged against physical, but against spiritual enemies. Our desire should be that all our physical enemies get saved! We are not sent out on some religious crusade to kill those of other religions. No! We are to pray for our enemies that they will also come to know our Lord and Saviour Jesus Christ so that their souls also may be saved from the eternal fires of hell!

The Christian's warfare is spiritual, and he must fight his battles by faith, casting down wicked imaginations and bringing his thoughts in line with the mind of Christ (2 Corinthians 10:3-6). He must resist temptations by the way God has provided (1 Corinthians 10:13). He must "war a good warfare; Holding faith and a good conscience" (1 Timothy 1:18-20). He must pray for all men, because God wills that all men be saved (1 Timothy 2:1-4).

As a Christian matures and grows in grace and in his knowledge of Jesus Christ, he is to "**endure hardness, as a good soldier of Jesus Christ**" (2 Timothy 2:3). He should also grow to the point of being able "to teach others also" (2 Timothy 2:3-7).

The Apostle Peter wrote of the fleshly lusts, which war against the soul: "Dearly beloved, I beseech *you* as strangers and pilgrims, abstain from fleshly lusts, which war against the soul; Having your conversation honest among the Gentiles: that, whereas they speak against you as evildoers, they may by *your* good works, which they shall behold, glorify God in the day of visitation" (1 Peter 2:11-12).

FIND THE WILL OF GOD AND DO IT!

How may I, as a born again believer, please God? Or, how may I bring pleasure to the Lord? Should this not be my greatest desire in life? No one else has or could have done what the Lord has done for me! I owe him my very life! I love him, because he first "**loved me, and gave himself for me**" (Galatians 2:20). For me to know how to bring pleasure to the Lord is not at all complicated. I may please God by reading and studying and meditating on his word, so that I may find and know the will of God. And once I know the will of God, then I must walk in the light of his revealed will. To discover [prove] the will of God is not a suggestion to a believer; it is a command: "**I beseech you therefore, brethren, by the mercies of God, that ye present your bodies a living sacrifice, holy, acceptable unto God, *which is* your reasonable service. And be not conformed to this world: but be ye transformed by the renewing of your mind, that ye may prove** [discover] **what *is* that good, and acceptable, and perfect, <u>will of God</u>**" (Romans 12:1-2).

It was the "**will of God**" for the Lord Jesus Christ to give "**himself for our sins, that he might deliver us from this present evil world**" (Galatians 1:3-5).

Epaphras, laboured in prayers for his fellow church members at Colosse, that they "**may stand perfect and complete in <u>all the will of God</u>**" (Colossians 4:12).

The Apostle Paul wrote many things to the believers telling them how they ought to walk and to please God (1 Thessalonians 4:1-2). Paul was very specific when he wrote to the church at Thessalonica, saying, "**<u>For this is the will of God</u>, *even* your sanctification, that ye should abstain from fornication: That every one of you should know how to possess his vessel in sanctification and honour; Not in the lust of concupiscence, even as the Gentiles which know not God: That no *man* go beyond and defraud his brother in *any* matter: because that the Lord *is* the avenger of all such, as we also have forewarned you and testified**" (1 Thessalonians 4:3-6).

In other words, refrain and keep yourself from fornication, which is ANY form of sexual activity outside of the marriage bed.

"**Marriage *is* honourable in all, and the bed undefiled: but whoremongers and adulterers God will judge**" (Hebrews 13:4).

Be thankful!

"**In every thing give thanks: for <u>this is the will of God</u> in Christ Jesus concerning you**" (1 Thessalonians 5:18).

Be submissive to civil authority.

"**Submit yourselves to every ordinance of man for the Lord's sake: whether it be to the king, as supreme; Or unto governors, as unto them that are sent by him for the punishment of evildoers, and for the praise of them**

that do well. <u>For so is the will of God</u>, that with well doing ye may put to silence the ignorance of foolish men: As free, and not using *your* liberty for a cloke of maliciousness, but as the servants of God" (1 Peter 2:13-16).

In other words, stop playing the cops and robbers game! It's very unsuitable of one who calls himself a Christian to act like a rebellious and foolish lost man! You cannot act in such a way and bring pleasure to the Lord. Instead you will bring upon yourself the judgment of God. We are commanded: "**Let every soul be subject unto the higher powers. For there is no power but of God: the powers that be are ordained of God. Whosoever therefore resisteth the power, resisteth the ordinance of God: and they that resist shall receive to themselves damnation**" (Romans 13:1-2).

You may indeed suffer for well doing, for the word of God says, "**Yea, and all that will live godly in Christ Jesus shall suffer persecution**" (2 Timothy 3:12). And it may be the will of God for you to suffer for well doing. But that would be far better than to suffer for evil doing! The Apostle Peter wrote, "**For *it is* better, if <u>the will of God</u> be so, that ye suffer for well doing, than for evil doing**" (1 Peter 3:16-17).

Stop sinning and live according to the will of God.

"**Forasmuch then as Christ hath suffered for us in the flesh, arm yourselves likewise with the same mind: for he that hath suffered in the flesh hath ceased from sin; That he no longer should live the rest of *his* time in the flesh to the lusts of men, but to <u>the will of God</u>**" (1 Peter 4:1-2; see also 1 John 2:15-17).

Be willing to suffer reproach, to be treated with scorn or contempt, for the name of Jesus Christ (1 Peter 4:14-19).

HOW CAN LOST MEN PLEASE GOD?

Lost, unregenerated men "**cannot cease from sin**" (2 Peter 2:14), because they are not in the Spirit, but in the flesh: "**So then they that are in the flesh <u>cannot please God</u>**" (Romans 8:8).

We believe the only pleasure that natural, unregenerated [unsaved] men can bring to God at this present time in world history is for them to hear and believe "**the glorious gospel of Christ, who is the image of God**" (2 Corinthians 4:4), "**how that Christ died for our sins according to the scriptures; And that he was buried, and that he rose again the third day according to the scriptures**" (1 Corinthians 15:3-4), and to receive and believe on his Son Jesus Christ by faith (John 1:12-13; Ephesians 1:12-14) "**to the saving of the soul**" (Hebrews 10:29).

The Lord has left born again members of his "**body, the church**" (Colossians 1:18) on earth with the command and commission: "**Go ye into all the world, and preach the gospel to every creature**" (Mark 16:15). This is because the Lord is "**not willing that any should perish, but that all should come to repentance**" (2 Peter 3:9). The Lord has "**no pleasure in the death of the wicked**" (Ezekiel 18:23, 32, 33:11)! But if you will believe on the Lord Jesus Christ it will be "your Father's good pleasure to give you the kingdom" (Luke 12:32)! "**Likewise, I say unto you, there is joy in the presence of the angels of God over one sinner that repenteth**" (Luke 15:10).

Chapter 11

Fellowship of the Spirit

Philippians 2:1-4 tell us, "If *there be* therefore any consolation in Christ, if any comfort of love, if any fellowship of the Spirit, if any bowels and mercies, Fulfil ye my joy, that ye be likeminded, having the same love, *being* of one accord, of one mind. *Let* nothing *be done* through strife or vainglory; but in lowliness of mind let each esteem other better than themselves. Look not every man on his own things, but every man also on the things of others."

INTRODUCTION

In the first four verses of the second chapter of Philippians, Paul exhorts believers to be in agreement, using words such as *fellowship*, *likeminded*, being of *one accord*, and of *one mind*. The prophet Amos asks the question: "**Can two walk together, except they be agreed?**" (Amos 3:3). The obvious and honest answer to this question is, "No." Therefore, believers cannot have "one mind" unless their "minds" are in tune with the same spiritual words! Between AD 1611 and AD 1881 was a period in church history that witnessed tremendous spiritual revivals in the Christian churches and missionary work in the world. During that period of time the Christian church only had one Holy Bible in the English language: the King James Bible, first published in 1611. All English speaking people, therefore were reading, teaching, and preaching from the same Holy Bible.

In 1881, Westcott and Hort translated a *new* version of the New Testament from two corrupt Greek manuscripts. Their New Testament was only the first of many corrupted water down versions of the "Bible." The modern versions of the "Bible" continue to cause divisions among believers and stir up ridicule among unbelievers today. As we shall see, the great falling away of the faith in these last days can ultimately be attributed to the work of Satan, "**the spirit that now worketh in the children of disobedience**" (Ephesians 2:2).

A STRONG CONSOLATION

Philippians 2:1 begins with the words, "If *there be* therefore any consolation in Christ…" *Consolation* is that which affords comfort, encouragement, and a refreshment of spirit. The Lord Jesus Christ himself is called, "**the consolation of Israel**" (Luke 2:25). He is "**the God of patience and consolation**" (Romans 15:5). Not only are we saved "by grace through faith" (Ephesians 2:8), but the grace of God teaches us in Titus 2:11-14, "that, denying ungodliness and worldly lusts, **we should live soberly, righteously, and <u>godly</u>**, in this present world; Looking for that blessed hope, and the glorious appearing of the great God and our Saviour Jesus Christ; Who gave himself for us, that he might redeem us from all iniquity, and purify unto himself a peculiar people, zealous of good works."

Concerning persecution for the faith, the scriptures are very clear: "**Yea, and all that will live godly in Christ Jesus shall suffer persecution**" (2 Timothy 3:12). Moreover, those who suffer for Christ's sake will also receive from the Lord his *consolation* in the midst of the trials: "**For as the sufferings of Christ abound in us, so our <u>consolation</u> also aboundeth by Christ**" (2 Corinthians 1:5). "**And our hope of you *is* stedfast, knowing, that as ye are partakers of the sufferings, so *shall ye be* also of the <u>consolation</u>**" (2 Corinthians 1:7). "**Now our Lord Jesus Christ himself, and God, even our Father, which hath loved us, and hath given *us* <u>everlasting consolation</u> and good hope through grace, [c]omfort your hearts, and stablish you in every good word and work**" (2 Thessalonians 2:16-17). In other words, serving God in "this present evil world" (Galatians 1:4) will result in persecution and suffering to us, but God will help us in our trouble by his consolation and comfort.

All "**the children of God by faith in Christ Jesus**" (Galatians 3:26) are "**heirs of God**" (Romans 8:17), and stand: "**In hope of eternal life, which God,**

that cannot lie, promised before the world began" (Titus 1:2). Furthermore, we read: "**Wherein God, willing more abundantly to shew unto the heirs of promise the immutability of his counsel, confirmed *it* by an oath: That by two immutable things, in which *it was* impossible for God to lie, we might have a strong consolation, who have fled for refuge to lay hold upon the hope set before us: Which *hope* we have as an anchor of the soul, both sure and stedfast, and which entereth into that within the veil; Whither the forerunner is for us entered, *even* Jesus, made an high priest for ever after the order of Melchisedec**" (Hebrews 6:17-20). The Lord Jesus Christ, "**the hope set before us,**" is our "**strong consolation.**" Notice that the consolation is only to them who are "**in Christ,**" and not to any one else.

GOD COMFORTS HIS CHILDREN

Philippians 2:1 continues to say, "…if any comfort of love…"

David declared: "**Yea, though I walk through the valley of the shadow of death, I will fear no evil: for thou *art* with me; thy rod and thy staff they comfort me**" (Psalm 23:4).

We are comforted by God's word: "**This *is* my comfort in my affliction: for thy word hath quickened me**" (Psalm 119:50). "**For whatsoever things were written aforetime were written for our learning, that we through patience and comfort of the scriptures might have hope**" (Romans 15:4). The soon coming of the Lord Jesus Christ for his born again believers is "**our blessed hope**" (Titus 2:13): "**For the Lord himself shall descend from heaven with a shout, with the voice of the archangel, and with the trump of God: and the dead in Christ shall rise first: Then we which are alive *and* remain shall be caught up together with them in the clouds, to meet the Lord in the air: and so shall we ever be with the Lord. Wherefore comfort one another with these words**" (1 Thessalonians 4:16-18).

We are comforted by the Holy Ghost: "**Then had the churches rest throughout all Judaea and Galilee and Samaria, and were edified; and walking in the fear of the Lord, and in the comfort of the Holy Ghost, were multiplied**" (Acts 9:31).

Our heavenly Father is called, "**the God of all comfort; Who comforteth us in all our tribulation, that we may be able to comfort them which are in any trouble, by the comfort wherewith we ourselves are comforted**

<u>**of God**</u>" (2 Corinthians 1:3-4). "**Now our Lord Jesus Christ himself, and God, even our Father, which hath loved us, and hath given *us* <u>everlasting consolation</u> and good hope through grace, [<u>c</u>]<u>omfort your hearts</u>, and stablish you in every good word and work**" (2 Thessalonians 2:16-17). "**Finally, brethren, farewell. Be perfect, <u>be of good comfort</u>, be of one mind, live in peace; and the God of love and peace shall be with you**" (2 Corinthians 13:11).

FELLOWSHIP OF THE SPIRIT

Then Philippians 2:1 says, "…if any fellowship of the Spirit…" When a man is "**born of the Spirit**" (John 3:8), he is "**a new creature: old things are passed away; behold, all things are become new**" (2 Corinthians 5:17). He is joined unto the Lord, and "**is one spirit**" (1 Corinthians 6:17). The scripture says: "**But ye are not in the flesh, but <u>in the Spirit</u>, if so be that the Spirit of God dwell in you. Now if any man have not the Spirit of Christ, he is none of his**" (Romans 8:9). "**And…the love of God is shed abroad in our hearts by the Holy Ghost which is given unto us**" (Romans 5:5). This love of God causes us to sincerely love all of our brothers in Christ. This is a strong indicator of whether one has truly been "**born of the Spirit**," for John asks, "**If a man say, I love God, and hateth his brother, he is a liar: for he that loveth not his brother whom he hath seen, how can he love God whom he hath not seen**?" (1 John 4:20). The real test of this is whether a man loves going to church with his brothers in Christ more than hanging out with his old friends who do not love the Lord!

WITNESS OF THE SPIRIT

I can testify that a very profound change took place in me when I believed on the Lord Jesus Christ, on the very day when my spiritual eyes were opened! Now I can rejoice in the scriptures that confirm the permanent residency of the Spirit of God in me! If we have been born of the Spirit, then the following scriptures are a great blessing to know: "<u>**The Spirit itself beareth witness with our spirit, that we are the children of God**</u>" (Romans 8:16). "**Likewise the Spirit also helpeth our infirmities: for we know not what we should pray for as we ought: but the Spirit itself maketh intercession for us with groanings which cannot be uttered**" (Romans 8:26). "<u>**Hereby know we that we dwell in him, and he in us, because he hath given us of his Spirit**</u>" (1 John 4:13). "<u>**And because ye are sons, God hath sent forth the Spirit of his Son into your hearts, crying, Abba, Father**</u>" (Galatians 4:6). "**And he that keepeth his**

commandments dwelleth in him, and he in him. <u>And hereby we know that he abideth in us, by the Spirit which he hath given us</u>" (1 John 3:24). "**Know ye not that ye are the temple of God, and *that* <u>the Spirit of God dwelleth in you</u>?**" (1 Corinthians 3:16). "**The grace of the Lord Jesus Christ, and the love of God, and the <u>communion of the Holy Ghost</u>, *be* with you all. Amen**" (2 Corinthians 13:14).

THE MERCIES OF GOD

Philippians 2:1 ends the sentence by saying "…if any bowels and mercies." The *bowels* were regarded within each person as the base of the more violent passions, such as anger and love; but by the Hebrews the *bowels* were regarded as the base of the more tender affections, especially kindness, benevolence, and compassion. Mercy is one of the distinguishing attributes of God. It is that attribute which causes God to have pity and compassion, and to treat an offender better than he deserves. Mercy results in a sinner not receiving that which he deserves as punishment from God. The psalmist wrote: "**For thou, Lord, *art* good, and ready to forgive; and <u>plenteous in mercy</u> unto all them that call upon thee**" (Psalm 86:5); in addition he wrote: "**But thou, O Lord, *art* a God full of compassion, and gracious, longsuffering, and <u>plenteous in mercy</u> and truth**" (Psalm 86:15).

After David numbered Israel contrary to God's will, the LORD gave David a choice of punishments, and "**David said unto Gad** [Prophet to king David (1 Chronicles 21:9; 2 Samuel 24:11)]**, I am in a great strait: let me fall now into the hand of the LORD; <u>for very great *are* his mercies</u>: but let me not fall into the hand of man**" (1 Chronicles 21:11-13).

Nehemiah rehearsed the many mercies of God toward the children of Israel in the wilderness. Speaking to the LORD, he said, "**Yet thou in <u>thy manifold mercies</u> forsookest them not in the wilderness**" (Nehemiah 9:19). Likewise, after all of Israel's murmurings and disobedience, Nehemiah wrote, "**Nevertheless for <u>thy great mercies'</u> sake thou didst not utterly consume them, nor forsake them; <u>for thou *art* a gracious and merciful God</u>**" (Nehemiah 9:31).

After David's grievous sin in the matter of Bathsheba and her husband, David called on the LORD, saying, "**Have <u>mercy</u> upon me, O God, according to thy lovingkindness: <u>according unto the multitude of thy tender mercies blot out my transgressions</u>**" (Psalm 51:1).

Jeremiah wrote, "***It is of* the LORD'S mercies that we are not consumed, because his compassions fail not**" (Lamentations 3:22).

Micah wrote: "**Who *is* a God like unto thee, that pardoneth iniquity, and passeth by the transgression of the remnant of his heritage? he retaineth not his anger for ever, because he delighteth *in* mercy**" (Micah 7:18).

SAVED ACCORDING TO GOD'S MERCY

The scriptures are so plain, and yet the world is filled with false religions who burden people with requirements for religious works in an utterly vain and worthless attempt to work for "**the gift of God**" (Romans 6:23). These are false and wicked religions, for we read: "**Not by works of righteousness which we have done, but according to his mercy he saved us, by the washing of regeneration, and renewing of the Holy Ghost; Which he shed on us abundantly through Jesus Christ our Saviour; That being justified by his grace, we should be made heirs according to the hope of eternal life. *This is* a faithful saying, and these things I will that thou affirm constantly, that they which have believed in God might be careful to maintain good works. These things are good and profitable unto men**" (Titus 3:5-8). The "good works" begin only after a man is "born of the Spirit" (John 3:8), for the "good works" are the work of God working in the believer (Philippians 2:13): "**For by grace are ye saved through faith; and that not of yourselves: *it is* the gift of God: Not of works, lest any man should boast**. [Salvation is by faith in God's grace. Only after salvation do our good works with God begin] **For we are his workmanship, created in Christ Jesus unto good works, which God hath before ordained that we should walk in them**" (Ephesians 2:8-10).

Paul to the Ephesians wrote: "**But God, who is rich in mercy, for his great love wherewith he loved us, Even when we were dead in sins, hath quickened us together with Christ, (by grace ye are saved;) And hath raised *us* up together, and made *us* sit together in heavenly *places* in Christ Jesus: That in the ages to come he might shew the exceeding riches of his grace in *his* kindness toward us through Christ Jesus**" (Ephesians 2:4-7).

In light of the great richness of God's mercy to save the likes of some of us, it is only reasonable that we should strive to be like our most loving and merciful God. The apostle commands: "**Put on therefore, as the elect of God, holy and beloved, bowels of mercies, kindness, humbleness of mind, meekness, longsuffering; Forbearing one another, and forgiving one another, if any**

man have a quarrel against any: even as Christ forgave you, so also *do* ye" (Colossians 3:12-13).

UNITY OF THE SPIRIT

Philippians 1:1 talks about the "ifs," and promptly addresses those "ifs" in Philippians 2:2 by giving us some instructions, saying, "Fulfil ye my joy, that ye be likeminded, having the same love, *being* of one accord, of one mind." To be "likeminded" is to have the same mind, the same spirit: to be in one accord as we glorify God in our bodies and in our spirits, "which are God's" (1 Corinthians 6:20). The Apostle Paul also wrote to the believers in Rome: "**Now the God of patience and consolation grant you to be likeminded one toward another according to Christ Jesus: That ye may with one mind *and* one mouth glorify God, even the Father of our Lord Jesus Christ**" (Romans 15:5-6). Believers should be, "**Endeavouring to keep the unity of the Spirit in the bond of peace**" (Ephesians 4:3). The Lord Jesus said, "**It is the spirit that quickeneth; the flesh profiteth nothing: the words that I speak unto you, *they* are spirit, and *they* are life**" (John 6:63).

God also gave gifted men to the church whose ministry should result in "**the unity of the faith**." "**And he** [God] **gave some, apostles; and some, prophets; and some, evangelists; and some, pastors and teachers; For the perfecting of the saints, for the work of the ministry, for the edifying of the body of Christ: Till we all come in the unity of the faith, and of the knowledge of the Son of God, unto a perfect man, unto the measure of the stature of the fulness of Christ**" (Ephesians 4:11-13).

CONFUSION

If believers are reading, teaching, and preaching from different bibles, which they suppose to be the words of God, but are, in truth, only the words of men, this will certainly bring confusion among the people of God. We know that this is the deceptive work of the devil, "**For God is not *the author* of confusion**" (1 Corinthians 14:33)! We read in God's word the promise that he would preserve his word for all generations: "**The words of the LORD *are* pure words: *as* silver tried in a furnace of earth, purified seven times. Thou shalt keep them, O LORD, thou shalt preserve them from this generation for ever**" (Psalm 12:6-7). According to these two verses, I can fully expect to be able to find the pure and preserved word of God written down for me in my generation! Even though unfaithful men have corrupted and watered down God's word, and published many so-called bibles, I have the scriptural ability to know which Bible is the authentic Holy Bible.

We know that the scripture was written when "**holy men of God spake *as they were* moved by the Holy Ghost**" (2 Peter 1:21), and we know that "**All scripture *is* given by inspiration of God, and *is* profitable for doctrine, for reproof, for correction, for instruction in righteousness: That the man of God may be perfect, throughly furnished unto all good works**" (2 Timothy 3:16-17).

The Lord Jesus spoke to his apostles about the coming of the Holy Ghost, saying, "**Howbeit when he, the Spirit of truth, is come, he will guide you into all truth: for he shall not speak of himself; but whatsoever he shall hear, *that* shall he speak: and he will shew you things to come. He shall glorify me: for he shall receive of mine, and shall shew *it* unto you**" (John 16:13-14). Therefore, the Holy Bible may be identified as the Bible which *most* glorifies the Lord Jesus Christ. There can be no doubt among honest men who study this matter that the King James Bible is far ahead of all other bible versions in glorifying the Lord Jesus Christ. This is the reason why our ministry only purchases and makes King James Bibles available to inmates. Please understand that we are not saying that the other versions do not convey truth: they certainly do. What we do believe is that the King James Bible is the *pure* word of God, for: "**Every word of God *is* pure: he *is* a shield unto them that put their trust in him**" (Proverbs 30:5), and: "**Thy word *is* very pure: therefore thy servant loveth it**" (Psalm 119:140). Would you not rather know what God said than to read what *man* said God said?

Everyone who has tampered with, and thus corrupted the word of God, will face serious consequences, for the scripture warns such men: "**For I testify unto every man that heareth the words of the prophecy of this book, If any man shall add unto these things, God shall add unto him the plagues that are written in this book: And if any man shall take away from the words of the book of this prophecy, God shall take away his part out of the book of life, and out of the holy city, and *from* the things which are written in this book**" (Revelation 22:18-19).

The Apostle Paul declared: "**Now we have received, not the spirit of the world, but the spirit which is of God; that we might know the things that are freely given to us of God. Which things also we speak, not in the words which man's wisdom teacheth, but which the Holy Ghost teacheth;**

comparing spiritual things with spiritual" (1 Corinthians 2:12-13). In other words, the Holy Bible was inspired by the Holy Ghost, while the other versions of the Bible are the "**words which man's wisdom teacheth,**" And "**the wisdom of this world is foolishness with God. For it is written, He taketh the wise in their own craftiness**" (1 Corinthians 3:19).

GOD'S MAGNIFIED WORD

The inspired psalmist David wrote: "**I will worship toward thy holy temple, and praise thy name for thy lovingkindness and for thy truth: for <u>thou hast magnified thy word above all thy name</u>**" (Psalm 138:2). Speaking of the name of Jesus Christ, the Holy Bible declares: "**Wherefore God also hath highly exalted him, and given him <u>a name which is above every name</u>: That at the name of Jesus every knee should bow, of *things* in heaven, and *things* in earth, and *things* under the earth; And *that* every tongue should confess that Jesus Christ *is* Lord, to the glory of God the Father**" (Philippians 2:9-11). "**Neither is there salvation in any other: for there is none other name** [the name of "Jesus Christ of Nazareth" (Acts 4:10)] **under heaven given among men, whereby we must be saved**" (Acts 4:12)!

Without the pure, preserved, inspired, and magnified word of God, we could have no confidence in the word of God, the Holy Bible. The new and corrupted versions of the "Bible" destroy the confidence of men in God's word. This is, of course, the goal of Satan! For example, the New International Version says: "...for you have so exalted your solemn decree that it surpasses your fame" (Psalm 138 NIV), instead of "**for <u>thou hast magnified thy word above all thy name</u>**" (Psalm 138:2)! Another place, instead of: "Thou shalt keep them ["the words of the LORD" (Psalm 12:6)], O LORD, thou shalt preserve them from this generation for ever" (Psalm 12:7), the NIV says: "You, LORD, will keep the needy safe and will protect us forever from the wicked" (Psalm 12:7 NIV)! These are words that are not even close to the truth! Yet again where the Holy Bible clearly says, "**And Joseph and his mother marvelled at those things which were spoken of him** [Jesus]" (Luke 2:33), the NIV blasphemously declares Joseph to be the father of Jesus, saying: "The child's father and mother marvelled at what was said about him" (Luke 2:33 NIV)! The Lord Jesus Christ has no earthly father. His Father is God in heaven, and they are "one" (John 10:30)!

According to the Holy Bible, Jesus Christ is clearly revealed as God made flesh (John 1:1, 14): "**And without controversy great is the mystery**

of godliness: God was manifest in the flesh, justified in the Spirit, seen of angels, preached unto the Gentiles, believed on in the world, received up into glory" (1 Timothy 3:16). Most all of the corrupt "Bibles" totally confuse the clearly worded scriptures and remove important words which emphatically prove Jesus to be God, like the following: "Beyond all question, the mystery from which true godliness springs is great: He appeared in the flesh" (1 Timothy 3:16 NIV). "He" is substituted for the important pronoun "God"!

With reference to the Godhead (Acts 17:29; Romans 1:20; Colossians 2:9), the Holy Bible declares: "**For there are three that bear record in heaven, the Father, the Word** [Jesus Christ, the Son (John 1:1)], **and the Holy Ghost: and these three are one**" (1 John 5:7). The NIV reads: "For there are three that testify" (1 John 5:7 NIV). These words were taken from verse 8, so that you would not notice that verse 7 in their corrupted "Bible" has been completely removed! God's word is pure, not deceptive!

STAY HUMBLE

Nevertheless, we must go on with the sermon. Philippians 2:3-4 says, "*Let* nothing *be done* through strife or vainglory; but in lowliness of mind let each esteem other better than themselves. Look not every man on his own things, but every man also on the things of others."

The word vainglory in the 1828 Webster's Dictionary is defined as self-vanity "excited by one's own performances; empty pride; undue elation of mind." Both strife and pride are destructive to Christian love and stir up carnal conflicts. We should be quick to judge our own faults, and be charitable in our judgments of others. We should esteem the good that we see in others above that which is in ourselves. We must be concerned not only for our own credit, and ease, and safety, but for those of others also. We should rejoice in the prosperity of others as truly as in our own.

In other words, we must love our neighbour as ourselves, and work no ill toward him (Romans 13:9-10). Jesus summed up all the commandments of God into two great commandments: To love God with all your heart, soul and mind. And the second like unto the first, "Thou shalt love thy neighbour as thyself" (Matthew 22:37-39). Instead of working ill toward our neighbor, we should love him. We can learn how to love our neighbor by demonstrating charity toward our neighbor. Paul, writing to the carnal church of Corinth, expounded on the topic of charity in his first letter. Unfortunately, the Corinthian church lacked love, and therefore, Paul explained in great detail what love is, and penned down the words: "Though I speak with the tongues of men and of angels, and have not charity, I am become *as* sounding brass, or a tinkling cymbal. And though I have *the gift of* prophecy, and understand all mysteries, and all knowledge; and though I have all faith, so that I could remove mountains, and have not charity, I am nothing. And though I bestow all my goods to feed *the poor*, and though I give my body to be burned, and have not charity, it profiteth me nothing. Charity suffereth long, *and* is kind; charity envieth not; charity vaunteth not itself, is not puffed up, Doth not behave itself unseemly, seeketh not her own, is not easily provoked, thinketh no evil; Rejoiceth not in iniquity, but rejoiceth in the truth; Beareth all things, believeth all things, hopeth all things, endureth all things. Charity never faileth..." (1 Corinthians 13:1-8).

As we see, love is more than speaking a kind word to someone, but is expressed in humility through that of good deeds and in truth (1 John 3:18). Love is an action and grace of humility. Not to love our neighbor is to express pride; but to express actions of charity toward our neighbor is to have humility and care for him. Both James and Peter declare that God resists the proud, but that he gives grace to the humble (James 4:6; 1 Peter 5:5). Therefore, "**Humble yourselves therefore under the mighty hand of God, that he may exalt you in due time**: **Casting all your care upon him; for he careth for you**" (1 Peter 5:6-7).

BE SAVED TODAY!

If you have not been "**born of the Spirit**" (John 3:8), and delivered "**from the power of darkness, and...translated...into the kingdom of his dear Son**" (Colossians 1:13), then I hope you will read the gospel according to John, which was "**written, that ye might believe that Jesus is the Christ, the Son of God; and that believing ye might have life through his name**" (John 20:31).

Chapter 12

Law or Grace

Second Timothy 2:15 is a command to Timothy, and to all believers, to study the word of God. It also commands us to rightly divide the word of truth. If the Holy Bible is not rightly divided, it can be used to teach many things which do not apply to the church today. Much confusion will arise as a result. And we know that, "**God is not *the author* of confusion, but of peace, as in all churches of the saints**" (1 Corinthians 14:33).

RIGHTLY DIVIDING BETWEEN LAW AND GRACE

John 1:17 says, "**For the law was given by Moses, *but* grace and truth came by Jesus Christ.**"

It is very important to understand that the law of Moses was not given to the church! God gave the law of Moses to the children of Israel in the wilderness (Deuteronomy 5:1-5; Exodus 20:1-2). The LORD, speaking through the prophet Malachi, commanded, "Remember ye the law of Moses my servant, which I commanded unto him in Horeb **for all Israel**, *with* the statutes and judgments" (Malachi 4:4). God gave the law **for all Israel**, and not for all nations, and certainly not for the church today, as the following scriptures will make abundantly clear!

God did not bring the church, which is Christ's body (Colossians 1:18, 24; Ephesians 5:29-30), "out of the land of Egypt, out of the house of bondage" (Exodus 20:2) to give them the Ten Commandments! He brought **Israel** out of Egyptian bondage and gave **them** the Ten Commandments. "**But when the fulness of the time was come** [more than fifteen hundred years after the law was given to Moses]**, God sent forth his Son, made of a woman, made under the law, [t]o redeem them that were under the law, that we might receive the adoption of sons**" (Galatians 4:4-5). Can you imagine how wicked and contrary to "the gospel of the grace of God" (Acts 20:24) any false doctrine would be that would attempt to place an adopted son of God (Romans 8:15; Ephesians 1:5) back under the law from which the Lord Jesus Christ has delivered him (Romans 7:6)? The law was fulfilled and satisfied in Jesus Christ, nailed to his cross, and has been taken out of the way (Colossians 2:14) for all those who have been born again and baptized by his Spirit into his body (1 Corinthians 12:13).

BEFORE THE CROSS

The Lord Jesus himself said, "**For God sent not his Son into the world to condemn the world; but that the world through him might me saved**" (John 3:17). In another place we read, "**that Christ Jesus came into the world to save sinners**" (1 Timothy 1:15). We also know that Jesus did "**taste death for every man**" (Hebrews 2:9). We also read, "**But God commendeth his love toward us, in that, while we were yet sinners, Christ died for us**" (Romans 5:8). It is abundantly clear that the way of salvation for the whole world is through Christ's death on the cross for our sins (1 Corinthians 15:3-4).

Nevertheless before his death on the cross, Christ came unto Israel as their promised Messiah (Daniel 9:25-26) to fulfill the law and the prophets concerning himself (Luke 24:25-27). Therefore, before the cross, his primary ministry was to Israel (Matthew 15:24). Before the cross, Jesus instructed his disciples, "**saying, Go not into the way of the Gentiles, and into *any* city of the Samaritans enter ye not: But go rather to the lost sheep of the house of Israel**" (Matthew 10:5-6).

There were a few exceptional Gentiles who were blessed by the Lord's earthly ministry. The Lord made the woman of Canaan's daughter whole after she demonstrated great faith and humility before him (Matthew 15:21-28). Jesus healed the servant of the Roman centurion who also demonstrated great faith in the Lord (Matthew 8:5-13). The Lord Jesus went out of his way to meet and save the Samaritan woman at Jacob's well (John 4:1-45). Many other Samaritans came out to see him as a result of her testimony and were saved. There may have been many other exceptions where the Lord healed and saved Gentiles during his earthly ministry, but his primary mission was "**unto the lost sheep of the house of Israel**" (Matthew 15:24).

AT THE CROSS

The Old Testament ends at the cross, and the New Testament begins at the cross (Matthew 26:28).

Above we affirmed by the scriptures that the law of Moses, with respect to all believers in Christ, was abolished in the flesh of Jesus Christ on the cross (Ephesians 2:14-17). We also know that the New Testament could not begin until the death of the Lord Jesus on the cross. Hebrews 9:15-17 says, "And for this cause he is the mediator of the new testament, that by means of death, for the redemption of the transgressions *that were* under the first testament, they which are called might receive the promise of eternal inheritance. For where a testament *is*, there must also of necessity be the death of the testator. For a testament *is* of force after men are dead: otherwise it is of no strength at all while the testator liveth."

Therefore, the Old Testament was still in effect during the earthly ministry of the Lord Jesus before his death, burial, and resurrection. Hence the Lord told the Jews, and not the church, "**Think not that I am come to destroy the law, or the prophets: I am not come to destroy, but to fulfil**" (Matthew 5:17). The Lord Jesus Christ was the only man on earth who ever fulfilled the law by keeping it perfectly. He "**was in all points tempted like as *we are, yet* without sin**" (Hebrews 4:15). The prophet Isaiah wrote of his first coming when he wrote, "**the LORD is well pleased for his righteousness' sake; he will magnify the law, and make it honourable**" (Isaiah 42:21). The Lord came to fulfill the law, and then to die for the sins of the world under the condemnation of the law, thus removing the condemnation of the law from all born again believers. In taking the law out of the way, the Lord now offers eternal life as a "free gift" (Romans 5:15-18; 6:23) to all who believe on him alone for salvation.

Today, during this "**dispensation of the grace of God**" (Ephesians 3:2), "**there are certain men crept in unawares, who were before of old ordained to this condemnation, ungodly men, turning the grace of our God into lasciviousness, and denying the only Lord God, and our Lord Jesus Christ**" (Jude 1:4). Men who attempt to add law to grace and bring the born again believers back under bondage are denying the "**grace of our God**." It is extremely shameful how many minds have been "**corrupted from the simplicity that is in Christ**" (2 Corinthians 11:3) by the "**vain jangling**" of those who, in our time, desire "**to be teachers of the law; understanding neither what they say, nor whereof they affirm**" (1 Timothy 1:6-7)! They attempt to unlawfully bring "**righteous**" men in Christ back under the law from which God has delivered them, not knowing, "**that the law is not made for a righteous man, but for the lawless and disobedient...**" (1 Timothy 1:8-11). Therefore, "**Beware lest any man spoil you through philosophy and vain deceit, after the tradition of men, after the rudiments of the world, and not after Christ**" (Colossians 2:8).

THE ERROR OF THE RELIGIOUS PHARISEES

In the early days of the church, "**there rose up certain of the sect of the Pharisees which believed, saying, That it was needful to circumcise them** [the Gentile believers], **and to command *them* to keep the law of Moses**" (Acts 15:5). The Apostle Peter rose up and gave the account of how the Gentiles had believed after he had preached the gospel unto them. He said that God had given them the Holy Ghost even as he had to the Jews, and that he had put no difference between the Jews and Gentiles, "**purifying their hearts by faith. Now therefore why tempt ye God, to put a yoke** [the law of Moses] **upon the neck of the disciples, which neither our fathers nor we were able to bear? But we believe that through the <u>grace</u> of the Lord Jesus Christ we shall be saved, even as they**" (Acts 15:9-11). Peter stated plainly that both Jews and Gentiles were saved by grace; "**And if by grace, then *is it* no more of works** [of the law (Galatians 2:16; 3:2, 5, 10)]**: otherwise grace is no more grace. But if *it be* of works, then is it no more grace: otherwise work is no more work**" (Romans 11:6). In other words, when men attempt to add any work requirement whatsoever to God's grace, then "**grace is no more grace**" (Romans 11:6). When men trust in any work that they must do in order to receive salvation from the Lord, they void God's grace. They stumble at the word (1 Peter 2:7-8).

Speaking of unbelieving Israel, Paul wrote: "**For they being ignorant of God's righteousness, and going about to establish their own righteousness, have not submitted themselves unto the righteousness of God**" (Romans 10:3). Salvation is, "**Not by works of righteousness which we have done, but according to his mercy he saved us**, by the washing of regeneration, and renewing of the Holy Ghost" (Titus 3:5). Peter also said that the law was a "**yoke of bondage**" which no man could bear! Only the Lord Jesus Christ kept the law perfectly and fulfilled the law! Praise God for his precious Son whom God made **"to be sin for us, who knew no sin, that we might be made the righteousness of God in him"** (2 Corinthians 5:21).

"But now the righteousness of God without the law is manifested, being witnessed by the law and the prophets; Even the righteousness of God *which is* by faith of Jesus Christ unto all and upon all them that believe: for there is no difference" (Romans 3:21-22).

After Peter had spoken, Paul and Barnabas also declared what miracles God had worked among the Gentiles by them. Then James recalled what the scripture says about the calling out of the Gentiles (Acts 15:14-18). He then concluded that the Gentiles are not under the law of Moses. The passage in Acts 15:22-29 continues telling the story, saying, "Then pleased it the apostles and elders, with the whole church, to send chosen men of their own company to Antioch with Paul and Barnabas; *namely*, Judas surnamed Barsabas, and Silas, chief men among the brethren: And they wrote *letters* by them after this manner; The apostles and elders and brethren *send* greeting unto the brethren which are of the Gentiles in Antioch and Syria and Cilicia: **Forasmuch as we have heard, that certain which went out from us have troubled you with words, subverting** [overthrowing; entirely destroying] **your souls, saying, *Ye must* be circumcised, and keep the law: to whom we gave no *such* commandment**: It seemed good unto us, being assembled with one accord, to send chosen men unto you with our beloved Barnabas and Paul, Men that have hazarded their lives for the name of our Lord Jesus Christ. We have sent therefore Judas and Silas, who shall also tell *you* the same things by mouth. **For it seemed good to the Holy Ghost, and to us, to lay upon you no greater burden than these necessary things; That ye abstain from meats offered to idols, and from blood, and from things strangled, and from fornication: from which if ye keep yourselves, ye shall do well. Fare ye well.**"

The Holy Ghost and the apostles of Jesus Christ plainly told the Gentiles that the Pharisees had troubled them with false words, subverting their souls. Then they singled out a broad form of the seventh commandment, "**Neither shalt thou commit adultery**" (Deuteronomy 5:18) from the other ten, and commanded the Gentiles to "**abstain from fornication**" (Acts 15:29). Fornication is the broad term that includes adultery and all other unlawful sexual activities outside of marriage. Later the Apostle Paul wrote to the church in Thessalonica, "**For this is the will of God, *even* your sanctification, that ye should abstain from fornication**" (1 Thessalonians 4:3). In other words, obedience to this commandment will set the born again believer apart for God and separate him from the wicked in the world, many of which are given over to fornication (Jude 1:7).

Nine of the Ten Commandments are found repeated in the New Testament. I have placed all ten commands below with their Old Testament references as well as their New Testament references. However, please note that one of the commands contains no reference in the New Testament.

I. Thou shalt have none other gods before me (Exodus 20:3; Deuteronomy 5:7; Acts 17:22-31; Hebrews 1:6; Revelation 4:10; 19:10).
II. Thou shalt not make thee any graven image... (Exodus 20:4; Deuteronomy 5:8-10; 1 Corinthians 5:10-11; 6:9-10; 10:7; Galatians 5:20; 1 John 5:21).
III. Thou shalt not take the name of the Lord thy God in vain (Exodus 20:7; Deuteronomy 5:11; 1 Timothy 6:1).
IV. Keep the sabbath day, to sanctify it (Exodus 20:8; Deuteronomy 5:12). **This commandment is not repeated for the church in the New Testament**.
V. Honour thy father and thy mother... (Exodus 20:12; Deuteronomy 5:16; Ephesians 6:2).
VI. Thou shalt not kill (Exodus 20:13; Deuteronomy 5:17; Romans 13:9).
VII. Neither shalt thou commit adultery (Exodus 20:14; Deuteronomy 5:18; Romans 13:9).
VIII. Neither shalt thou steal (Exodus 20:15; Deuteronomy 5:19; Romans 13:9).
IX. Neither shalt thou bear false witness against thy neighbor (Exodus 20:16; Deuteronomy 5:20; Romans 13:9).
X. Neither shalt thou covet thy neighbor's house... (Exodus 20:17; Deuteronomy 5:21; Romans 13:9).

The fourth commandment is **a sign between God and Israel** (Exodus 31:13-17; Ezekiel 20:20) ***and is not repeated in the New Testament as a commandment for the church to keep!***

God explains this sign in Exodus 31:13-17, saying, "Speak thou also unto the children of Israel, saying, Verily my sabbaths ye shall keep: for it *is* a sign between me and you throughout your generations; that *ye* may know that I *am* the LORD that doth sanctify you. Ye shall keep the sabbath therefore; for it *is* holy unto you: every one that defileth it shall surely be put to death: for whosoever doeth *any* work therein, that soul shall be cut off from among his people. Six days may work be done; but in the seventh *is* the sabbath of rest, holy to the LORD: whosoever doeth *any* work in the sabbath day, he shall surely be put to death. Wherefore the children of Israel shall keep the sabbath, to observe the sabbath throughout their generations, *for* a perpetual covenant. It *is* a sign between me and the children of Israel for ever: for *in* six days the LORD made heaven and earth, and on the seventh day he rested, and was refreshed."

Again, God reaffirms this command to the nation of Israel, saying in Ezekiel 20:19-20, "I *am* the LORD your God; walk in my statutes, and keep my judgments, and do them; And hallow my sabbaths; and they shall be a sign between me and you, that ye may know that I *am* the LORD your God."

Paul the apostle, after listing the last five of the Ten Commandments in Romans 13:9, concludes by saying, "...**and if there be any other commandment, it is briefly comprehended in this saying, namely, Thou shalt love thy neighbour as thyself. Love worketh no ill to his neighbour: therefore love is the fulfilling of the law**" (Romans 13:9-10). Also, in another place we read, "**For all the law is fulfilled in one word, *even* in this; Thou shalt love thy neighbor as thyself**" (Galatians 5:14; see also Romans 8:3-4; 14:5-6). If it was imperative or necessary for the church to keep the sabbath day, these passages would have been perfect places to include that commandment to the church, but it is not mentioned at all! Some have taught that believers will not be able to enter into heaven unless they "Keep the sabbath day, to sanctify it" (Deuteronomy 5:12). But what does the Holy Ghost and the apostles say to this ridiculous attempt to bring true believers back under the bondage of the law? Read Acts 15:1-29 again. Then read Galatians chapter 3. That anyone, who is in Christ, would need further justification through the works of the law before he could enter into heaven is ridiculous in light of the fact that God "**hath** [already] **raised us** [the children of God by faith in Christ Jesus (Galatians 3:26)] **up together, and made us sit together in heavenly places in Christ Jesus**" (Ephesians 2:6)! The Lord Jesus Christ is our "**passover**" (1 Corinthians 5:7) and our "**rest**" (Matthew 11:28-30), into whom we have entered, and we have ceased from our own works (Hebrews 4:10). "**For it is God which worketh in you both to will and to do of *his* good pleasure**" (Philippians 2:13). Our salvation is in him, and not in the works of the law! The Lord Jesus Christ is "**the way, the truth, and the life**" (John 14:6). "**He that hath the Son hath life; *and* he that hath not the Son of God hath not life**" (1 John 5:12).

With respect to all born again believers in Christ, Moses' law was "**abolished**" by the Lord Jesus Christ on the cross (2 Corinthians 3:12-14;

Ephesians 2:14-17). No born again believer is under the law (Romans 6:14-15). Before we were saved, we were under the law, "**But when the fulness of the time was come, God sent forth his Son, made of a woman, made under the law, To redeem them that were under the law, that we might receive the adoption of sons**" (Galatians 4:4-5).

"For he testifieth, Thou *art* a priest for ever after the order of Melchisedec. **For there is verily a disannulling of the commandment going before for the weakness and unprofitableness thereof. For the law** [Moses' law] **made nothing perfect, but the bringing in of a better hope** [the Lord Jesus Christ] ***did***; by the which we draw nigh unto God" (Hebrews 7:17-19).

The law has not been abolished for all men; but only for righteous men: "**But we know that the law *is* good, if a man use it lawfully**; **Knowing this, that the law is not made for a righteous man**, but for the lawless and disobedient, for the ungodly and for sinners, for unholy and profane, for murderers of fathers and murderers of mothers, for manslayers, [f]or whoremongers, for them that defile themselves with mankind, for menstealers, for liars, for perjured persons, and if there be any other thing that is contrary to sound doctrine; According to the glorious gospel of the blessed God, which was committed to my trust" (1 Timothy 1:8-11).

The law is still in effect over lost men. "Now we know that what things soever the law saith, it saith to **them who are under the law** [lost, unsaved men]: that every mouth may be stopped, and all the world may become guilty before God" (Romans 3:19).

"But the scripture hath concluded all under sin, that the promise by faith of Jesus Christ might be given to them that believe. **But before faith came, we were kept under the law, shut up unto the faith which should afterwards be revealed. Wherefore the law was our schoolmaster *to bring us* unto Christ, that we might be justified by faith. But after that faith is come, we are no longer under a schoolmaster** [the law]. For ye are all the children of God by faith in Christ Jesus" (Galatians 3:22-26).

One glorious day when all the wicked are cast into the lake of fire, and all the righteous are present with the Lord, the law will "**vanish away**" (Hebrews 8:12-13)! **Abolish** means to make void; to **annul**. The law has been annulled for all of God's children.

AFTER THE CROSS

The Gospel Is Sent to the Gentiles:

After Christ's resurrection, the Lord commissioned his disciples, saying, "**Go ye into all the world, and preach the gospel** [Acts 20:24; 1 Corinthians 15:3-4] **to every creature**" (Mark 16:15). Just before he ascended up into heaven, the Lord Jesus told his disciples that they would soon receive power, after that the Holy Ghost came upon them, and that they would be witnesses for him "**in Jerusalem, and in all Judea, and in Samaria, and unto the uttermost part of the earth**" (Acts 1:8). About ten days after that, on the day of Pentecost, the Holy Ghost came upon the disciples, after which they began to preach and teach the resurrected Christ with much boldness (Acts 4:31). It was after this that the angel of the Lord sent Philip to meet the Ethiopian eunuch, preach Jesus Christ to him, and baptize him (Acts 8:26-39).

Then the Lord Jesus appeared to Saul, who became Paul the apostle, saved him, had him baptized (Acts 9:18-19), gave him the revelation of the gospel of the grace of God (Galatians 1:11-12; Acts 20:24), and sent him to bear his name "**before the Gentiles, and kings, and the children of Israel**" (Acts 9:15).

Then we read how the Lord worked to arrange the meeting between Peter and Cornelius' household so that they could hear the gospel and believe (Acts 10).

Jesus' Ministry Is Redirected:

After the resurrection of Christ, instead of continuing to concentrate on the Jews, the Lord began to send out his disciples into all the world to "preach the gospel to every creature" (Mark 16:15). We have been in the church age for almost two thousand years now (Matthew 16:18). Before the cross men were under the law of Moses. There are six teachings that changed after the resurrection, and they are as follows:

1. Before the cross, Jesus instructed the seventy that he sent out to Israel to preach the "gospel of the kingdom," "Go not from house to house" (Luke 10:7). If a preacher today preached the "gospel of the kingdom" instead of the "gospel of the grace of God" (Acts 20:24; 1 Corinthians 15:3-4), he would be accursed (Galatians 1:6-9). Not only that, but after the resurrection, the Apostle Paul taught publicly and "went from house to house" (Acts 20:20).

2. Before the cross, Jesus commanded the twelve not to go into the way of the Gentiles, but only to the lost sheep of the house of Israel (Matthew 10:5-6). After the resurrection, the Lord commanded them, "Go ye into all the world, and preach the gospel to every creature" (Mark 16:15).
3. In the sermon on the mount Jesus warned, "and whosoever shall say to his brother, Raca, shall be in danger of the council" (Matthew 5:22). Today Christians have no council to be in danger of. Jesus is the head of the church (Ephesians 1:22).
4. Jesus also warned, "but whosoever shall say, Thou fool, shall be in danger of hell fire" (Matthew 5:22). Christians are not in danger of hell fire, even for calling a man a fool (read Romans 1:22; 1 Corinthians 15:36; Galatians 3:1, Paul properly called out fools by their rightful name).
5. Jesus also spoke of bringing a gift to the altar (Matthew 5:23-24). Christian churches do not have an altar upon which to offer a gift.
6. The sermon on the mount (Matthew 5—7) was given by the King of the Jews to the Jews. It amounts to the constitution of Christ's coming kingdom on earth, when he will reign for a thousand years over this present earth (Revelation 20:4-6). Although many things that are said by the Lord may be spiritually applied today, some of the doctrines are not primarily for the present church age. Only that portion of the preaching of Jesus Christ that is "according to the revelation of the mystery" (Romans 16:25) "of the gospel" (Ephesians 6:19) will carry over to this present dispensation of the grace of God.

CONCLUSION

When anyone comes to the Holy Bible and does not rightly divide the word of truth, he will no doubt be confused, but when the Holy Bible is rightly divided, then everything fits into its proper and rightful place. One of the most common causes of error in our day comes from not realizing that the New Testament of our Lord and Saviour Jesus Christ has replaced the Old Testament given by God to Israel through Moses. "**For the law was given by Moses, *but* grace and truth came by Jesus Christ**" (John 1:17).

The Holy Bible clearly teaches that, as we approach the end, the world will get worse and worse: "**But evil men and seducers shall wax worse and worse, deceiving, and being deceived**" (2 Timothy 3:13). See also Luke 17:26-30.

Those of us who have been born again and placed in Christ by the baptism of the Holy Spirit (1 Corinthians 12:13) are "**Looking for that blessed hope, and**

the glorious appearing of the great God and our Saviour Jesus Christ; Who gave himself for us, that he might redeem us from all iniquity, and purify unto himself a peculiar people, zealous of good works" (Titus 2:13-14)! How about you? Will you be caught up to meet the Lord in the air (1 Thessalonians 4:16-18), or will you be left behind to face the "great tribulation" (Matthew 24:21), the most devastating and terrifying time that this earth will ever see?

No man knows the day or hour of Christ's coming for his blood-bought church, for he is coming "**as a thief in the night**" (1 Thessalonians 5:2; 2 Peter 3:10). The Bible warns all men, "Boast not thyself of to morrow; for thou knowest not what a day may bring forth" (Proverbs 27:1). Tomorrow could be too late!

"**We then, *as* workers together *with him*, beseech *you* also that ye receive not the grace of God in vain. (For he saith, I have heard thee in a time accepted, and in the day of salvation have I succoured thee: behold, now *is* the accepted time; behold, now *is* the day of salvation.**)" (2 Corinthians 6:1-2).

"**And they said, Believe on the Lord Jesus Christ, and thou shalt be saved, and thy house**" (Acts 16:31).

Chapter 13

Glory in This

It is written in Jeremiah 9:23-24, saying, "Thus saith the LORD, Let not the wise *man* glory in his wisdom, neither let the mighty *man* glory in his might, let not the rich *man* glory in his riches: But let him that glorieth glory in this, that he understandeth and knoweth me, that I *am* the LORD which exercise lovingkindness, judgment, and righteousness, in the earth: for in these *things* I delight, saith the LORD."

To glory in something is to rejoice in it and give praise for it, or to boast and brag about it. It's fine to boast about the Lord's work among his people, giving glory to him (Psalms 34:2; 44:8), but to boast and brag and speak proudly about what you have done or what you possess is nothing more than foolish pride, which the Lord hates (Proverbs 6:16-19; 8:13). This kind of boasting shows our own ignorance. The truth is that we do not have anything in this world that wasn't received from God. Likewise, we have nothing to brag about!

"**For who maketh thee to differ *from another*? and what hast thou that thou didst not receive** [from above (James 3:17)]**? now if thou didst receive *it*, why dost thou glory [boast or brag], as if thou hadst not received *it*?**" (1 Corinthians 4:7).

The Bible warns us "that in the last days perilous times shall come, for men shall be lovers of their own selves, covetous, **boasters**, **proud**, blasphemers..." (2 Timothy 3:1-5). We can also read the Bible's list of the characteristics of lost people in this world whom God has turned over to a reprobate [abandoned in sin; lost to virtue and grace] mind (Romans 1:28-32). Among many other wicked things, they are "backbiters, haters of God, despiteful, **proud, boasters**..." (Romans 1:30).

Notice in Romans 1:30 that being proud and boasting go together. A proud man deceives himself when he thinks himself to be something when he is nothing (Galatians 6:3). A proud, boastful, and conceited man lives in denial of the God who made him and gives him life and breath (Acts 17:25) and all things to enjoy (1 Timothy 6:17). But "God resisteth the proud, and giveth grace to the humble" (1 Peter 5:5). God has even made salvation by his grace through faith in Jesus Christ, and "not of works, **lest any man should boast**" (Ephesians 2:8-9).

A. THREE THINGS NOT TO GLORY IN

1. The Wisdom of this World

Our sermon's text, Jeremiah 9:23, begins by saying, "**Thus saith the LORD, Let not the wise *man* glory in his wisdom**..." The wisdom of this world is foolishness with God (1 Corinthians 3:19). A man who boasts about his worldly wisdom is certainly deceiving himself. This worldly "wisdom descendeth not from above, but is earthly, sensual, devilish" (James 3:15). It would be better for this man to become a fool in the eyes of this world (1 Corinthians 3:18) that he might receive the true wisdom that cometh from above (James 3:17). "The Lord knoweth the thoughts of the wise, that they are vain" (1 Corinthians 3:20).

Job's friends thought they were counseling Job with words of wisdom. Job told them, "No doubt but ye are the people, and wisdom shall die with you" (Job 12:2). Concerning younger Elihu's long speech to Job, God said, "Who is this that darkeneth counsel by words without knowledge?" (Job 38:2). God also told Job's three elder friends, "...for ye have not spoken of me the thing that is right, as my servant Job hath" (Job. 42:7).

EVOLUTIONARY FOOLS—There are many examples today of men who, "**professing themselves to be wise, they became fools**, [a]nd changed the glory of the uncorruptible God into an image made like to corruptible man, and to birds, and fourfooted beasts, and creeping things" (Romans 1:22-23). But God says, "**Woe unto *them that are* wise in their own eyes, and prudent in their own sight**!" (Isaiah 5:21).

Most of the so-called wise men of the world are able to supply themselves with a very comfortable life as they journey down the broad way to destruction! Evolutionary biologist Richard Dawkins, professor at Oxford University in England, is highly acclaimed by the world. He believes that God is a delusion, religion is a virus, and America [especially fundamental Bible believing Christians] has slipped back into the Dark Ages. Earlier this year, Dawkins signed an agreement with British television to make a documentary about the destructive role of religion in modern history, tentatively titled "The Root of All Evil." Gordy Slack interviewed Dawkins in his hotel room during the Atheist Alliance International annual conference in Los Angeles. A few select quotes from this interview follow:

> Gordy Slack—"Still, so many people resist believing in evolution. Where does the resistance come from?"[4]
>
> Richard Dawkins—"It comes, I'm sorry to say, from religion. And from bad religion. You won't find any opposition to the idea of evolution among <u>sophisticated, educated theologians</u> [worldly and unsaved professors of religion who have believed the "profane *and* vain babblings, and oppositions of science falsely so called" (1 Timothy 6:20) instead of the word of God]. It comes from an <u>exceedingly retarded, primitive version of religion</u> [true born again Bible believing Christians], which unfortunately is at present undergoing an epidemic in the United States. Not in Europe, not in Britain, but in the United States."[5]
>
> Richard Dawkins—"There is just no evidence for the existence of God. Evolution by natural selection is a process that works up from simple beginnings, and simple beginnings are easy to explain...the relevance of evolutionary biology to atheism is that evolutionary biology gives us the only known mechanism whereby the illusion of design, or apparent design, could ever come into the universe anywhere."[6]
>
> Gordy Slack—"You are working on a new book tentatively called "The God Delusion." Can you explain it?"[7]
>
> Richard Dawkins—"A delusion is something that people believe in despite a total lack of evidence..."[8]

But enough of Dawkins' "wisdom of this world." This is the talk of a man who has become vain in his imaginations, whose foolish heart has been darkened! No evidence of a Creator! So, let's see what the scriptures say:

Psalm 19:1 says, "**The heavens declare the glory of God; and the firmament sheweth his handywork.**" Romans 1:19-21 says, "Because that which may be known of God is manifest in them; for God hath shewed *it* unto them. **For the invisible things of him from the creation of the world are clearly seen, being understood by the things that are made, *even* his eternal power and Godhead; so that they are without excuse**: Because that, when they knew God, they glorified *him* not as God, neither were thankful; but became vain in their imaginations, and their foolish heart was darkened." Proverbs 28:26 says, "**He that trusteth in his own heart is a fool**: but whoso walketh wisely, he shall be delivered." And Jeremiah 17:5 says, "Thus saith the LORD; **Cursed *be* the man that trusteth in man, and maketh flesh his arm, and whose heart departeth from the LORD.**"

GOD WILL DESTROY THE WISDOM OF THE WISE

"For it is written, I will destroy the wisdom of the wise, and will bring to nothing the understanding of the prudent. Where *is* the wise? where *is* the scribe? where *is* the disputer of this world? hath not God made foolish the wisdom of this world? For after that in the wisdom of God the world by wisdom knew not God, it pleased God by the foolishness of preaching to save them that believe. For the Jews require a sign, and the Greeks seek after wisdom: But we preach Christ crucified, unto the Jews a stumblingblock, and unto the Greeks foolishness; But unto them which are called, both Jews and Greeks, **Christ the power of God, and the wisdom of God**. Because the foolishness of God is wiser than men; and the weakness of God is stronger than men. For ye see your calling, brethren, how that **not many wise men after the flesh, not many mighty, not many noble, *are called***: But God hath chosen the foolish things of the world to confound the wise; and God hath chosen the weak things of the world to confound the things which are mighty; And base things of the world, and things which are despised, hath God chosen, *yea*, and things which are not, to bring to nought things that are: That no flesh should glory in his presence. **But of him are ye in Christ Jesus, who of God is made unto us wisdom, and righteousness, and sanctification, and redemption: That, according as it is written, He that glorieth, let him glory in the Lord**" (1 Corinthians 1:19-31).

Again, the scriptures reiterate, "**But he that glorieth, let him glory in the Lord**" (2 Corinthians 10:17).

2. The Power of this World

The second section of our sermon's text, Jeremiah 9:23, continues the thought, saying, "...**neither let the mighty *man* glory in his might**..."

Moses warned the children of Israel not to forget all that the Lord had done for them and never to come to the place where they would say, "**My power and the might of *mine* hand** hath gotten me this wealth. But thou shalt remember the LORD thy God: **for *it is* he that giveth thee power to get wealth**, that he may establish his covenant which he sware unto thy fathers, as *it is* this day" (Deuteronomy 8:17-18).

Goliath was the proud Philistine giant who boasted against God and against Israel. He gloried in his own power and might. But the bigger they are, the harder they fall! He said unto David, "Am I a dog, that thou comest to me with staves? And the Philistine cursed David by his gods. And the Philistine said to David, Come to me, and I will give thy flesh unto the fowls of the air, and to the beasts of the field" (1 Samuel 17:43-44). But David prevailed over the Philistine with a sling and with a stone and by the power of God!

"And **Pharaoh** said, Who *is* the LORD, that I should obey his voice to let Israel go? I know not the LORD, neither will I let Israel go" (Exodus 5:2). God showed Pharaoh his mighty power through the plagues he brought upon Egypt, judged his gods, killed his firstborn son, then drowned Pharaoh and his army in the Red Sea (Exodus 14:27-28; 15:19; Psalm 136:15)!

"The king [**Nebuchadnezzar**] spake, and said, **Is not this great Babylon, that I have built for the house of the kingdom by the might of my power, and for the honour of my majesty?** While the word *was* in the king's mouth, there fell a voice from heaven, *saying*, O king Nebuchadnezzar, to thee it is spoken; The kingdom is departed from thee" (Daniel 4:30-31). Then the Lord reduced him to the likes of an animal in the field and made him eat grass for seven years (Daniel 4:32-33). But the result was that Nebuchadnezzar eventually humbled himself and came to worship the true and living God (Daniel 4:34-37).

"But he [God] giveth more grace. Wherefore he saith, **God resisteth the proud, but giveth grace unto the humble**" (James 4:6).

"**Some *trust* in chariots, and some in horses: but we will remember the name of the LORD our God**" (Psalm 20:7).

God has appointed to all men "once to die, but after this the judgment" (Hebrews 9:27). No mighty man will boast forever. On judgment day he will be humbled and give an account of himself to Almighty God (Romans 14:12; 1 Peter 4:5).

3. The Wealth of this World

A third point of Jeremiah 9:23 says, "**let not the rich *man* glory in his riches**" before continuing into the next verse.

Great riches have ruined the lives of a great number of people, who have trusted that they were right with God because of the temporary blessings of the abundance of things that they possessed on earth (1 Timothy 6:5; Luke 12:15). Therefore the Lord Jesus said, "It is easier for a camel to go through the eye of a needle, than for a rich man to enter into the kingdom of God" (Matthew 19:24).

"**But they that will be rich fall into temptation and a snare, and *into* many foolish and hurtful lusts, which drown men in destruction and perdition. For the love of money is the root of all evil** [and NOT religion, Mr. Dawkins!]: **which while some coveted after, they have erred from the faith, and pierced themselves through with many sorrows**" (1 Timothy 6:9-10).

Jesus told of the rich man who boasted in his great riches. And because of his riches, he boasted of many years to come during which time he had plans to live in abundance. But that very night God called him a fool and took his life (Luke 12:15-21)! I would also encourage you to read also about the rich man who went to hell (Luke 16:19-31).

"**Charge them that are rich in this world, that they be not highminded, nor trust in uncertain riches, but in the living God, who giveth us richly all things to enjoy; That they do good, that they be rich in good works, ready to distribute, willing to communicate; Laying up in store for themselves a good foundation against the time to come, that they may lay hold on eternal life**" (1 Timothy 6:17-19).

Meanwhile, "**Labour not to be rich**: cease from thine own wisdom. **Wilt thou set thine eyes upon that which is not? for *riches* certainly make themselves wings; they fly away as an eagle toward heaven**" (Proverbs 23:4-5).

No amount of riches will be able to deliver men from the terrible judgment of God in the day of his wrath (Zephaniah 1:18). James also warns the rich concerning a soon and coming day, saying, "Go to now, *ye* rich men, weep and howl for your miseries that shall come upon *you*. Your riches are corrupted, and your garments are motheaten. Your gold and silver is cankered; and the rust of them shall be a witness against you, and shall eat your flesh as it were fire. Ye have heaped treasure together for the last days. Behold, the hire of the labourers who have reaped down your fields, which is of you kept back by fraud, crieth: and the cries of them which have reaped are entered into the ears of the Lord of sabaoth. Ye have lived in pleasure on the earth, and been wanton; ye have nourished your hearts, as in a day of slaughter" (James 5:1-6).

In the day when God judges "the world in righteousness by *that* man whom he hath ordained [the Lord Jesus Christ]" (Acts 17:31), then hell will enlarge herself, and open her mouth without measure: "**and <u>their glory</u>, and their multitude, and <u>their pomp</u>, and <u>he that rejoiceth</u>** [he that glories in his own wisdom, might, and riches]**, shall descend into it. And the mean man shall be brought down, and <u>the mighty man</u> shall be humbled, and the eyes of <u>the lofty</u> shall be humbled: But the LORD of hosts shall be exalted in judgment, and God that is holy shall be sanctified in righteousness**" (Isaiah 5:14-16).

Solomon had riches and power and wisdom, but he discovered that it was all vanity (Ecclesiastes). It was all worthless and temporary. His strong advice to all men at the end of his life was: "**Let us hear the conclusion of the whole matter: Fear God, and keep his commandments: for this *is* the whole *duty* of man. For God shall bring every work into judgment, with every secret thing, whether *it be* good, or whether *it be* evil**" (Ecclesiastics 12:13-14).

B. GLORY IN THIS

Jeremiah 9:24 says, "**But let him that glorieth glory in this, that he understandeth and knoweth me, that I *am* the LORD which exercise lovingkindness, judgment, and righteousness, in the earth: for in these *things* I delight, saith the LORD.**"

I. THAT YOU UNDERSTAND AND KNOW THE LORD

In Jesus' parable of the talents, the servant who hid the one talent that he had received from the Lord did NOT understand and know the Lord! He said, "Lord, I knew thee that thou art an hard man, reaping where thou hast not sown, and gathering where thou hast not strawed: And I was afraid, and went and hid thy talent in the earth: lo, *there* thou hast *that is* thine" (Matthew 25:24-25).

This servant by his own words reveals the fact that he did not know the Lord. The Lord is not "an hard man" who steals another man's crop! He is One who labors. He is the Lord who delights in exercising **lovingkindness, judgment, and righteousness, in the earth** (Jeremiah 9:24)! You will never know a more loving and compassionate person besides the Lord Jesus Christ! It's his mercy that makes your salvation possible. It's his grace that brought him into the world to do the work to die on a cruel cross for your sins (2 Corinthians 8:9; 1 Corinthians 15:3-4). It's his goodness that leads sinners to repentance (Romans 2:4). It's his mighty power that makes him **the Saviour of the world** (1 John 4:14) and the **one mediator between God and men** (1 Timothy 2:5).

In a similar parable, the servant that hid the pound he had received of the Lord, said, "For I feared thee, because **thou art an austere man**: thou takest up that thou layedst not down, and reapest that thou didst not sow" (Luke 19:21). "Austere" means severe, harsh, rigid, and stern, such as persons who are an austere master with an austere look. The Lord said unto him, "Out of thine own mouth will I judge thee, *thou* wicked servant. Thou knewest that I was an austere man, taking up that I laid not down, and reaping that I did not sow: Wherefore then gavest not thou my money into the bank, that at my coming I might have required mine own with usury?" (Luke 19:22-23). In other words, Jesus could have said, "Thou wicked servant, you have seen me and received my blessings, but you don't know me. You accuse me of being severe and harsh and a thief. You have proved with your own words that you do not know me!"

Likewise, Jesus warned, "Not every one that saith unto me [Jesus], Lord, Lord, shall enter into the kingdom of heaven; but he that doeth the will of my Father which is in heaven." On the Day of Judgment, "Many will say to me [Jesus] in that day, Lord, Lord, have we not prophesied in thy name? and in thy name have cast out devils? and in thy name done many wonderful works? And then will I profess unto them, I never knew you: depart from me, ye that work iniquity" (Matthew 7:21-23).

The question now is, "Do you know the Lord?" I know that you have heard about the Lord, but do you KNOW HIM? Do you know that he is God manifest in the flesh (John 1:1, 14; 1 Timothy 3:16; Hebrews 1:8)? Have you been born of the Spirit (John 3:3-7)? Do you have the Spirit of Christ (Romans 8:9) living within you? Do you keep his commandments by the power of the Holy Ghost?

For the Bible says, "**And hereby we do know that we know him, if we keep his commandments**. **He** [the person] **that saith, I know him** [the Lord],

and keepeth not his commandments, is a liar, and the truth is not in him" (1 John 2:3-4).

As well, "**And we know that the Son of God is come, and hath given us an understanding, that we may know him that is true, and we are in him that is true, *even* in his Son Jesus Christ. This is the true God, and eternal life**" (1 John 5:20).

I fear that there are many today like the servant above who say that they know the Lord, but it is only a head knowledge and not a heart knowledge. The Bible says of them, "**They profess that they know God; but in works they deny *him*, being abominable, and disobedient, and unto every good work reprobate**" (Titus 1:16). In other words, they say they know the Lord, but their lives bear no evidence of being separated unto God. They bear no fruit of the Spirit (Galatians 5:22-23). No one would suspect them of being real blood-washed, Spirit filled, children of God. They have no victory over sins (Matthew 1:21). Their mouths are **full of cursing and bitterness** (Romans 3:14). Jesus said of such, "*Ye* hypocrites, well did Esaias prophesy of you, saying, This people draweth nigh unto me with their mouth, and honoureth me with *their* lips; but their heart is far from me" (Matthew 15:7-8).

II. THE LORD'S WORK IN THE EARTH

To repeat, Jeremiah 9:24 ends with the mighty statement of God, saying, "**I *am* the LORD which exercise lovingkindness, judgment, and righteousness, in the earth: for in these *things* I delight, saith the LORD**."

a. LOVINGKINDNESS

After declaring his mercy on the rebels who repented and called upon the LORD (Psalm 107:10-14) and on the fools who called upon the LORD in their affliction (Psalm 107:17-20) and on the seamen who called upon the LORD in their distress (Psalm 107:23-30), the scripture says, "Whoso *is* wise, and will observe these *things*, even **they shall understand the lovingkindness of the LORD**" (Psalm 107:43).

The Lord swore to David concerning all the children of God through faith in Jesus Christ, that although he will **visit their transgression with the rod, and their iniquity with stripes. Nevertheless my lovingkindness will I not utterly take from him, nor suffer my faithfulness to fail. My covenant will**

I not break, nor alter the thing that is gone out of my lips (Psalm 89:30-34). We who know the Lord and his lovingkindness now live, **[i]n hope of eternal life, which God, that cannot lie, promised before the world began** (Titus 1:2). We have absolute and eternal security in **the great God and our Saviour Jesus Christ** (Titus 2:13).

b. JUDGMENT, AND RIGHTEOUSNESS

Jesus Christ is the righteous judge of the quick [living] and the dead [lost] (Acts 10:42; 2 Timothy 4:1) people. "**Because he hath appointed a day, in the which he will judge the world in righteousness by *that* man whom he hath ordained; *whereof* he hath given assurance unto all *men*, in that he hath raised him from the dead**" (Act 17:31).

"**O let the nations be glad and sing for joy: for thou shalt judge the people righteously, and govern the nations upon earth**. Selah" (Psalm 67:4). I would also encourage you to read Psalms 7:11; 9:7-8; 58:10-11; 96:10-13 and Revelation 19:11-13.

c. I GLORY IN THE CROSS

Galatians 6:14 says, "**But God forbid that I should glory, save in the cross of our Lord Jesus Christ, by whom the world is crucified unto me, and I unto the world**."

I glory in this, that on a rainy day in June of 1979, while reading a Bible in my house, the Lord called me by his gospel (2 Thessalonians 2:13-14), convicted me of sin by his Holy Spirit (John 16:7-9), gave me faith through his holy word (Romans 10:17), and saved me by his grace (Ephesians 2:8-9). I was nothing more than a poor lost hell bound sinner who was not looking for God. But God gave me knowledge of the gospel, faith, and repentance to the acknowledging of the truth (2 Timothy 2:26) on the day of my salvation. I glory in the Lord today, and one day I will stand with "much people in heaven, saying, Alleluia; Salvation, and **glory, and honour, and power, unto the Lord our God**..." (Revelation 19:1).

I glory in this, that "**I know whom I have believed**, and am persuaded that he is able to keep that which I have committed unto him against that day" (2 Timothy 1:12). I know him that is true, and I am in **him that is true, even in his Son Jesus Christ. This is the true God, and eternal life** (1 John 5:20).

"Yea doubtless, and I count all things *but* loss **for the excellency of the knowledge of Christ Jesus my Lord**..." (Philippians 3:8).

The Lord Jesus, who has "all power in heaven and in earth" (Matthew 28:18) is **my strength** (Psalm 19:14). He whose **understanding is infinite** (Psalm 147:5) is my **wisdom** (1 Corinthians 1:30). He who owns all things (Psalm 89:11) supplies all my **need according to his riches in glory** (Philippians 4:19). In Christ all things are mine (1 Corinthians 3:21). **My soul shall make her boast in the LORD: the humble shall hear *thereof*, and be glad** (Psalm 34:2).

Do you know him? John wrote his gospel, **that ye might believe that Jesus is the Christ, the Son of God; and that believing ye might have life through his name** (John 20:31). You may not have much time before Jesus comes for his own people. I hope that you will read the gospel according to John today and consider his words!

Chapter 14

ETERNAL SECURITY OF THE SOUL

The eternal security of the born again believer continues to be a subject of great controversy. Eternal security has been debated by "believers" since the very beginning of the church. Those who believe that all born again believers have eternal life, and cannot for any reason lose it, **should earnestly contend for the faith that was once delivered to the saints** (Jude 1:3) against those who teach that a born again believer can lose his salvation for any reason. The following study is given in hopes that the child of God will be edified by the word of God, and that the Lord will give him understanding concerning this very important subject. We are not going to enter into a debate over the clear teaching of the word of God. We are simply presenting the following truths on the subject in hopes that the Holy Spirit will teach you the truth—that the soul of the born again child of God has unconditional eternal life, given to him at the moment he was **born of God** (1 John 3:9; 4:7; 5:1, 4, 18).

THE THREE PARTS OF MAN

You must understand the composition of man in order to rightly understand the doctrines of salvation, redemption, and eternal security revealed in the scriptures. Otherwise much confusion will result, because the scripture will not be rightly divided (2 Timothy 2:15). In other words, if one does not know that in the beginning of the world God created man in his own image (Genesis 1:26) and made him with three distinct parts (1 Thessalonians 5:23), many scriptures on eternal security will be misunderstood.

"**And God said, Let us** [plural pronoun signifying "the Father, the Word, and the Holy Ghost" (1 John 5:7)] **make man in our** [Father, Word, and Holy Ghost] **image, after our likeness**: and let them have dominion over the fish of the sea, and over the fowl of the air, and over the cattle, and over all the earth, and over every creeping thing that creepeth upon the earth" (Genesis 1:26).

Since God himself is three in one (1 John 5:7) therefore man himself, made in God's image, is three in one (1 Thessalonians 5:23). "For there are **three** that bear record in heaven, the **Father**, the **Word**, and the **Holy Ghost**: and these three are **one**" (1 John 5:7). "And the very God of peace sanctify you wholly; and *I pray God* your **whole spirit** and **soul** and **body** be preserved blameless unto the coming of our Lord Jesus Christ" (1 Thessalonians 5:23). Every man consists of spirit, soul, and body. It is essential to keep this trinity of man in mind as we look at the scriptures regarding salvation and eternal redemption.

JESUS CHRIST DIED FOR ALL OUR SINS

Jesus Christ died once on the cross for all the sins of every human being (2 Corinthians 5:15; 1 Timothy 2:5-6; Acts 10:43; 1 John 2:2; Hebrews 2:9)—past, present, and future. However, this does not result in the automatic salvation of the entire human race, although salvation is available to all men. God's forgiveness of your sins depends upon your personal response to the gospel. When you receive and believe on Jesus Christ, then the blood of Jesus Christ cleanses you from all your sins (Revelation 1:5). When you are born of God, you receive God's forgiveness and have the righteousness of Jesus Christ placed upon your account.

As you will read below, your soul and spirit are born again, but your body of flesh is not yet redeemed. If you do not understand this, then you will not be able to understand the doctrine of the eternal security of the soul. You will read verses that speak of the punishment of the flesh because of the sins of the flesh, and you will confuse these verses to mean the punishment of your **soul** for your sins. God would never punish the soul for sins after Jesus Christ has already died for them! If you do not rightly divide the word of truth in these matters, then you will not be able to clearly understand the glorious truth of the eternal security of the soul.

A born again believer will never have to pay for sins in his soul, because Jesus Christ has already paid for them. Nonetheless, he must suffer the consequences for the sins he commits in his body (flesh) after his salvation. In the following verses we will see a distinction between the body (flesh) and the soul.

THE REAL YOU—AN ETERNAL SOUL

The words of Jesus provide clarity about the real you in Matthew 16:26 and Luke 9:25. Matthew 16:26 says, "For what is a man profited, if he shall gain the whole world, and lose his own soul? or what shall a man give in exchange for his soul?" Comparable, Luke 9:25 says, "For what is a man advantaged, if he gain the whole world, and lose himself, or be cast away?"

By comparing Matthew 16:26 with Luke 9:25, we get the Bible's definition of man's soul. We discover that a man's **own soul** is **himself**! You are an eternal soul. Your body is only the temporary house for your soul in this physical world. Speaking of his flesh, Job spoke to God and said, "**Thou hast clothed me** [his soul] **with skin and flesh, and hast fenced me with bones and sinews** [his body]" (Job 10:11). Your eternal soul will never cease to exist, however your temporary body will return to the dust (Genesis 3:19).

The tragedy is that lost men live for the pleasures of sins that are primarily derived from the sensual pleasures of the body. They live for the short-lived pleasures of a body that will go back to dust. Most have no concern at all for their eternal souls! Dr. Bob Jones Sr. once said: "Don't sacrifice the permanent on the altar of the immediate."[9] Lost men sacrifice their eternal soul on the altar of the immediate gratification of their flesh, on that which is only temporary! In short, you are going to lose your body to the dust. And if you do not repent from your unbelief and turn to God in faith, you will lose your soul to the never ending torments of the damned in the lake of fire! The Lord Jesus put it this way in Matthew 16:25: "**For whosoever will save his life** [life of sin] **shall lose it: and whosoever will lose his life** [life of sin] **for my sake shall find it** [eternal life with God]."

SALVATION OF THE SOUL

James 5:19-20 says, "Brethren, if any of you do err from the truth, and one convert him; Let him know, that he which converteth the sinner from the error of his way shall save a soul from death, and shall hide a multitude of sins." The converted sinner's **soul** is saved from death. No one's **body** will be saved from death (Hebrews 9:27), with the exception of those who are **alive and remain unto the coming of the Lord** (1 Thessalonians 4:15-17; 1 Corinthians 15:51-53), whose bodies will be **"changed, in a moment, in the twinkling of an eye"** (1 Corinthians 15:51-53)—the rapture. The Lord Jesus will "**change our vile body, that it may be fashioned like unto his glorious body**" (Philippians 3:20-21). In other words, when a sinner is converted to faith in Jesus Christ from the error of his unbelief, his **soul** will be saved from "**the lake of fire. This is the second death**" (Revelation 20:14).

Hebrews 10:38-39 says, "Now the just shall live by faith: but if *any man* draw back, my soul shall have no pleasure in him. But we are not of them who draw back unto perdition; but of them that believe to the saving of the soul." Paul says that we are "of them that believe to the saving of the **soul**." Again, we see that it is the **soul**—and not the body—that is saved by believing the gospel.

In answer to the Philippian jailor's question, "**Sirs, what must I do to be saved?**" Paul and Silas said, "**Believe on the Lord Jesus Christ, and thou shalt be saved, and thy house**" (Acts 16:30-31). The jailor's **soul** was saved when he believed, but his body was not saved or changed. The body is not saved when a person is born again! If the body were saved from death at salvation, then we would see a huge number of very old saints still walking the earth, some of them in more than nineteen hundred year old bodies!

James 1:21 says, "Wherefore lay apart all filthiness and superfluity of naughtiness, and receive with meekness the engrafted word, which is able to save your souls." Again, we see that the **soul**—and not the body—is saved by receiving the word of God.

REDEMPTION OF THE SOUL

First Peter 1:17-23 says, "And if ye call on the Father, who without respect of persons judgeth according to every man's work, pass the time of your sojourning *here* in fear: Forasmuch as ye know that ye were not redeemed with corruptible things, *as* silver and gold, from your vain conversation *received* by tradition from your fathers; But with the precious blood of Christ, as of a lamb without blemish and without spot: Who verily was foreordained before the foundation of the world, but was manifest in these last times for you, [w]ho by him do believe in God, that raised him up from the dead, and gave him glory; that your faith and hope might be in God. Seeing ye have purified your souls in obeying the truth through the Spirit unto unfeigned love of the brethren, *see that ye* love one another with a pure heart fervently: Being born again, not of corruptible seed, but of incorruptible, by the word of God, which liveth and abideth for ever."

Here we read that believers have been **redeemed with the precious blood of Christ, as of a lamb without blemish and without spot** (1 Peter 1:19). The believer's **souls** were redeemed and purified "**in obeying the truth through the Spirit** [to obey the gospel is to believe the gospel report (Romans 10:16)]" (1 Peter 1:22). Their **soul** was "**born again, not of corruptible seed** [flesh], **but of incorruptible, by the word of God**" (1 Peter 1:23). Their body was not born again. I would encourage you to open your Bible and also read Psalms 34:22; 49:15; 72:14; 86:13; Isaiah 38:17 for more understanding of this topic.

REDEMPTION OF THE BODY

First Peter 1:23-25 says, "Being born again, not of corruptible seed, but of incorruptible, by the word of God, which liveth and abideth for ever. For all flesh *is* as grass, and all the glory of man as the flower of grass. The grass withereth, and the flower thereof falleth away: But the word of the Lord endureth for ever. And this is the word which by the gospel is preached unto you."

The body has not yet been redeemed, but only the soul of those true believers who have been "born again" (John 3:3-7), "born...of God" (John 1:12-14) has been redeemed. In 1 Peter 1:24 Peter goes on to define the flesh **as grass** that **withereth**! The physical body is like the grass that withers. It is corruptible, getting old, and headed for death and the grave and then back to dust. The body of a born again saint of God is not yet redeemed! If you have trusted the finished work of the Lord Jesus Christ through the blood of Jesus Christ your **soul** has been redeemed, but your body is still waiting for its future redemption when the Lord comes for his church and gathers them together to meet him in the air (1 Thessalonians 4:16-18).

Romans 8:17-23 says, "And if children, then heirs; heirs of God, and joint-heirs with Christ; if so be that we suffer with *him*, that we may be also glorified together. For I reckon that the sufferings of this present time *are* not worthy *to be compared* with the glory which shall be revealed in us. For the earnest expectation of the creature waiteth for the manifestation of the sons of God. For the creature was made subject to vanity, not willingly, but by reason of him who hath subjected *the same* in hope, [b]ecause the creature itself also shall be delivered from the bondage of corruption into the glorious liberty of the children of God. For we know that the whole creation groaneth and travaileth in pain together until now. And not only *they*, but ourselves also, which have the firstfruits of the Spirit, even we ourselves groan within ourselves, waiting for the adoption, *to wit*, the redemption of our body."

Believers are waiting for the redemption of our **body**! **"The sufferings of this present time"** (Romans 8:18) refer to the suffering believers still experience in their corruptible and aging bodies while they wait for the coming of the Lord Jesus Christ, **"Who shall change our vile body, that it may be fashioned like unto his glorious body"** (Philippians 3:21). The whole creation groans and travails **in pain together until now. And not only *they*, but ourselves also, which have the firstfruits of the Spirit, even we ourselves groan within ourselves, waiting for the adoption, *to wit*, the redemption of our <u>body</u>"** (Romans 8:22-23). Then glory will be revealed in us, and the suffering we now experience will be forgotten.

So far, we see that all men are eternal souls living in temporary bodies. Born again men are redeemed souls living in unredeemed bodies. Or to put it another way, born again men are saved souls living in unsaved bodies; they are regenerated incorruptible souls living in unregenerated corruptible bodies.

Saved men are purified souls living in corruptible bodies! No wonder there is a conflict between the flesh and the spirit! **"For the flesh lusteth against the Spirit, and the Spirit against the flesh: and these are contrary the one to the other: so that ye cannot do the things that ye would"** (Galatians 5:17). Jesus therefore warned, "Watch and pray, that ye enter not into temptation: **the spirit indeed *is* willing, but the flesh *is* weak**" (Matthew 26:41). "That **which is born of the flesh is flesh; and that which is born of the Spirit is spirit**" (John 3:6).

Because of this warfare between the flesh and the Spirit in the born again man, the saved soul must learn to bring the body under subjection to the will of God (1 Corinthians 9:27). In writing to the Corinthian church, Paul spoke of himself as an example of how all Christians ought to handle their bodies. He said, "**But I keep under my body, and bring *it* into subjection**: lest that by any means, when I have preached to others, I myself should be a castaway" (1 Corinthians 9:27).

This is why Christians are commanded to walk after the Spirit and not after the flesh. If we walk after the flesh after our soul has been redeemed, our flesh will suffer the consequences of sin. Romans 8:13 warns us, **"For if ye live after the flesh, ye shall die: but if ye through the Spirit do mortify the**

deeds of the body, ye shall live." In addition, God instructs us through the writing of Paul to the Christians in Rome: "**Neither yield ye your members** [members of your body] ***as* instruments of unrighteousness unto sin: but yield yourselves unto God, as those that are alive from the dead, and your members *as* instruments of righteousness unto God**" (Romans 6:13). We are instructed to do this because "Forasmuch then as Christ hath suffered for us in the flesh, arm yourselves likewise with the same mind: **for he that hath suffered in the flesh hath ceased from sin; That he no longer should live the rest of *his* time in the flesh to the lusts of men, but to the will of God**" (1 Peter 4:1-2).

It is important for the believer to remember that his flesh remains under the law of sowing and reaping (Galatians 6:7-8). After the salvation of your soul, your flesh is still capable of sin. However, you are no longer under its dominion and control (Romans 6:14). Nevertheless, you are still free to choose your actions. If you choose to live after the flesh, you will only bring to yourself the consequences of sin: sorrow, sickness, chastisement of God, imprisonment, and punishment from the Lord, including the possible early death of your body (1 Corinthians 11:29-30)! But your redeemed soul will never die! Why? Because "Jesus said unto her, I am the resurrection, and the life: he that believeth in me, though he were dead, yet shall he live: **And whosoever liveth and believeth in me shall never die. Believest thou this?**" (John 11:25-26).

SEALED

After you heard the word of truth, the gospel of your salvation and trusted in Jesus Christ to save you, your soul was redeemed and sealed by the Holy Spirit until the day of the redemption of your body (Ephesians 1:7, 13-14). Jesus died so he could eventually redeem your entire person: your "**whole spirit and soul and body**" (1 Thessalonians 5:23)! But at the present time, only your spirit and soul have been redeemed. You are waiting for the redemption of your body. Therefore, your spirit and soul are saved, but your body of flesh is not saved.

The Bible says, "**In whom we** [our souls] **have redemption through his blood, the forgiveness of sins, according to the riches of his grace...In whom ye also *trusted*, after that ye heard the word of truth, the gospel of your salvation: in whom also after that ye believed, ye** [your souls] **were sealed with that holy Spirit of promise, [w]hich is the earnest** [security or down payment] **of our inheritance until the redemption of the purchased possession** ["your whole spirit and soul and body" (1 Thessalonians 5:23)], **unto the praise of his glory**" (Ephesians 1:7, 13-14).

"**And grieve not the holy Spirit of God, whereby ye are sealed unto the day of redemption** [of your bodies]," Ephesians 4:30 tells us. The saved man's soul has been sealed by "that holy Spirit of promise" to keep the destructive influence of his corruptible body of flesh from defiling the soul.

WHAT HAS BEEN SAVED?

When asked if they have been saved, several men have told me, "Yes, I was saved from dying of an overdose;" or, "God spared my life in a terrible car accident;" or, "God saved me from destroying myself on the streets by sending me back to prison!" It may be true that God did save them from physical death to give them another opportunity for their souls to be saved. I try to tell them that this is nothing but "**the goodness of God that leadeth thee to repentance**" (Romans 2:4).

Remember, according to Peter, if you are saved by the grace of God, your soul is clothed in flesh—our body—which is "**as grass**" (1 Peter 1:24). "For which cause we faint not; but though our outward man [body of flesh] perish, yet the inward *man* [the soul and spirit] is renewed day by day. For our light affliction [in our bodies], which is but for a moment [this brief lifetime only], worketh for us a far more exceeding *and* eternal weight of glory [which is eternal]; While we look not at the things which are seen, but at the things which are not seen: for the things which are seen *are* temporal [the flesh]; but the things which are not seen [soul and spirit] *are* eternal" (2 Corinthians 4:16-18).

"For we know that if our earthly house of *this* tabernacle were dissolved [our fleshly body], we have a building of God, an house not made with hands, eternal in the heavens [our new glorified body like Christ's body (Philippians 3:20-21)]. For in this [corruptible and mortal body (1 Corinthians 15:53-54)] we groan, earnestly desiring to be clothed upon with our house which is from heaven [our incorruptible and immortal body (1 Corinthians 15:53-54)]: If so be that being clothed we shall not be found naked. For we that are in *this* tabernacle [corruptible body] do groan, being burdened: not for that we would be unclothed, but clothed upon, that mortality might be swallowed up of life. Now he that hath wrought us for the selfsame thing *is* God, who also hath given unto us the earnest [assurance and firstfruits] of the Spirit" (2 Corinthians 5:1-5).

YOUR SOUL CANNOT SIN

First John 3:9 tells us, "**Whosoever is born of God doth not commit sin; for his seed remaineth in him: and he cannot sin, because he is born of God**."

The question that arises is, "Who is born of God?" By now, we understand that the soul and spirit have been born of God, but not the flesh. So, according to this clear verse, the soul and spirit of the born again believer CANNOT SIN! When the believer sins it is his flesh that sins, and it is his flesh which will suffer the consequences of his sin.

THE EXAMPLE OF LOT

Sometime you may want to read the Old Testament account of Lot's life (Genesis 11-19). You will find that Lot was a very self-centered and carnal [fleshly] man. Judging from this account most would conclude that Lot was not a saved man. His life story gives a very poor testimony. He committed some very horrible sins. Yet we discover in the New Testament that Lot was a just, righteous, and godly man in the sight of God! Read the following scriptures and the imbedded comments written by Peter inspired by God:

"For if God spared not the angels that sinned, but cast *them* down to hell, and delivered *them* into chains of darkness, to be reserved unto judgment; And spared not the old world, but saved Noah the eighth *person*, a preacher of righteousness, bringing in the flood upon the world of the ungodly; And turning the cities of Sodom and Gomorrha into ashes condemned *them* with an overthrow, making *them* an ensample unto those that after should live ungodly; And delivered **just Lot** ["just" could mean "only," or it could mean that Lot was a just man, justified of God. Since God delivered Lot and his wife and two daughters from Sodom and Gomorrha, it could not mean "only Lot." So Lot was a just man before God], vexed with the filthy conversation of the wicked: (For that **righteous man** [Lot had God's righteousness imputed to him by faith, just as his uncle Abraham (Romans 4)] dwelling among them, in seeing and hearing, vexed *his* **righteous soul** from day to day with *their* unlawful deeds;) [Lot put himself in a situation that was irritating and troubling to him. Lot is an example of those who do not obey God's command to separate from wicked men] The Lord knoweth how to deliver the **godly** out of temptations, and to reserve the unjust unto the day of judgment to be punished" (2 Peter 2:4-9).

CONCLUSION

There is always the danger that unstable men will take the teaching of the eternal security of the soul and use it as a license to sin. Some slanderously reported that Paul taught, "**Let us do evil, that good may come**" (Romans 3:8). Paul said that their "**damnation is just**" (Romans 3:8), meaning that they will reap what they sow, whether they are lost hypocrites or true believers who have been subverted by false doctrine. If you are a born again believer you have the eternal security of being saved and redeemed for ever, because God has forgiven all your sins and bought you to himself by the blood of Jesus Christ (1 Corinthians 6:20; 7:23; Acts 20:28). God's word is truth. Nevertheless, if you choose not to walk after the Spirit, but after the flesh, you shall of the flesh reap corruption (Galatians 6:7-8)!

Do you want to end up like Lot, who committed incest with two of his daughters after drinking the wine they served him? You will reap what you sow! As a born again believer you can lose your testimony, your peace, your joy, your freedom, your family, your health, your mind, your eternal rewards, your eternal glory, and you can end up being the least in the kingdom of heaven. Yes, thank God, you will be in heaven, but if you choose to live after the flesh, you will **grieve** (Ephesians 4:30) and **quench** (1 Thessalonians 5:19) and **resist** the Holy Spirit (Acts 7:51), vex your righteous **soul** with the filthy conversation of the wicked (2 Peter 2:7), and be one of the most miserable creatures on earth. The Lord wants you to have an abundant life here on earth (John 10:10)!

If you have not been born again by the Spirit of God, then you may "**enjoy the pleasures of sin for a season**" (Hebrews 11:25) in your flesh. But then you will die, and at the great white throne judgment God will cast your soul and body into hell [the lake of fire] (Matthew 10:28; Revelation 20:11-15)!

Nevertheless, God is not willing that you should perish, but that you should come to repentance (2 Peter 3:9). Therefore God **now commandeth all men everywhere to repent** (Acts 17:30) and **believe on the name of his Son Jesus Christ** (1 John 3:23). I pray that you will not sacrifice your eternal soul on the altar of the immediate gratification of that which will soon go back to the dust!

"**Believe on the Lord Jesus Christ and thou shalt be saved, and thy house**" (Acts 16:31).

Chapter 15

The Will of God Part 1

Any person who pretends to know the will of God for your life outside of the revealed will of God in the scriptures is to be avoided like a deadly plague. It does not matter who they are! I have talked with men whose story went something like the following. One man said that a woman pastor told him that he would be greatly used by the Lord in the ministry. When I asked why he was doing time in prison, he said that he had been "shacking up" with a "nice Christian lady" who had a drug habit. He was trying to "help" her. When the parole officer came to visit, he found her drugs stashed away and so he was sent back to prison on a parole violation.

Now what is wrong with this picture? First of all the woman pastor was out of the will of God for assuming the position of pastor (1 Timothy 2:12). Second, she was either lying or delusional to presume to know what God's will was for him. Third, he was completely out of the will of God by committing fornication (1 Thessalonians 4:3). Fourthly, he has no discernment or wisdom whatsoever if he thinks that a "lady" who uses drugs and shacks up with the likes of him is a "nice Christian lady"! Now I do not know whether this man is truly born of the Spirit or not, but he certainly does not talk or act like a Christian. The only way for this man, or any other man, to find the specific will of God for his life is first to find and submit to the will of God that is clearly revealed in the scriptures.

The only reliable place to find the will of God is in the Holy Bible. It is not a confusing or complicated matter to know the will of God. He tells us plainly and simply in the scriptures what his will is for all of his children. He also reveals that his will for unsaved individuals is that they might be saved.

If all born again believers would submit themselves to the revealed will of God in every point, no doubt there would be great revival in the churches. Dwight L. Moody, an American evangelist in the latter part of the 19th century said, "The world has yet to see what God can do with and for and through and in and by the man who is fully and wholly consecrated to him. I will try my utmost to be that man." Mr. Moody held meetings in the United States and Great Britain and saw thousands come to a saving knowledge of Jesus Christ.

On the other hand, if you are not interested in doing the will of God, all of the following information about the will of God will not help you. Hopefully you want to do the will of God, and so you will be blessed, encouraged, and motivated by the Spirit of God to submit to his will according to the things which are found in God's word. It is God's will:

I. TO SAVE AND DELIVER US

"**Grace *be* to you and peace from God the Father, and *from* our Lord Jesus Christ, Who gave himself for our sins, that he might deliver us from this present evil world, according to <u>the will of God</u> and our Father**" (Galatians 1:3-4).

It is God's will that all men might be saved (1 Timothy 2:3-4) and delivered from this present evil world. "**For God sent not his Son into the world to condemn the world; but that the world** [all men] **through him might be saved**" (John 3:17).

"**This *is* a faithful saying, and worthy of all acceptation, that Christ Jesus came into the world to save sinners; of whom I am chief**" (1 Timothy 1:15).

We know that the Lord is "**<u>not willing that any should perish</u>, but that all should come to repentance**" (2 Peter 3:9). God has "**no pleasure in the death of the wicked**" (Ezekiel 18:23, 33:11). Therefore if you chase after and pursue evil unto your own death (Proverbs 11:19) and die the death of a wicked man and go to hell, that is clearly not God's will, but it will be your own rebellious choice!

God's will is not only to save men's souls from the eternal torments of hell, but that they who are saved might be delivered from "**this present evil world**" (Galatians 1:4), which the scripture defines as "**<u>the lust of the flesh, and the lust of the eyes, and the pride of life</u>**" (1 John 2:15-17). "**This present evil world**" is a reference to all lost [unsaved] humanity who walk after the flesh in darkness and in rebellion to God's will! This is the world we all entered into when we were "**born of the flesh**" (John 3:6). We all continued in to live in this darkness until some of us were "**born of the Spirit**" (John 3:6-8). This spiritual birth took place when we received and believed [trusted] on the Lord Jesus Christ to save our souls (John 1:12-13). That is when we were "**born again, not of corruptible seed, but of incorruptible, by the word of God, which liveth and abideth for ever**" (1 Peter 1:23).

The following verses, and many more like them, make it abundantly clear that God's will for his children is to depart from evil and live holy lives for his glory.

"**For the grace of God that bringeth salvation hath appeared to all men, <u>Teaching us that, denying ungodliness and worldly lusts, we should live soberly, righteously, and godly, in this present world</u>; Looking for that blessed hope, and the glorious appearing of the great God and our Saviour Jesus Christ; <u>Who gave himself for us, that he might redeem us from all iniquity, and purify unto himself a peculiar people, zealous of good works</u>**" (Titus 2:11-14).

"**According as his divine power hath given unto us all things that *pertain* unto life and godliness, through the knowledge of him that hath called us to glory and virtue: Whereby are given unto us exceeding great and precious promises: that by these ye might be partakers of the divine nature, <u>having escaped the corruption that is in the world through lust</u>**" (2 Peter 1:3-4).

"**Wherefore gird up the loins of your mind, be sober, and hope to the end for the grace that is to be brought unto you at the revelation of Jesus Christ; As obedient children, <u>not fashioning yourselves according to the former lusts</u>** [this present evil world: the lust of the flesh and the lust of the eyes and the pride of life] **<u>in your ignorance</u>: But as he which hath called you is holy, so be**

ye holy in all manner of conversation; Because it is written, Be ye holy; for I am holy" (1 Peter 1:13-16).

"**For by grace are ye saved through faith; and that not of yourselves:** ***it is*** **the gift of God: Not of works, lest any man should boast. For we are his workmanship, created in Christ Jesus unto good works, which God hath before ordained that we should walk in them**" (Ephesians 2:8-10).

In other words, if God has before ordained [appointed and established] that all of his children should walk in good works, then there is no doubt that to walk in good works is the will of God for them.

II. TO FELLOWSHIP WITH OTHER BELIEVERS

At the beginning of his letter to the Romans, the Apostle Paul prayed for a prosperous journey "**by the will of God**" to come unto the Romans (Romans 1:9-10). Toward the end of his letter he wrote, "**That I may be delivered from them that do not believe in Judaea; and that my service which** ***I have*** **for Jerusalem may be accepted of the saints; That I may come unto you with joy by the will of God, and may with you be refreshed**" (Romans 15:31-32). In other words Paul was saying that it was by or according to God's will and it was his desire also to come out from ministering to the heathen for awhile and be refreshed in his spirit by being in the assembly of believers there in Rome.

We know that it is the will of God for all believers to separate from the unbelievers at various times and to assemble together in local churches to be refreshed and comforted together by our mutual faith (Romans 1:12) and to be edified by the preaching and teaching there (1 Thessalonians 5:11; Ephesians 4:11-16). We are given commandment not to neglect church attendance:

"**And let us consider one another to provoke unto love and to good works: Not forsaking the assembling of ourselves together, as the manner of some** ***is*****; but exhorting** ***one another*****: and so much the more, as ye see the day approaching**" (Hebrews 10:24-25).

As "**just Lot**" was "**vexed** [provoked; irritated; troubled; agitated; disquieted; and afflicted] **with the filthy conversation of the wicked**" (2 Peter 2:7), so are the souls of the justified children of God vexed in this "**present evil world**." Therefore it is a great blessing to believers when they can separate from the unbelievers at work and in the community at least two or three times each week and go to church where they can rejoice in the midst of other believers who have come together to praise, worship, and honour our Lord and Saviour Jesus Christ! Then, after they are refreshed and instructed, they can go back into the world to be witnesses for our Lord Jesus Christ and to preach the gospel (Mark 16:15). This is God's will and a great blessing for all believers who are "**labourers together with God**" (1 Corinthians 3:9).

III. TO SERVE GOD AND OTHERS

The Apostle Paul, writing to the Corinthians concerning the churches of Macedonia, said that they "**first gave their own selves to the Lord, and unto us <u>by the will of God</u>**" (2 Corinthians 8:5). It is God's will that the believer give himself first to the love and service of God and then to love his neighbour as himself. These churches of Macedonia were obeying the two greatest commandments given by the Lord:

"**Jesus said unto him, <u>Thou shalt love the Lord thy God with all thy heart, and with all thy soul, and with all thy mind</u>. <u>This is the first and great commandment</u>. <u>And the second *is* like unto it, Thou shalt love thy neighbour as thyself</u>. On these two commandments hang all the law and the prophets**" (Matthew 22:37-40).

If you want real joy then always put **J**esus in first place, **O**thers next, and **Y**ourself last. If you will do this, "**God shall supply all your need according to his riches in glory by Christ Jesus**" (Philippians 4:19).

"**But seek ye first the kingdom of God, and his righteousness; and all these things shall be added unto you**" (Matthew 6:33).

According to James 4:6-10 the way to get close to God is to humble yourself and submit yourself to God, and then God will lift you up. Then there will be real joy: not the cheap joy of putting yourself first before God and others. The joy God gives is far better than the joy you seek for yourself. There is great joy in serving God and others!

IV. TO SERVE THOSE WITHIN YOUR REACH

"**For David, after he had <u>served his own generation by the will of God</u>, fell on sleep, and was laid unto his fathers, and saw corruption**" (Acts 13:36).

David served his own generation by the will of God. David did good in the world. He kept God's precepts (Psalms 119:63, 69, 100, 134). As the faithful servant of God, David *served* and *pleased men,* "**as whatever the king did pleased the people**" (2 Samuel 3:36). He served for the good of men, but did not serve according to the will of men. As king of Israel, he *served his own generation.* The LORD said of David that he was "**a man after mine own heart**" (Acts 13:22).

"David was a great blessing to the age wherein he lived; he was the *servant* of his generation: many are the curse, and plague, and burden of their generation. Even those that are in a lower and narrower sphere must look upon it that they live to *serve their generation;* and those that will do good in the world must make themselves *servants of* all (1 Corinthians 9:19). We were not born for ourselves, but are members of communities, to which we must study to be serviceable."[10]

It is the will of God for every child of God to serve their family, their church, and their community. Have you been responsible for bringing children into the world? "**Children are an heritage of the Lord**" (Psalm 127:3). It is the will of God for you to serve your children and "**to bring them up in the nurture and admonition of the Lord**" (Ephesians 6:4). Do you have a wife? Then you are commanded to love your wife, "**even as Christ also loved the church, and gave himself for it**" (Ephesians 5:25). Are your parents still living? Then you are commanded, "**Honour thy father and thy mother: that thy days may be long upon the land which the LORD thy God giveth thee**" (Exodus 20:12). The LORD spoke of Abraham and said, "**For I know him, that he will command his children and his household after him, and they shall keep the way of the LORD, to do justice and judgment; that the LORD may bring upon Abraham that which he hath spoken of him**" (Genesis 18:19). Abraham was a family man who served his family. Are you supplying the needs of your family as a wise and faithful servant of God? The Lord Jesus asked, "**Who then is a faithful and wise servant, whom his lord hath made ruler over his household, to give them meat in due season?**" (Matthew 24:45).

Are you an active member of a local church? Do you attend services regularly, pray for your pastor and your church, and support your church financially? "**As we have therefore opportunity, let us do good unto all *men*** [all men in your community], **especially unto them who are of the household of faith** [members of the church]" (Galatians 6:10).

V. TO BE THANKFUL

"**In every thing give thanks: for this is the will of God in Christ Jesus concerning you**" (Thessalonians 5:18).

Not only give thanks *in* every thing, but give thanks *for* every thing!

"**Giving thanks always for all things unto God and the Father in the name of our Lord Jesus Christ**" (Ephesians 5:20).

By being thankful in and for all things we will continue to offer the sacrifice of praise to God!

"**By him therefore let us offer the sacrifice of praise to God continually, that is, the fruit of *our* lips giving thanks to his name**" (Hebrews 13:15).

Always pray with thanksgiving!

"**Be careful for nothing; but in every thing by prayer and supplication with thanksgiving let your requests be made known unto God**" (Philippians 4:6).

The children of Israel forfeited the promised land and were forced by God to wander in the wilderness for forty years, because they provoked the Lord by their murmuring and complaining (Exodus 14). They were an unthankful and disobedient people, and they suffered greatly for their unbelief and wicked rebellion. Likewise, it is for those of God's children today who constantly complain and blame God for their difficulties. Such men are bitter and angry. Therefore, they miss the benefits of the kingdom of God in this present world, which are, "**righteousness, and peace, and joy in the Holy Ghost**" (Romans 14:16-17)! Child of God, there is always more to be thankful for than to complain about! So thank God for salvation and all his other wonderful benefits (Psalm 68:19). The Lord does not appreciate the murmurers and complainers among his blood-bought children (Jude 1:15-16) who exhibit the same ungrateful attitude as the unbelievers!

VI. TO LIVE A GODLY LIFE

"**For so is the will of God, that with well doing ye may put to silence the ignorance of foolish men: As free, and not using *your* liberty for a cloke of maliciousness, but as the servants of God**" (1 Peter 2:15-16).

If you are a Christian you will find that many foolish unbelievers will bring up arguments against your faith. One thing I have been slow to learn is that you cannot win an argument with a foolish man. The greatest weapon I have against their ignorance is a godly, Christ-honoring, life. If I live a consistent holy life before the unbelievers perhaps they will stop talking and take notice that I really do care about them and that I am a Christian indeed. Only by a truly consistent godly life can I hope to put to silence the ignorant talk of foolish men.

"Recompense to no man evil for evil. Provide things honest in the sight of all men. If it be possible, as much as lieth in you, live peaceably with all men. Dearly beloved, avenge not yourselves, but *rather* give place unto wrath: for it is written, Vengeance *is* mine; I will repay, saith the Lord. Therefore if thine enemy hunger, feed him; if he thirst, give him drink: for in so doing thou shalt heap coals of fire on his head. Be not overcome of evil, but overcome evil with good" (Romans 12:17-21).

It is true that if I live a godly life before unbelievers that I will most likely suffer persecution (2 Timothy 3:12), but by faith I should rejoice in this persecution and thank God for it, because great is my reward in heaven, provided I take the persecution and continue to walk in righteousness for the glory of God.

"Blessed are ye, when *men* shall revile you, and persecute *you*, and shall say all manner of evil against you falsely, for my sake. Rejoice, and be exceeding glad: for great *is* your reward in heaven: for so persecuted they the prophets which were before you" (Matthew 5:11-12).

"Let your light so shine before men, that they may see your good works, and glorify your Father which is in heaven" (Matthew 5:16).

SUMMARY

So far we have learned that the will of God is for all men to be saved. Have you been saved? If not then you are out of the will of God. After salvation we have seen that the will of God for all of his blood bought children is: (1) to be delivered from this present evil world, (2) to seek the fellowship of other believers in order to be refreshed for the work of the ministry, (3) to serve God and others, (4) to serve all those within our reach, (5) to give God thanks for all things, and (6) to live godly lives in this present evil world. This is the plain and simple will of God for believers. We will take up the remaining points in the next sermon outline, *The Will of God Part 2*.

If you are not already a child "**of God by faith in Christ Jesus**" (Galatians 3:26), then God is commanding you now to repent (Acts 17:30) and to "**believe on the name of his Son Jesus Christ**" (1 John 3:23). For the Lord is "**not willing that any should perish, but that all should come to repentance**" (2 Peter 2:9).

"**And they said, Believe on the Lord Jesus Christ, and thou shalt be saved, and thy house**" (Acts 16:31).

Chapter 16

The Will of God Part 2

The Christian life is not supposed to be complicated and difficult, but some people do "**bring in damnable heresies**" (2 Peter 2:1) and "**doctrines of devils**" (1 Timothy 4:1-5) and corrupt the minds of believers away "**from the simplicity that is in Christ**" (2 Corinthians 11:3). The only way for the believer to know the will of God is to know what God said and not to go by feelings, signs, dreams, omens, and the opinions of those who boast themselves of having superior knowledge! Although there is nothing wrong with asking for counsel from another brother in the Lord or a pastor or teacher, you should make sure that their counsel comes from and is backed up by the word of God.

In the first message on the will of God we discovered that it was the will of God that Jesus Christ die for our sins and that (1) we might be delivered from this present evil world (Galatians 1:4); (2) that we come apart from unbelievers and be refreshed in church by other believers so that we might prosper in our journey as ambassadors in this world (Romans 1:9-10; 15:31-32); (3) that we serve God and serve others (2 Corinthians 8:5); (4) that we serve our own generation (Acts 13:36); (5) that we be thankful for and in every thing (1 Thessalonians 5:18); and (6) that we live godly lives (1 Peter 2:15-16).

Now we will look at a few other verses and find that it is God's will:

I. TO SUFFER FOR WELL DOING

"**For *it is* better, if the will of God be so, that ye suffer for well doing, than for evil doing. For Christ also hath once suffered for sins, the just for the unjust, that he might bring us to God, being put to death in the flesh, but quickened by the Spirit**" (1 Peter 3:17-18).

"**Wherefore let them that suffer according to the will of God commit the keeping of their souls *to him* in well doing, as unto a faithful Creator**" (1 Peter 4:19).

It should be obvious that it is not God's will that you suffer for doing evil! But it is God's will that we endure with the right attitude the suffering that we might receive for doing right, so that men might come to Jesus Christ because of our godly testimony. For example, the Apostle Paul preached the gospel in Philippi. As a result of his preaching Paul was beaten, thrown in jail, and put in stocks. Here is a good man suffering at the hands of evil men. That was not God's will! God's will is for all men to repent and believe on Jesus Christ and get saved and not for them to beat and persecute his children! Nevertheless Paul and Silas took their mistreatment and suffering with patience and love and thankfulness to God. They sang hymns and prayed to God with their hands and feet confined in stocks there in the Philippian jail. They endured hardness as good soldiers of Jesus Christ (2 Timothy 2:3). Because of their godly attitude and behavior, God sent a miraculous earthquake which brought about the salvation of the Philippian jailer and his family (Acts 16:16-40).

It is not God's will for you to suffer at the hands of evil men; but if you do suffer for well doing, God's will is that you endure the suffering with patience and a godly attitude. It is God's will that when suffering comes our way that it comes not because of evil doing, but as the consequences of doing right in a world gone wrong. And it is God's will that when we suffer for doing right that we continue to do right, so that our testimony is strengthened and our testimony is confirmed when we say, "Even in this, God is good! Even in this, I'm not turning my back on Jesus! Even in this, I'm going to go on for the Lord!" Christian, if you have to take some grief, let it be for going with the Holy Bible and not against the Holy Bible; let it be for standing on the word of God and crossing somebody's opinion rather than standing with someone's opinion and crossing the word of God! You will suffer grief, persecution, and mistreatment in this world, but make sure that you suffer for preaching the gospel and living for God and not for lying, stealing, disobeying civil authorities, fornication, or murder!

The Lord Jesus Christ bore your sins on the cross so that he could save you and deliver you "from this present evil world" (Galatians. 1:4). He did not revile and curse the Roman soldiers who nailed him to the cross. He asked his Father to forgive them (Luke 23:34)! What Jesus suffered at the hands of men did not change his heart of love toward men. That was God's will. Do not allow the suffering that you receive for well doing change you, but stay right with God and remain in his will to take the suffering patiently. Many men have been converted to faith in Jesus Christ after observing the patient deaths of martyrs whose bodies were tortured and burned at the stake or given over to the ferocious and hungry lions in the coliseums of Rome! Read Hebrews 11:35-40 for more examples of faith in times of distress.

II. TO ABSTAIN FROM FORNICATION AND FRAUD

"**For this is the will of God, *even* your sanctification, that ye should abstain from fornication: That every one of you should know how to possess his vessel in sanctification and honour; Not in the lust of concupiscence, even as the Gentiles which know not God: That no *man* go beyond and defraud his brother in *any* matter: because that the Lord *is* the avenger of all such, as we also have forewarned you and testified**" (1 Thessalonians 4:3-6).

The amoral [no morals] behavior of young people today is the result of their belief of the lie of evolution with which they have been brainwashed in their public schools and by the news and entertainment media. They live like the animals they have been taught that they are. They eagerly pursue their carnal desires with no thought of the terrible consequences that sin will bring upon their lives and the lives of their victims.

"The CDC estimates that there are approximately 19 million new STD infections each year—almost half of them among young people 15 to 24 years of age. And these reported cases are only a fraction of actual cases, since up to 80 percent of infections have no symptoms and remain undetected, meaning that their victims unknowingly continue to spread them to others."[11]

"Thirty-nine years ago the Supreme Court of the United States handed down one of the worst decisions our nation has ever seen – *Roe v. Wade*. Since this horrific decision that called the destruction of human life a "right," 54 million babies have been aborted."[12]

Sodomy in all forms is also growing like a cancer in our already sick and dying society.

This present evil world is turning the brains of people into mush. The TV and movies and DVDs spew out the filthy messages of their fornicating "stars," their filthy talk, and trashy living, and make you think you've missed something if you aren't living like them. These people "**remain in the congregation of the dead**" (Proverbs 21:16)! They lure the multitudes to follow them through the darkness to the eternal "**mist of darkness**" (2 Peter 2:17) which God has prepared for all unrepentant sinners!

Thank God that he has given commandments to his people so that we can live our lives separated from this present evil world! Listen, before the day of my salvation in 1979 I lived in this present evil world as a member of "**the congregation of the dead**" (Proverbs 21:16), constantly chasing after self-gratification. I was on the road to destruction and was quickly becoming a burned out, despondent, drunken, pot smoking, lazy good for nothing fog head! Then the word of God brought light to my spirit and called me to salvation through faith in the Lord Jesus Christ! Now I'm living real life in Christ, and I have "**everlasting life**" (John 6:47). I know what I'm talking about. I have now lived about thirty years of my life on both sides: the first was lived in total spiritual darkness, the last in "**the light of the glorious gospel of Christ, who is the image of God**" (2 Corinthians 4:4)! I wouldn't go back to the darkness to enjoy "the pleasures of sin" (Hebrews 11:25) for any reason whatsoever!

The pleasures of sin are only for a season, a very brief and fleeting season. James asked, "**For what *is* your life? It is even a vapour, that appeareth for a little time, and then vanisheth away**" (James 4:14). The pleasures of sin are only for a moment of time while "the wages of sin is death" (Romans 6:23). This is the second death where lost men's souls will suffer forever in the lake of fire (Revelation 14:11; 20:14-15). Will you sacrifice your eternal soul to the eternal torments of the damned for a brief moment of sinful pleasure?

God's will is that one man marries one woman and remains in that marriage for life. This husband and wife relationship can be the most satisfying of all human relationships; but in these perilous times and last days not too many are marrying according to the will of God. Today people who claim to be Christians are going to *eHarmony.com* to find a wife! They will trust some psychological trait-matching program, which tries to match up couples so that they will be alike in as many areas as possible, instead of trusting God to send them his choice for their lifelong spouse. God's choice will give the man a wife who will be a help to him (Genesis 2:18). She may be strong in areas where he is weak and weak in areas where he is strong! They will be well matched if God's will is submitted to by both husband and wife, and they can have a little heaven on earth. I could never experience such a blessing, for I must reap now what I sowed during the dark days of my life. Nevertheless, I have known a few married couples who are very happy and content, who love one another more with each passing year. One of these couples just celebrated their fiftieth wedding anniversary! Many of you will not even live that long if you continue to rebel against the will of God!

III. TO PRAY FOR ONE ANOTHER

"**Likewise the Spirit also helpeth our infirmities: for we know not what we should pray for as we ought: but the Spirit itself maketh intercession for us with groanings which cannot be uttered. And he that searcheth the hearts knoweth what *is* the mind of the Spirit, because he maketh intercession for the saints according to *the will of* God**" (Romans 8:26-27).

"**Who *is* he that condemneth? *It is* Christ that died, yea rather, that is risen again, who is even at the right hand of God, who also maketh intercession for us**" (Romans 8:34).

If it is the will of God the Father for the Holy Spirit and for the Lord Jesus Christ to pray for the saints, and the saints have the Holy Spirit of Christ in them (Colossians 1:27; Romans 8:9), then it certainly must be the will of God for the saints to pray for one another! Read the following New Testament commandments to the church:

"**Pray without ceasing**" (1 Thessalonians 5:17).

"**Continue in prayer, and watch in the same with thanksgiving; Withal praying also for us, that God would open unto us a door of utterance, to speak the mystery of Christ, for which I am also in bonds: That I may make it manifest, as I ought to speak**" (Colossians 4:2-4).

"**Confess *your* faults one to another, and pray one for another, that ye may be healed. The effectual fervent prayer of a righteous man availeth much**" (James 5:16).

The great prophet Samuel told Israel that it would have been a sin against the LORD for him not to pray for them, saying, "**Moreover as for me, God forbid that I should sin against the LORD in ceasing to pray for you: but I will teach you the good and the right way**" (1 Samuel 12:23).

The Apostle Paul said that he was praying for the church in Colosse without ceasing (Colossians 1:9). We Christians need to stop talking about one another in negative ways, gossiping, and griping, carrying bitterness and anger against one another, and start praying for one another! You will not be able to stay in bitterness and anger against someone for whom you are truly and sincerely praying! You will not fall into hate for someone you are praying for. You will not desire the destruction and ruin of someone you are praying for. You cannot wish harm upon someone whose well-being you are continually seeking from God in prayer.

CONCLUSION

Finally, there are three things the Holy Bible says *about* the will of God concerning the believer:

1. WE ARE TO KNOW IT

"**I beseech you therefore, brethren, by the mercies of God, that ye present your bodies a living sacrifice, holy, acceptable unto God, *which is* your reasonable service. And be not conformed to this world: but be ye transformed by the renewing of your mind, that ye may prove what *is* that good, and acceptable, and perfect, will of God**" (Romans 12:1-2). By continuing in and by studying the word of God (John 8:31-32; 1 Timothy 2:15) the believer's mind will be transformed from carnal and worldly thinking and will be renewed to know the truth. In this way the believer "**may prove** [make certain and know] **what *is* that good, and acceptable, and perfect, will of God**."

Some have taught that this verse (verse 2) teaches three separate degrees of God's will: (1) good, (2) acceptable, or (3) perfect. This is not so. God's will is all three and not one or the other. God's will is good, acceptable, and perfect. God commands, "**Be ye holy; for I am holy**" (1 Peter 1:16). God's will cannot be good or acceptable unless it is holy and perfect.

If you have a Holy Bible, and you read it daily, then you should not be "**carried about with every wind of doctrine**" (Ephesians 4:14) that comes to you from men whose religious opinions are not based upon the scriptures! You cannot possibly "**be renewed in the spirit of your mind**" (Ephesians 4:23) by listening to the misinformed words of other men! The spirit of your mind must be renewed by the words of God, which are spirit (John 6:63)! Not only are we commanded to know the will of God, as well we are commanded:

2. WE ARE TO DO IT HEARTILY

"**Not with eyeservice, as menpleasers; but as the servants of Christ, <u>doing the will of God from the heart</u>; With good will doing service, as to the Lord, and not to men: Knowing that whatsoever good thing any man doeth, the same shall he receive of the Lord, whether *he be* bond or free**" (Ephesians 6:6-8).

"**<u>And whatsoever ye do, do *it* heartily</u>, as to the Lord, and not unto men; Knowing that of the Lord ye shall receive the reward of the inheritance: for ye serve the Lord Christ**" (Colossians 3:23-24).

If you do not want to know and do the will of God, then certainly you will not do it from your heart, but if you truly love the Lord Jesus Christ who died and resurrected for you and saved your soul from hell, then you will have a heart's desire to please him and obey his commandments (John 14:15).

3. WE ARE TO DO IT COMPLETELY

"**Epaphras, who is *one* of you, a servant of Christ, saluteth you, always labouring fervently for you in prayers, <u>that ye may stand perfect and complete in all the will of God</u>**" (Colossians 4:12).

The Lord Jesus told Satan, "**It is written, That man shall not live by bread alone, but <u>by every word of God</u>**" (Luke 4:4). You are falling way short of the will of God if all you do is read the Psalms every day, or the Proverbs every day. You and I need to saturate our minds with the word of God. At a minimum, you should have a plan by which you can read through the Holy Bible at least once each year.

"**All scripture *is* given by inspiration of God, and *is* profitable for doctrine, for reproof, for correction, for instruction in righteousness: That the man of God may be perfect, throughly furnished unto all good works**" (2 Timothy 3:16-17).

You must read ***all*** the scripture if you will know sound doctrine, if you will be reproved and corrected by the Lord in order to be conformed to the image of his Son, and if you will receive instruction in righteousness. You cannot know all the will of God without reading and studying the entire Holy Bible, much less can you hope to do all the will of God if you do not know what it is.

If you have not been "**born of the Spirit**" (John 3:6-8), then the will of God for you is very clear. God is "**not willing**" that you should perish (2 Peter 3:9) in the lake of fire for ever. Therefore he commands all men everywhere to repent (Acts 17:31) from their rebellion and unbelief and to "**believe on the name of his Son Jesus Christ**" (1 John 3:23).

"**And they said, Believe on the Lord Jesus Christ, and thou shalt be saved, and thy house**" (Acts 16:31).

Chapter 17

God's Powerful Word

We begin our sermon outline with the scriptural text of 1 Thessalonians 2:10-13, which says, "Ye *are* witnesses, and God *also*, how holily and justly and unblameably we behaved ourselves among you that believe: As ye know how we exhorted and comforted and charged every one of you, as a father *doth* his children, That ye would walk worthy of God, who hath called you unto his kingdom and glory. For this cause also thank we God without ceasing, because, when ye received the word of God which ye heard of us, ye received *it* not *as* the word of men, but as it is in truth, the word of God, which effectually worketh also in you that believe." With this passage in mind, we shall examine each of it's verses with the intention to learn how we are to handle and apply God's holy word in our lives.

BLAMELESS

Let's look at the first verse again. First Thessalonians 2:10 says, "Ye *are* witnesses, and God *also*, how holily and justly and unblameably we behaved ourselves among you that believe."

Paul under the inspiration of the Holy Ghost used the word *holily*. Paul was saying that he and Silvanus and Timotheus had behaved among the Thessalonians as holy men of God; that is, they had sanctified themselves [set themselves apart] to be consecrated or devoted to the service of God. Under the Law of Moses, atonement was made for the altar and other items in the tabernacle, to *sanctify* them, that they might be *holy* (Exodus 29:37; 30:29; 40:10). The LORD told the children of Israel: "For I *am* the LORD your God: **ye shall therefore sanctify yourselves** [set yourselves apart]**, and ye shall be holy** [dedicated and devoted to God]; **for I *am* holy**: neither shall ye defile yourselves with any manner of creeping thing that creepeth upon the earth" (Leviticus 11:44). Later in the New Testament, Peter wrote in reference to this verse: "**But as he which hath called you is holy, so be ye holy in all manner of conversation**; **Because it is written, Be ye holy; for I am holy**" (1 Peter 1:15-16).

To be *holy* is to be whole, entire or perfect, in a moral sense. Hence, pure in heart, temper or dispositions; free from sin and sinful affections. This definition can only be applied to God, for **holy** signifies perfectly pure, spotless, undefiled, and complete in moral character. Only "**the man Christ Jesus**" (1 Timothy 2:5) meets those qualifications, "***who is* holy, harmless, undefiled, separate from sinners, and made higher than the heavens**" (Hebrews 7:26)! Even born again men can never be perfectly holy in this life, because they are not sinless (1 John 1:8). We call a man *holy* when his heart is conformed in some degree to the image of God, and his life is regulated by the word of God. Hence, *holy* is used as being nearly equal to good, or godly.

The next word that the Apostle Paul penned down was *justly*. These three men, Paul Silvanus and Timotheus, had behaved in a manner of life suitable to justified men [a man who has been justified by God through faith in Jesus Christ (Romans 3:28; Galatians 2:16; 3:24)]. To behave *justly* is to behave according to the truth of God's word; honestly; fairly; and with integrity.

In describing their behavior among the Thessalonians, Paul also used the word *unblameably*. Here, Paul could declare that he and his two companions had given no cause to the believers at Thessalonica to find fault with them. They were *blameless*, but they were not *sinless*, "**For *there is* not a just man upon earth, that doeth good, and sinneth not**" (Ecclesiastics 7:20). Speaking to believers, the Apostle John clearly states: "**If we say that we have no sin, we deceive ourselves, and the truth is not in us**. If we confess our sins, he is faithful and just to forgive us *our* sins, and to cleanse us from all unrighteousness. **If we say that we have not sinned, we make him a liar, and his word is not in us**" (1 John 1:8-10). Sinless perfection, while living in this corruptible flesh, is impossible; but to walk unblameably is possible, if we confess and forsake our sins as we walk through this life. Then we shall have the mercy of God: "**He that covereth his sins shall not prosper: but whoso confesseth and forsaketh *them* shall have mercy**" (Proverbs 28:13). Paul desired that God would sanctify these believers also, and that their "**whole spirit and soul and body** [would] **be preserved blameless unto the coming of our Lord Jesus Christ**" (1 Thessalonians 5:23; 3:13).

THE WORD WAS PREACHED

The beginning of 1 Thessalonians 2:11 says, "As ye know how we exhorted and comforted and charged every one of you…"

To *exhort* means to incite by words or advice; to encourage or urge by arguments to a good deed or to any desired conduct or course of action. Paul exhorted Timothy: "**Preach the word; be instant in season, out of season; reprove, rebuke, exhort with all longsuffering and doctrine**" (2 Timothy 4:2). Paul exhorted the Thessalonians that they should walk and please God as they had been taught (1 Thessalonians 4:1), and that they should, "warn them that are unruly, comfort the feebleminded, support the weak, be patient toward all *men*" (1 Thessalonians 5:14). Paul wrote Timothy: "**I exhort therefore, that, first of all, supplications, prayers, intercessions, *and* giving of thanks, be made for all men**" (1 Timothy 2:1). Writing to all believers, Jude wrote: "**Beloved, when I gave all diligence to write unto you of the common salvation, it was needful for me to write unto you, and exhort *you* that ye should earnestly contend for the faith which was once delivered unto the saints**" (Jude 1:3).

To *comfort* means to strengthen; to invigorate; to cheer or enliven; to strengthen the mind when depressed or enfeebled; to console; to give new vigor to the spirits; to cheer, or relieve from depression, or trouble. Paul wrote that he had sent Timotheus: "**to establish you, and to comfort you concerning your faith**" (1 Thessalonians 3:2). Paul gave them the doctrine how the church will be caught up to meet the Lord in the air (1 Thessalonians 4:16-17), and said: "**Wherefore comfort one another with these words**" (1 Thessalonians 4:16-18). Paul also commanded the Thessalonians: "**Wherefore comfort yourselves together, and edify one another, even as also ye do**" (1 Thessalonians 5:11), and that they should "**comfort the feebleminded, support the weak, be patient toward all *men***" (1 Thessalonians 5:14). In his second letter, Paul prayed that God will: "**Comfort your hearts, and stablish you in every good word and work**" (2 Thessalonians 2:16-17). God and his word is the source of all comfort (2 Corinthians 1:3-4).

To *charge* is to lay on or impose, as a duty or command to be kept. Paul wrote to Timothy: "**I <u>charge</u> *thee* therefore before God, and the Lord Jesus Christ, who shall judge the quick and the dead at his appearing and his kingdom; Preach the word; be instant in season, out of season; reprove, rebuke, exhort with all longsuffering and doctrine**" (2 Timothy 4:1-2).

AS A FATHER

The end of 1 Thessalonians 2:11 says, "…as a father *doth* his children."

Paul considered his converts as his sons in the faith. He wrote to the believers in Corinth: "**I write not these things to shame you, but <u>as my beloved sons</u> I warn *you*. For though ye have ten thousand instructors in Christ, yet *have ye* not many <u>fathers</u>: for in Christ Jesus I have begotten you through the gospel. Wherefore I beseech you, be ye followers of me. For this cause have I sent unto you Timotheus, who is <u>my beloved son</u>, and faithful in the Lord, who shall bring you into remembrance of my ways which be in Christ, as I teach every where in every church**" (1 Corinthians 4:14-17).

A LIFE WORTHY OF GOD

The beginning of 1 Thessalonians 2:12 says, "That ye would walk worthy of God…"

Only the Lord Jesus Christ is worthy "**to receive glory and honour and power**," for he has created all things, and for his pleasure "**they are and were created**" (Revelation 4:11). John heard billions of voices in heaven, "**Saying with a loud voice, <u>Worthy</u> is the Lamb that was slain to receive power, and riches, and wisdom, and strength, and honour, and glory, and blessing**" (Revelation 5:12)! We praise God now by "giving thanks to his name" (Hebrews 13:15), and by good works (Hebrews 13:16).

To "**walk worthy of God**" would be to walk having the qualities of life and character that are suitable to one who is one of "**the sons of God**" (1 John 3:2); in other words, "**to walk and to please God**" (1 Thessalonians 4:1). In his second letter to the Thessalonians, Paul wrote that he was praying for them, "**that our God would count you <u>worthy</u> of *this* calling, and fulfil all the good pleasure of *his* goodness, and the work of faith with power: That the name of our Lord Jesus Christ may be glorified in you, and ye in him, according to the grace of our God and the Lord Jesus Christ**" (2 Thessalonians 1:11-12). If

God does not work in the believer (Philippians 2:13), then the believer cannot walk worthy of his calling, for the Lord Jesus said, "**without me ye can do nothing**" (John 15:5). Only a born again believer, who is filled with the Spirit (Ephesians 5:18), is able to bring glory to God. Peter also encouraged the born again believers, writing: "**But ye *are* a chosen generation, a royal priesthood, an holy nation, a peculiar people; that ye should shew forth the praises of him who hath called you out of darkness into his marvellous light**: Which in time past *were* not a people, but *are* now the people of God: which had not obtained mercy, but now have obtained mercy" (1 Peter 2:9-10).

The Lord Jesus commanded: "**Let your light so shine before men, that they may see your good works, and glorify your Father which is in heaven**" (Matthew 5:16). Paul exhorted the Ephesians: "**that ye walk <u>worthy</u> of the vocation** [the calling by the will of God] **wherewith ye are called**" (Ephesians 4:1), "**And walk in love, as Christ also hath loved us, and hath given himself for us an offering and a sacrifice to God for a sweetsmelling savour**" (Ephesians 5:2); "**For ye were sometimes darkness, but now *are ye* light in the Lord: walk as children of light**" (Ephesians 5:8). To the Philippians Paul wrote: "**Only let your conversation** [general course of manners; behavior; deportment; especially as it respects morals] **be as it becometh the gospel of Christ: that whether I come and see you, or else be absent, I may hear of your affairs, that ye stand fast in one spirit, with one mind striving together for the faith of the gospel**" (Philippians 1:27). And to the Colossians, Paul wrote: "**That ye might walk <u>worthy</u> of the Lord unto all pleasing, being fruitful in every good work, and increasing in the knowledge of God**" (Colossians 1:10), and: "**As ye have therefore received Christ Jesus the Lord, *so* walk ye in him**" (Colossians 2:6). And John wrote: "**He that saith he abideth in him ought himself also so to walk, even as he walked**" (1 John 2:6); and: "**Herein is our love made perfect, that we may have boldness in the day of judgment: because as he is, so are we in this world**" (1 John 4:17). To walk worthy of God should be the desire of every born again believer. We are commanded: "**Whether therefore ye eat, or drink, or whatsoever ye do, do all to the glory of God**" (1 Corinthians 10:31).

CALLED BY THE GOSPEL

The last part of 1 Thessalonians 2:12 says, "…who hath called you unto his kingdom and glory."

God calls all men by the gospel of the grace of God (Acts 20:24). The gospel, "**how that Christ died for our sins according to the scriptures; And that he**

was buried, and that he rose again the third day according to the scriptures" (1 Corinthians 15:3-4) "**is the power of God unto salvation to every one that believeth**" (Romans 1:16). This is the one and *only* saving gospel! Someone had come into the church in Galatia to *bewitch* [charm, deceive, and mislead] them with *another gospel* (Galatians 3:1), and pervert the gospel of Christ. Paul wrote to them: "I marvel that ye are so soon removed from him that called you into the grace of Christ unto another gospel: Which is not another; but there be some that trouble you, and would pervert the gospel of Christ. **But though we, or an angel from heaven, preach any other gospel unto you than that which we have preached unto you, let him be accursed**. As we said before, so say I now again, **If any *man* preach any other gospel unto you than that ye have received, let him be accursed**" (Galatians 1:6-9).

The "**gospel of the grace of God**" (Acts 20:24) is the only soul saving gospel. All other so called *gospels* will damn your soul to hell! The scriptures make this abundantly clear. In his second letter, Paul wrote to them: "But we are bound to give thanks alway to God for you, brethren beloved of the Lord, because God hath from the beginning chosen you to salvation through sanctification of the Spirit and belief of the truth: **Whereunto he called you by our gospel, to the obtaining of the glory of our Lord Jesus Christ** (2 Thessalonians 2:13-14)." In Romans, we read, "**and whom he called, them he also justified: and whom he justified, them he also glorified**" (Romans 8:30). Paul told the Corinthians: "**for in Christ Jesus I have begotten you through the gospel**" (1 Corinthians 4:15). James tells us that God, "**Of his own will begat he us with the word of truth, that we should be a kind of firstfruits of his creatures**" (James 1:18). And Peter states: "**Being born again, not of corruptible seed, but of incorruptible, by the word of God, which liveth and abideth for ever**" (1 Peter 1:23). The Apostle Paul wrote, "**That we should be to the praise of his glory, who first trusted in Christ. In whom ye also *trusted*, after that ye heard the word of truth, the gospel of your salvation: in whom also after that ye believed, ye were sealed with that holy Spirit of promise**" (Ephesians 1:12-13).

We are called by the Spirit of God: "***There is* one body, and one Spirit, even as ye are called in one hope of your calling**" (Ephesians 4:4). For the Lord Jesus said: "**It is the spirit that quickeneth; the flesh profiteth nothing: the words that I speak unto you, *they* are spirit, and *they* are life**" (John 6:63). God has "**saved us, and called *us* with an holy calling, not according to our works, but according to his own purpose and grace, which was given us in Christ Jesus before the world began**" (2 Timothy 1:9). By the gospel, God has called us "**unto the fellowship of his Son Jesus Christ our Lord**"

(1 Corinthians 1:9), that we "**should shew forth the praises of him who hath called you out of darkness into his marvellous light**" (1 Peter 2:9). After we obeyed, by believing the gospel (Romans 10:9; Acts 8:37; 16:31), we read that God "**hath delivered us from the power of darkness, and hath translated *us* into the kingdom of his dear Son**" (Colossians 1:13). And God will finish the work that he began in us when we were born again: "**Being confident of this very thing, that he which hath begun a good work in you will perform *it* until the day of Jesus Christ**" (Philippians 1:6). For "**Faithful *is* he that calleth you, who also will do *it***" (1 Thessalonians 5:24). After our salvation, we read that God "**hath made us meet** [suitable and qualified] **to be partakers of the inheritance of the saints in light**" (Colossians 1:12). The Lord will give "**the reward of the inheritance**" (Colossians 3:24) for faithful service.

THE POWER OF THE WORD

The beginning of 1 Thessalonians 2:13 says, "For this cause also thank we God without ceasing, because, when ye received the word of God which ye heard of us, ye received *it* not *as* the word of men, but as it is in truth, the word of God..."

The only *words* that any of us can safely and confidently trust with all of our hearts are the words of God of the Holy Bible, which is the *only* reliable source of truth! Men are commanded: "**Trust in the LORD with all thine heart; and lean not unto thine own understanding In all thy ways acknowledge him, and he shall direct thy paths**" (Proverbs 3:5-6). For the natural man's "**heart *is* deceitful above all *things*, and desperately wicked: who can know it?**" (Jeremiah 17:9). Therefore: "**Thus saith the LORD; Cursed *be* the man that trusteth in man, and maketh flesh his arm, and whose heart departeth from the LORD**" (Jeremiah 17:5)! But he goes on to declare: "**Blessed *is* the man that trusteth in the LORD, and whose hope the LORD is**" (Jeremiah 17:7).

Based on these scriptures, are you blessed or cursed? Are you trusting in your self? "**He that trusteth in his own heart is a fool: but whoso walketh wisely, he shall be delivered**" (Proverbs 28:26). To walk wisely is to walk in the light of God's word. David wrote: "**Thy word *is* a lamp unto my feet, and a light unto my path**" (Psalm 119:105). And again: "**The entrance of thy words giveth light; it giveth understanding unto the simple**" (Psalm 119:130). The Apostle Peter made it very plain, that God's written word is more *sure* than hearing the Father's voice out of the cloud (Matthew 17:5)! Peter wrote: "**We have also a more sure word of prophecy; whereunto ye do well that ye take**

heed, as unto a light that shineth in a dark place, until the day dawn, and the day star arise in your hearts" (2 Peter 1:19).

I have heard many unsaved men say: "The Bible is just a book written by men!" This statement is true, as far as it goes, but the scripture says: "For the prophecy came not in old time by the will of man: but **holy men of God spake *as they were* moved by the Holy Ghost**" (2 Peter 1:21). God set certain "holy men of God" apart and inspired them to write the scriptures. "**All scripture *is* given by inspiration of God, and *is* profitable for doctrine, for reproof, for correction, for instruction in righteousness: That the man of God may be perfect, throughly furnished unto all good works**" (2 Timothy 3:16-17). And not only did God inspire men to write the scriptures, in addition he promised to preserve his word for all generations, so that today we can have the pure word of God. "**The words of the LORD *are* pure words: *as* silver tried in a furnace of earth, purified seven times. Thou shalt keep them, O LORD, thou shalt preserve them from this generation for ever**" (Psalm 12:6-7). This ministry distributes only the King James Bible, and not any of the other *modern* bible versions, because we believe by faith that it is the Holy Bible in English. I believe that it is God's pure and preserved word. The modern bibles are "**the words which man's wisdom teacheth**" (1 Corinthians 2:13), but the King James Bible are the words "**which the Holy Ghost teacheth**" (1 Corinthians 2:13). If you would like more information on this subject, then ask me for a copy of the Sermon Outline called *Identifying the Holy Bible.*

The end of 1 Thessalonians 2:13 says, "...which effectually worketh also in you that believe."

Since *faith* "**is the victory that overcometh the world**" (1 John 5:4), and "**faith *cometh* by hearing, and hearing by the word of God**" (Romans 10:17), the word of God will work in the believer and give him victory over sin. But he must read it, believe it, and obey it (James 1:22) to have success. The "**world**" that may be overcome by faith is defined as, "**the lust of the flesh, and the lust of the eyes, and the pride of life**" (1 John 2:15-16).

The Lord Jesus told the Pharisees that they had made "the word of God of none effect" through their tradition (Mark 7:13). Again he said unto them, "**Full well ye reject the commandment of God, that ye may keep your own tradition**" (Mark 7:9). It is very regretful how many in these "latter times" have departed from the faith, "giving heed to seducing spirits, and doctrines of devils; Speaking lies in hypocrisy; having their conscience seared with a hot iron; Forbidding to marry, *and commanding* to abstain from meats, which God hath created to be received with thanksgiving of them which believe and know the truth" (1 Timothy 4:1-3)! But those who walk in the light are not surprised, since the word of God prophesied that it would be this way!

In the parable of the sower, we find four things that can cause the believer to become unfruitful (Matthew 13:22): (1) "**the cares of this world**" (Mark 4:19), (2) "**the deceitfulness of riches**" (Mark 4:19), (3) "**the lusts of other things**" (Mark 4:19), and (4) "**the pleasures of this life**" (Luke 8:14). But believers are commanded: "**Walk in the Spirit, and ye shall not fulfil the lust of the flesh**" (Galatians 5:16). And we know that if we walk "**after the Spirit,**" the righteousness of the law will be fulfilled in us (Romans 8:4).

CONDEMNED MEN DESPISE THE WORD

After Jeremiah spoke God's word to the Jews in Egypt, they replied: "***As for* the word that thou hast spoken unto us in the name of the LORD, we will not hearken unto thee**" (Jeremiah 44:16)! The Lord Jesus gave a warning to those who would not hear the words of his disciples, saying: "**And whosoever shall not receive you, nor hear your words, when ye depart out of that house or city, shake off the dust of your feet. Verily I say unto you, It shall be more tolerable for the land of Sodom and Gomorrha in the day of judgment, than for that city**" (Matthew 10:14-15). The men of Sodom and Gomorrha are still "**suffering the vengeance of eternal fire**" (Jude 1:7)! But the Lord Jesus said that those who reject his words will be judged even more harshly!

The Jews in the synagogue of Antioch in Pisidia were upset when they saw Gentiles come to hear the word of God: "**But when the Jews saw the multitudes, they were filled with envy, and spake against those things which were spoken by Paul, contradicting and blaspheming**" (Acts 13:45), but many of the Gentiles believed (Acts 13:48). After hearing Paul preach the gospel to them, "Then certain philosophers of the Epicureans, and of the Stoicks, encountered him. And some said, What will this babbler say? other some, He seemeth to be a setter forth of strange gods: because he preached unto them Jesus, and the resurrection" (Acts 17:18). After his sermon to them on Mars hill, there was a mixed reaction: "**And when they heard of the resurrection of the dead, some mocked: and others said, We will hear thee again of this *matter***" (Acts 17:32). "**Howbeit certain men clave unto him, and believed**" (Acts 17:34). God opened the heart of Lydia, and "she attended unto the things which were spoken of Paul" (Acts 16:14). She was then baptized (Acts 16:15).

WILL YOU DESPISE OR RECEIVE THE WORD?

What will you do with the word of God? Will you refuse to hear it? Will you contradict and blaspheme [revile or speak evil of] it? Will you mock and despise it? Galatians 6:7-8 gives this warning: "**Be not deceived; God is not mocked: for whatsoever a man soweth, that shall he also reap. For he that soweth to his flesh shall of the flesh reap corruption; but he that soweth to the Spirit shall of the Spirit reap life everlasting.**" Proverbs 13:13 says, "**Whoso despiseth the word shall be destroyed: but he that feareth the commandment shall be rewarded.**" The Lord Jesus Christ warned: "**He that rejecteth me, and receiveth not my words, hath one that judgeth him: the word that I have spoken, the same shall judge him in the last day**" (John 12:48). If you are an unbeliever, you do not have to wait until the last day to be condemned, for you are "**condemned already**" (John 3:18)! But there is hope for you, because God has "**no pleasure in the death of the wicked; but that the wicked turn from his way and live**" (Ezekiel 33:11). Therefore God "**now commandeth all men every where to repent**" (Acts 17:30), and "**That we should believe on the name of his Son Jesus Christ, and love one another, as he gave us commandment**" (1 John 3:23). The Lord is "**not willing that any should perish, but that all should come to repentance** [turn from unbelief to belief]" (2 Peter 3:9).

On the first day of Pentecost after the resurrection of Jesus Christ, Peter preached the gospel, "**and the same day there were added *unto them* about three thousand souls**" (Acts 2:41), because they believed the gospel. Later, Peter preached the gospel to Cornelius and his family and friends, who believed and were saved (Acts 10:37-48). The Jews in the synagogue at Berea "**were more noble than those in Thessalonica, in that they received the word with all readiness of mind, and searched the scriptures daily, whether those things were so. Therefore many of them believed; also of honourable women which were Greeks, and of men, not a few**" (Acts 17:11-12). Whether if you are sitting in a prison cell or at home, you have the time to read the scriptures and check them out for yourself to see if these things are true. The truth is, you will either find yourself in eternal torments in "the lake of fire" (Revelation 20:10, 14-15), or enjoying the pleasures of the Lord for ever (Psalm 16:11). Your eternal destiny depends upon whether you receive or reject the Lord Jesus Christ.

"**Believe on the Lord Jesus Christ, and thou shalt be saved**" (Acts 16:31).

Chapter 18

THE WORD OF GOD

John 1:1-14 tells us, "In the beginning was the Word, and the Word was with God, and the Word was God. The same was in the beginning with God. All things were made by him; and without him was not any thing made that was made. In him was life; and the life was the light of men. And the light shineth in darkness; and the darkness comprehended it not. There was a man sent from God, whose name *was* John. The same came for a witness, to bear witness of the Light, that all *men* through him might believe. He was not that Light, but *was sent* to bear witness of that Light. *That* was the true Light, which lighteth every man that cometh into the world. He was in the world, and the world was made by him, and the world knew him not. He came unto his own, and his own received him not. But as many as received him, to them gave he power to become the sons of God, *even* to them that believe on his name: Which were born, not of blood, nor of the will of the flesh, nor of the will of man, but of God. And the Word was made flesh, and dwelt among us, (and we beheld his glory, the glory as of the only begotten of the Father,) full of grace and truth."

"Word" is only one of many names given in the Bible for the Son of God, the Lord Jesus Christ, who is himself God, according to the scriptures. The name, "Word," is found exactly seven times in the New Testament. This matches the seven occurrences of "Jehovah" in the Old Testament. Three of these occurrences appear as compound names: "Jehovahjireh" (Genesis 22:14), "Jehovahnissi" (Exodus 17:15), and "Jehovahshalom" (Judges 6:24). Jesus Christ is Jehovah in the flesh!

Colossians 2:9 says, "**For in him** [Jesus Christ] **dwelleth all the fulness of the Godhead bodily**."

Let's look at several things about the "Word" found in this passage and in three other verses in the New Testament.

I. THE WORD IS GOD

John 1:1 says, "In the beginning was the Word [the Son], and the Word [the Son] was with God [the Father and the Holy Ghost], and the Word [the Son] was God [God the Son]."

The Word is "from everlasting." We know this because Micah 5:2 tells us, "But thou, Bethlehem Ephratah, *though* thou be little among the thousands of Judah, *yet* out of thee shall he come forth unto me *that is* to be ruler in Israel; **whose goings forth *have been* from of old, from everlasting**." Again, the Bible tells us in Isaiah 9:6, "For unto us a child is born [the man Christ Jesus], unto us a son is given [the eternal Son of God]: and the government shall be upon his shoulder: and his name shall be called Wonderful, Counsellor, The mighty God, **The everlasting Father**, The Prince of Peace."

John 1:1 is the first verse in the Bible where "Word" is found with a capital letter. It is found three times in this first verse reminding us of the trinity of God. The Lord Jesus, after his resurrection, commanded his disciples, "Go ye therefore, and teach all nations, baptizing them in the <u>name</u> of the Father, and of the Son, and of the Holy Ghost" (Matthew 28:19). Notice that the word "name" is singular, because there is only one God. However, God is manifest to us in three persons: "**For there are three that bear record in heaven, the Father, the Word, and the Holy Ghost: and these <u>three</u> are <u>one</u>**" (1 John 5:7).

Notice also that the *order* of the three is the same in these two verses, the only difference being the use of the name "Word" in 1 John 5:7 in the place of "Son" in Matthew 28:19. The Son, the Word, is an equal member of the Godhead with the Father and the Holy Ghost. Philippians 2:5-6 says, "Let this mind be in you, which was also in Christ Jesus: Who, being in the form of God, thought it not robbery to be **equal with God**."

II. THE WORD WAS IN THE BEGINNING

John 1:2 says, "The same was in the beginning with God."

The Word was God in the beginning, the Word is God now, and the Word will be God forever! Hebrews 13:8 declares, "**Jesus Christ the same yesterday, and today, and for ever**."

You might well ask the question, "In the beginning of what?" The Word, the Son of God, was there with the Father and the Holy Ghost in the beginning of the creation of the heaven and the earth! He is the "everlasting God" (Romans 16:26; Psalm 90:2) who never had a beginning! He is the eternal God. Time, with the passing of days and weeks and years according to the sun's movement, is a dimension which God set apart for His eternal purpose of creating, testing, and redeeming mankind (which he made in his own image) to himself.

Revelation 4:11 says, "**Thou art worthy, O Lord, to receive glory and honour and power: for thou hast created all things, and for thy pleasure they are and were created**."

You have been born in "time" for God's pleasure. However, should YOU make the choice in your lifetime for evil instead of for God, then you must suffer the punishment of being separated from God in the lake of fire throughout eternity! If you choose to remain a rebel, this gives God no pleasure. God exclaims in Ezekiel 33:11: "Say unto them, **As I live, saith the Lord GOD, I have no pleasure in the death of the wicked; but that the wicked turn from his way and live**: turn ye, turn ye from your evil ways; for why will ye die, O house of Israel?"

If you should choose to reject God's Son as your Saviour and to rebel against His perfect plan for your life, this leaves God no alternative but to allow you to continue your rejection of him and deliver to you the "wages of sin," which is "the second death" (Romans 6:23; Revelation 20:14-15)!

When God's plan in "time" and on this earth has been completed, the present heavens and earth will be destroyed, and God will create a "new heaven and a new earth" (Revelation 21:1) wherein only righteousness will dwell (2 Peter 3:13). All of God's children look forward to that time!

III. THE WORD IS THE CREATOR

John 1:3 says, "All things were made by him [the "Word"]; and without him [the "Word"] was not any thing made that was made."

We have already seen that "the Word was God" (John 1:1), so there should be no problem understanding that the Son of God created all things, and that the reference to God in Genesis 1:1 is also a reference to God the Son: "**In the beginning God** ["the Word was God" (John 1:1)] **created the heaven and the earth**" (Genesis 1:1).

We find this truth stated again in the New Testament: Colossians 1:16-17 says, "**For by him** [the "Son" (Colossians 1:13)] **were all things created, that are in heaven, and that are in earth, visible and invisible, whether they be thrones, or dominions, or principalities, or powers: all things were created by him, and for him**: **And he is before all things, and by him all things consist**."

IV. THE WORD IS "THAT ETERNAL LIFE"

John 1:4-5 says, "In him was life; and the life was the light of men. And the light shineth in darkness; and the darkness comprehended it not."

John writes again of the Lord Jesus Christ in his first general epistle, calling him "the Word of life" (1 John 1:1). This is the fifth occurrence so far where we have seen the Lord called the "Word."

The scriptures in 1 John 1:1-3 say, "That which was from the beginning, which we have heard, which we have seen with our eyes, which we have looked upon, and our hands have handled, of **the Word of life**; (For the life was manifested, and we have seen it, and bear witness, and show unto you **that eternal life**, which was with the Father, and was manifested unto us;) That which we have seen and heard declare we unto you, that ye also may have fellowship with us: and truly our fellowship is with the Father, and with his Son Jesus Christ."

God so loved the world that he sent His Son into the world with the commandment to lay down his life for sinners! John 10:17-18 says, "Therefore doth my Father love me, because I lay down my life, that I might take it again. No man taketh it from me, but I lay it down of myself. I have power to lay it down, and I have power to take it again. This commandment have I received of my Father."

God has given us a perfect record of his Son. Those who do not believe the record are calling God a liar! "**He that believeth on the Son of God hath the witness in himself: he that believeth not God hath made him a liar; because he believeth not the record that God gave of his Son**" (1 John 5:10).

Let no man be deceived to imagine that he can know the true and living God outside of Jesus Christ! No man can come to God unless he comes to the Son and acknowledges him as God! He is the only way to the Father! The Father accepts no other way than through his Son!

In John 14:6, "**Jesus saith unto him, I am the way, the truth, and <u>the life</u>: no man cometh unto the Father, but by me.**" In John 11:25-26, "Jesus said unto her, **I am the resurrection, and <u>the life</u>**: he that believeth in me, though he were dead, yet shall he live: And whosoever liveth and believeth in me shall never die. Believest thou this?" Again, 1 John 5:12 explains, "He **that hath the Son hath <u>life</u>; and he that hath not the Son of God hath not life.**"

Make no mistake about it; you are alive today because of Jesus Christ! This world exists because of Jesus Christ! It is being held together by Jesus Christ! You have food to eat because of Jesus Christ! You are not yet burning in hell because of the grace and mercy of Jesus Christ! Yet there is more to life than meets the natural eye. Jesus Christ came into the world to save sinners, sinners who are walking in darkness: sinners who say they see, but are if fact spiritually dead in their sins and trespasses (Ephesians 2:1).

V. THE WORD IS THE LIGHT

John 1:4-9 says, "In him was life; and the life was the light of men. And the light shineth in darkness; and the darkness comprehended it not. There was a man sent from God, whose name was John. The same came for a witness, to bear witness of the Light, that all men through him might believe. He was not that Light, but was sent to bear witness of that Light. That was the true Light, which lighteth every man that cometh into the world."

John 8:12 tells us, "**Then spake Jesus again unto them, saying, I am the light of the world: he that followeth me shall not walk in darkness, but shall have the light of life.**"

But evil men love darkness and hate the light! John 3:17-20 explains, "**For God sent not his Son into the world to condemn the world; but that**

the world through him might be saved. He that believeth on him is not condemned: but he that believeth not is condemned already, because he hath not believed in the name of the only begotten Son of God. And this is the condemnation, that light is come into the world, and men loved darkness rather than light, because their deeds were evil. For every one that doeth evil hateth the light, neither cometh to the light, lest his deeds should be reproved. But he that doeth truth cometh to the light, that his deeds may be made manifest, that they are wrought in God."

John 1:10 says, "He [Jesus] was in the world, and the world was made by him, and the world knew him not." The world did not know the Light when he came to earth the first time, neither do they recognize born again believers to be the sons of God at this present time (1 John 3:1)!

John 1:11 tells us that, "He [Jesus] came unto his own, and his own received him not." His own chosen people, the nation of Israel, whom he had saved out of heathenism and out of bondage in Egypt and had blessed through his prophets by giving them promises in his word that he would come to them and would pay the price of the ransom for them, rejected him and crucified him! Nonetheless, this was all done according to the eternal foreknowledge of God from the foundation of the world. Peter preaching to a bunch of Jews reviewed the life and death of Jesus Christ by stating in his sermon, "Him, being delivered by the determinate counsel and foreknowledge of God, ye have taken, and by wicked hands have crucified and slain: Whom God hath raised up, having loosed the pains of death: because it was not possible that he should be holden of it" (Acts 2:23-24).

Evil men love darkness. They hate Jesus Christ, because they hate the light. They hate God. They despise God's word. Therefore, God declares in Proverbs 13:13, "**Whoso despiseth the <u>word</u> shall be destroyed: but he that feareth the commandment shall be rewarded**." Why? Because "[t]**he entrance of thy <u>words</u>** [God's words] **giveth light; it giveth understanding unto the simple**" (Psalm 119:130).

God has a place called "outer darkness" (Matthew 8:12) reserved for those who love darkness! God describes these lovers of darkness as: "**Raging waves of the sea, foaming out their own shame; wandering stars, to whom is reserved the blackness of darkness for ever**" (Jude 1:13).

We thank God for the "But" of the next verse, because that's exactly where all sinners can find God's mercy. John 1:12 says, "But as many as received him, to them gave he power to become the sons of God, even to them that believe on his name: Which were born, not of blood, nor of the will of the flesh, nor of the will of man, but of God" (John 1:12-13).

God has given us the Holy Bible so that we can know about and believe on his Son and receive eternal life through faith in his name. God is offering to every sinner a "free gift" (Romans 5:15-19). This gift is God's only begotten Son! Those who receive him are said to be born of God. They are born again of incorruptible seed, by the word of God. First Peter 1:23-25 says, "**Being born again, not of corruptible seed, but of incorruptible, by <u>the word of God</u>, which liveth and abideth for ever**. For all flesh is as grass, and all the glory of man as the flower of grass. The grass withereth, and the flower thereof falleth away: But the word of the Lord endureth for ever. And this is the word which by the gospel is preached unto you." I would encourage you to also read John 3:3-7 for a further biblical explanation of this profound statement.

The word of God that we preach to you is called "**the gospel of the grace of God**" (Acts 20:24) which is "...**how that Christ died for our sins according to the scriptures; And that he was buried, and that he rose again the third day according to the scriptures**" (1 Corinthians 15:3-4). Because of this Paul was confidentially able to affirm "**For I am not ashamed of the gospel of Christ: for it is the power of God unto salvation to every one that believeth; to the Jew first, and also to the Greek**" (Romans 1:16).

VI. THE WORD WAS MADE FLESH

John 1:14 says, "And the Word was made flesh, and dwelt among us, (and we beheld his glory, the glory as of the only begotten of the Father,) full of grace and truth."

The incarnation of the eternal Son of God was part of God's plan before the foundation of the world. God knew that Adam would sin, and God knew that the only possible way for Adam and his offspring to be redeemed from the penalty of eternal death for sin would be the death of an innocent substitute in their stead. God himself would have to provide the innocent substitute. God made this all possible when he made a body for his Son, the Lord Jesus Christ.

"Wherefore when he cometh into the world, he saith, Sacrifice and offering thou wouldest not, but a body hast thou prepared me." (Hebrews 10:5).

The Lord Jesus Christ, the Word, became flesh to die for the sins of the world. He was "**made a little lower than the angels for the suffering of death**" (Hebrews 2:9). Then God "**made him to be sin for us, who knew no sin; that we might be made the righteousness of God in him**" (2 Corinthians 5:21). Those who repent and turn from their sins and receive him as Saviour receive a pardon for their sins and eternal life through him!

"By the which will we are sanctified through the offering of the body of Jesus Christ once for all" (Hebrews 10:10).

The truth of God (the Word) being made flesh is without controversy. We are not here to argue with you about God's word, but to preach to you the glorious gospel of Christ, which "is the power of God unto salvation to every one that believeth…" (Romans 1:16). "**And without controversy great is the mystery of godliness: God was manifest in the flesh, justified in the Spirit, seen of angels, preached unto the Gentiles, believed on in the world, received up into glory**" (1 Timothy 3:16).

VII. THE WORD IS COMING AGAIN!

The final reference in the Bible to the Word is found in the last book of the Bible. Revelation 19:11-16 says, "And I saw heaven opened, and behold a white horse; and he that sat upon him was called Faithful and True, and in righteousness he doth judge and make war. His eyes were as a flame of fire, and on his head were many crowns; and he had a name written, that no man knew, but he himself. And he was clothed with a vesture dipped in blood: and his name is called **The Word of God**. And he hath on his vesture and on his thigh a name written, **KING OF KINGS, AND LORD OF LORDS**."

The Lord Jesus Christ came the first time to bring peace between sinners and God. At His second coming, he will take vengeance upon those who have rejected him. Second Thessalonians 1:7-9 explains, "**And to you who are troubled rest with us, when the Lord Jesus shall be revealed from heaven with his mighty angels, [i]n flaming fire taking vengeance on them that know not God, and that obey not the gospel of our Lord Jesus Christ: Who shall be punished with everlasting destruction from the presence of the Lord, and from the glory of his power**."

This KING OF KINGS, AND LORD OF LORDS is none other than JEHOVAH: "That men may know that thou, whose name alone is JEHOVAH, art the most high over all the earth" (Psalm 83:18).

CONCLUSION

Will you submit to the Almighty God by believing and obeying the gospel or will you take your place with the rest of the wicked who reject the counsel of God against themselves (Luke 7:30)? God commands you to repent (Acts 17:30-31), but leaves the choice up to you. Jesus said, "He that rejecteth me, and receiveth not my words, hath one that judgeth him: the word that I have spoken, the same shall judge him in the last day" (John 12:48).

Before the Lord Jesus Christ comes again in flaming fire to take vengeance upon his enemies he is coming as a thief in the night to deliver his people out of the world just before the antichrist is revealed and the worst time the world has ever seen begins. The majority of the world has not taken the Holy Bible, the written word of God, seriously; therefore, they continue to reject God's warnings and commandments.

What about you? The written word of God is the true record concerning the incarnate "Word of God." It is my prayer if you are lost and have never obeyed the gospel from your heart that you will receive Jesus Christ today. The Bible says: "**That if thou shalt confess with thy mouth the Lord Jesus, and shalt believe in thine heart that God hath raised him from the dead, thou shalt be saved**" (Romans 10:9).

Chapter 19

Why Read the Bible?

As I talk to men about reading their Bible, I find that the daily program for many men consists simply in reading a daily devotional and their favorite Psalm! I offer these few words and scriptures in an attempt to show how essential it is for believers to read their Bible everyday. I was personally born again while alone in my house reading a Bible, and I have known of many men who have also been miraculously saved simply by reading the scriptures. Therefore, let me encourage you who do not believe in the Lord Jesus Christ to read the Holy Bible also.

There are several reasons why we should read the Bible every single day. Those reasons are as follows:

I. TO KNOW THE TRUTH

A. FOR SANCTIFICATION

Jesus prayed to his Father for his disciples saying, "**Sanctify them through thy truth: thy word is truth**" (John 17:17). The Lord Jesus Christ told the Jews which believed on him, "**If ye continue in <u>my word</u>, then are ye my disciples**

indeed; And ye shall know the truth, and the truth shall make you free" (John 8:31-32).

Psalm 138:2 says, "I will worship toward thy holy temple, and praise thy name for thy lovingkindness and **for thy truth: for thou hast magnified thy word above all thy name**."

The Apostle Paul refers to **the gospel of your salvation** as **the word of truth** (Ephesians 1:13). Again, he refers to **the word of the truth of the gospel** (Colossians 1:5). Paul commands Timothy, "**Study to shew thyself approved unto God, a workman that needeth not to be ashamed, rightly dividing the word of truth**" (2 Timothy 2:15).

I cannot imagine why a man who knows Jesus Christ and has the Spirit of Christ in him (Colossians 1:27; Romans 8:9) would not desire to know all the truth of the Bible! Believers are commanded: "**As newborn babes, desire the sincere milk of the word, that ye may grow thereby**" (1 Peter 2:2). Simply reading your favorite Psalm everyday is not enough! Paul writes to Timothy, "**All scripture is given by inspiration of God, and is profitable for doctrine, for reproof, for correction, for instruction in righteousness: That the man of God may be perfect, throughly furnished unto all good works**" (2 Timothy 3:16-17).

When the devil tempted Jesus in the wilderness, Jesus **answered and said, It is written, Man shall not live by bread alone, but by every word that proceedeth out of the mouth of God** (Matthew 4:4). Today we are living in a wilderness of sin and deception. We need every word of God to guide and direct our paths. Only then will our path be **as the shining light**.

Proverbs 4:18 says, "**But the path of the just is as the shining light, that shineth more and more unto the perfect day**."

B. FOR SALVATION

The word of God is the "seed" that is sown in the "world" that brings forth the "fruit" of salvation in the hearts of men (Matthew 13:3-23). Men are **born again, not of corruptible seed, but of incorruptible, by the word of God, which liveth and abideth for ever** (1 Peter 1:23). Men beget physical children by physical seed. God begets spiritual children with spiritual seed. The Lord commanded his disciples, "**Go ye into all the world, and preach the gospel**

to every creature" (Mark 16:15), for the Lord is **not willing that any should perish, but that all should come to repentance** (2 Peter 3:9). God has chosen his word to be the **seed** by which he begets spiritual children into his kingdom from among the men of the world. James 1:18 says, "**Of his own will begat he us with the word of truth, that we should be a kind of firstfruits of his creatures**."

The Apostle Paul wrote to the Corinthian believers who had believed after they heard the gospel at his preaching, saying: "**For though ye have ten thousand instructors in Christ, yet have ye not many fathers: for in Christ Jesus I have begotten you through the gospel**" (1 Corinthians 4:15).

While in prison Paul the apostle met a runaway servant named Onesimus, who was the servant of Philemon a fellow Christian brother of Paul's. Paul had sown the seed of the word of God by preaching the gospel unto Onesimus, and God had saved him by faith. In his letter to Philemon, Paul called him, **my son Onesimus, whom I have begotten in my bonds** (Philemon 10).

The Apostle Peter wrote that God **hath begotten us again unto a lively hope by the resurrection of Jesus Christ from the dead** (1 Peter 1:3).

The Apostle John wrote that those who are born again—begotten of God—will love God and also any other man **that is begotten of him** (1 John 5:1).

II. TO HAVE FELLOWSHIP WITH JESUS CHRIST

If born again believers do not walk in the light of God's word, it is impossible for them to be in fellowship with the Lord. The LORD, through the prophet Amos, asked the question, "**Can two walk together, except they be agreed?**" (Amos 3:3). The answer is, "No!" You cannot walk together and have communion with the Lord Jesus Christ unless you are walking in agreement with his word. And how can you walk in the light of—or in agreement with—his word if you do not even know what his word says? You're headed for many pitfalls, sorrows, and perhaps an early death if you do not walk in the light of God's word. You will miss the joy and peace and excitement in this life that comes from serving the Lord if you trade your birthright for the vanity of this life. Not only that, but you will be a loser at the judgment seat of Christ (1 Corinthians 3:15). Instead of reigning together with Christ during his thousand year reign on the earth, you will be appointed your portion with the hypocrites (Matthew 24:51) and unbelievers (Luke 12:46).

The following was written to believers:

First John 1:6-7 — "**If we say that we have fellowship with him, and walk in darkness, we lie, and do not the truth: But if we walk in the light, as he is in the light, we have fellowship one with another, and the blood of Jesus Christ his Son cleanseth us from all sin**.

To walk in the light means to walk in agreement with God's word, which is light (Psalms 119:105, 130; Proverbs 6:23; 2 Peter 1:19).

Psalm 119:105 says, "**Thy word is a lamp unto my feet, and a light unto my path**."

Psalm 119:130 says, "**The entrance of thy words giveth light; it giveth understanding unto the simple**."

Proverbs 6:23 says, "**For the commandment is a lamp; and the law is light**; and reproofs of instruction are the way of life."

Second Peter 1:19 says, "We have also a more sure **word** of prophecy; whereunto ye do well that ye take heed, **as unto a light that shineth in a dark place**, until the day dawn, and the day star arise in your hearts."

III. TO BE FILLED WITH THE SPIRIT

By comparing two scriptures, we see that the results of (1) being filled with the Spirit (Ephesians 5:18-19) and (2) letting the word of Christ dwell in you richly (Colossians 3:16) are the same. Since the words of Christ **are spirit** (John 6:63) it follows that in order to be filled with the Spirit one must let the word of Christ dwell in him richly. The only way that is going to happen is when you read, listen to, study, meditate on, and obey God's word every day. To be filled with the Spirit means that the Spirit of Christ has the control of every part of your heart and life.

IV. TO ESCAPE THE DESTROYER

The only way to avoid the lies and deceptions and corruptions of the devil is by reading and obeying God's word. The devil has many paths and ways which seem right to men, but the end of those ways is death and eternal destruction (Proverbs 14:12). The devil is the mastermind behind all false religions.

Psalm 17:4-5 says, "**Concerning the works of men, <u>by the word of thy lips</u> I have kept me from the paths of the destroyer. Hold up my goings in thy paths, that my footsteps slip not.**"

Psalm 119:105 says, " **<u>Thy word is a lamp unto my feet, and a light unto my path</u>**."

James commands us to "**Resist the devil, and he will flee from you**." But first, he says, "**Submit yourselves therefore to God**" (James 4:7). Submission means obedience to God's word, which is impossible unless you are reading it. Peter also warns us saying, "**your adversary the devil, as a roaring lion, walketh about, seeking whom he may devour: Whom resist stedfast in the faith**" (1 Peter 5:8-9). To resist the devil **steadfast in the faith** requires a working knowledge of the word of God, because **faith cometh by hearing, and hearing by the word of God** (Romans 10:17). There is no way around it; if you do not continue to read the Bible you will be easy prey for the devil, and he will literally destroy your life.

V. TO BE BLESSED

Psalm 1:1-3 says, "**Blessed is the man that walketh not in the counsel of the ungodly, nor standeth in the way of sinners, nor sitteth in the seat of the scornful. <u>But his delight is in the law of the LORD</u>; and <u>in his law doth he meditate day and night</u>. And he shall be like a tree planted by the rivers of water, that bringeth forth his fruit in his season; his leaf also shall not wither; and whatsoever he doeth shall prosper**."

VI. TO BE BUILT UP

Acts 20:32 says, "And now, brethren, I commend you to God, and to **the word of his grace, which is able to build you up, and to give you an inheritance among all them which are sanctified**."

VII. TO RECEIVE THE LORD'S COUNSEL

If you will continue to read the Bible, you will find that you have no need to ask a man what you should do. You will be **taught of God** (John 6:45; 1 Thessalonians 4:9). The word of God will give you all the counsel and direction you will ever need.

Psalm 119:24 says, "**Thy testimonies also are my delight and my counsellors**."

Proverbs 6:20-24 says, " My son, keep thy father's commandment, and forsake not the law of thy mother: Bind them continually upon thine heart, and tie them about thy neck. When thou goest, it shall lead thee; when thou sleepest, it shall keep thee; and when thou awakest, it shall talk with thee. **For the commandment is a lamp; and the law is light; and reproofs of instruction are the way of life**: **To keep thee from the evil woman, from the flattery of the tongue of a strange woman**."

VIII. TO INCREASE IN FAITH

Romans 10:17 says, "**So then faith cometh by hearing, and hearing by the word of God**."

IX. TO GROW IN GRACE AND KNOWLEDGE

Second Peter 3:18 says, "**But grow in grace, and in the knowledge of our Lord and Saviour Jesus Christ. To him be glory both now and for ever. Amen**."

First Peter 2:1-3 says, "Wherefore laying aside all malice, and all guile, and hypocrisies, and envies, and all evil speakings, **As newborn babes, desire the sincere milk of the word, that ye may grow thereby**: If so be ye have tasted that the Lord is gracious."

X. TO RENEW AND TRANSFORM YOUR MIND

The only way to know the will of God is through the Bible. If you are obedient to the commandments of the Lord your mind will be renewed and your life transformed from walking in sin after the flesh to walking in holiness in the Spirit.

Romans 12:1-2 says, "I beseech you therefore, brethren, by the mercies of God, that ye present your bodies a living sacrifice, holy, acceptable unto God, which is your reasonable service. And be not conformed to this world: but **be ye transformed by the renewing of your mind, that ye may prove what is that good, and acceptable, and perfect, will of God**."

Second Corinthians 4:16-18 says, "For which cause we faint not; but though our outward man perish, **yet the inward man is renewed day by day**. For our light affliction, which is but for a moment, worketh for us a far more exceeding and eternal weight of glory; **While we look not at the things which are seen,**

but at the things which are not seen: for the things which are seen are temporal; but the things which are not seen are eternal."

Ephesians 4:21-24 says, "If so be that ye have heard him, and have been taught by him, as **the truth is in Jesus**: That ye put off concerning the former conversation the old man, which is corrupt according to the deceitful lusts; **And be renewed in the spirit of your mind**; And that ye put on the new man, which after God is created in righteousness and true holiness."

Colossians 3:8-11 says, "But now ye also put off all these; anger, wrath, malice, blasphemy, filthy communication out of your mouth. Lie not one to another, seeing that ye have put off the old man with his deeds; **And have put on the new man, which is renewed in knowledge after the image of him that created him**: Where there is neither Greek nor Jew, circumcision nor uncircumcision, Barbarian, Scythian, bond nor free: but Christ is all, and in all."

Galatians 5:16-18 says, "This I say then, **Walk in the Spirit, and ye shall not fulfil the lust of the flesh**. For the flesh lusteth against the Spirit, and the Spirit against the flesh: and these are contrary the one to the other: so that ye cannot do the things that ye would. **But if ye be led of the Spirit, ye are not under the law**."

XI. TO BE SEPARATED FROM THE WICKED

John 17:17 says, "**Sanctify them through thy truth: thy word is truth**."

Ephesians 5:25-27 says, "Husbands, love your wives, even as Christ also loved the church, and gave himself for it; **That he might sanctify and cleanse it with the washing of water by the word**, **That he might present it to himself a glorious church, not having spot, or wrinkle, or any such thing; but that it should be holy and without blemish**."

First John 5:4-5 says, "For whatsoever is born of God overcometh the world: **and this is the victory that overcometh the world, even our faith. Who is he that overcometh the world, but he that believeth that Jesus is the Son of God?**"

Proverbs 4:14-15 says, "**Enter not into the path of the wicked, and go not in the way of evil men. Avoid it, pass not by it, turn from it, and pass away**."

First Corinthians 5:9-13 says, "**I wrote unto you in an epistle not to company with fornicators**: Yet not altogether with the fornicators of this world, or with the covetous, or extortioners, or with idolaters; for then must ye needs go out of the world. **But now I have written unto you not to keep company, if any man that is called a brother be a fornicator, or covetous, or an idolater, or a railer, or a drunkard, or an extortioner; with such an one no not to eat**. For what have I to do to judge them also that are without? do not ye judge them that are within? But them that are without God judgeth. **Therefore put away from among yourselves that wicked person**."

Second Thessalonians 3:6 says, "Now we command you, brethren, in the name of our Lord Jesus Christ, that ye **withdraw yourselves from every brother that walketh disorderly**, and not after the tradition which he received of us."

Second Thessalonians 3:14 says, "**And if any man obey not our word by this epistle, note that man, and have no company with him, that he may be ashamed**."

Second Corinthians 6:14-18 says, "**Be ye not unequally yoked together with unbelievers: for what fellowship hath righteousness with unrighteousness? and what communion hath light with darkness? And what concord hath Christ with Belial? or what part hath he that believeth with an infidel? And what agreement hath the temple of God with idols? for ye are the temple of the living God; as God hath said, I will dwell in them, and walk in them; and I will be their God, and they shall be my people. Wherefore come out from among them, and be ye separate, saith the Lord, and touch not the unclean thing; and I will receive you, And will be a Father unto you, and ye shall be my sons and daughters, saith the Lord Almighty**."

XII. TO ESCAPE EARLY DEATH

The saved man who rebels and lives after the flesh shall die an early death.

Romans 8:13 says, "**For if ye live after the flesh, ye shall die: but if ye through the Spirit do mortify the deeds of the body, ye shall live**."

But the man who loves the Lord and keeps his commandments (John 14:15) will be satisfied with a long life.

Psalm 91:14-16 says, "**Because he hath set his love upon me, therefore will I deliver him: I will set him on high, because he hath known my name. He shall call upon me, and I will answer him: I will be with him in trouble; I will deliver him, and honour him. With long life will I satisfy him, and shew him my salvation.**"

Proverbs 3:1-2 says, "**My son, forget not my law; but let thine heart keep my commandments**: For length of days, and long life, and peace, shall they add to thee."

CONCLUSION

If you have not been born of the Spirit of God through faith in the Lord Jesus Christ, then I recommend that you read the gospels of Matthew, Mark, Luke, and John in the Holy Bible, especially the gospel according to John. This gospel was written to give you faith so that you might be born again and receive everlasting life (John 20:31).

If you are already saved, I hope and pray that this sermon will encourage you to establish a regular habit of reading your Bible completely through at least once per year. If you only read two pages per day you would read the Bible once in a year. Everyday you might want to try reading one or two Psalms, a chapter of Proverbs that matches the day of the month, and at least a chapter each in the Old Testament (Genesis through Malachi) and in the New Testament (Matthew through Revelation). And don't forget:

"**But be ye doers of the word, and not hearers only, deceiving your own selves**" (James 1:22).

Jesus said: "**[T]he words that I speak unto you, they are spirit, and they are life** (John 6:63).

Chapter 20

The Truth Shall Make You Free

The passage of scripture in John 8:12-32 tells us, "Then spake Jesus again unto them, saying, I am the light of the world: he that followeth me shall not walk in darkness, but shall have the light of life. The Pharisees therefore said unto him, Thou bearest record of thyself; thy record is not true. Jesus answered and said unto them, Though I bear record of myself, *yet* my record is true: for I know whence I came, and whither I go; but ye cannot tell whence I come, and whither I go. Ye judge after the flesh; I judge no man. And yet if I judge, my judgment is true: for I am not alone, but I and the Father that sent me. It is also written in your law, that the testimony of two men is true. I am one that bear witness of myself, and the Father that sent me beareth witness of me. Then said they unto him, Where is thy Father? Jesus answered, Ye neither know me, nor my Father: if ye had known me, ye should have known my Father also. These words spake Jesus in the treasury, as he taught in the temple: and no man laid hands on him; for his hour was not yet come. Then said Jesus again unto them, I go my way, and ye shall seek me, and shall die in your sins: whither I go, ye cannot come. Then said the Jews, Will he kill himself? because he saith, Whither I go, ye cannot come. And he said unto them, Ye are from beneath; I am from above: ye are of this world; I am not of this world. I said therefore unto you, that ye shall die in your sins: for if ye believe not that I am *he*, ye shall die in your sins. Then said they unto him, Who art thou? And Jesus saith unto them, Even *the same* that I said unto you from the beginning. I have many things to say and to judge of you: but he that sent me is true; and I speak to the world those things which I have heard of him. They understood not that he spake to them of the Father. Then said Jesus unto them, When ye have lifted up the Son of man, then shall ye know that I am *he*, and *that* I do nothing of myself; but as my Father hath taught me, I speak these things. And he that sent me is with me: the Father hath not left me alone; for I do always those things that please him. As he spake these words, many believed on him. Then said Jesus to those Jews which believed on him, If ye continue in my word, *then* are ye my disciples indeed; And ye shall know the truth, and the truth shall make you free."

INTRODUCTION

In this passage, as the Lord Jesus Christ was teaching the Jews, there were many Jews which "**believed on him**" (John 8:30). We have no doubt at all that they were saved. First of all, because the report is given by the Holy Ghost, the author of the scriptures, and not by some man who may only have professed to have believed, but did not believe with all his heart, and whose faith was vain (1 Corinthians 15:1-2; James 2:20). Secondly, because the Lord Jesus himself said: "Verily, verily, I say unto you, **He that believeth on me hath everlasting life**" [John 6:47 (see also John 3:18; 6:40)]

Thirdly, because the holy scriptures proclaim that the one and only way to be saved is by believing on the Lord Jesus Christ (Acts 16:31). God begat the Jews which believed on Jesus Christ, "**with the word of truth**" (James 1:18). God's word had accomplished what God intended: "**For as the rain cometh down, and the snow from heaven, and returneth not thither, but watereth the earth, and maketh it bring forth and bud, that it may give seed to the sower, and bread to the eater: So shall my word be that goeth forth out of my mouth: it shall not return unto me void, but it shall accomplish that which I please, and it shall prosper *in the thing* whereto I sent it**" (Isaiah 55:10-11).

In John 8:31-32, Jesus Christ spoke to these believing Jews, and therefore saved Jews. I want to direct your attention to these two verses in this sermon. The Lord Jesus Christ made many clear statements regarding the gift of eternal life to all those that believe on him. But now he addresses those Jews which believed on him concerning discipleship.

I. DISCIPLESHIP IS CONDITIONAL

A. "IF YE CONTINUE IN MY WORD" (John 8:31)

1. We must continue to read the word.

Deuteronomy 17:18-20 says, "And it shall be, when he [the king of Israel] sitteth upon the throne of his kingdom, that he shall write him a copy of this law in a book out of *that which is* before the priests the Levites: And it shall be with him, and **he shall read therein all the days of his life: that he may learn to fear the LORD his God, to keep all the words of this law and these statutes, to do them**: That his heart be not lifted up above his brethren, and that he turn not aside from the commandment, *to* the right hand, or *to* the left: to the end that he may prolong *his* days in his kingdom, he, and his children, in the midst of Israel."

Revelation 5:9-10 says, "And they sung a new song, saying, Thou art worthy to take the book, and to open the seals thereof: for thou wast slain, and hast redeemed us to God by thy blood out of every kindred, and tongue, and people, and nation; **And hast made us unto our God <u>kings and priests</u>: and we shall reign on the earth**."

Psalm 119:117 says, "Hold thou me up, and I shall be safe: and **I will have respect unto thy statutes continually**."

Acts 6:4 says, "But we [the apostles] will give ourselves continually to prayer, and **to the ministry of the word**."

Acts 17:11 says, "These were more noble than those in Thessalonica, in that they received the word with all readiness of mind, and **<u>searched the scriptures daily</u>**, whether those things were so."

First Timothy 4:13 says, "Till I come, **<u>give attendance to reading</u>**, to exhortation, to doctrine."

2. We must continue to read ALL of the word (Luke. 4:4)

"And Jesus answered him, saying, It is written, That man shall not live by bread alone, but by **<u>every word of God</u>**" (Luke 4:4).

"**<u>All scripture</u>** *is* given by inspiration of God, and *is* profitable for doctrine, for reproof, for correction, for instruction in righteousness: That the man of God may be perfect, **throughly furnished unto all good works**" (2 Timothy 3:16-17).

3. We must continue to study the word.

"**Study to shew thyself approved unto God, a workman that needeth not to be ashamed, rightly dividing the word of truth**" (2 Timothy 2:15).

4. We must continue to meditate on the word.

"This book of the law shall not depart out of thy mouth; **but thou shalt meditate therein day and night, that thou mayest observe to do according to all that is written therein: for then thou shalt make thy way prosperous, and then thou shalt have good success**" (Joshua 1:8).

"Blessed *is* the man that walketh not in the counsel of the ungodly, nor standeth in the way of sinners, nor sitteth in the seat of the scornful. **But his delight *is* in the law of the LORD; and in his law doth he meditate day and night**. And he shall be like a tree planted by the rivers of water, that bringeth forth his fruit in his season; his leaf also shall not wither; and whatsoever he doeth shall prosper" (Psalm 1:1-3).

"**O how love I thy law! it *is* my meditation all the day**. Thou through thy commandments hast made me wiser than mine enemies: for they *are* ever with me. I have more understanding than all my teachers: **for thy testimonies *are* my meditation**" (Psalm 119:97-99).

5. We must continue to obey the word.

"**And if any man obey not our word by this epistle, note that man, and have no company with him, that he may be ashamed**" (2 Thessalonians 3:14).

"**But be ye doers of the word, and not hearers only, deceiving your own selves**" (James 1:22).

"And Samuel said, Hath the LORD *as great* delight in burnt offerings and sacrifices, as in obeying the voice of the LORD? **Behold, to obey *is* better than sacrifice, *and* to hearken than the fat of rams**" (1 Samuel 15:22).

B. “THEN ARE YE MY DISCIPLES INDEED” (John 8:31)

Unless a believer continues in God’s word, he will not understand the conditions and requirements of true discipleship. The Holy Ghost cannot guide him into all truth except the child of God reads all truth. He will end up being tossed to and fro by every wind of doctrine (Ephesians 4:14) and will end up following some man into a ditch (Luke 6:39). Some of the requirements of discipleship are:

1. A disciple loves God more than any thing or any one else, including his own life (Luke 14:26; Matthew 10:37).
2. He is willing to forsake all for the gospel’s sake (Luke 14:33).
3. He expects to suffer persecution (2 Timothy 3:12).
4. He fixes his eyes upon Jesus and does not look back to the world (Isaiah 50:7; Hebrews 12:1-2; Luke 9:62).

II. KNOWING THE TRUTH IS CONDITIONAL

Our sermon scriptures make the declaration, **“If ye continue in my word... ye shall know the truth”** (John 8:31-32). **God’s word is the truth** (John 17:17), and the only way to know it is to continue to read, study, meditate, and do it. In addition, **God only gives knowledge of the truth to those who obey it.** For a further in depth study, look at John 7:17; Psalms 111:10; 119:99-100; James 1:22.

“If any man will do his will, he shall know of the doctrine, whether it be of God, or *whether* I speak of myself” (John 7:17).

“But be ye doers of the word, and **not hearers only, deceiving your own selves**” (James 1:22).

III. BEING MADE FREE IS CONDITIONAL

Our sermon scriptures make another declaration, **“If ye continue in my word...the truth shall make you free”** (John 8:32).

When I was saved, I was “set” free (delivered) “from the power of darkness” (Colossians 1:13). I was “set” free from eternal death (John 5:24) and from God’s condemnation (John 5:24). As God looks at his saints, according to his foreknowledge, he can say that they have been **made** “free from sin” (Romans

6:18-22) and "free from the law of sin and death" (Romans 8:2; Galatians 5:1). However, as long as the saint lives in this corruptible body, he must "continue" to fight the good fight of faith, for he will not be completely free from committing sins (1 John 1:8, 10) until after he is delivered to heaven at his own death or at the rapture (2 Corinthians 5:8; 1 Thessalonians 4:16-18).

The Holy Bible (KJV) uses the word "<u>make</u> you free." However, verses 31 and 32 in the New International [Per]Version read as follows: "To the Jews who had believed him, Jesus said, "If you hold to my teaching, you are really my disciples. Then you will know the truth, and the truth will **set** you free."

The primary meaning of the word "make" is, "To cause to act or do, to press, drive, strain or compel, as in the phrases, make your servant work, make him go" (Noah Webster 1828 Dictionary). This is exactly the sense of what Jesus Christ is saying to those Jews that believed on him. He is telling them that if they continue in his word, the word of God, the truth, will cause them to "act or do;" it will "press, drive, strain or compel" them to do the right thing in the sight of God and will therefore progressively "make them free." On the other hand to "set" free, means "to release from confinement, imprisonment or bondage; to liberate; to emancipate" (Noah Webster 1828 Dictionary). Every living born again believer is a work in progress. As he submits to the word of God he is progressively made more and more free from sin. He will not be "set" free from sin until he gets a new body at the resurrection of the just!

A. THE WORD OF GOD WILL WORK EFFECTUALLY IN THE SAINT THAT BELIEVES IT

"For this cause also thank we God without ceasing, because, when ye received the word of God which ye heard of us, ye received *it* not *as* the word of men, but as it is in truth, **the word of God, which effectually worketh also in you that believe**" (Thessalonians 2:13).

B. THE WORD OF GOD WILL BUILD UP THE SAINT WHO CONTINUES IN IT

"And now, brethren, I commend you to God, and **to the word of his grace, which is able to build you up, and to give you an inheritance among all them which are sanctified**" (Acts 20:32).

C. THE WORD OF GOD WILL GUIDE THE SAINT WHO TAKES HEED TO IT

"**Thy word** ***is*** **a lamp unto my feet, and a light unto my path**" (Psalm 119:105).

D. THE WORD OF GOD WILL KEEP THE SAINT FROM FALLING WHO OBEYS IT

"Wherefore the rather, brethren, give diligence to make your calling and election sure: **for if ye do these things, ye shall never fall**" (2 Peter 1:10).

E. THE WORD OF GOD WILL COUNSEL THE SAINT WHO CONSULTS IT DAILY

"**Thy testimonies also** ***are*** **my delight** ***and*** **my counsellors**" (Psalm 119:24).

F. THE WORD OF GOD WILL SHIELD THE SAINT WHO HAS ON THE WHOLE ARMOUR OF GOD

"**Every word of God** ***is*** **pure: he** ***is*** **a shield unto them that put their trust in him**" (Proverbs 30:5).

G. THE WORD OF GOD BLESSES THE SAINT THAT KEEPS IT

"But he said, Yea rather, blessed *are* they that **hear the word of God, and keep it**" (Luke 11:28).

H. THE WORD OF GOD WILL BEAR FRUIT TO THE SAINT WHO PREACHES IT

"**Preach the word**; be instant in season, out of season; reprove, rebuke, exhort with all longsuffering and doctrine. For the time will come when they will not endure sound doctrine; but after their own lusts shall they heap to themselves teachers, having itching ears; And they shall turn away *their* ears from the truth, and shall be turned unto fables" (2 Timothy 4:2-4).

I. THE WORD OF GOD INCREASES THE FAITH OF THE SAINT WHO HEARS IT

"**So then faith** ***cometh*** **by hearing, and hearing by the word of God**" (Romans 10:17).

J. THE ABIDING WORD OF GOD IN THE SAINT OVERCOMES THE WICKED "one"

"I have written unto you, fathers, because ye have known him *that is* **from the beginning. I have written unto you, young men, because ye are strong, and the word of God abideth in you, and ye have overcome the wicked one" (1 John 2:14).**

K. THE WORD OF GOD MAY BRING MARTYRDOM TO THE SAINT, BUT WILL ALSO EARN HIM A CROWN OF LIFE

"And I saw thrones, and they sat upon them, and judgment was given unto them: and *I saw* the souls of them that were beheaded for the witness of Jesus, and for the word of God, and which had not worshipped the beast, neither his image, neither had received *his* mark upon their foreheads, or in their hands; **and they lived and reigned with Christ a thousand years**" (Revelation 20:4).

"Fear none of those things which thou shalt suffer: behold, the devil shall cast *some* of you into prison, that ye may be tried; and ye shall have tribulation ten days: be thou faithful unto death, **and I will give thee a crown of life**" (Revelation 2:10).

L. THE WORD OF GOD WILL SANCTIFY AND CLEANSE THE SAINT WHO WASHES IN IT

"Husbands, love your wives, even as Christ also loved the church, and gave himself for it; **That he might sanctify and cleanse it with the washing of water by the word**" (Ephesians 5:25-26).

M. THE WORD OF GOD WILL GIVE GROWTH TO THE SAINT WHO DESIRES IT

"**As newborn babes, desire the sincere milk of the word, that ye may grow thereby**" (1 Peter 2:2).

N. THE WORD OF GOD WILL KEEP SIN FROM THE SAINT WHO HIDES THE WORD IN HIS HEART

"Thy **word have I hid in mine heart, that I might not sin against thee**" (Psalm 119:11).

O. THE WORD OF GOD HELPS THE SAINT TO GROW

The word of God helps us to "grow in grace, and in the knowledge of our Lord and Saviour Jesus Christ" (2 Peter 3:18). This knowledge of Christ and the love of Christ constrains us and causes us to submit to God and walk after his commandments as faithful stewards and servants, living for him and not for ourselves (2 Corinthians 5:14-15).

P. THE WORD OF GOD WILL CORRECT ANY ERROR IN THE DISCIPLE'S UNDERSTANDING

"Cease, my son, to hear the instruction *that causeth* to err from the words of knowledge" (Proverbs 19:27).

A CHARGE TO BELIEVERS

"I charge *thee* therefore before God, and the Lord Jesus Christ, who shall judge the quick and the dead at his appearing and his kingdom; Preach the word; be instant in season, out of season; reprove, rebuke, exhort with all longsuffering and doctrine. For the time will come when they will not endure sound doctrine; but after their own lusts shall they heap to themselves teachers, having itching ears; And they shall turn away *their* ears from the truth, and shall be turned unto fables. But watch thou in all things, endure afflictions, do the work of an evangelist, make full proof of thy ministry" (2 Timothy 4:1-5).

The church today has been caused to err in many ways. There are false brethren, false bibles, false teachers and doctrines, and many false gospels. The ONLY antidote for error is the "word of God," for the word of God is pure, preserved, and perfect (Psalm 12:6-7; 1 Corinthians 13:10). If you walk in the light of the word of God, you will have fellowship "with the Father, and with his Son Jesus Christ" (1 John 1:3-7).

"Jesus answered and said unto them, **Ye do err, not knowing the scriptures**, nor the power of God" (Matthew 22:29).

"Nevertheless we, according to his promise, look for new heavens and a new earth, wherein dwelleth righteousness. Wherefore, beloved, seeing that ye look for such things, be diligent that ye may be found of him in peace, without spot, and blameless. And account *that* the longsuffering of our Lord *is* salvation;

even as our beloved brother Paul also according to the wisdom given unto him hath written unto you; As also in all *his* epistles, speaking in them of these things; in which are some things hard to be understood, which they that are unlearned and unstable wrest, as *they do* also the other scriptures, unto their own destruction. Ye therefore, beloved, seeing ye know *these things* before, **beware lest ye also, being led away with the error of the wicked, fall from your own stedfastness. But grow in grace, and *in* the knowledge of our Lord and Saviour Jesus Christ. To him *be* glory both now and for ever. Amen**" (2 Peter 3:13-18).

"We are of God: **he that knoweth God heareth us** [disciples indeed hear the scriptures which "holy men of God spake as they were moved by the Holy Ghost" (2 Peter 1:21)]**; he that is not of God heareth not us. Hereby know we the spirit of truth, and the spirit of error**" (1 John 4:6).

IV. PERSONAL FREEDOM BY THE WORD OF GOD

Since the day of my salvation, the word of God has freed me from many things:

1. Freed me from doubting the purity of the word of God regarding salvation and the eternal security of my soul.
2. Freed me from believing the false gospels that add "good works" to the finished work of Jesus Christ.
3. Free me from joining two churches which taught a false gospel.
4. Freed me from trusting myself (Proverbs 28:26; 3:5-6).
5. Freed me from the fear of man (Psalm 118:6; Proverbs 29:25; Matt. 10:28).
6. Freed me from the fear of death (John 5:24; Revelation 20:14-15; Hebrews 2:14-15).
7. Freed me from continuing to teach the word of God erroneously.

CONCLUSION

I was gloriously born of the Spirit (John 3:3-7) on a rainy day in June while alone reading a Bible in my house. I have read through and listened to the Bible many times. The word of God continues to make me more and more free from many things (Proverbs 4:18; John 8:31-32), too numerous to list or talk about here. I thank God for his precious and preserved pure word that works in me and cleanses me each and every day. I thank God that I can continue to grow in grace and in the knowledge of my Lord and Saviour by continuing in his word everyday (Psalm 143:8; Lamentations 3:22-23). Jesus Christ said, "**If ye love me, keep my commandments**" (John 14:15). The only way to keep his commandments is to know what his commandments are, and the only way to know them is to continue in his word! This wisdom "**is better than rubies; and all the things that may be desired are not to be compared to it**" (Proverbs 8:11). Will you seek wisdom in God's word, or be destroyed for lack of knowledge (Hosea 4:6)? The choice is yours!

"[S]**irs, what must I do to be saved? And they said, Believe on the Lord Jesus Christ, and thou shalt be saved**, and thy house" (Acts 16:30-31).

Chapter 21

Trust

WHAT IS TRUST?

Trust is defined by scripture as *confidence*: "***It is*** **better to trust in the LORD than to put confidence in man.** ***It is*** **better to trust in the LORD than to put confidence in princes**" (Psalm 118:8-9). See also Micah 7:5 and Philippians 3:4. *Trust* is also defined by the Noah Webster 1828 Dictionary as "*confidence*; a reliance or resting of the mind on the integrity, veracity, justice, friendship or other sound principle of another person." *Faith* is to *trust* in "the record that God gave of his Son" (1 John 5:10), for "faith cometh by hearing, and hearing by the word of God" (Romans 10:17). To *trust* God means to *believe* in God and in his word.

MISPLACED TRUST

1. Trusting human power and might:

Moses warned the children of Israel of the curses that would come upon them, because they did not listen and attend to the voice of the LORD, "to keep his commandments and his statutes which he [God] commanded" (Deuteronomy

28:45). According to Moses, these curses would come upon them, because they did not serve the LORD "with joyfulness, and with gladness of heart" (Deuteronomy 28:47). Because they refused to serve the LORD, the LORD would bring enemies against them, and they would serve their enemies (Deuteronomy 28:48). The children of Israel would be cursed, because they trusted in their high and fenced walls (Deuteronomy 28:52). Israel trusted in their own strength and fortifications instead of trusting in the LORD!

The prophet Isaiah wrote: "**Woe to them that go down to Egypt for help; and stay on horses, and trust in chariots, because *they are* many; and in horsemen, because they are very strong; but they look not unto the Holy One of Israel, neither seek the LORD!**" (Isaiah 31:1). But the psalmist proclaims that he will trust in the LORD: "**Some *trust* in chariots, and some in horses: but we will remember the name of the LORD our God. They are brought down and fallen: but we are risen, and stand upright**" (Psalm 20:7-8); and, "Through thee [God] will we push down our enemies: through thy name will we tread them under that rise up against us. **For I will not trust in my bow, neither shall my sword save me. But thou hast saved us from our enemies, and hast put them to shame that hated us**" (Psalm 44:5-7).

2. Trusting wealth and riches for redemption:

"**They that trust in their wealth, and boast themselves in the multitude of their riches**; **None *of them* can by any means <u>redeem</u> his brother, nor give to God a <u>ransom</u> for him**: (For the redemption of their soul *is* precious, and it ceaseth for ever:) That he should still live for ever, *and* not see corruption" (Psalm 49:6-9). Through the prophet Hosea the LORD declared to the children of Israel: "**I will <u>ransom</u> them from the power of the grave; I will <u>redeem</u> them from death: O death, I will be thy plagues; O grave, I will be thy destruction: repentance shall be hid from mine eyes**" (Hosea 13:14).

After the resurrection of the Lord Jesus Christ, it is written: "**Neither by the blood of goats and calves, but by his own blood he entered in once into the holy place, having obtained <u>eternal redemption *for us*</u>**" (Hebrews 9:12). Therefore all born again believers today "**have <u>redemption through his blood</u>, the forgiveness of sins, according to the riches of his grace**" (Ephesians 1:7; Colossians 1:14).

Soon in the future after the translation [the carrying away of God's children to heaven] of the church into heaven (1 Thessalonians 4:16-18) they will sing "a new song, saying, "**Thou art worthy to take the book, and to open the seals thereof: for thou wast slain, and hast redeemed us to God by thy blood out of every kindred, and tongue, and people, and nation**" (Revelation 5:9). A *ransom* is the price paid for *redemption*. And so it is written: "For *there is* one God, and one mediator between God and men, the man Christ Jesus; **Who gave himself a ransom for all, to be testified in due time**" (1 Timothy 2:5-6).

Wealth and riches can supply you with earthly needs and desires, but they are corruptible things that cannot redeem your soul. The Apostle Peter wrote: "**Forasmuch as ye know that ye were not redeemed with corruptible things, *as* silver and gold, from your vain conversation *received* by tradition from your fathers; But with the precious blood of Christ, as of a lamb without blemish and without spot**" (1 Peter 1:18-19). The Lord once said to his disciples: "Children, **how hard is it for them that trust in riches to enter into the kingdom of God!**" (Mark 10:24).

3. Trusting false gods:

"The idols of the heathen *are* silver and gold, the work of men's hands. They have mouths, but they speak not; eyes have they, but they see not; They have ears, but they hear not; neither is there *any* breath in their mouths. **They that make them are like unto them: *so is* every one that trusteth in them**" (Psalm 135:15-18). "**They shall be turned back, they shall be greatly ashamed, that trust in graven images, that say to the molten images, Ye *are* our gods**" (Isaiah 42:17). Israel had begun to serve the gods of the heathen Egyptians. When calamity and destruction comes to the heathen nations, the LORD will say to Israel: "Where *are* their gods, *their* rock in whom they trusted, [w]hich did eat the fat of their sacrifices, *and* drank the wine of their drink offerings? [L]et them rise up and help you, *and* be your protection" (read Deuteronomy 32:26-38).

4. Trusting in man:

"**Thus saith the LORD; Cursed *be* the man that trusteth in man, and maketh flesh his arm, and whose heart departeth from the LORD**" (Jeremiah 17:5). Man cannot help you with the most important needs in your life. Only God can meet those needs. Men are subject to death at any moment, but the Lord Jesus Christ is "alive for evermore" (Revelation 1:18) and has "all power…in heaven and in earth" (Matthew 28:18)! Therefore, "**Put not your trust in princes, *nor* in the son of man, in whom *there is* no help**. His breath goeth forth, he returneth to his earth; in that very day his thoughts perish" (Psalm 146:3-4). The scriptures also command the wise not to trust in brothers and neighbors (Jeremiah 9:4), nor in a friend or a wife or any of his family members (Micah 7:5-6)! All men are sinners; so why trust sinners when you can trust the Saviour?

5. Trusting in self or in religious works:

"**He that trusteth in his own heart is a fool**: but whoso walketh wisely, he shall be delivered" (Proverbs 28:26). The Lord Jesus spoke a "**parable unto certain which trusted in themselves that they were righteous, and despised others**" (read Luke 18:9-14). God was not listening to the prayer of the self-righteous Pharisee, but he, God, justified [declared righteous] the repentant and humbled publican, who acknowledged that he was a sinner.

Paul himself had been a self-righteous Pharisee, but his conversion on the road to Damascus had changed all that! Paul wrote: "**But we had the sentence of death in ourselves, that <u>we should not trust in ourselves, but in God which raiseth the dead</u>: Who delivered us from so great a death, and doth deliver: <u>in whom we trust that he will yet deliver *us*</u>**" (2 Corinthians 1:9-10). Again, the Apostle Paul wrote: "Though I might also have confidence in the flesh. **If any other man thinketh that he hath whereof he might trust in the flesh, I more**" (Philippians 3:4). Then he proceeds to list his personal attributes (Philippians 3:5-6). Then, in the next two verses, he wrote: "**But what things were gain to me, those I counted loss for Christ. Yea doubtless, and I count all things *but* loss for the excellency of the knowledge of Christ Jesus my Lord: for whom I have suffered the loss of all things, and do count them *but* dung, that I may win Christ**" (Philippians 3:7-8).

TRUSTING THE TRUTH

In his God given wisdom, Solomon wrote in his proverbs: "**Trust in the LORD with all thine heart; and lean not unto thine own understanding. In all thy ways acknowledge him, and he shall direct thy paths**" (Proverbs 3:5-6). Ruth the Moabitish woman who returned from Moab with Naomi came to trust in the LORD. When she met Boaz, he said to her: "The LORD recompense thy work, and a full reward be given thee of the LORD God of Israel, under whose wings thou art come to **trust**" (Ruth 2:12). Boaz eventually married Ruth, and their firstborn son, named Obed, was the grandfather of David, king of Israel. The book of Ruth is a wonderful story of redemption by the kinsman redeemer, and a wonderful picture of the redemption of Jesus Christ given to all who trust in him!

After the LORD had delivered David out of the hand of all his enemies and out of the hand of Saul, he wrote a song: "And he said, The LORD *is* **my rock**, and **my fortress**, and **my deliverer**; The God of my rock; **in him will I trust**: *he is* **my shield**, and **the horn of my salvation**, **my high tower**, and **my refuge**, **my saviour**; thou savest me from violence. I will call on the LORD, *who is* worthy to be praised: so shall I be saved from mine enemies...***As for* God, his way *is* perfect; the word of the LORD *is* tried: he *is* a buckler to all them that trust in him**. For who *is* God, save the LORD? and who *is* a rock, save our God? God *is* my strength *and* power: and he maketh my way perfect" (2 Samuel 22:2-4; 31-33).

Let's break down that song which David wrote. He said that the LORD is:

1. "**My rock**"—the "rock" in Horeb (Exodus 17:6) was a type of the Lord Jesus Christ, for the Apostle Paul wrote that Israel "**drank of that spiritual Rock that followed them: and that Rock was Christ**" (1 Corinthians 10:4).
2. "**My fortress...my high tower**"—a fortress is any fortified place; a fort; a castle; a strong hold; a place of defense or security. "**The name of the LORD *is* a strong tower: the righteous runneth into it, and is safe**" (Proverbs 18:10). The name of the LORD is *Jesus*, which is the only name "under heaven given among men, whereby we must be saved" (Acts 4:12). Are you safe forever in Jesus Christ? Do you call upon him and *trust* him daily?
3. "**My deliverer**"—the Apostle Paul, writing to all born again believers, wrote that God has "**delivered us from so great a death, and doth deliver: in whom we trust that he will yet deliver *us***" (2 Corinthians 1:10). Paul also wrote that God: "**hath delivered us from the power of darkness, and hath translated *us* into the kingdom of his dear Son**" (Colossians 1:13). Another time to the believers in Thessalonica, Paul wrote that they were waiting "**for his Son from heaven, whom he raised from the dead, *even* Jesus, which delivered us from the wrath to come**" (1 Thessalonians 1:10). Have you been delivered from "the second death" (Revelation 20:14; 21:8), which speaks of the eternal damnation of all Christ rejecters (John 12:48)? Has God delivered you from the power of darkness, or do you remain condemned, because you love darkness rather than light, because your deeds are evil (John 3:19)?
4. "**My shield**"—in another place David wrote, "**Thou *art* my hiding place and my shield: I hope in thy word**" (Psalm 119:114). If you

have been "crucified with Christ" (Galatians 2:20) and "If ye then be risen with Christ" (Colossians 3:1), then "your life is hid with Christ in God" (Colossians 3:1-3). I do not know about you, but I am safely hiding behind "my shield," the Lord Jesus Christ, who has "all power… in heaven and in earth" (Matthew 28:18)!

5. "**The horn of my salvation**"—The *horn* of an animal signifies their strength and is the principle means of both their attack and defense (Deuteronomy 33:17). The Lord's salvation is strong and everlasting, and no one can by any means separate a redeemed child of God from his "**great God and our Saviour Jesus Christ**" (Romans 8:35-39; Titus 2:13).
6. "**My refuge**"—a refuge is a shelter to protect. The redeemed of God have "fled for refuge to lay hold upon the hope set before us: Which *hope* we have as an anchor of the soul, both sure and stedfast, and which entereth into that within the veil; Whither the forerunner is for us entered, *even* Jesus, made an high priest for ever after the order of Melchisedec" (Hebrews 6:18-20). The LORD is "a refuge for the oppressed, a refuge in times of trouble" (Psalm 9:9), and he is a refuge for the poor (Psalm 14:6).
7. "**My saviour**"—The Lord Jesus Christ is "the Saviour of the world" (1 John 4:14). Is he your Saviour?

TRUST AND OBEY

Hezekiah king of Judah "**did *that which was* right in the sight of the LORD**, according to all that David his father did. He removed the high places, and brake the images, and cut down the groves, and brake in pieces the brasen serpent that Moses had made: for unto those days the children of Israel did burn incense to it: and he called it Nehushtan. **He trusted in the LORD God of Israel; so that after him was none like him among all the kings of Judah, nor *any* that were before him**" (2 Kings 18:3-5). Notice how Hezekiah's trust in God's word caused him to destroy the wicked places and items of idolatrous worship. Those who really trust the LORD and believe his word know that God will chasten them if they sin willfully against him (Hebrews 12:6). They know this, because they trust that his word is true. They know that if they live after the flesh they will die an early death (Romans 8:13). Therefore because they truly do trust the LORD, they will both love (John 14:15) and fear (Deuteronomy 5:29) the LORD, and keep his commandments (John 5:23)!

Job "was perfect and upright, and one that feared God, and eschewed evil" (Job 1:1). Therefore, when he was greatly afflicted by Satan, with God's permission, Job could say: "**Though he slay me, yet will I trust in him**: **but I will maintain mine own ways before him**" (Job 13:15).

ALL WHO TRUST IN GOD ARE BLESSED

"**Kiss the Son, lest he be angry, and ye perish *from* the way, when his wrath is kindled but a little. Blessed *are* all they that put their trust in him**" (Psalm 2:12). The word "kiss" here is used in accordance with the Oriental custom, for it was in this way that respect was indicated for one of superior rank. Kissing was also a way for the heathen to give reverence and respect to their idols (1 Kings 19:18; Hosea 13:2). To *kiss* was the ancient and eastern mode of doing homage or allegiance to a king. Sometimes the Persians would kiss his hand, or his dress, or his feet. When Samuel the prophet anointed Saul as the king of Israel, we read: "**Then Samuel took a vial of oil, and poured *it* upon his head, and kissed him, and said, *Is it* not because the LORD hath anointed thee *to be* captain over his inheritance?**" (1 Samuel 10:1). The practice of kissing the hand of a monarch is not uncommon in European courts as a token of allegiance. This was also common among the Persians.

To "Kiss the Son" would be a suitable expression of recognition and allegiance to the Son of God, who is "the King of kings, and Lord of lords" (1 Timothy 6:15), who alone is worthy to receive glory. John was given a vision of future events in heaven when he saw the twenty and four elders saying: "**Thou art worthy, O Lord, to receive glory and honour and power: for thou hast created all things, and for thy pleasure they are and were created**" (Revelation 4:11). Then John saw the redeemed church in heaven, "**Saying with a loud voice, Worthy is the Lamb that was slain to receive power, and riches, and wisdom, and strength, and honour, and glory, and blessing**" (Revelation 5:12). All men should receive and embrace the Lord Jesus Christ as their Saviour and honour him as their soon coming King! I am truly blessed, because all my trust is in "**the great God and our Saviour Jesus Christ**" (Titus 2:13)! See also Psalms 5:11-12; 9:8-10.

THOSE WHO TRUST THE LORD ARE PRESERVED

"**But I have trusted in thy mercy**; my heart shall rejoice in thy salvation. I will sing unto the LORD, because he hath dealt bountifully with me" (Psalm 13:5-6). David prayed: "**Preserve me, O God: for in thee do I put my trust**" (Psalm 16:1). Later, David was inspired to write: "**O love the LORD, all ye his saints: *for* the LORD preserveth the faithful, and plentifully rewardeth the proud**

doer" (Psalm 31:23); and: "**For the LORD loveth judgment, and forsaketh not his saints; they are preserved for ever: but the seed of the wicked shall be cut off**" (Psalm 37:28). All born again believers stand: "**In hope of eternal life, which God, that cannot lie, promised before the world began**" (Titus 1:2).

TRUSTING IN THE LORD GIVES STRENGTH AND BLESSINGS

King David said that he would not be *moved* nor *slide*, because his trust was in the LORD (Psalms 21:7; 26:1). God delivers and prevents confusion among those who trust in him (Psalm 22:4-5). Those that trust in God are *helped* (Psalm 28:7). God has laid up *goodness* for them that trust in him (Psalm 31:19), and *mercy* surrounds them (Psalm 32:10). The man that trusts in the LORD is *greatly blessed*, and his heart *rejoices* in him (Psalms 34:8; 33:21). "The LORD redeemeth the soul of his servants: and **none of them that trust in him shall be desolate** [wasted]" (Psalm 34:22). The psalmist promises: "**Trust in the LORD, and do good; *so* shalt thou dwell in the land, and verily thou shalt be fed**" (Psalm 37:3). Another great promise: "But the salvation of the righteous *is* of the LORD: *he is* their strength in the time of trouble. And the LORD shall help them, and deliver them: **he shall deliver them from the wicked, and save them, because they trust in him**" (Psalm 37:39-40). "**Blessed *is* that man that maketh the LORD his trust**, and respecteth not the proud, nor such as turn aside to lies" (Psalm 40:4). "**They that trust in the LORD *shall be* as mount Zion, *which* cannot be removed, *but* abideth for ever**" (Psalm 125:1).

TO TRUST GOD IS TO BELIEVE GOD

It is impossible to trust in God if you do not believe his word! After seeing so many great miracles, the children of Israel continued to murmur and complain in their unbelief. Concerning their journey in the wilderness, Asaph records later that the children of Israel said, "Behold, he smote the rock, that the waters gushed out, and the streams overflowed; can he give bread also? can he provide flesh for his people? Therefore the LORD heard *this*, and was wroth: so a fire was kindled against Jacob, and anger also came up against Israel; **Because they <u>believed</u> not in God, and <u>trusted</u> not in his salvation**: Though he had commanded the clouds from above, and opened the doors of heaven, [a]nd had rained down manna upon them to eat, and had given them of the corn of heaven" (Psalm 78:20-24).

Read the following verses to see the wonderful benefits to those who trust in the LORD: God is the Saviour of all those who trust in him: "**Behold, <u>God</u>**

***is* my salvation; I will trust, and not be afraid: for the LORD JEHOVAH *is* my strength and *my* song; he also is become my salvation. Therefore with joy shall ye draw water out of the wells of salvation**" (Isaiah 12:2-3). "He that handleth a matter wisely shall find good: **and whoso trusteth in the LORD, happy *is* he**" (Proverbs 16:20). "The fear of man bringeth a snare: **but whoso putteth his trust in the LORD shall be safe**" (Proverbs 29:25). "**Every word of God *is* pure: he *is* a shield unto them that put their trust in him**" (Proverbs 30:5). "**Thou wilt keep *him* in perfect peace, *whose* mind *is* stayed *on thee*: because he trusteth in thee. Trust ye in the LORD for ever: for in the LORD JEHOVAH *is* everlasting strength**" (Isaiah 26:3-4). "**Blessed *is* the man that trusteth in the LORD, and whose hope the LORD is**" (Jeremiah 17:7). The LORD told Jeremiah in the dungeon: "For I will surely deliver thee, and thou shalt not fall by the sword, but thy life shall be for a prey unto thee: **because thou hast put thy trust in me, saith the LORD**" (Jeremiah 39:18).

THE LORD KNOWS THOSE WHO TRUST HIM

In the Old Testament it is written: "**The LORD *is* good, a strong hold in the day of trouble; and he knoweth them that trust in him**" (Nahum 1:7). Then in the New Testament we find the same thought: "Nevertheless the foundation of God standeth sure, having this seal, **The Lord knoweth them that are his**. And, Let every one that nameth the name of Christ depart from iniquity [sin]" (2 Timothy 2:19). "Them that are his" are all those who have believed and trusted in Christ. Writing to "the faithful in Christ Jesus" (Ephesians 1:1), Paul outlined the sequence of their salvation, when he wrote: "In whom [Christ] also we have obtained an inheritance, being predestinated according to the purpose of him who worketh all things after the counsel of his own will: **That we should be to the praise of his glory, who first trusted in Christ. In whom ye also *trusted*, after that ye heard the word of truth, the gospel of your salvation: in whom also after that ye believed, ye were sealed with that holy Spirit of promise**, [w]hich is the earnest of our inheritance until the redemption of the purchased possession, unto the praise of his glory" (Ephesians 1:11-14).

Have you ever clearly heard the gospel, the good news, "**how that Christ died for our sins according to the scriptures; And that he was buried, and that he rose again the third day according to the scriptures**" (1 Corinthians 15:3-4)? Did you know that this "**gospel of Christ…is the power of God unto salvation to every one that believeth**" (Romans 1:16)?

I personally trusted in Christ after reading the gospel accounts of Matthew, Mark, Luke, and John while alone in my house in 1979. Now I can agree wholeheartedly with the psalmist David, who wrote, "**What time I am afraid, I will trust in thee. In God I will praise his word, <u>in God I have put my trust</u>; I will not fear what flesh can do unto me**" (Psalm 56:3-4); and I agree with the Apostle Paul, who wrote: "**For we are the circumcision** [we have been "circumcised with the circumcision made without hands, in putting off the body of the sins of the flesh by the circumcision of Christ" (Colossians 2:11)] **which worship God in the spirit, and rejoice in Christ Jesus, and have no confidence** [trust] **in the flesh**" (Philippians 3:3).

Therefore "**we** [who are in Christ] **both labour and suffer reproach, because we trust in the living God, who is the Saviour of all men, specially of those that believe**" (1 Timothy 4:10). "**For we are labourers together with God**…" (1 Corinthians 3:9). "**We then, *as* workers together *with him*, beseech *you* also that ye receive not the grace of God in vain**. (For he saith, I have heard thee in **a time accepted, and in the day of salvation** have I succoured thee: **behold, now *is* the accepted time; behold, now *is* the day of salvation**.)" (2 Corinthians 6:1-2). "Now then we are ambassadors for Christ, as though God did beseech *you* by us: we pray *you* in Christ's stead, **be ye reconciled to God. For he hath made him *to be* sin for us, who knew no sin; that we might be made the righteousness of God in him**" (2 Corinthians 5:20-21). Trust Christ today!

"**Believe on the Lord Jesus Christ, and thou shalt be saved**" (Acts 16:31).

Chapter 22

Victorious Walk

Today's sermon outline shall be based upon the scriptural text of Romans 8:1-9 which concerns how a believer in Christ Jesus can have a victorious walk in his Christianity. The scriptures say, "*There is* therefore now no condemnation to them which are in Christ Jesus, who walk not after the flesh, but after the Spirit. For the law of the Spirit of life in Christ Jesus hath made me free from the law of sin and death. For what the law could not do, in that it was weak through the flesh, God sending his own Son in the likeness of sinful flesh, and for sin, condemned sin in the flesh: That the righteousness of the law might be fulfilled in us, who walk not after the flesh, but after the Spirit. For they that are after the flesh do mind the things of the flesh; but they that are after the Spirit the things of the Spirit. For to be carnally minded *is* death; but to be spiritually minded *is* life and peace. Because the carnal mind *is* enmity against God: for it is not subject to the law of God, neither indeed can be. So then they that are in the flesh cannot please God. But ye are not in the flesh, but in the Spirit, if so be that the Spirit of God dwell in you. Now if any man have not the Spirit of Christ, he is none of his."

WHICH CONDEMNATION? (Romans 8:1)

The beginning of verse 1 states, "*There is* therefore now no condemnation..." The "condemnation" in this verse is NOT speaking of eternal damnation!

According to Noah Webster 1828 dictionary, one definition of condemn is "to determine or judge to be wrong, or guilty; to disallow; to disapprove." The condemnation of verse 1 refers to God's judgment upon the believer, who walks after the flesh and does NOT walk after the Spirit. Some new bibles omit the last phrase, "**who walk not after the flesh, but after the Spirit**." By removing this phrase, the modern versions lead one to believe the error that there is no condemnation *of any sort* to the believer who walks after the flesh! There will most certainly be condemnation (judgment) to all believers in this life because of sin which they commit in their bodies after their salvation (Hebrews 12:8). And any disobedient believer, who has NOT confessed and forsaken his sins on earth (1 John 1:9; Proverbs 28:13) will receive for the wrong which he hath done (Colossians 3:25), either in this life or when he stands at the judgment seat of Christ (Romans 14:10; 2 Corinthians 5:10) to give account of his bad works (1 Corinthians 3:15). There he will see all of his bad works go up in smoke when God tries them by fire.

OBEDIENCE OR REBELLION? (Romans 8:1)

The ending of verse 1 states, "...who walk not after the flesh, but after the Spirit."

I once heard a radio preacher teach that this verse means that all those who are "in Christ Jesus" NEVER walk after the flesh, but that they ALWAYS walk after the Spirit! But if that were true, then all "just" men would walk in the Spirit at all times. And if this were true, they would never sin! This would be a great thing, but it is simply not the truth. It will never happen in this life! "**For *there is* not a just man upon earth, that doeth good, and sinneth not**" (Ecclesiastics 7:20). Walking in the Spirit should be the desire of all believers, but there is not one man, with the exception of Jesus Christ, who ever accomplished the goal of walking in the Spirit every moment of his life on earth (Ecclesiastics 7:20; 1 John 1:8-10).

The correct interpretation of verse 1 may be confirmed by looking a little further down in this same chapter. Read verses 12 and 13: "Therefore, brethren, we are debtors, not to the flesh, to live after the flesh. For if ye live after the flesh, ye shall die: but if ye through the Spirit do mortify the deeds of the body, ye shall live." In other words, saved "brethren" do not owe anything to the flesh, "to live after the flesh." To live after the flesh means to live according to the direction and dictates of the flesh: to return to the bondage of corruption by allowing the fleshly (carnal) mind to dictate the actions of the body rather than the Spirit of God according to the word of God. If saved men do live "after the flesh," they may even die prematurely. They will be condemned by the Lord, because they have willfully sinned against God (Hebrews 10:26-30).

Therefore verse 1 means that if a saved man will walk after the Spirit, then God will not have to judge (condemn) him; but if he walks after the flesh, then God will judge (condemn) him. However if a believer will judge himself according to God's word, then he **should not be judged. But when we are judged, we are chastened of the Lord, that we should not be condemned** [eternally] **with the world** (1 Corinthians 11:31-32). God may even condemn him to die (Romans 8:13). "Them which are in Christ Jesus" (Romans 8:1) are those who have already passed from death unto life. And the Lord Jesus promised that such a man "**shall not come into** [eternal] **condemnation**" (John 5:24). Therefore the condemnation of the believer in verse 1 refers to the temporary chastisement of the Lord (Galatians 6:7-8; 1 Corinthians 11:29-30; 1 Timothy 3:6; Titus 2:7-8; Romans 13:2; 1 Timothy 5:11-12), but the condemnation of the world is eternal torments in the lake of fire, which is the second death (Revelation 20:14-15). As you can see, there is a great deal of difference between the condemnation of the born again believer and the condemnation of the lost sinner!

What does it mean to walk **after the Spirit**? Can every man do this? No! Only the born again child of God, who has the Holy Ghost permanently indwelling him, has the power to walk **after the Spirit**. Only born again men have a desire to walk after the Spirit. To walk **after the Spirit** means to live according to the direction and dictates of the Spirit, which he wrote in the Bible (2 Peter 1:21). It simply means to walk in the light of God's word (1 John 1:7; Psalms 119:105, 130). The words of God **are spirit, and they are life** (John 6:63). The carnal man has no desire to walk after the commandments of the Lord.

Believers **who walk not after the flesh, but after the Spirit** (Romans 8:1) can expect no condemnation from the **Lord** (1 Corinthians 11:31), from the **law** (Romans 8:2) or from **self** (Romans 14:22; 1 John 3:21).

WALKING UNDER A NEW LAW (Romans 8:2)

Verse 2 starts out by stating, "For the law of the Spirit of life in Christ Jesus…"

One of Noah Webster's definitions of the word "law" in the Noah Webster 1828 Dictionary is, "that which governs or has a tendency to rule; that which has the power of controlling." Unbelievers are not subject to the law of the Spirit of life. Only born again believers, who are **in Christ Jesus** may be subject to the controlling power of the Spirit of Christ, which is in them (Romans 8:9; Colossians 1:27). **The law of the Spirit of life <u>in Christ Jesus</u>**, includes **the royal law**, which is, "**Thou shalt love thy neighbour as thyself**" (James 2:8). This is the second of the two commandments upon which hang all the law and the prophets (Matthew 22:37-40). The royal law, which appears exactly seven times in the Bible (Leviticus 19:18; Matthew 19:19; 22:39; Mark 12:31; Romans 13:9; Galatians 5:14; James 2:8), is the perfect law of the King of kings, the Lord Jesus Christ (Revelation 19:16).

As many as receive the Lord Jesus Christ through true repentance and faith (Acts 20:21; Hebrews 6:1), are given **power to become the sons of God** (John 1:12-13). God gives the Holy Spirit to all them that believe. **Hereby know we that we dwell in him, and he in us, because he hath given us of his Spirit** (1 John 4:13; 3:24).

The last part of verse 2 says, "...hath made me free from the law of sin and death." Furthermore, when men **repent** (Luke 13:3, 5) and receive Jesus Christ by faith, they pass from death unto life (John 5:24). Before their salvation they were **dead in trespasses and sins** (Ephesians 2:1), and they were condemned to the lake of fire, which is the second death, because of their sins under the law (Revelation 20:14-15). Every sinner is under the captivity of "**the law of sin**" (Romans 7:23) which works in the members of his body, "**the old man**" (Colossians 3:9; Romans 6:6). But at the moment of salvation, "**our old man is crucified with him, that the body of sin might be destroyed**" (Romans 6:6), and we are baptized into one body by the Holy Spirit (1 Corinthians 12:13). At this time we become "**members of his** [Christ's] **body, of his flesh, and of his bones**" (Ephesians 5:30). And you can be certain that the body of Christ is not brought under the captivity of the law of sin!

Also all those in Christ Jesus have been redeemed **from the curse of the law** (Galatians 3:13). Under **the law of the Spirit of life in Christ Jesus**, no one can ever be cast out of Christ (John 6:37). No one [soul and spirit] can ever die under the law of the Spirit of life in Christ Jesus (John 11:25-26)! Nevertheless, the Lord does chasten and scourge every son whom he receiveth (Hebrews 12:6). God corrects his children who walk after the flesh, sometimes even unto the death of the body (1 John 5:16). Nevertheless, they will always be his children!

The New Testament is **not of the letter, but of the spirit: for the letter killeth, but the spirit giveth life** (2 Corinthians 3:6). In other words, the law killeth, but the Spirit giveth life. **For the law was given by Moses, but grace and truth came by Jesus Christ** (John 1:17). The law is called, **the ministration of death, written and engraven in stones** (2 Corinthians 3:7), whereas **the law of the Spirit of life in Christ Jesus**, the New Testament, is called, **the ministration of the spirit** (2 Corinthians 3:8) and **the ministration of righteousness** (2 Corinthians 3:9). The Lord Jesus Christ said, **I am come that they might have life, and that they might have it more abundantly** (John 10:10). True life and living is only found in Christ (John 3:36; 11:25-26; 1 John 5:12).

FULFILLING THE LAW (Romans 8:3-4)

The beginning of verse 3 starts off by stating, "For what the law could not do…"

This brings us to the point that the weakness was not in the law itself, but in the flesh of those who were under the law. The law was never intended to give life or to make men righteous (Galatians 3:21). The law was given to prove to all men that they are sinners, that **all the world may become guilty before God** (Romans 3:19), and to be a **schoolmaster to bring us unto Christ, that we might be justified by faith** (Galatians 3:24). The law brings the knowledge of sin to men. That's why wicked men hate the sight of the Ten Commandments posted in a public place! It reproves them of their sins! However, no man could ever be justified by keeping the law (Romans 3:20). The Bible says, "**Wherefore the law is holy, and the commandment holy, and just, and good**" (Romans 7:12). But all men are sinners (Romans 3:23), who are unholy, unjust, and evil! And besides that, there is nothing a sinner can do to make himself holy, just, and good! Only God, by his grace through faith in Jesus Christ, can make a man holy, just, and good!

This now leads us into the next point of verse 3. The middle section of verse 3 continues by stating, "...God sending his own Son in the likeness of sinful flesh..."

The verse which follows the most popular Bible verse in the world (John 3:16) says, "**For God sent not his Son into the world to condemn the world; but that the world through him might be saved**" (John 3:17). **Christ Jesus came into the world to save sinners** (1 Timothy 1:15). The Lord Jesus came, not to establish another religion, but to save sinners! The Lord Jesus did not have corruptible flesh (Psalm 16:10; Acts 2:31; 13:35-37) as all other men do (Romans 8:21; 1 Corinthians 15:42). He did not have the same sin nature as all of Adam's natural born children do, because God is his Father. God **created a**

new thing in the earth (Jeremiah 31:22) when he prepared a body for his Son in the womb of a virgin woman (Isaiah 7:14; 9:6; Hebrews 10:5). The Bible clearly proclaims that Jesus Christ, also called the Word, is God, and that **the Word was made flesh and dwelt among us** (John 1:1, 14; 1 Timothy 3:16). Yet the Son of God appeared to be like all other men when he came into the world the first time. The world did not know him (John 1:10). His own Jewish people rejected him (John 1:11). Isaiah prophesied, "**For he shall grow up before him as a tender plant, and as a root out of a dry ground: he hath no form nor comeliness; and when we shall see him, there is no beauty that we should desire him**" (Isaiah 53:2).

Verse 3 ends with, "…condemned sin in the flesh."

God condemned OUR sin in the flesh of his Son Jesus Christ! The gospel we preach is **how that Christ died for our sins according to the scriptures; And that he was buried, and that he rose again the third day according to the scriptures** (1 Corinthians 15:3-4). God **made him to be sin for us, who knew no sin; that we might be made the righteousness of God in him** (2 Corinthians 5:21). Jesus Christ **was in all points tempted like as we are, yet without sin** (Hebrews 4:15). He is the only man to ever walk the face of this earth [w]**ho did no sin, neither was guile found in his mouth** (1 Peter 2:22). He never once sinned, [b]**ut he was wounded for our transgressions, he was bruised for our iniquities** (Isaiah 53:5). **The LORD hath laid on him the iniquity of us all** (Isaiah 53:6). **For the transgression of my people was he stricken** (Isaiah 53:8). **He was numbered with the transgressors; and he bare the sin of many, and made intercession for the transgressors** (Isaiah 53:12). **He was manifested to take away our sins; and in him is no sin** (1 John 3:5). The Lord Jesus Christ is **holy, harmless, undefiled, separate from sinners, and made higher than the heavens** (Hebrews 7:26).

The next verse of our sermon, verse 4, states, "That the righteousness of the law might be fulfilled in us, who walk not after the flesh, but after the Spirit."

The Spirit of God fulfills the righteousness of the law in the born again believer (Philippians 2:13) who is submitted to God's word (Colossians 1:27; 1 Corinthians 15:10; Ephesians 3:20; Isaiah 26:12; James 4:7) and is walking in the light of it (Psalm 119:105). Such a man is walking **after the Spirit**. The righteousness of the law CANNOT be fulfilled by the believer who is walking after the flesh (Galatians 5:19-21).

Love is the fulfilling of the law (Romans 13:10; Galatians 5:14). And this is **the love of God** [which] **is shed abroad in our hearts by the Holy Ghost which is given unto us** (Romans 5:5). This love is the first mentioned fruit of the Spirit (Galatians 5:22).

Verse 5 tells us, "For they that are <u>after the flesh</u> do mind the things of the flesh; but they that are <u>after the Spirit</u> the things of the Spirit."

One of Noah Webster's definitions of the word "AFTER" is, "According to the direction and influence of. To walk after the flesh; to live after the flesh, as explained in Romans 8." The Noah Webster 1828 Dictionary continues to define "after" as "to follow after, in scripture, [as an example] is to pursue, or imitate; to serve, or worship."

Therefore they that are AFTER the flesh are they who are living according to the direction and influence of the flesh. And they that are AFTER the Spirit are they who are living according to the direction and influence of the Spirit. Carnal believers are fleshly believers who MIND the things of the flesh. In other words, they attend to and fix their thoughts on the flesh and are inclined to follow the desires and lusts of the flesh. When a man is first saved, he is called a newborn babe in Christ (1 Peter 2:2). He is commanded to **desire the sincere milk of the word** that he may grow thereby. He will naturally tend to walk after the flesh more at the beginning of his new life in Jesus Christ than he will later after his mind has been renewed by the word of God (Romans 12:1-2; John 8:31-32). A mature believer, on the other hand, will walk AFTER the Spirit. He will read and meditate on his Bible everyday, and he will congregate with other believers, such as attending church regularly (Hebrews 10:25), and he will fix his mind on Jesus Christ and incline himself to follow the leading of the Spirit of God through the word of God.

DEATH OR LIFE AND PEACE? (Romans 8:6)

The beginning of verse 6 tell us, "For to be carnally minded *is* death..."

This is the living death of the unbeliever, which leads to eternal death. The carnal mind not only leads to death or misery, but also this verse says that the carnal mind is death itself; there is woe and condemnation when a man is devoted to the corrupt passions of the flesh. To be carnally minded is to be under the dominion of the fleshly impulses of the body. It is a bondage of the most deceiving sort (1 Timothy 5:6; Proverbs 21:16). We who have passed from that terrible spiritual "death" (the fruitless wandering out of the way of understanding) unto life in Christ Jesus recall how truly miserable we were as we rushed around to fulfill the lusts of the flesh, which never really satisfied us! Not only that, but also these fleshly lusts brought forth sin: **and sin, when it is finished, bringeth forth death** (James 1:14-15).

It is the spirit that makes alive, but the flesh (the carnal mind) profits NOTHING! Jesus Christ said, "**It is the spirit that quickeneth; the flesh profiteth nothing: the words that I speak unto you, they are spirit, and they are life**" (John 6:63).

The last part of the verse gloriously tells us "...but to be spiritually minded *is* life and peace."

This is the abundant life of the Spirit filled believer who has **peace with God through** [faith in] **our Lord Jesus Christ** (Romans 5:1) and **the peace of God, which passeth all understanding** (Philippians 4:7). To be spiritually minded is to think on things that are true, honest, just, pure, lovely, of good report, and of virtue (Philippians 4:8). To be spiritually minded is to be constantly growing in grace and knowledge of our Lord and Saviour Jesus Christ through daily Bible reading, studying, and meditating upon the word of God. To be spiritually minded is to love God's law and pursue a life of submission to it, being **doers of the word, and not hearers only** (James 1:22; Isaiah 26:3; Psalm 119:165). The very beginning of a spiritual mind is faith, which comes by the word and by the Spirit of God (Romans 10:17; 5:1-2).

Our next verse of the sermon, verse 7, explains why as verse 6 puts it, to be carnally minded is death. Verse 7 states, "Because the carnal mind *is* enmity against God: for it is not subject to the law of God, neither indeed can be."

The unsaved natural man **receiveth not the things of the Spirit of God: for they are foolishness unto him: neither can he know them, because they are spiritually discerned** (1 Corinthians 2:14). In other words, the carnal mind hates God and his word! It rebels against God's word and has no desire to become obedient to God's law. Before I was saved by the grace of God, I was an enemy of God (Romans 5:10), and I was **dead in trespasses and sins** (Ephesians 2:1). I lived as an enemy of God. I thought as an enemy of God. Now I am a friend of God and have a new purpose in life, and that is to help other unbelieving enemies of God find the grace and salvation of Jesus Christ.

Verse 8 continues with the same thought and reveals the hopelessness of someone with a carnal mind. Verse 8 says, "So then they that are in the flesh cannot please God."

These are they who are yet carnal and unsaved. They have not been born again (John 3:3-7). As sugar is mixed in tea and cannot be separated by normal means, so the carnal man is **in the flesh**. He is part of his flesh, he is mixed in with it, like he is married to it (Romans 7:1-6). All of the so-called "good deeds" of unsaved (unregenerated) men count for nothing with God. The scripture says that even **the plowing of the wicked is sin** (Proverbs 21:4). Any activity of the wicked is sin, because God is now commanding **all men everywhere to repent** (Acts 17:30). Therefore anything else that they do is rebellion against the clear commandment of God to repent. The wicked man, by continuing in his rebellion against God is treasuring up unto himself **wrath against the day of wrath and revelation of the righteous judgment of God** (Romans 2:5). The lost man is **condemned already, because he hath not believed in the name of the only begotten Son of God** (John 3:18). **He that believeth not the Son shall not see life; but the wrath of God abideth on him** (John 3:36)!

Nothing that a lost man can do **in the flesh** will please God. Only true broken hearted **repentance toward God and faith toward our Lord Jesus Christ** (Acts 20:21; 17:30; 1 John 3:23; Hebrews 11:6) will please God, because the Lord is **not willing that any should perish, but that all should come to repentance** (2 Peter 3:9).

This now takes us to the last verse of our sermon. The beginning of verse 9 states, "But ye are not in the flesh..."

At the time of their regeneration, all born again children of God **are circumcised with the circumcision made without hands, in putting off the body of the sins of the flesh by the circumcision of Christ** (Colossians 2:11). This is called **the operation of God** (Colossians 2:12) whereby God, with his quick, and powerful word divides **the soul and spirit** from **the joints and marrow** [the body] (Hebrews 4:12).

The next section of verse 9 continues by saying, "...but in the Spirit..."

God puts **off the body of the sins of the flesh** of the believer so that he can **be married to another, even to him who is raised from the dead** (Romans 7:4). Therefore when the new believer is born again he becomes a **new creature** in Christ (2 Corinthians 5:17). He is now joined unto the Lord and is **one spirit** with the Lord (1 Corinthians 6:17). However, even though the regenerated new creature "in Christ" is NOT **in the flesh** in the sense that he is joined to his flesh, as being mixed in with it, or married to it; he must still yet **walk in the flesh** (2 Corinthians 10:3). But he does not **walk** (Romans 8:1, 4) or **live AFTER** [according to the direction and influence of] **the flesh** (Romans 8:12-13), and he does **not war AFTER** [according to the direction and influence of] **the flesh** (2 Corinthians 10:3). He is like a person living in an old condemned house, with definite future promises of moving into a new house (2 Corinthians 5:1-4). He is now waiting to be delivered **from the body of this death** (Romans 7:24-25), when the Lord Jesus Christ will descend from heaven and **change our vile body, that it may be fashioned like unto his glorious body** (Philippians 3:21; 1 Corinthians 15:51-53). Then we will **be clothed upon with our house which is from heaven** (2 Corinthians 5:2).

Verse 9 continues to say, "...if so be that the Spirit of God dwell in you..."

The indwelling Holy Spirit of God is called **the firstfruits of the Spirit** (Romans 8:23). He is also called **the earnest of the Spirit** (2 Corinthians 1:22; 5:5; Ephesians 1:13-14). Earnest is "that which is in advance, and gives promise of something to come" (Noah Webster 1828 Dictionary). God gives all born again believers his Holy Spirit to abide with them forever (John 14:16; Ephesians 4:30). God confirms our salvation to us by the presence of his Spirit in our hearts. **Hereby know we that we dwell in him, and he in us, because he hath given us of his Spirit** (1 John 4:13). The evidence that we have the Spirit of Christ is that we will **mind the things of the Spirit** (Romans 8:5), and bear **the fruit of the Spirit** (Galatians 5:22-23). Jesus Christ said, "**Wherefore by their fruits ye shall know them**" (Matthew 7:20). Because of the power of the indwelling Spirit of God, the new believer will also begin to gain complete and miraculous victories over sins.

The end of verse 9 states, "Now if any man have not the Spirit of Christ, he is none of his."

Jesus told a religious ruler of the Jews, named Nicodemus, "**Except a man be born again, he cannot see the kingdom of God** (John 3:3), and **he cannot enter into the kingdom of God**" (John 3:5). The Spirit of Christ is received when the repentant and believing soul is born again. Therefore, all those who do not have the Spirit of Christ are lost (Jude 1:17-19). They are in danger of hell fire, and have a great need!

FINAL QUESTION

You are in great danger if you have read this sermon and are not saved. However, you can be sure that God does not want you to perish in the lake of fire forever (2 Peter 3:9). God showed his love to you when he put your sins upon his only Son Jesus Christ and had him crucified in your place (John 3:16; Romans 5:8; 1 Corinthians 15:3-4). God **now commandeth all men every where to repent** (Acts 17:30) and to **believe on the name of his Son Jesus Christ** (1 John 3:23). What will you do with the Lord Jesus Christ? You will either receive him and be saved (John 1:12-13), or you will reject him (John 12:48) and be condemned forever in the lake which burneth with fire and brimstone (Revelation 10:15).

The gospel of John was written **that ye might believe that Jesus is the Christ, the Son of God; and that believing ye might have life through his name** (John 20:31). If you are not saved, I recommend that you read the gospel of John and allow the word of God to bring light into your darkness (Psalm 119:130; John 8:12). Do not allow Satan, the world, and your darkened heart to rule you any longer! Do not boast or brag about what you might do tomorrow. You do not know what tomorrow may bring. Billions are suffering the torments of hell at this very moment who thought they had plenty of time! You will either suffer the torments of the damned (Revelation 14:11), or you will enjoy the pleasures of the Lord forever (Psalm 16:11; 36:8)!

Romans 6:23 says, "**For the wages of sin is death; but the gift of God is eternal life through Jesus Christ our Lord**."

Revelation 22:17 encourages you and me with the words, "**And the Spirit and the bride say, Come. And let him that heareth say, Come. And let him that is athirst come. And whosoever will, let him take the water of life freely**."

Chapter 23

Spiritual Workout

Philippians 2:12-13 says, "Wherefore, my beloved, as ye have always obeyed, not as in my presence only, but now much more in my absence, work out your own salvation with fear and trembling. For it is God which worketh in you both to will and to do of *his* good pleasure."

FAITHFUL BELIEVERS

Our sermon starts out with looking at the first section of Philippians 2:12, which says, "Wherefore, my beloved, as ye have always obeyed, not as in my presence only, but now much more in my absence…" One would observe by reading these words of the Apostle Paul that evidently these believers were truly serving God, "Not with eyeservice, [or] as menpleasers; but as the servants of Christ, doing the will of God from the heart" (Ephesians 6:6), and "in singleness of heart, fearing God" (Colossians 3:22). Whether Paul was there with them, or not, they were walking in obedience to God. They were not hypocrites as others, who "profess that they know God; but in works they deny *him*, being abominable, and disobedient, and unto every good work reprobate" (Titus 1:16). They had "obeyed from the heart that form of doctrine which was delivered" (Romans 6:17) to them.

THE WORK OF GRACE

Our second section of Philippians 2:12 continues to say "...work out your own salvation..."

This is a command that *believers* are to work *out* that which God has placed within them by his grace through faith: "**For by grace are ye saved through faith; and that not of yourselves: *it is* the gift of God: Not of works, lest any man should boast**" (Ephesians 2:8-9). Men are saved when they believe the gospel of God's grace. The scripture does NOT say, "Work *on* your own salvation," or "Work *for* your own salvation," because "Salvation is of the LORD" (Jonah 2:9)! The salvation of the soul has never been attained by the good works of men. The scriptures are very clear about that. Religious people fall into the same deception as the Jews did. Paul said of them: "**For they being ignorant of God's righteousness, and going about to establish their own righteousness, have not submitted themselves unto the righteousness of God. For Christ *is* the end of the law for righteousness to every one that believeth**" (Romans 10:3-4).

When God justifies a man through faith, he pardons and clears him from all guilt, washes away his sins in the blood of Jesus Christ (Revelation 1:5), and puts the righteousness of Christ on his account. And so we read: "**Knowing that a man is not justified by the works of the law, but by the faith of Jesus Christ, even we have believed in Jesus Christ, that we might be justified by the faith of Christ, and not by the works of the law: for by the works of the law shall no flesh be justified**" (Galatians 2:16). Another time: "Be not thou therefore ashamed of the testimony of our Lord, nor of me his prisoner: but be thou partaker of the afflictions of the gospel according to the power of God; Who hath saved us, and called *us* with an holy calling, **not according to our works, but according to his own purpose and grace, which was given us in Christ Jesus before the world began**" (2 Timothy 1:8-9). Yet again: "**Not by works of righteousness which we have done, but according to his mercy he saved us, by the washing of regeneration, and renewing of the Holy Ghost; Which he shed on us abundantly through Jesus Christ our Saviour; That being justified by his grace, we should be made heirs according to the hope of eternal life**" (Titus 3:5-7).

The last section of Philippians 2:12 says, "...with fear and trembling."

Some commentaries on the scriptures degrade the word *fear* to mean reverential trust. This definition does not come from the scriptures, but from man's faulty watering down of God's word. *Fear* according to the Noah Webster 1828 Dictionary is "a painful emotion or passion excited by an expectation of evil, or the apprehension of impending danger. Fear is accompanied with a desire to avoid or ward off the expected evil. Fear is an uneasiness of mind, upon the thought of future evil likely to befall us. Fear is the passion of our nature which excites us to provide for our security, on the approach of evil." When coupled, as it is here, with "trembling," there can be no doubt that the fear of the Lord in the believer is the subject here.

The kings and judges of the earth are warned of the possibility of being dashed in pieces, and of perishing from the way, because of the wrath of the Son of God. Therefore, they are told to serve the LORD with *fear,* and to rejoice with *trembling.* They are to fear God for their very lives! The psalmist records the words of the Father to the Son, saying: "Thou *art* my Son; this day have I begotten thee. Ask of me, and I shall give *thee* the heathen *for* thine inheritance, and the uttermost parts of the earth *for* thy possession. **Thou shalt break them with a rod of iron; thou shalt dash them in pieces like a potter's vessel. Be wise now therefore, O ye kings: be instructed, ye judges of the earth. Serve the LORD with fear, and rejoice with trembling. Kiss the Son, lest he be angry, and ye perish *from* the way, when his wrath is kindled but a little. Blessed *are* all they that put their trust in him**" (Psalm 2:7-12).

BELIEVERS HAVE GOOD REASON TO FEAR GOD

The Lord Jesus Christ told his apostles not to fear men, but to fear God, saying: "**And fear not them which kill the body, but are not able to kill the soul: but rather fear him which is able to destroy both soul and body in hell**" (Matthew 10:28). But what do the born again children of God have to fear? The perfect love of God toward them in Jesus Christ has cast out all fear of eternal judgment for them (1 John 4:18). Yet we read that believers are told: "Having therefore these promises, dearly beloved, let us cleanse ourselves from all filthiness of the flesh and spirit, **perfecting holiness in the fear of God**" (2 Corinthians 7:1).

The Hebrew believers are told: "And let us consider one another to provoke unto love and to good works: Not forsaking the assembling of ourselves together, as the manner of some *is*; but exhorting *one another*: and so much the more, as ye see the day approaching. **For if we sin wilfully after that we have received the knowledge of the truth, there remaineth no more sacrifice for sins, [b] ut a certain fearful looking for of judgment and fiery indignation, which**

shall devour the adversaries" (Hebrews 10:24-27). The Lord will not devour his children, but he will devour the *adversaries* of the LORD: "**The adversaries of the LORD shall be broken to pieces; out of heaven shall he thunder upon them**: the LORD shall judge the ends of the earth; and he shall give strength unto his king, and exalt the horn of his anointed" (1 Samuel 2:10). "**Thine hand shall be lifted up upon thine adversaries, and all thine enemies shall be cut off**" (Micah 5:9). "God *is* jealous, and the LORD revengeth; the LORD revengeth, and *is* furious; **the LORD will take vengeance on his adversaries, and he reserveth *wrath* for his enemies**" (Nahum 1:2).

The writer of Hebrews continues: "**He that despised Moses' law died without mercy under two or three witnesses: Of how much sorer punishment, suppose ye, shall he be thought worthy, who hath trodden under foot the Son of God, and hath counted the blood of the covenant, wherewith he was sanctified, an unholy thing, and hath done despite unto the Spirit of grace? For we know him that hath said, Vengeance *belongeth* unto me, I will recompense, saith the Lord. And again, The Lord shall judge his people. *It is* a fearful thing to fall into the hands of the living God**" (Hebrews 10:28-31). Please notice what the scripture is saying: "**The Lord shall judge his people**." They are in the hands of the living God (John 10:27-30). They should fear and tremble while they praise and rejoice in God's mercy!

WHY SHOULD BORN AGAIN BELIEVERS FEAR GOD?

1. God will judge and chasten them for their disobedience. Speaking of the Lord's Supper, Paul wrote: "**For he that eateth and drinketh unworthily, eateth and drinketh damnation to himself, not discerning the Lord's body. For this cause many *are* weak and sickly among you, and many sleep. For if we would judge ourselves, we should not be judged. But when we are judged, we are chastened of the Lord, that we should not be condemned with the world**" (1 Corinthians 11:29-32). Those who were eating and drinking the Lord's Supper unworthily received the Lord's chastening in the form of sickness and early death.
2. They may lose the rewards they have laboured for: "**Look to yourselves, that we lose not those things which we have wrought, but that we receive a full reward**" (2 John 1:8).
3. To escape the judgment of God upon themselves and their family: "By faith Noah, being warned of God of things not seen as yet, **moved with fear**, prepared an ark to the saving of his house; by the which he condemned the world, and became heir of the righteousness which

is by faith" (Hebrews 11:7). Noah feared destruction by the flood, so he obeyed God and built the ark. The Apostle Peter wrote: "And if ye call on the Father, who without respect of persons judgeth according to every man's work, **pass the time of your sojourning *here* in fear**" (1 Peter 1:17).

4. Because "the fear of the Lord" is a good thing: "Behold, the fear of the Lord, that is wisdom; and to depart from evil *is* understanding" (Job 28:28); "The fear of the LORD *is* clean, enduring for ever: the judgments of the LORD *are* true *and* righteous altogether" (Psalm 19:9). "The fear of the LORD *is* the beginning of wisdom: a good understanding have all they that do *his commandments*: his praise endureth for ever" (Psalm 111:10). "The fear of the LORD *is* the beginning of knowledge: *but* fools despise wisdom and instruction" (Proverbs 1:7). "The fear of the LORD *is* to hate evil: pride, and arrogancy, and the evil way, and the froward mouth, do I [God] hate" (Proverbs 8:13). "The fear of the LORD *is* the beginning of wisdom: and the knowledge of the holy *is* understanding" (Proverbs 9:10). "The fear of the LORD prolongeth days: but the years of the wicked shall be shortened" (Proverbs 10:27). "In the fear of the LORD *is* strong confidence: and his children shall have a place of refuge. The fear of the LORD *is* a fountain of life, to depart from the snares of death" (Proverbs 14:26-27). "The fear of the LORD *is* the instruction of wisdom; and before honour *is* humility" (Proverbs 15:33). "By mercy and truth iniquity is purged: and by the fear of the LORD *men* depart from evil" (Proverbs 16:6). "The fear of the LORD *tendeth* to life: and *he that hath it* shall abide satisfied; he shall not be visited with evil" (Proverbs 19:23). "By humility *and* the fear of the LORD *are* riches, and honour, and life" (Proverbs 22:4). "Let not thine heart envy sinners: but *be thou* in the fear of the LORD all the day long" (Proverbs 23:17). "Then had the churches rest throughout all Judaea and Galilee and Samaria, and were edified; and walking in the fear of the Lord, and in the comfort of the Holy Ghost, were multiplied" (Acts 9:31).

GOD WORKS IN THE BELIEVER

Philippians 2:13 says, "For it is God which worketh in you both to will and to do of *his* good pleasure." When these believers received the Lord Jesus Christ by believing "the gospel of the grace of God" (Acts 20:24), "**how that Christ died for our sins according to the scriptures; And that he was buried, and that he rose again the third day according to the scriptures**" (1 Corinthians

15:3-4), God gave them "power to become the sons of God" (John 1:12-14). This "power" is the permanent indwelling of the Holy Spirit in every born again believer. When writing to the Ephesian believers, the Apostle Paul outlined the progressive sequence that leads to every believer's salvation: "That we should be to the praise of his [God's] glory, who first trusted in Christ. In whom ye also *trusted*, after that ye heard the word of truth, the gospel of your salvation: in whom also after that ye believed, ye were sealed with that holy Spirit of promise, [w]hich is the earnest of our inheritance until the redemption of the purchased possession, unto the praise of his glory" (Ephesians 1:12-14).

And we have the promise: "**But if the Spirit of him that raised up Jesus from the dead dwell in you, he that raised up Christ from the dead shall also quicken your mortal bodies by his Spirit that dwelleth in you**" (Romans 8:9-11). God quickens our mortal bodies and works in us by his grace to labor abundantly with God. The Apostle Paul wrote: "**But by the grace of God I am what I am: and his grace which *was bestowed* upon me was not in vain; but I laboured more abundantly than they all: yet not I, but the grace of God which was with me**" (1 Corinthians 15:10). As well, Paul wrote to the believers at Corinth: "**And God *is* able to make all grace abound toward you; that ye, always having all sufficiency in all *things*, may abound to every good work**" (2 Corinthians 9:8).

The God of peace works inside the born again believer: "Now the God of peace, that brought again from the dead our Lord Jesus, that great shepherd of the sheep, through the blood of the everlasting covenant, [m]ake you perfect in every good work to do his will, **working in you that which is wellpleasing in his sight, through Jesus Christ; to whom *be* glory for ever and ever. Amen**" (Hebrews 13:20-21).

Therefore the Spirit of God, the Spirit of Christ, dwells in all born again believers, and, "**if any man have not the Spirit of Christ, he is none of his**" (Romans 8:9)! Many scriptures confirm the presence of God's Spirit in the born again believer. Some of those scriptures are: "**One God and Father of all, who *is* above all, and through all, and in you all**" (Ephesians 4:6). "**Know ye not that ye are the temple of God, and *that* the Spirit of God dwelleth in you?**" (1 Corinthians 3:16). "**What? know ye not that your body is the temple of the Holy Ghost *which is* in you, which ye have of God, and ye are not your own?**" (1 Corinthians 6:19). "**To whom God would make known what *is* the riches of the glory of this mystery among the Gentiles; which is Christ in you, the hope of glory**" (Colossians 1:27). "**Ye are of God, little children, and**

have overcome them: because greater is he that is in you, than he that is in the world" (1 John 4:4).

The presence of the Spirit of God in the believer not only gives him *power*, but also gives him *assurance* of his relationship with God: "**Hereby know we that we dwell in him, and he in us, because he hath given us of his Spirit**" (1 John 4:13). Believers, who walk in the light of God's word (1 John 1:7) are confident that God will finish what he has started in them: "**Being confident of this very thing, that he which hath begun a good work in you will perform *it* until the day of Jesus Christ**" (Philippians 1:6). If you do not have God's Spirit, then you are not one of God's children! "**Examine yourselves, whether ye be in the faith; prove your own selves. Know ye not your own selves, how that Jesus Christ is in you, except ye be reprobates?**" (2 Corinthians 13:5). Only you yourself can "make your calling and election sure" (2 Peter 1:10)!

After we are saved by believing "the gospel of the grace of God" (Acts 20:24), the work of the Lord Jesus Christ on the cross on our behalf, then the scripture goes on to say: "**For we are his workmanship, created in Christ Jesus unto good works, which God hath before ordained that we should walk in them**" (Ephesians 2:10). God's will for every born again believer is for him to walk in obedience to his commandments, and to demonstrate to the world the goodness, grace, and power of God! A believer walking after the Holy Spirit will glorify the Lord Jesus Christ (John 16:14), who only is worthy "to receive glory and honour" (Revelation 4:11). The Lord Jesus Christ said, "**Let your light so shine before men, that they may see your good works, and glorify your Father which is in heaven**" (Matthew 5:16).

SANCTIFIED BY THE WORD OF TRUTH

After the Ephesians were saved and "sanctified by faith" (Acts 26:18) that is in Christ, Paul told these Ephesian elders: "And now, brethren, I commend you to God, and to the word of his grace, which is able to build you up, and to give you an inheritance among all them which are sanctified" (Acts 20:32). There is an inheritance awaiting all those who will walk after the Spirit of God and labor together with God (1 Corinthians 3:9) during the remainder of their lives here on earth. Furthermore, there can be no further sanctification of the believer without the word of God. The Lord Jesus prayed for his disciples: "**Sanctify them through thy truth: thy word is truth**" (John 17:17). The Lord told the Jews which believed on him: "**If ye continue in my word, *then* are ye my disciples indeed; And ye shall know the truth, and the truth shall make**

you free" (John 8:31-32). Paul wrote to the Thessalonians' believers: "**For this cause also thank we God without ceasing, because, when ye received the word of God which ye heard of us, ye received *it* not *as* the word of men, but as it is in truth, the word of God, which effectually worketh also in you that believe**" (1 Thessalonians 2:13). The word of God will have great effect upon you if you read and obey all of it that pertains to you! Quoting Deuteronomy 8:3, the Lord Jesus told the devil: "**It is written, Man shall not live by bread alone, but by every word that proceedeth out of the mouth of God**" (Matthew 4:4).

FILLED WITH THE SPIRIT

While it is certainly true that every born again believer is indwelt by the Holy Spirit, every believer is not filled with the Spirit! Believers are commanded: "**And be not drunk with wine, wherein is excess; but be filled with the Spirit; Speaking to yourselves in psalms and hymns and spiritual songs, singing and making melody in your heart to the Lord**" (Ephesians 5:18-19). Paul also wrote to the believers in the Colossian church: "**Let the word of Christ dwell in you richly in all wisdom; teaching and admonishing one another in psalms and hymns and spiritual songs, singing with grace in your hearts to the Lord**" (Colossians 3:16). It is important to notice that the results of letting the word of Christ dwell in you, and being filled with the Spirit are the same! The believer who is filled with the words of God will also be filled with the Spirit of God, simply because the words of the Lord: "***they* are spirit, and *they* are life**" (John 6:63)!

SPIRITUAL GROWTH

All born again believers begin their spiritual walk, after the Spirit, as newborn babies. Therefore they are commanded: "**As newborn babes, desire the sincere milk of the word, that ye may grow thereby: If so be ye have tasted that the Lord *is* gracious**" (1 Peter 2:2-3). All believers have tasted that the Lord is gracious, because we were saved by God's grace! Furthermore, after being born of the Spirit, "**we are his workmanship, created in Christ Jesus unto good works, which God hath before ordained that we should walk in them**" (Ephesians 2:10).

The Apostle Peter gives the spiritual progression of a born again believer who continues in the word of God and is obedient to it. By his obedience to the word, the faithful believer is given the power to walk in this world without falling: "**And beside this, giving all diligence, add to your faith virtue; and to virtue knowledge; And to knowledge temperance; and to temperance patience; and to patience godliness; And to godliness brotherly kindness; and to brotherly kindness charity. For if these things be in you, and abound, they make *you that ye shall* neither *be* barren nor unfruitful in the knowledge of our Lord Jesus Christ. But he that lacketh these things is blind, and cannot see afar off, and hath forgotten that he was purged from his old sins. Wherefore the rather, brethren, give diligence to make your calling and election sure: for if ye do these things, ye shall never fall: For so an entrance shall be ministered unto you abundantly into the everlasting kingdom of our Lord and Saviour Jesus Christ**" (2 Peter 1:5-11).

THE EVER FLOWING WELL OF LIVING WATER

Over fourteen hundred years before Christ, when Moses struck the rock in the wilderness, the water came out of it for the people to drink (Exodus 17:5-6). This was a prophetical picture or "similitude" (Hosea 12:10) of the crucifixion of Christ, out of whom would flow the living water of the Holy Ghost. The Apostle Paul wrote: "Moreover, brethren, I would not that ye should be ignorant, how that all our fathers were under the cloud, and all passed through the sea; And were all baptized unto Moses in the cloud and in the sea; And did all eat the same spiritual meat; **And did all drink the same spiritual drink: for they drank of that spiritual Rock that followed them: and that Rock was Christ**" (1 Corinthians 10:1-4).

Over seven hundred years before the birth of Jesus Christ, the prophet Isaiah referred to this "living water," when he wrote: "**Behold, God *is* my salvation; I will trust, and not be afraid: for the LORD JEHOVAH *is* my strength and *my* song; he also is become my salvation. Therefore with joy shall ye draw water out of the wells of salvation**" (Isaiah 12:2-3).

Over six hundred years before Christ, the prophet Jeremiah wrote of the rebellion of the children of Israel who had forsaken the LORD, who is the fountain of living waters: "**For my people have committed two evils; they have forsaken me the fountain of living waters, *and* hewed them out cisterns, broken cisterns, that can hold no water**" (Jeremiah 2:13). In addition, Jeremiah wrote: "**O LORD, the hope of Israel, all that forsake thee shall be ashamed, *and* they that depart from me shall be written in the earth, because they have forsaken the LORD, the fountain of living waters**" (Jeremiah 17:13).

The Lord Jesus Christ went out of his way so that a poor sinful woman of Samaria might receive the gift of eternal life from him. He met her at Jacob's well (John 4:6). After the woman questioned why the Lord had asked her for a drink, "**Jesus answered and said unto her, If thou knewest the gift of God, and who it is that saith to thee, Give me to drink; thou wouldest have asked of him, and he would have given thee living water. The woman saith unto him, Sir, thou hast nothing to draw with, and the well is deep: from whence then hast thou that living water? Art thou greater than our father Jacob, which gave us the well, and drank thereof himself, and his children, and his cattle? Jesus answered and said unto her, Whosoever drinketh of this water shall thirst again: But whosoever drinketh of the water that I shall give him shall never thirst; but the water that I shall give him shall be in him a well of water springing up into everlasting life**" (John 4:10-14).

CONCLUSION

The Lord spoke to the people of that "**living water**," which he identified as "**the Holy Ghost**": "In the last day, that great *day* of the feast, Jesus stood and cried, saying, If any man thirst, let him come unto me, and drink. He that believeth on me, as the scripture hath said, **out of his belly shall flow rivers of living water. (But this spake he of the Spirit, which they that believe on him should receive: for the Holy Ghost was not yet *given*; because that Jesus was not yet glorified.**)" (John 7:37-39).

The question now arises, will you receive Jesus Christ, the fountain of living waters today? Waiting could result in your eternal damnation!

"**Believe on the Lord Jesus Christ, and thou shalt be saved**" (Acts 16:31).

Chapter 24

Pressing On

If there is a war for anything in life than you can be sure that any Christian will experience a full-scale assault from the kingdom of hell against him and his faith in Christ. It is my hope that as you read this sermon outline that you will be encouraged and challenged to press on and continue the good fight of faith by the power of the Lord Jesus Christ. Our sermon outline shall come from the scriptural text of Philippians 3:7-14, which says, "But what things were gain to me, those I counted loss for Christ. Yea doubtless, and I count all things *but* loss for the excellency of the knowledge of Christ Jesus my Lord: for whom I have suffered the loss of all things, and do count them *but* dung, that I may win Christ, And be found in him, not having mine own righteousness, which is of the law, but that which is through the faith of Christ, the righteousness which is of God by faith: That I may know him, and the power of his resurrection, and the fellowship of his sufferings, being made conformable unto his death; If by any means I might attain unto the resurrection of the dead. Not as though I had already attained, either were already perfect: but I follow after, if that I may apprehend that for which also I am apprehended of Christ Jesus. Brethren, I count not myself to have apprehended: but *this* one thing *I do*, forgetting those things which are behind, and reaching forth unto those things which are before, I press toward the mark for the prize of the high calling of God in Christ Jesus."

We begin at Philippians 3:7, which says, "But what things were gain to me, those I counted loss for Christ." The things that "were gain" to Paul were the things of the flesh, mentioned in the previous three verses. Make a note that the world would highly esteem these things, but Paul understands that they are merely temporal things that he is privileged to count as a loss for Christ. Those things mentioned were: (1) he was a circumcised man of the stock of Israel; (2) he was "an Hebrew of the Hebrews"; (3) "as touching the law, a Pharisee"; (4) he was a religious zealot persecuting the church; and (5) he was blameless as pertaining to the righteousness of the law.

Paul confidently is able to say he counts these things as a loss for Christ because he has come to understand God's perspective: that God is not in the least impressed with a man's *genealogy*. It makes no difference to God whether you were born into the household of a king, or that you were born of a poor beggar! It makes no difference to God whether your skin is white, yellow, red, brown, or black. Anyone who boasts of his genealogy is foolish and proud. For we are all born into sin, being the offspring of Adam: "**Wherefore, as by one man sin entered into the world, and death by sin; and so death passed upon all men, for that all have sinned**" (Romans 5:12).

Furthermore, God is not impressed with your *religion*! The Lord Jesus Christ did not come into the world to start a religion; he "**came into the world to save sinners**" (1 Timothy 1:15), and he is building a "church" (Matthew 16:18) on the "sure foundation" (Isaiah 28:16) of himself (Matthew 16:18). And the members of his church "**are all the children of God by faith in Christ Jesus**" (Galatians 3:26).

Also God is not interested in your so called religious "works of righteousness," for "**we are all as an unclean *thing*, and all our righteousnesses *are* as filthy rags; and we all do fade as a leaf; and our iniquities, like the wind, have taken us away**" (Isaiah 64:6). This was the great error of the religious Jews, who also had "a zeal of God, but not according to knowledge. Romans 10:2-4 says, "**For they being ignorant of God's righteousness, and going about to establish their own righteousness, have not submitted themselves unto the righteousness of God. For Christ *is* the end of the law for righteousness to every one that believeth.**" In his letter to Titus, Paul admitted that we all started wrong, and that we must all be justified by God's grace: "For we ourselves also were sometimes foolish, disobedient, deceived, serving divers lusts and pleasures, living in malice and envy, hateful, *and* hating one another. But after that the kindness and love of God our Saviour toward man appeared, [**n]ot by works of righteousness which we have done, but according to his mercy he**

saved us, by the washing of regeneration, and renewing of the Holy Ghost; Which he shed on us abundantly through Jesus Christ our Saviour; That being justified by his grace, we should be made heirs according to the hope of eternal life" (Titus 3:3-7). Paul again makes it very clear to the Ephesians that salvation is by the grace of God through faith in the Lord Jesus Christ and his gospel: "**For by grace are ye saved through faith; and that not of yourselves: *it is* the gift of God: Not of works, lest any man should boast**" (Ephesians 2:8-9).

The first major section of Philippians 3:8 says, "Yea doubtless, and I count all things *but* loss for the excellency of the knowledge of Christ Jesus my Lord: for whom I have suffered the loss of all things, and do count them *but* dung,..."

Paul, when he was saved, gave up many things in regard to this earthly life. He abandoned the hope of honour and distinction as a religious ruler of the Jews; he sacrificed every prospect of gain or ease; and he gave up his friends, and separated himself from those whom he loved. We do not know the exact extent of his losses when he began to follow Jesus Christ. He was probably excommunicated by the Jews, and disowned by his own family. Some Jewish families even today disown their sons and daughters who believe on the Lord Jesus Christ. Nevertheless, Paul here admits that "the excellency of the knowledge of Christ" is not to be compared with the vain things of this life that will soon fade away and be gone forever!

After suffering many things for the cause and service and glory of Jesus Christ, Paul wrote: "**For our light affliction, which is but for a moment, worketh for us a far more exceeding *and* eternal weight of glory; While we look not at the things which are seen, but at the things which are not seen: for the things which are seen *are* temporal; but the things which are not seen *are* eternal**" (2 Corinthians 4:17-18). Many times Paul announced that suffering was a part of serving the Lord in this life: "**Yea, and all that will live godly in Christ Jesus shall suffer persecution**" (2 Timothy 3:12); "**And if children, then heirs; heirs of God, and joint–heirs with Christ; if so be that we suffer with *him*, that we may be also glorified together. For I reckon that the sufferings of this present time *are* not worthy *to be compared* with the glory which shall be revealed in us**" (Romans 8:17-18).

Speaking to the people and to his disciples, the Lord Jesus Christ said: "**Whosoever will come after me, let him deny himself, and take up his cross, and follow me. For whosoever will save his life shall lose it; but whosoever**

shall lose his life for my sake and the gospel's, the same shall save it. For what shall it profit a man, if he shall gain the whole world, and lose his own soul? Or what shall a man give in exchange for his soul? Whosoever therefore shall be ashamed of me and of my words in this adulterous and sinful generation; of him also shall the Son of man be ashamed, when he cometh in the glory of his Father with the holy angels" (Mark 8:34-38).

THE VANITY OF THIS WORLD

Solomon gave the right perspective on the things of this world in the book of Ecclesiastes, when he wrote: "**Vanity of vanities, saith the Preacher, vanity of vanities; all *is* vanity**" (Ecclesiastics 1:2). By "all" Solomon includes all works "under the sun" (Ecclesiastics 1:14) of this earth, the pleasure, grandeur, wisdom, the life of man, childhood, youth, and length of days, the forgetfulness brought about by the grave, wandering and unsatisfied desires, riches and possessions, and the unrighteousness committed by the human governments of the world. Then Solomon gives his conclusion and recommendations to all: "**Let us hear the conclusion of the whole matter: Fear God, and keep his commandments: for this *is* the whole *duty* of man. For God shall bring every work into judgment, with every secret thing, whether *it be* good, or whether *it be* evil**" (Ecclesiastics 12:13-14). In other words, if you waste your life on the vain, temporal, things of this earth, not fearing God, then you will eventually be condemned as an unbelieving sinner and cast into "**the lake which burneth with fire and brimstone: which is the second death**" (Revelation 21:8)!

So Paul wrote: "**I have suffered the loss of all things, and do count them *but* dung.**" He counted his earthly life but dung—the excrement, or feces, of animals! Paul knew that the knowledge of Jesus Christ, and all that comes with that glorious knowledge, is far better than anything this old vain world has to offer! Paul wrote to the Corinthians: "**Let no man deceive himself. If any man among you seemeth to be wise in this world, let him become a fool, that he may be wise. For the wisdom of this world is foolishness with God. For it is written, He taketh the wise in their own craftiness. And again, The Lord knoweth the thoughts of the wise, that they are vain**" (1 Corinthians 3:18-20).

Some of the world's most foolish men actually have very brilliant minds, and yet "**they became vain in their imaginations, and their foolish heart** [has become] **darkened**" (Romans 1:21). They also have "the understanding darkened, being alienated from the life of God through the ignorance that is in them, because of the blindness of their heart" (Ephesians 4:18). These men are greatly deceived! The gospel "**is hid to them that are lost: In whom the god of this world** [Satan] **hath blinded the minds of them which believe not, lest the light of the glorious gospel of Christ, who is the image of God, should shine unto them**" (2 Corinthians 4:3-4). Before his miraculous conversion, Paul—no doubt also a man with a brilliant mind, had such a blinded heart that he really believed that he was doing service to God by persecuting and murdering God's people (John 16:2)!

WINNING CHRIST

Philippians 3:8 finishes with the words, "...that I may win Christ." It is essential to realize that Paul is *not* speaking here about winning or gaining his eternal salvation, for that is a "free gift" (Romans 5:15-18) received by faith, for "the gospel of Christ...is the power of God unto salvation to every one that believeth; to the Jew first, and also to the Greek" (Romans 1:16). Paul was already saved, and he knew it (Romans 8:38-39). In the context of this passage, we can find what Paul was striving to win. In general he was "striving together for the faith of the gospel" (Philippians 1:27).

Continuing on with our sermon, Philippians 3:9 says, "And be found in him, not having mine own righteousness, which is of the law, but that which is through the faith of Christ, the righteousness which is of God by faith." Paul knew that no man, no offspring of the first Adam, was righteous on his own merits: "**As it is written, There is none righteous, no, not one**" (Romans 3:10), "**For all have sinned, and come short of the glory of God**" (Romans 3:23). He would have to agree with the declaration of God through the prophet Isaiah, who wrote: "**But we are all as an unclean *thing*, and all our righteousnesses *are* as filthy rags; and we all do fade as a leaf; and our iniquities, like the wind, have taken us away**" (Isaiah 64:6).

At one time Paul had been a Pharisee of Israel, and had been blinded to the truth of the gospel of Christ. Then years later after his conversion he wrote to the church in Rome that the Israelites "**have a zeal of God, but not according to knowledge. For they being ignorant of God's righteousness, and going about to establish their own righteousness, have not submitted themselves unto the righteousness of God. For Christ *is* the end of the law for righteousness to every one that believeth**" (Romans 10:2-4). In addition, he was inspired by God to write: "**But now the righteousness of God without the law is manifested, being witnessed by the law and the prophets; Even the righteousness of God *which is* by faith of Jesus Christ unto all and upon all them that believe: for there is no difference**" (Romans 3:21-22).

Next in our sermon, Paul wrote in Philippians 3:10, "That I may know him [Christ], and the power of his resurrection, and the fellowship of his sufferings, being made conformable unto his death."

KNOWLEDGE

What did Paul mean when he wrote that he wanted to win Christ? To *win* means to *gain*. Paul desired to gain more knowledge of Christ. Paul wanted to *win* "**the excellency of the knowledge of Christ Jesus**" (Philippians 3:8). In Paul's case, this knowledge would have to come from the previously written Old Testament scriptures, by special revelation from Jesus Christ (Galatians 1:12; 1 Corinthians 15:3-4; 1 Corinthians 11:23), by experience (1 Timothy 3:11; 4:17), and by prophecy (Romans 12:6; 1 Corinthians 12:10; 1 Timothy 1:18). For us today, we gain knowledge through the now completed Holy Bible and by our walk with the Lord as we labour together with God (1 Corinthians 3:9). In Philippians 3:10, Paul wrote: "**That I may know him**…"

To *meet* the Lord Jesus Christ through his word by faith as our Saviour is only the beginning of a lifetime of growing "**in grace, and *in* the knowledge of our Lord and Saviour Jesus Christ**" (2 Peter 3:8). We will never cease to grow in our knowledge of him, for: "**Great *is* our Lord, and of great power: his understanding *is* infinite**" (Psalm 147:5)!

POWER

Paul wanted to *know* and experience "**the power of his resurrection**" (Philippians 3:10). Paul knew that he was "risen with Christ" (Colossians 3:1). Now he was seeking "those things which are above, where Christ sitteth on the right hand of God" (Colossians 3:1). Paul wrote to the believers in Christ: "Therefore we are buried with him by baptism into death: that **like as Christ was raised up from the dead by the glory of the Father, even so we also should walk in newness of life. For if we have been planted together in the likeness of his death, we shall be also *in the likeness* of *his* resurrection: Knowing this, that our old man is crucified with *him*, that the body of sin might be destroyed, that henceforth we should not serve sin. For he that is dead is freed from sin**. Now if we be dead with Christ, we believe that we shall also live with him: Knowing that Christ being raised from the dead dieth no more; death hath no more dominion over him. For in that he died, he died unto sin once: but in that he liveth, he liveth unto God. **Likewise reckon ye also yourselves to be dead indeed unto sin, but alive unto God through**

Jesus Christ our Lord" (Romans 6:4-11). Paul was seeking for the power to live his life for the glory of God!

All born again believers have the Spirit of Christ. Paul wrote concerning the mystery of the indwelling Christ in all believers, saying: "To whom God would make known what *is* the riches of the glory of this mystery among the Gentiles; **which is Christ in you, the hope of glory**" (Colossians 1:27). The Spirit of Christ *only* indwells those who have received Jesus Christ by faith and have been "born of the Spirit" (John 3:8), for "**if any man have not the Spirit of Christ, he is none of his**" (Romans 8:9). Paul wrote to Timothy that "**God hath not given us the spirit of fear; but of power, and of love, and of a sound mind. Be not thou therefore ashamed of the testimony of our Lord, nor of me his prisoner: but be thou partaker of the afflictions of the gospel according to the power of God**" (2 Timothy 1:7-8).

The Lord Jesus Christ is "**the power of God, and the wisdom of God**" (1 Corinthians 1:23-24). Therefore Paul desired to "win Christ," to gain the power of the Spirit of Christ that dwelled in him. Every believer should attend a Bible believing church and submit himself to the preaching of Jesus Christ and "**the glorious gospel of Christ**" (2 Corinthians 4:4; Hebrews 10:25). "**For the preaching of the cross is to them that perish foolishness; but unto us which are saved it is the power of God**" (1 Corinthians 1:18). The Apostle Paul told the Corinthians: "And my speech and my preaching *was* not with enticing words of man's wisdom, but **in demonstration of the Spirit and of power: That your faith should not stand in the wisdom of men, but in the power of God**" (1 Corinthians 2:4-5). In his second letter to the Corinthians, Paul wrote concerning Christ, "**For though he was crucified through weakness, yet he liveth by the power of God. For we also are weak in him, but we shall live with him by the power of God toward you**" (2 Corinthians 13:4).

The Apostle Paul also prayed for the church at Ephesus: "Wherefore I also, after I heard of your faith in the Lord Jesus, and love unto all the saints, Cease not to give thanks for you, making mention of you in my prayers; **That the God of our Lord Jesus Christ, the Father of glory, may give unto you the spirit of wisdom and revelation in the knowledge of him: The eyes of your understanding being enlightened; that ye may know what is the hope of his calling, and what the riches of the glory of his inheritance in the saints, And what *is* the exceeding greatness of his power to us–ward who believe, according to the working of his mighty power, Which he wrought in Christ, when he raised him from the dead, and set *him* at his own right hand**

in the heavenly *places*, [f]ar above all principality, and power, and might, and dominion, and every name that is named, not only in this world, but also in that which is to come: And hath put all *things* under his feet, and gave him *to be* the head over all *things* to the church, [w]hich is his body, the fulness of him that filleth all in all" (Ephesians 1:15-23). You and I must have his power to resist the temptation to fulfill the desires of our lustful flesh. Without the power of the Spirit of Christ, you and I are weak and easily defeated by the snares and wicked imaginations of the devil. But, thank God, "**greater is he that is in you, than he that is in the world**" (1 John 4:4).

The power of the Spirit of the risen Christ enables believers to forsake lust and live according to the will of God: "**Forasmuch then as Christ hath suffered for us in the flesh, arm yourselves likewise with the same mind: for he that hath suffered in the flesh hath ceased from sin; That he no longer should live the rest of *his* time in the flesh to the lusts of men, but to the will of God**" (1 Peter 4:1-2). And, praise the Lord, born again believers "**are kept by the power of God through faith unto salvation ready to be revealed in the last time**" (1 Peter 1:5).

FELLOWSHIP

Paul desired to know "**the fellowship of his sufferings**" (Philippians 3:10). This fellowship of Christ's sufferings will certainly come to all who will live for him: "**Yea, and all that will live godly in Christ Jesus shall suffer persecution**" (2 Timothy 3:12)! This world hates Jesus Christ, therefore it will hate you if you live for and preach Jesus Christ to them (John 15:18). Paul and Barnabas "returned again to Lystra, and *to* Iconium, and Antioch, [c]**onfirming the souls of the disciples, *and* exhorting them to continue in the faith, and that we must through much tribulation enter into the kingdom of God**" (Acts 14:21-22). Paul also told the believers in Thessalonica that we are appointed to afflictions and tribulation (1 Thessalonians 3:3-4).

Peter said that we should be ready to take it patiently when we suffer for doing well: "**For even hereunto were ye called: because Christ also suffered for us, leaving us an example, that ye should follow his steps**" (1 Peter 2:20-21). Peter also wrote: "**But and if ye suffer for righteousness' sake, happy *are ye*: and be not afraid of their terror, neither be troubled**" (1 Peter 3:14). According to Peter, all believers will face fiery trials, which will make us "**partakers of Christ's sufferings; that, when his glory shall be revealed, ye may be glad also with exceeding joy**" (1 Peter 4:12-13). Peter goes on to instruct: "If ye be reproached for the name of Christ, happy *are ye*; for the spirit of glory and of God resteth upon you: on their part he is evil spoken of, but on your part he is glorified. But let none of you suffer as a murderer, or *as* a thief, or *as* an evildoer, or as a busybody in other men's matters. **Yet if *any man suffer* as a Christian, let him not be ashamed; but let him glorify God on this behalf**" (1 Peter 4:12-16).

BEING MADE CONFORMABLE

God has predestinated *all* who are in Christ Jesus "***to be* conformed to the image of his Son, that he might be the firstborn among many brethren**" (Romans 8:29). As we "grow in grace, and in the knowledge of our Lord and Saviour Jesus Christ" (2 Peter 3:18), we come to know and experience the power of Christ's resurrection and the fellowship of his sufferings in our present lives, as we wait "for the adoption, *to wit*, the redemption of our body" (Romans 8:23). These trials, sufferings, temptations, and tribulations serve to conform us more and more into the image of our Saviour Jesus Christ.

Further, into our sermon, we come along to Philippians 3:11-12. The scriptures say, "If by any means I might attain unto the resurrection of the dead. Not as though I had already attained, either were already perfect: but I follow after, if that I may apprehend that for which also I am apprehended of Christ Jesus."

According to the Webster 1828 Dictionary, to "attain" means to reach; to come to or arrive at, by motion, bodily exertion, or efforts towards a place or object. It is abundantly clear that Paul was not speaking of simply reaching a *place* in the "resurrection of the just" (Luke 14:14) by his own efforts! Paul himself wrote: "**For we know that if our earthly house of *this* tabernacle were dissolved, we have a building of God, an house not made with hands, eternal in the heavens…Now he that hath wrought us for the selfsame thing *is* God, who also hath given unto us the earnest of the Spirit…For we must all appear before the judgment seat of Christ; that every one may receive the things *done* in *his* body, according to that he hath done, whether *it be* good or bad**" (2 Corinthians 5:1-10). By his own blood, the Lord Jesus Christ "**entered in once into the holy place, having obtained eternal redemption *for us***" (Hebrews 9:12). We were apprehended by God who called us by the gospel, and after being saved by grace through faith in the Lord Jesus Christ (Ephesians 2:8-9), we are now "**his workmanship, created in Christ Jesus unto good works, which God hath before ordained that we should walk in them**" (Ephesians 2:10). Therefore, we see that God has a purpose for each of our lives.

Paul is simply saying that he is following after Christ so that he may accomplish that which Christ has ordained for him to do. The same principle is found in Hebrews, where Paul exhorts the Hebrew believers: "**let us go on unto perfection**" (Hebrews 6:1). Again, with the same principle in mind, Paul wrote to Timothy: "**Therefore I endure all things for the elect's sakes, that they may also obtain the salvation which is in Christ Jesus <u>with eternal glory</u>**" (2 Timothy 2:10). The "elect" had already obtained salvation, but the apostle desired to see them obtain a resurrection [salvation] "**with eternal glory**," that is, "**a better resurrection**" (Hebrews 11:35).

PRESSING TOWARD THE MARK

The last section of our sermon deals with Philippians 3:13-14. In these verses Paul writes, "Brethren, I count not myself to have apprehended: but *this* one thing *I do*, forgetting those things which are behind, and reaching forth unto those things which are before, I press toward the mark for the prize of the high calling of God in Christ Jesus."

Some of us were saved at an older age after committing much sin in our lives. Although I know now that I "**have redemption through his blood, the forgiveness of sins, according to the riches of his grace**" (Ephesians 1:7), nevertheless, like David, I can still say, "**I acknowledge my transgressions: and my sin *is* ever before me**" (Psalm 51:3). Often Satan, "the accuser of our brethren" (Revelation 12:10), or one of his fellow devils, will bring into my thoughts sins that have been forgiven, but not forgotten by me; and I will try to forget them once again, knowing that God himself has chosen to remember them no more (Jeremiah 31:34; Hebrews 8:12; 10:17). Accordingly, as long as we are in this sinful flesh, we must continue the process of "forgetting" the past life and all of its sins. We must continually be "**Casting down imaginations, and every high thing that exalteth itself against the knowledge of God, and bringing into captivity every thought to the obedience of Christ**" (2 Corinthians 10:5). We must obey Paul's instruction to Timothy: "**Fight the good fight of faith, lay hold on eternal life, whereunto thou art also called, and hast professed a good profession before many witnesses**" (1 Timothy 6:12). Timothy already had eternal life. Paul was telling him to lay hold on it by faith, and live this present life "**in the power of his** [Christ's] **resurrection**" (Philippians 3:10).

In his last letter to Timothy, written from prison, we see that Paul actually did apprehend that for which he was apprehended (Philippians 3:12). Paul actually did reach the mark that he was pressing toward (Philippians 3:14). As

Paul awaited his execution by the Romans—historically he was reported to have been decapitated by Nero's guillotine. In prison he wrote to Timothy: "**For I am now ready to be offered, and the time of my departure is at hand** [Paul was ready "to depart, and to be with Christ; which is far better" (Philippians 1:23)]. **I have fought a good fight, I have finished *my* course, I have kept the faith**: **Henceforth there is laid up for me a crown of righteousness, which the Lord, the righteous judge, shall give me at that day: and not to me only, but unto all them also that love his appearing**" (2 Timothy 4:6-8).

CONCLUSION

Are you "**Looking for that blessed hope, and the glorious appearing of the great God and our Saviour Jesus Christ**" (Titus 2:13)? When the Lord comes, will you be caught up to meet him in the air (1 Thessalonians 4:16-18), or will God send you a strong delusion when the antichrist is revealed, to damn you, because you had not a love of the truth that you might be saved (2 Thessalonians 2:8-12)? The gospel, "**how that Christ died for our sins according to the scriptures; And that he was buried, and that he rose again the third day according to the scriptures**" (1 Corinthians 15:3-4), "**is the power of God unto salvation to every one that believeth**" (Romans 1:16).

"**Believe on the Lord Jesus Christ, and thou shalt be saved**" (Acts 16:31).

Chapter 25

Let Us Go On

Hebrews 6:1-12 tells us, "Therefore leaving the principles of the doctrine of Christ, let us go on unto perfection; not laying again the foundation of repentance from dead works, and of faith toward God, Of the doctrine of baptisms, and of laying on of hands, and of resurrection of the dead, and of eternal judgment. And this will we do, if God permit. For *it is* impossible for those who were once enlightened, and have tasted of the heavenly gift, and were made partakers of the Holy Ghost, And have tasted the good word of God, and the powers of the world to come, If they shall fall away, to renew them again unto repentance; seeing they crucify to themselves the Son of God afresh, and put *him* to an open shame. For the earth which drinketh in the rain that cometh oft upon it, and bringeth forth herbs meet for them by whom it is dressed, receiveth blessing from God: But that which beareth thorns and briers *is* rejected, and *is* nigh unto cursing; whose end *is* to be burned. But, beloved, we are persuaded better things of you, and things that accompany salvation, though we thus speak. For God *is* not unrighteous to forget your work and labour of love, which ye have shewed toward his name, in that ye have ministered to the saints, and do minister. And we desire that every one of you do shew the same diligence to the full assurance of hope unto the end: That ye be not slothful, but followers of them who through faith and patience inherit the promises."

This passage has often been misunderstood. Some have believed it to be speaking of salvation. However when we look at the passage in the light of the scriptures, we will see that the subject is not salvation at all, but rather Christian service. As we shall see, the subject is about the Christian going on in his daily walk with Jesus Christ in order to reach the mark set for him in his earthly life by the Lord.

I. THE PRINCIPLES (Hebrews 6:1-2)

Hebrews 6:1 starts off by saying, "**Therefore leaving the principles of the doctrine of Christ**..." This does not mean that we are to discard and forget about these principles. No, it means that we are to go beyond them, to move on past the milk stage of maturity (1 Peter 2:2) to the meat stage of our Christian growth. The word "Therefore" points back to what he had just said previously in Hebrews 5:12-14: that these Hebrew Christians had fallen short of the growth that was expected of them, and that they were still babies and "**unskilful in the word of righteousness**" (Hebrews 5:13). Perhaps they had failed to continue in the word (John 8:31-32), or if they had, they were not faithful doers of the word (James 1:22). Paul, like Peter, is telling these Hebrew Christians to add to their faith and build good works upon the foundation of Jesus Christ (1 Corinthians 3:11-13; 2 Peter 1:5-11).

God promises rewards and an abundant entrance into the kingdom of Jesus Christ for those who "**go on unto perfection**" in their lives, adding to their faith "**good works, which God hath before ordained that we should walk in them**" (Ephesians 2:10; 2 Peter 1:10-11). The man who does not add to his faith will be blind and ignorant, and may not even remember that he was saved (2 Peter 1:9)!

The "principles" are the "milk of the word" (1 Peter 2:2), called, "the first principles" (Hebrews 5:12). God does not want his people to remain babies! He wants them to mature and grow up! It is a tragic and regretful to see a man who has been saved for many years still to be in the baby stage of his Christian growth. He obviously does not love the Lord as he should or he would have obeyed God's commandment to grow (1 Peter 2:2).

Hebrews 6:1 continues with the thought, saying, "...**let us go on unto perfection...**" It is these words that I want us to center our thoughts upon; these words are the encouragement and subject of this entire passage. This is what we will do "**if God permit**" (Hebrews 6:3).

To "go on unto perfection" means that we are to constantly remain in the process of maturing into a child of God who is being conformed to the image of Jesus Christ (Romans 8:29). This is accomplished by submitting ourselves to God's word in our lives (Romans 12:1-2; James 4:7). Only by obeying the Lord's commandments (1 Corinthians 14:37) can we demonstrate that we love him (John 14:15), and only by obedience will we be able, by the grace of God, to grow up beyond the baby stage and mature into men of understanding (1 Corinthians 14:20).

Those Christians who never grow up spiritually are "choked with cares and riches and pleasures of this life, and bring no fruit to perfection" (Luke 8:14). They get sidetracked from the things that are essential for Christian growth. Some of those essentials needed for spiritual growth are Bible study (2 Timothy 2:15), church attendance (Hebrews 10:25), prayer and Bible reading (John 15:4-7), witnessing, and so on. The Christians who neglect the things of God never "go on unto perfection" (Hebrews 6:1) for the glory of God, and therefore have no results.

The next part of Hebrews 6:1 says,"...**not laying again the foundation**." The foundation for salvation is repentance and faith toward God, according to Acts 20:21.

Even if one could lose salvation, which one certainly cannot (1 John 5:13; John 6:37, 47; et al), the foundation cannot be laid again. The redemption that was purchased for us by the blood of Jesus Christ is eternal (Hebrews 9:12)!

THE SIX FIRST PRINCIPLES

Hebrews 6:1-2 informs us that there are six fundamental principles that a Christian should come to understand and know so that he can grow into a mature child of God for God's glory. Not understanding these basic principles not only hinders a Christian from growing in the grace of God, but is one of the reasons why so many people are deceived to believe the lies of cults and heresies who use the name of Jesus. These six principles are as follows:

1. **"Repentance from dead works."** This principle refers to repentance at salvation, since it is from "dead works" and from unbelief that we are saved from. Second Corinthians 7:10 says, "For godly sorrow worketh repentance to salvation not to be repented of: but the sorrow of the world worketh death." Only those individuals who have a godly sorrow unto

repentance, and who believe in their hearts on the Lord Jesus Christ, are truly saved. They are the individuals who "[God] *hath quickened*, who [Christians] were dead in trespasses and sins" (Ephesians 2:1).

2. **"Faith toward God."** Both repentance and faith are foundational for salvation. The apostle Paul reminded the Ephesian elders that he testified "both to the Jews, and also to the Greeks, **repentance** toward God, and **faith** toward our Lord Jesus Christ" (Acts 20:21). "For by grace are ye saved through faith; and that not of yourselves: *it is* the gift of God" (Ephesians 2:8). Galatians 3:26 tells us that Christians are children of God by faith in Christ Jesus. The reason is because without faith *it is* impossible to please *him*: for he that cometh to God must believe that he is, and *that* he is a rewarder of them that diligently seek him (Hebrews 11:6).
3. **"The doctrine of baptisms."** There are seven different baptisms in the Bible. An understanding of these is basic to the foundation for a Christian.
4. **"Laying on of hands."** When Paul and Barnabas were sent out on their first missionary journey, the disciples "fasted and prayed, and laid their hands on them" (Acts 13:3).
5. **"Resurrection of the dead."** A fundamental doctrine of the faith is that all people shall be resurrected. Acts 24:15 says, "And have hope toward God, which they themselves also allow, that there shall be a resurrection of the dead, both of the just and unjust."
6. **"Eternal judgment."** The doctrine of hell and the lake of fire is a first principle that is necessary to understand for spiritual maturity and bringing God glory. (Matthew 25:41, 46; Revelation 20:11-15)!

II. THE PROBLEM (Hebrews 6:3)

Hebrews 6:3 states, "**And this will we do, if God permit**." What will we do if God permit? Get saved? No, we are already saved! We who are already saved will "**go on unto perfection**" (Hebrews 6:1), "**if God permit**"! The "if" implies that some Christians are not permitted to go on unto perfection. These are Christians who refuse to add to their faith (2 Peter 1:5-11) and grow in maturity. Some of them refuse to believe the first principles, eternal hell or eternal salvation as examples. These people are destined to be spiritually "retarded" all of their lives, never growing up in the things of God. They will be miserable and without victory in their lives and constantly under the chastening hand of God. Although they do not lose their salvation, they lose their fellowship with the Lord here, and they will lose their rewards in heaven at "**the judgment seat of Christ**" (2 Corinthians 5:10).

Paul brought his body under subjection so that he would not become a "castaway" (1 Corinthians 9:27). Paul did not want God to put him on the shelf and take him out of service. Paul did not want to be someone who is not allowed to go on unto perfection. Paul said that he had not yet reached the perfection or the mark that God had set for him. But Paul was not working for salvation; he was pressing "**toward the mark for the prize of the high calling of God in Christ Jesus**" (Philippians 3:13-14).

AN IMPOSSIBILITY (Hebrews 6:4-6)

This section of scripture has been used by many heretics, cults, and deceivers to mislead and deceive people away from the truth of God's word and into a lie. The following are some of the false teachings commonly taught from this passage:

1. These are Christians who lost their salvation.
2. These are only professing believers who never really got saved.
3. The passage only applies to Jews in the tribulation period.
4. The verses are only hypothetical and purely conjectural.

Each of these false interpretations ignores the context of the passage, which is written to believers concerning their going on unto perfection. There is no doubt the passage is written to genuine believers because:

1. Paul includes himself in the group he writes to, using the words "us" (Hebrews 6:1) and "we" (Hebrews 6:3).
2. They have been "enlightened" (Hebrews 6:4).
3. They "have tasted of the heavenly gift" (Hebrews 6:4). To taste is to experience. New born babes in Christ "have tasted that the Lord is gracious" (1 Peter 2:2-3). The Lord Jesus Christ "tasted death for every man" (Hebrews 2:9).
4. They "were made partakers of the Holy Ghost" (Hebrews 6:4).
5. They "have tasted the good word of God" (Hebrews 6:5).
6. They have tasted "the powers of the world to come" (Hebrews 6:5). The world to come is only revealed by the Holy Ghost (1 Corinthians 2:9-10) who is only given to those who have received Jesus Christ (John 7:38-39).

Look again at the main emphasis of this passage: Hebrews 6:1-6 says, "**Therefore leaving the principles of the doctrine of Christ, let us go on unto**

perfection...And this will we do, if God permit...For it is impossible for those who were once enlightened...If they shall fall away, to renew them again unto repentance..."

A man who is content to remain a babe in Christ will reach a point when God's longsuffering with regard to his growth will come to an end. At this point, God will no longer allow him to "**go on unto perfection**" (Hebrews 6:1). As a result he will remain an immature baby Christian all of his life. At first he refuses to go on in obedience to God's command, then the time comes when God will not permit him to "go on unto perfection" (Hebrews 6:1), even though he wants to! God will not repent and allow the man to go on unto perfection, even if the man himself repents!

III. THE EXAMPLE OF ISRAEL

The scriptures give us a perfect example of this principle. The testimonies of the people of Israel happened unto them for ensamples: and they are written for our admonition, upon whom the ends of the world are come (1 Corinthians 10:11). God had a plan of perfection for the children of Israel when he brought them out of Egypt under the leadership of Moses. The account of the exodus, the wandering in the wilderness, and the taking of the Promised Land are an example of the redemption that God has provided for all men through the Lord Jesus Christ. They were redeemed by the blood of the lamb (Exodus 12:13; Ephesians 1:7). They "**were all baptized unto Moses in the cloud and in the sea**" (1 Corinthians 10:2; Acts 8:35-38). God's goal for the children of Israel on this earth was to give them victory in the land of Canaan, but the people refused to believe God. As a result, God would not permit them to go into the Promised Land! He would not permit them "**to go on unto perfection**" (Hebrews 6:1). Let's look at the major steps of this example.

A. GOD TOLD THEM HIS PLAN

Exodus 3:17 says, "And I [God] have said, I will bring you up out of the affliction of Egypt unto the land of the Canaanites, and the Hittites, and the Amorites, and the Perizzites, and the Hivites, and the Jebusites, unto a land flowing with milk and honey."

As God told the Israelites his plan for them, the Lord too has told us his plan for our lives: an abundant life (John 10:10)!

B. GOD PROMISED TO GIVE THEM THE LAND AND TO GO BEFORE THEM AND FIGHT FOR THEM

Exodus 33:1-2 says, "And the LORD said unto Moses, Depart, and go up hence, thou and the people which thou hast brought up out of the land of Egypt, unto the land which I sware unto Abraham, to Isaac, and to Jacob, saying, Unto thy seed will I give it: **And I will send an angel before thee**; and I will drive out the Canaanite, the Amorite, and the Hittite, and the Perizzite, the Hivite, and the Jebusite."

Just as God promised them victory, the Lord promises us victory too (1 Corinthians 15:57), because he has gone before us (Hebrews 6:18-20)!

C. THEY REBELLED AGAINST GOD IN UNBELIEF

But when the spies, who had been sent into the promised land to spy it out, had returned, they brought an evil report which caused the people to turn aside from the commandment of the Lord.

Numbers chapter 13 gives us an account of the whole story. Numbers 13:31-33 tells us of the disbelief, saying, "But the men that went up with him said, We be not able to go up against the people; for they are stronger than we. And they brought up an evil report of the land which they had searched unto the children of Israel, saying, The land, through which we have gone to search it, is a land that eateth up the inhabitants thereof; and all the people that we saw in it are men of a great stature. And there we saw the giants, the sons of Anak, which come of the giants: and we were in our own sight as grasshoppers, and so we were in their sight."

I have heard men say, "It's too hard to live for the Lord!" That's an evil report. Whoever says that is trusting in their own strength and not in the promises of God. I can do nothing without Jesus Christ (John 15:5), but I "CAN do all things through Christ which strengtheneth me" (Philippians 4:13)!

D. GOD CURSED THE PEOPLE

God's longsuffering toward these people came to an end. He told them that all of the complainers and murmurers would be forced to wander in the wilderness for forty years until they were dead! Only their children and those who had not complained would be allowed to enter into the Promised Land

(Numbers 14:28-35). Not only that, but the spies who had brought the evil report were killed by a plague (Numbers 14:36-38).

E. THE PEOPLE TRIED TO FIND REPENTANCE

When the people heard the curse they confessed their sin and presumed to go up to take the land, but Moses warned them that the Lord was not with them. They went to battle against the Amalekites anyway, and the Amalekites won the battle (Numbers 14:39-45)! They had murmured one time too many times and God had put them aside. Now, it was impossible "to renew them again unto repentance" (Hebrews 6:6). God would not permit them to "go on unto perfection" (Hebrews 6:1). It was too late for them to hope that God would repent (change his mind) about letting them go into the Promised Land.

John 15:5 says, "...**for without me** [Christ] **ye can do nothing**."

F. THEY DID NOT LOSE SALVATION

Although God would not allow them to enter into the Promised Land—a picture of the abundant and victorious life—they were still saved by his grace. They, like Christians today, were not saved by works of righteousness; neither did they lose their salvation by bad works. Those who had faith in God had been given God's righteousness (Hebrews 11:7). Even after Israel's rebellion, we read how the Lord saw his own imputed righteousness in Israel when he looked upon them. Speaking to the Israelites, God said in Micah 6:5, "**O my people, remember now what Balak king of Moab consulted, and what Balaam the son of Beor answered him from Shittim unto Gilgal; that ye may know the righteousness of the LORD**."

Numbers 23:19-23 tells us, "God is not a man, that he should lie; neither the son of man, that he should repent: hath he said, and shall he not do it? or hath he spoken, and shall he not make it good? Behold, I have received commandment to bless: and he hath blessed: and I cannot reverse it. **He hath not beheld iniquity in Jacob, neither hath he seen perverseness in Israel**; the LORD his God is with him, and the shout of a king is among them. **Surely there is no enchantment against Jacob, neither is there any divination against Israel: according to this time it shall be said of Jacob and of Israel, What hath God wrought!**"

God worked the victory through his redeemer and gave it to Israel, even to them who rebelled and failed to go on unto perfection! Abram (later called

Abraham) believed God and he imputed it to him for righteousness (Genesis 15:6). Christians have the same righteousness imputed to them (Romans 4:24)!

IV. THE EXAMPLE OF MOSES

Moses was also prevented from going into the Promised Land, because, in type, "**he crucified the Son of God afresh, and put him to an open shame**" (Hebrews 6:6). The rock in the wilderness was a type or a picture of Jesus Christ (1 Corinthians 10:4).

The first time Moses got water from the "rock," he was told to strike the rock with his rod: Exodus 17:6 says, "Behold, I [God] will stand before thee there upon the rock in Horeb; and **thou shalt smite the rock, and there shall come water out of it, that the people may drink**. And Moses did so in the sight of the elders of Israel."

The second time Moses was not told to strike the rock, he was specifically told to speak to the rock: Numbers 20:8 says, "Take the rod, and gather thou the assembly together, thou, and Aaron thy brother, and **speak ye unto the rock before their eyes; and it shall give forth his water, and thou shalt bring forth to them water out of the rock**: so thou shalt give the congregation and their beasts drink." However, Moses, in anger, was disobedient to God and smote the rock. Because of this, God would not permit him to "**go on unto perfection**," that is, God would not allow Moses to enter into the Promised Land, which was God's original plan for Moses. Numbers 20:11-12 describes that disobedience and its consequences, saying, "**And Moses lifted up his hand, and with his rod he smote the rock twice**: and the water came out abundantly, and the congregation drank, and their beasts also. **And the LORD spake unto Moses and Aaron, Because ye believed me not, to sanctify me in the eyes of the children of Israel, therefore ye shall not bring this congregation into the land which I have given them**."

Thank God, the Lord Jesus Christ has already suffered once for all (Hebrews 10:10), and he will never have to suffer again on the cross! When a Christian willfully sins against God, he brings his Saviour to an open shame, like Moses did when he smote the "rock" the second time!

V. THE EXAMPLE OF ESAU

After Esau had sold his birthright to Jacob, and Jacob had received the blessing of the firstborn, then Esau went to his father Isaac begging him to repent (change his mind); but Esau found that it was too late! His father would not repent (change his mind) and give him the blessing. You can read the accounts in Genesis 25:19-34 and Genesis 27:34-41. Hebrews 12:16-17 says, "Lest there be any fornicator, or profane person, as Esau, who for one morsel of meat sold his birthright. For ye know how that afterward, when he would have inherited the blessing, he was rejected: for he found no place of repentance, though he sought it carefully with tears."

VI. THE EXAMPLE OF THE EARTH (Hebrews 6:7-8)

The "earth" in verse 7 is a reference to those that are on "good ground" which also are those Christians that "beareth fruit" (Matthew 13:23). The fruit that he bears are good works which will bring him a reward at the judgment seat of Christ (1 Corinthians 3:14).

The earth "**which beareth thorns**" (Hebrews 6:8) is a reference to those Christians who are "**among thorns...and the care of this world, and the deceitfulness of riches, choke the word, and he becometh unfruitful**" (Matthew 13:22). This Christian will be at the judgment seat of Christ (2 Corinthians 5:10) to see his bad works burned up! "**He shall suffer loss** [loss of rewards and privileges]**: but he himself** [his soul] **shall be saved; yet so as by fire**" (1 Corinthians 3:15).

CONCLUSION AND ENCOURAGEMENT

Hebrews 6:9-12 says, "But, beloved, we are persuaded better things of you, and things that accompany salvation, though we thus speak. For God *is* not unrighteous to forget your work and labour of love, which ye have shewed toward his name, in that ye have ministered to the saints, and do minister. And we desire that every one of you do shew the same diligence to the full assurance of hope unto the end: That ye be not slothful, but followers of them who through faith and patience inherit the promises."

"**Things that accompany salvation**" (Hebrews 6:9) are "**good works**" (Ephesians 2:8-10; Titus 2:11-14) which result from the fruit of the Spirit (Galatians 5:22-23) and from God working in the believer, "**both to will and to do of his good pleasure**" (Philippians 2:13).

Paul is writing to those who sadly have not gone beyond the possibility of repentance. He is writing to warn them to avoid the tragedy of not going unto perfection. Those that lose the joy and blessings of the abundant life here and now on earth (John 10:10), lose their rewards at the judgment seat of Christ when they get to heaven (2 John 1:8; 2 Corinthians 5:10; 1 Corinthians 3:15). Not only do these miss out on the great abundance God wants to give them, in addition they receive the chastisement of God and will be least in the kingdom of heaven on earth during the millennium (Matthew 5:19).

Paul is encouraging them not to be slothful and lazy, but to be diligent in their work for God. He said, God will not "**forget your work and labour of love**" (Hebrews 6:10; Colossians 3:23-25; 2 John 1:8).

Therefore, "**Let us go on unto perfection**..." (Hebrews 6:1). Let us submit ourselves unto God (Romans 12:1-2) and allow him to work in us "both to will and to do of his good pleasure" (Philippians 2:13). "**Whether therefore ye eat, or drink, or whatsoever ye do, do all to the glory of God**" (1 Corinthians 10:31).

If you have never been "**born of the Spirit**" (John 3:6-7), then you are pursuing evil to your own death (Proverbs 11:19)! "**Believe on the Lord Jesus Christ, and thou shalt be saved**" (Acts 16:31).

Chapter 26

Model Servants

Today's sermon topic is a very important one. If someone claims to be a follower of Jesus Christ, then one of his hopes should be to bring glory to his Father which is in heaven. In order for this hope to become evident, it is imperative that he walk in the light of God's word in fellowship with the Lord Jesus (1 John 1:7). By walking in the light, he will let men see his good works and hear his testimony of God's amazing grace through the outworking of God in his life. Then his Father in heaven can be glorified through him.

This is what today's sermon is all about. We begin this sermon with the scriptural text of 1 Thessalonians 2:1-9, which says, "For yourselves, brethren, know our entrance in unto you, that it was not in vain: But even after that we had suffered before, and were shamefully entreated, as ye know, at Philippi, we were bold in our God to speak unto you the gospel of God with much contention. For our exhortation *was* not of deceit, nor of uncleanness, nor in guile: But as we were allowed of God to be put in trust with the gospel, even so we speak; not as pleasing men, but God, which trieth our hearts. For neither at any time used we flattering words, as ye know, nor a cloke of covetousness; God *is* witness: Nor of men sought we glory, neither of you, nor *yet* of others, when we might have been burdensome, as the apostles of Christ. But we were gentle among you, even as a nurse cherisheth her children: So being affectionately desirous of you, we were willing to have imparted unto you, not the gospel of God only, but also our own souls, because ye were dear unto us. For ye remember, brethren, our labour and travail: for labouring night and day, because we would not be chargeable unto any of you, we preached unto you the gospel of God."

VAIN FAITH

Again, 1 Thessalonians 2:1 says, "For yourselves, brethren, know our entrance in unto you, that it was not in vain."

In chapter one, Paul said that the Thessalonians were "**ensamples to all that believe in Macedonia and Achaia**," and that "**they themselves shew of us what manner of entering in we had unto you, and how ye turned to God from idols to serve the living and true God**" (1 Thessalonians 1:7-9). Now Paul writes, saying that the Thessalonians themselves knew that Paul's ministry to them "**was not in vain**." It is essential for you to understand that the only man in the world who can be sure of your salvation is you yourself! If you are truly born again, God himself will be your witness, for it is written: "**The Spirit itself beareth witness with our spirit, that we are the children of God**" (Romans 8:16). All born again believers have "**the firstfruits of the Spirit**" (Romans 8:23). God has given to us "**the earnest** [the advance confirmation of the believer's eternal place in God's kingdom] **of the Spirit in our hearts**" (2 Corinthians 1:22, 5:5). Believers are said to be "**sealed with that holy Spirit of promise**" (Ephesians 1:13), and "**sealed unto the day of redemption**" (Ephesians 4:30). They were sealed after they heard the gospel of their salvation, "**how that Christ died for our sins according to the scriptures; And that he was buried, and that he rose again the third day according to the scriptures**" (1 Corinthians 15:3-4), and after they believed on the Lord Jesus Christ (Ephesians 1:12-13; Acts 16:31; Romans 10:9). "**Hereby know we that we dwell in him, and he in us, because he hath given us of his Spirit**" (1 John 4:13).

We also know that the Lord Jesus Christ himself shall confirm us unto the end, that we "***may be*** **blameless in the day of our Lord Jesus Christ**" (1 Corinthians 1:8), for we are "**sealed unto the day of redemption**" (Ephesians 4:30). "**He that hath the Son hath life; *and* he that hath not the Son of God hath not life**" (1 John 5:12). "**Now if any man have not the Spirit of Christ, he is none of his**" (Romans 8:9). All of the so-called *confirmation* of men, or their religions, means absolutely nothing in the eyes of God! No doubt many a man is now "suffering the vengeance of eternal fire" (Jude 1:7), because he was trusting in his *religion.* What every man needs is the confirmation of the Spirit of God!

So be very diligent to make "**your calling and election sure**" (2 Peter 1:10), for it is possible to believe the gospel in vain! "**Moreover, brethren, I declare unto you the gospel** (1 Corinthians 15:3-4) **which I preached unto you, which also ye have received, and wherein ye stand; By which also ye are saved, if ye keep in memory what I preached unto you, unless ye have <u>believed in vain</u>**" (1 Corinthians 15:1-2). I believe there are a great number of men who have believed the gospel in vain. A vain belief is one that is "empty; worthless; having no substance, value, or importance." For example, one very proud young prison inmate, who had just let out a string of obscenities and blasphemies, laughingly said to me, "We all believe in Jesus!" My friend, if you are comfortable to continue in sin, and yet say that you believe in Jesus, you have believed the gospel in vain! It has done you no good! True belief in the gospel is the work of the Holy Ghost of God who reproves [convicts or convinces] men of their sin of unbelief (John 16:7) and brings them to a place of true repentance to acknowledge the truth of the gospel (2 Timothy 2:24-26). When a man is truly born of the Spirit, his life and attitude will change. He will know that a profound change has taken place in his life, for "**if any man *be* in Christ, *he is* a new creature: old things are passed away; behold, all things are become new**" (2 Corinthians 5:17). In the church today are the wheat [the true born again believers] and the tares [the professing believers]. When the Lord comes to get his children [the wheat], the devil's children [tares] will be left behind (Matthew 13:24-30). "**We then, *as* workers together *with him*, beseech *you* also that ye receive not the grace of God in <u>vain</u>**" (2 Corinthians 6:1).

AFFLICTIONS OF THE GOSPEL

First Thessalonians 2:2 says, "But even after that we had suffered before, and were shamefully entreated, as ye know, at Philippi, we were bold in our God to speak unto you the gospel of God with much contention."

Before coming to Thessalonica, Paul and Silas had been in Philippi, which was a three day journey from Thessalonica. The account that Paul refers to here may be read in detail in Acts 16:12-40. At Philippi Paul and Silas spoke to the women at a riverside where Lydia, the first European convert to the faith, was baptized. After that, Paul cast out the unclean spirit from a damsel (a young woman) who spoke the truth by an unclean spirit. This caused great indignation among her masters. These masters forcefully took and brought Paul and Silas before the law and accused them of teaching against their customs. Paul and Silas were then beaten and cast into jail. At midnight, Paul and Silas prayed and sang praises to God, and God sent an earthquake and loosed all the bands of the prisoners. As a result of Paul's and Silas' testimony, the jailer and his family got saved and baptized. Paul and his companions also faced much contention [strife, controversy, argument] as they journeyed and preached the gospel at Thessalonica (Acts 17:5-9) and later at Athens (Acts 17:17-21).

An important principle we learn from this testimony is that all believers will face opposition as they witness the gospel to others. Nonetheless, we are commanded to contend for the faith (Jude 3). Of course, those who contend *against* the gospel do so because of spiritual blindness and pride (Proverbs 13:10). Paul wrote, "**we were bold in our God to speak unto you the gospel**." Likewise, we read that after the disciples at Jerusalem had prayed, "the place was shaken where they were assembled together; and they were all filled with the Holy Ghost, and they **spake the word of God with boldness**" (Acts 4:31). No doubt the apostles were filled with the Spirit of God, which gave them great boldness to earnestly defend and preserve the faith of the gospel. They would also be "**speaking the truth in love**" (Ephesians 4:15).

First Thessalonians 2:3 says, "For our exhortation *was* not of deceit, nor of uncleanness, nor in guile."

Exhortation means to excite by words; to urge by arguments to a good deed or to any laudable conduct or course of action. "**Not of deceit**" means the apostles were not misleading the hearers to believe something that is not true. To deceive is the work of evil men who continue to increase according to the scriptures: "But **evil** men and **seducers** shall wax worse and worse, **deceiving**, and being **deceived**" (2 Timothy 3:13). "**Nor uncleanness**" has a reference to moral impurity and sinfulness. "**Nor in guile**" means their delivery of the gospel was plain and straight forward. They were not being crafty, cunning, artificial, or feigned.

The first part of 1 Thessalonians 2:4 says, "But as we were allowed of God to be put in trust with the gospel..."

The "**gospel of the grace of God**" (Acts 20:24) was first revealed to the Apostle Paul by the Lord Jesus (Romans 16:25-26; Gal. 1:11-12). Paul wrote to the church in Galatia: "But I certify you, brethren, that the **gospel** which was preached of me is not after **man**. For I neither received it of **man**, neither was I taught *it*, but by the **<u>revelation</u>** of **<u>Jesus Christ</u>**" (Galatians 1:11-12). And Paul wrote to Timothy: "And I thank Christ Jesus our Lord, who hath enabled me, for that he counted me faithful, putting me into the ministry; Who [talking about himself] was before a blasphemer, and a persecutor, and injurious: but I obtained mercy, because I did *it* ignorantly in unbelief" (1 Timothy 1:12-13). Not only was the gospel revealed to Paul, but God entrusted Paul with the ministry of the gospel, and enabled him. All true disciples of the Lord Jesus Christ are also enabled by the Spirit of God and entrusted with the gospel (1 Corinthians 3:9; Philippians 2:13; Hebrews 13:21; 1 Thessalonians 2:4) to be profitable servants to the Lord.

God enabled and inspired the Apostle Paul to write the fourteen books from Romans through Hebrews. These books contain the essential foundation for the doctrine of the church today. One should never go to the Acts of the Apostles to find church doctrine, for the book of Acts covers the period of transition between the time when the Jews were under Moses' law to the early beginnings of the church under the grace of Christ (John 1:17). During the period of the acts of the apostles, God confirmed the word of the apostles with signs following (Mark 16:20).

Many *false* gospels have been spawned from the book of Acts. The false doctrine of "baptismal regeneration," which teaches that one must be baptized in water to be saved, came from a misinterpretation of Acts 2:38. Compare Acts 2:38 with Acts 10:43, where the same Peter preached: "**To him** [Jesus Christ] **give all the prophets witness, <u>that through his name whosoever believeth in him shall receive remission of sins</u>**" (Acts 10:43). And once a man's sins have been remitted [forgiven], and he has been born of the Spirit (John 3:6-8), and has received the Spirit of Christ (Romans 8:9; Acts 10:44-48), he should follow the Lord in believer's baptism, "**for** [because of] **the remission of sins**" (Acts 2:38). It is a false interpretation to say that Acts 2:38 means that one should be baptized "for [in order to receive] the remission of sins." The "for" does not mean that one should be baptized *in order to receive* the remission of sins. <u>The "for" means that one should be baptized *because of* the remission of sins</u>! That is, once a man has repented from his unbelief and believed on the Lord Jesus Christ, his sins are remitted [forgiven]. Then this man should be baptized. The Lord Jesus Christ "**<u>gave himself for our sins</u>, that he might deliver us from this present evil world, according to the will of God and our Father**" (Galatians 1:4). In other words, the Lord Jesus gave himself *because of* our sins, and not *in order to receive* our sins!

As well, the false doctrine that one must speak in tongues as a demonstration that they have received the Holy Ghost also comes from

Acts. But since it is clear that all who are in the church do not speak with tongues (1 Corinthians 12:28-31), and because "**tongues are for a sign**" (1 Corinthians 14:22), and "**the Jews require a sign**" (1 Corinthians 1:22), this teaching is also shown not to be true, especially in churches where there are no Jews.

The last part of 1 Thessalonians 2:4 says, "...even so we speak; not as pleasing men, but God, which trieth our hearts."

Paul wrote to the Galatian church: "**For do I now persuade men, or God? or do I seek to please men? for if I yet pleased men, I should not be the servant of Christ**" (Galatians 1:10). Paul had no desire to teach and preach the gospel in order to flatter and please men, or to win their applause, or gratify their passions. There are plenty of false teachers and preachers in this very day who make "the word of God of none effect" (Mark 7:13) by their ear tickling fables (2 Timothy 4:3-4) and slanderous get rich quick schemes. Paul was not one of them. But this is not to suppose that Paul desired to offend men; or that he regarded their esteem as of no value; or that he was indifferent whether they were pleased or displeased. The important concern is it was not the direct object of his preaching to please people. Paul's object was to declare the truth, and to obtain the pleasure of God, no matter what men might think of it. Paul knew that "**the preaching of the cross is to them that perish foolishness**" (1 Corinthians 1:18), and that all who preach the gospel will be a "**partaker of the afflictions of the gospel**" (2 Timothy 1:8). They will experience the "**offence of the cross**" (Galatians 5:11) and suffer "**much contention**" (1 Thessalonians 2:2). They will *not* have their "best life now," as one popular prosperity preacher teaches! The "best life," for all born again believers, will begin when they are caught up "**to meet the Lord in the air: and so shall we ever be with the Lord. Wherefore comfort one another with these words**" (1 Thessalonians 4:16-18).

Ministers who seek to please men instead of God are enemies of the men they seek to please, especially if they hold back from them the preaching of "**all the counsel of God**" (Acts 20:27). Paul was more interested in pleasing God, "**which trieth our hearts.**" Many scriptures teach us that the LORD searches the heart (Jeremiah 17:10; Romans 8:27), and that "**the word of God *is* quick, and powerful, and sharper than any twoedged sword, piercing even to the dividing asunder of soul and spirit, and of the joints and marrow, and *is* a discerner of the thoughts and intents of the heart**" (Hebrews 4:12).

BEWARE OF FLATTERING WORDS

First Thessalonians 2:5 says, "For neither at any time used we flattering words, as ye know, nor a cloke of covetousness; God *is* witness."

Paul was a well educated man who could have laid it on thick with a long string of high sounding words, but God wants the preaching of the gospel to be plain, that men may know of the "**simplicity that is in Christ**" (2 Corinthians 11:3). Paul wrote to the Corinthians, saying: "**And my speech and my preaching *was* not with enticing words of man's wisdom, but in demonstration of the Spirit and of power: That your faith should not stand in the wisdom of men, but in the power of God**" (1 Corinthians 2:4-5). Paul warned the Romans: "**Now I beseech you, brethren, mark them which cause divisions and offences contrary to the doctrine which ye have learned; and avoid them. For they that are such serve not our Lord Jesus Christ, but their own belly; <u>and by good words and fair speeches deceive the hearts of the simple</u>**" (Romans 16:17-18). "**A man that flattereth his neighbour spreadeth a net for his feet**" (Proverbs 29:5). You should also beware of the "strange woman, *even* from the stranger *which* flattereth with her words" (Proverbs 2:16; 6:23-24; 7:5, 21). You should also beware of flattering preachers!

Paul also did not use a "cloke of covetousness," simply because he was not a covetous man, nor was he coveting after anything that belonged to the Thessalonians. And Paul was fully aware that God was his witness. He wrote to the Romans: "**For God is my witness, whom I serve with my spirit in the gospel of his Son**, that without ceasing I make mention of you always in my prayers" (Romans 1:9), and again he wrote: "I say the truth in Christ, I lie not, **my conscience also bearing me witness in the Holy Ghost**" (Romans 9:1).

THE APOSTLES' HUMBLE SPIRIT

The first part of 1 Thessalonians 2:6 says, "Nor of men sought we glory, neither of you, nor *yet* of others..." In addition, it would be wise to consider the wisdom of Proverbs 25:27, which states: "***It is* not good to eat much honey: so *for men* to search their own glory *is not* glory**."

The Lord asked the Jews, who sought to kill the Lord Jesus, because he had made himself "**equal with God**" (John 5:18): "**How can ye believe, which receive honour one of another, and seek not the honour that *cometh* from God only?**" (John 5:44). In another place we read of these unbelieving

Jews, that "**they loved the praise of men more than the praise of God**" (John 12:43).

The Spirit filled believer will always seek to glorify the Lord Jesus Christ, and not himself (John 16:14), for Jesus Christ has sent him into the world to preach the gospel. The Father sent the Son into the world to save sinners (1 Timothy 1:15), therefore the Lord Jesus glorified his Father in every thing. Jesus declared: "**He that speaketh of himself seeketh his own glory: but he that seeketh his glory that sent him, the same is true, and no unrighteousness is in him**" (John 7:18). All believers are commanded: "**Let us not be desirous of vain glory, provoking one another, envying one another**" (Galatians 5:26).

The middle part of 1 Thessalonians 2:6 continues the thought and says, "... when we might have been burdensome..."

Paul, and Silvanus, and Timotheus, could have come to the Thessalonians expecting to be specially treated and cared for as apostles, but later in this letter, Paul told them: "**Neither did we eat any man's bread for nought; but wrought with labour and travail night and day, that we might not be chargeable to any of you: Not because we have not power, but to make ourselves an ensample unto you to follow us**" (2 Thessalonians 3:8-9). Paul worked to supply his own needs, and was not a burden to the church. Paul was living what he preached, when he wrote in the next verse: "**For even when we were with you, this we commanded you, that if any would not work, neither should he eat**" (2 Thessalonians 3:10). The Apostle Peter also instructed the elders of the church: "**Feed the flock of God which is among you, taking the oversight *thereof*, not by constraint, but willingly; not for filthy lucre, but of a ready mind; Neither as being lords over *God's* heritage, <u>but being ensamples to the flock</u>**" (1 Peter 5:1-3). Paul acknowledged that it would be right for him to be supported by the church, when he wrote to the Corinthians: "**Even so hath the Lord ordained that they which preach the gospel should live of the gospel**" (1 Corinthians 9:14). But Paul chose to work with his own hands so as not to be a burden to these Gentiles, making his ministry "void of offence" (Acts 24:16). Certainly, no one could accuse Paul of being "greedy of filthy lucre" (1 Timothy 3:8). Paul did receive unrequested contributions from the church at Philippi while he was in Thessalonica (Philippians 4:15-16).

The end of 1 Thessalonians 2:6 says, "...as the apostles of Christ."

Paul identifies himself, Silvanus, and Timotheus "as the apostles of Christ" (1 Thessalonians 2:6). Barnabas is also identified as an apostle (1 Corinthians 9:6; Acts 14:14). But neither of these four men were part of the twelve apostles. When Judas fell (Acts 1:15-26), the remaining eleven apostles chose Matthias to be his replacement; but when Herod "killed James the brother of John with the sword" (Acts 12:1-2), James was not replaced. The wall of the New Jerusalem has "twelve foundations, and in them the names of the twelve apostles of the Lamb" (Revelation 21:14). The twelve names will be those of the original eleven, in addition to Matthias who replaced Judas.

AS A GENTLE NURSE

First Thessalonians 2:7-8 says, "But we were gentle among you, even as a nurse cherisheth her children: So being affectionately desirous of you, we were willing to have imparted unto you, not the gospel of God only, but also our own souls, because ye were dear unto us."

"**Gentleness**" is a fruit of the Spirit, which all servants of God should demonstrate when they minister to others. Paul also wrote saying that he besought the Corinthians: "by the meekness and **gentleness of Christ**" (2 Corinthians 10:1). Paul wrote to Timothy that, "the servant of the Lord must not strive; but be **gentle unto all *men***..." (2 Timothy 2:24-26). James declared: "**But the wisdom that is from above is first pure, then peaceable, <u>gentle</u>, *and* easy to be intreated, full of mercy and good fruits, without partiality, and without hypocrisy**" (James 3:17).

Paul, and Silvanus, and Timotheus were willing to offer their lives for the salvation of those souls in Thessalonica. By this, they were demonstrating the love of God that had been shed abroad in their "**hearts by the Holy Ghost**" (Romans 5:5). They were obedient to the Lord's commandment: "**That ye love one another, as I have loved you. Greater love hath no man than this, that a man lay down his life for his friends. Ye are my friends, if ye do whatsoever I command you**" (John 15:12-14). In similar words, the Apostle Paul wrote to the Philippians: "**Yea, and if I be offered upon the sacrifice and service of your faith, I joy, and rejoice with you all**" (Philippians 2:17). And again to the Corinthians: "**And I will very gladly spend and be spent for you; though the more abundantly I love you, the less I be loved**" (2 Corinthians 12:15). Paul was ready to depart this life and go to be with Christ. He wrote: "**For to me to live *is* Christ, and <u>to die *is* gain</u>. But if I live in the flesh, this *is* the fruit of my labour: yet what I shall choose I wot not. For I am in a strait betwixt two, <u>having a desire to depart,</u>**

and to be with Christ; which is far better: Nevertheless to abide in the flesh *is* more needful for you" (Philippians 1:21-24). The Apostle Paul would never credit himself for his abundant labour for God, but rather gave credit to "**the grace of God which was with me**" (1 Corinthians 15:10). In another place he wrote: "**I am crucified with Christ: nevertheless I live; yet not I, but Christ liveth in me: and the life which I now live in the flesh I live by the faith of the Son of God, who loved me, and gave himself for me**" (Galatians 2:20).

The first part of 1 Thessalonians 2:9 says, "For ye remember, brethren, our labour and travail: for labouring night and day, because we would not be chargeable unto any of you..."

We have already commented on the subject of the apostles not being burdensome to the church in Thessalonica under verse 6 in this outline. So we shall not repeat what has already been spoken. You may review verse 6 for your own exhortation.

However, the section in the last part of 1 Thessalonians 2:9 must still be addressed. These last words state that, "...we preached unto you the gospel of God." Very short and simple words, but important wisdom and truth to consider and understand.

For when it was revealed to him that bonds and afflictions awaited him, Paul told the Ephesian elders that the ministry, which he received of the Lord Jesus was: "**to testify the gospel of the grace of God**" (Acts 20:24). This is the same as "**the gospel of Christ**," which is "**the power of God unto salvation to every one that believeth; to the Jew first, and also to the Greek**" (Romans 1:16)!

Likewise, have you "**obeyed the gospel**" by believing the report (Romans 10:15-17), "**the record that God gave of his Son**" (1 John 5:10), God's word concerning the death, burial, and resurrection of Jesus Christ for your sins (1 Corinthians 15:3-4)? I first trusted Christ, after I read the word of truth, the gospel of my salvation. I was then sealed with that holy Spirit of promise, which is the earnest of my inheritance until the redemption of by body, unto the praise of his glory (read Ephesians 1:12-14).

ARE YOU TROUBLED?

There is *rest* to be found in Jesus Christ, who said: "**Come unto me, all *ye* that labour and are heavy laden, and I will give you rest. Take my yoke upon**

you, and learn of me; for I am meek and lowly in heart: and ye shall find rest unto your souls. For my yoke *is* easy, and my burden is light" (Matthew 11:28-30).

In his second letter to the Thessalonians, Paul wrote: "**And to you who are troubled rest with us, when the Lord Jesus shall be revealed from heaven with his mighty angels, In flaming fire taking vengeance on them that know not God, and that obey not the gospel of our Lord Jesus Christ: Who shall be punished with everlasting destruction from the presence of the Lord, and from the glory of his power; When he shall come to be glorified in his saints, and to be admired in all them that believe (because our testimony among you was believed) in that day**" (2 Thessalonians 1:7-10).

The Lord Jesus Christ sent Paul to the Gentiles [all non-Jewish people]: "**To open their eyes, *and* to turn *them* from darkness to light, and *from* the power of Satan unto God, that they may receive forgiveness of sins, and inheritance among them which are sanctified by faith that is in me**" (Acts 26:17-18). May the Lord open your eyes today to the "**light of the glorious gospel of Christ, who is the image of God**" (2 Corinthians 4:4).

"**Believe on the Lord Jesus Christ, and thou shalt be saved**" (Acts 16:31).

Chapter 27

PURPOSE OF THE CHURCH IN THE WORLD

Ephesians 1:12-14 says, "That we should be to the praise of his glory, who first trusted in Christ. In whom ye also *trusted,* after that ye heard the word of truth, the gospel of your salvation: in whom also after that ye believed, ye were sealed with that holy Spirit of promise, Which is the earnest of our inheritance until the redemption of the purchased possession, unto the praise of his glory."

These verses are directed to those who have been born again by the Spirit of God; to those who know that there is absolutely nothing that they can do or offer to God for eternal life. They have received the gift of eternal life from God, because they have believed that Jesus Christ paid their sin debt on the cross. They have repented of their own personal pride and self-righteousness, and now they are trusting only in the "**righteousness of God *which is* by faith of Jesus Christ**" (Romans 3:22)!

According to these verses we were saved after we heard the word of truth, the gospel of Jesus Christ—"**how that Christ died for our sins according to the scriptures; And that he was buried, and that he rose again from the dead according to the scriptures**" (1 Corinthians 15:3-4), and believed in our hearts "**that God raised him from the dead**" (Romans 10:9). According to these verses, why did God save us? The answer is God saved us for "**the praise of his glory**" (Ephesians 1:12, 14); and after we believed we "**were sealed with that holy Spirit of promise**" (Ephesians 1:13). Why did God seal us with the Holy Spirit? So that he could safely leave us in this world to reach other lost people with the truth of the gospel, so that they can believe and be saved just like we were! Who else is going to witness and preach the true gospel to the lost other than born again believers? Certainly not lost, self-righteous religious people nor unbelievers!

We born again believers are sealed and kept in this world in answer to Jesus' prayer. Jesus asked the Father not to take his disciples out of the world, but to keep them from the evil (John 17:14-16). Why did God send his only begotten Son into the world? See the following verses:

"This *is* a faithful saying, and worthy of all acceptation, that **Christ Jesus came into the world to save sinners**; of whom I am chief" (1 Timothy 1:15).

"**For God sent not his Son into the world to condemn the world; but that the world through him might be saved**" (John 3:17).

Then Jesus continued his prayer and said to the Father, "**As thou hast sent me into the world, even so have I also sent them into the world**" (John 17:18). The Father sent his Son into the world that the world by him might be saved. Believers are now sent into the world with the gospel of the grace of God so that the world, through the gospel, might be saved. The Lord continued his prayer, saying, "**Neither pray I for these alone, but for them also which shall believe on me through their word; That they all may be one; as thou, Father, *art* in me, and I in thee, that they also may be one in us: that the world may believe that thou hast sent me.** And the glory which thou gavest me I have given them; that they may be one, even as we are one: I in them, and thou in me, that they may be made perfect in one; **and that the world may know that thou hast sent me, and hast loved them, as thou hast loved me**" (John 17:20-23). The Lord Jesus Christ wants all the world to know, "**For God so loved the world, that he gave his only begotten Son, that whosoever believeth in him should not perish, but have everlasting life**" (John 3:16)!

Before the Lord Jesus ascended back into heaven, he met with the first local church. He assembled together with them and said, "But ye shall receive power, after that the Holy Ghost is come upon you: **and ye shall be witnesses unto me both in Jerusalem, and in all Judaea, and in Samaria, and unto the uttermost**

part of the earth" (Acts 1:8). The local church therefore is commanded to reach the entire world with the gospel! This is the essential "**work of the ministry**" (Ephesians 4:12), the reason God has left his children in this "**present evil world**" (Galatians 1:4).

The Lord's command to his church to take the gospel to all the world is repeated several times. Jesus said to the eleven disciples, "**Go ye therefore and teach all nations**..." (Matthew 28:19-20). Again we read, "And said unto them, Thus it is written, and thus it behoved Christ to suffer, and to rise from the dead the third day: **And that repentance and remission of sins should be preached in his name among all nations**, beginning at Jerusalem. And ye are witnesses of these things" (Luke 24:46-48). Again, Jesus commanded his disciples, "**Go ye into all the world, and preach the gospel to every creature**" (Mark 16:15). The only way for anybody to be saved is to hear and to believe the gospel, "**for it is the power of God unto salvation to every one that believeth**" (Romans 1:16). But "**how shall they believe in him of whom they have not heard? and how shall they hear without a preacher? And how shall they preach, except they be sent? as it is written, How beautiful are the feet of them that preach the gospel of peace, and bring glad tidings of good things!**" (Romans 10:14-15). It is the duty and commission of the church to get the gospel witness to all the people of the world. So Jesus Christ has saved us, sealed us, and sent us into all the world to preach "**the gospel of the grace of God**" (Acts 20:24).

GOD'S GOOD PLEASURE

The scriptures teach us that the Lord Jesus Christ created all things for his pleasure (Revelation 4:11). Likewise, we also read that the Lord GOD said, "**I have no pleasure in the death of the wicked; but that the wicked turn from his way and live**..." (Ezekiel 33:11). God did not create anybody to damn them! God's desire is to have every man saved and to have a relationship with every man. We read that the Lord is "**not willing that any should perish, but that all should come to repentance**" (2 Peter 3:9).

Throughout the history of the world, it has always been God's desire that all men know him and believe on him and have a relationship with him. He has dispensed his grace and word to men at different times in different ways, but always with a desire to show mercy and grace to all men. God said that men should not glory in their wisdom, might, and riches, "**But let him that glorieth glory in this, that he understandeth and knoweth me, that I *am* the LORD**

which exercise lovingkindness, judgment, and righteousness, in the earth: for in these *things* I delight, saith the LORD" (Jeremiah 9:24).

Throughout history God has raised up individuals and separated groups of people for the purpose of using them to reveal himself to all the peoples of the world. Men and circumstances have changed, but God has never changed in his will for "**all men to be saved, and to come unto the knowledge of the truth**" (1 Timothy 2:4). "**For I *am* the LORD, I change not; therefore ye sons of Jacob are not consumed**" (Malachi 3:6). Again, "**Jesus Christ the same yesterday, and to day, and for ever**" (Hebrews 13:8).

THE BLESSING OF ABRAHAM

After the flood and after the rebellion and confusion of languages at the tower of Babel, God called Abram and established the Hebrew nation, called Israel, to be a witness to all peoples. God called Abram and promised to make of him a great nation, to bless him, and to make his name great, and to make him a blessing (Genesis 12:1-2). And the LORD continued and said, "**And I will bless them that bless thee, and curse him that curseth thee: and in thee shall <u>all families of the earth</u> be blessed**" (Genesis 12:3). Not just the families of Abraham, Isaac, and Jacob, but "**<u>all families of the earth</u>**." Later the LORD was more specific about his way of blessing the nations when he told Abraham, "... **and in thy <u>seed</u> shall <u>all the nations of the earth be blessed</u>**" (Genesis 26:4). Concerning this "**seed**," we later read, "**Now to Abraham and his <u>seed</u> were the promises made. He saith not, And to seeds, as of many; but as of one, And to thy <u>seed</u>, which is <u>Christ</u>**" (Galatians 3:16). The Lord Jesus Christ is "**the Saviour of the world**" (John 4:42; 1 John 4:14)! When Abraham believed God, his faith was accounted to him for righteousness. All the heathen who believe are also justified by faith and blessed with faithful Abraham. The blessing of Abraham came upon the Gentiles through Jesus Christ. Read Galatians 3:6-16.

GOD'S PURPOSE WITH PHARAOH

The LORD God's purpose in showing his great power against rebellious Pharaoh and his people in Egypt was told to Pharaoh by Moses, saying, "And in very deed for this *cause* have I raised thee up, for to shew *in* thee my power; and **that my name may be declared throughout all the earth**" (Exodus 9:16). God wanted his name to be known throughout all the earth! Paul the apostle also quoted this, saying, "For the scripture saith unto Pharaoh, Even for this same purpose have I raised thee up, that I might shew my power in thee, and **that my**

name might be declared throughout all the earth" (Romans 9:17). This one thing is very clear; God's desire is for all the earth to know him!

THEY HEARD THE MESSAGE

When the two spies from Israel came to Jericho and were hidden by Rahab the harlot, Rahab "said unto the men, I know that the LORD hath given you the land, and that your terror is fallen upon us, and that all the inhabitants of the land faint because of you. For we have heard how the LORD dried up the water of the Red Sea for you, when ye came out of Egypt; and what ye did unto the two kings of the Amorites, that *were* on the other side Jordan, Sihon and Og, whom ye utterly destroyed. **And as soon as we had heard *these things*, our hearts did melt, neither did there remain any more courage in any man, because of you: for the LORD your God, he *is* God in heaven above, and in earth beneath**" (Joshua 2:9-11). Rahab and her family were saved from destruction, because they believed on the LORD. This was God's will and purpose! The other people of Jericho also heard the report, but they did not believe! They were destroyed with the city of Jericho! It is the same in our country today! Most people have heard the good news of the death, burial, and resurrection of Jesus Christ for our sins, but only a few have believed and been saved by the grace of God! All unbelievers "**shall have their part in the lake which burneth with fire and brimstone: which is the second death**" (Revelation 21:8)! God does not will their destruction. God has provided a way for them to escape. But if they do not come to God through faith in Jesus Christ, the holy and righteous judgment of God demands their eternal destruction! We believers need to tell lost sinners the good news and their need to repent and "**believe the gospel**" (Mark 1:15)!

GOD'S PURPOSE FOR ISRAEL

The LORD gave his law to Moses for Israel to keep, and commanded them, "**Keep therefore and do *them*; for this *is* your wisdom and your understanding <u>in the sight of the nations</u>, which shall hear all these statutes, and say, Surely this great nation *is* a wise and understanding people. For what nation *is there so* great, who *hath* God *so* nigh unto them, as the LORD our God *is* in all *things that* we call upon him *for*? And what nation *is there so* great, that hath statutes and judgments *so* righteous as all this law, which I set before you this day?**" (Deuteronomy 4:6-8). The nation of Israel was to be a light to the Gentile nations by keeping God's commandments in the midst of them. The Lord Jesus Christ told the Jews, "**Let your light so shine before men, that they may see your good works, and glorify your Father which is in heaven**" (Matthew 5:16).

The psalmist of Israel wrote Psalm 96 exhorting Israel to sing a new song unto the LORD, and to "**shew forth his salvation from day to day. Declare his glory among the heathen, his wonders among all people**" (Psalm 96:2-3). In the same psalm David also wrote, "**Say among the heathen *that* the LORD reigneth: the world also shall be established that it shall not be moved: he shall judge the people righteously**" (Psalm 96:10). So not only was Israel commanded to keep Moses' law as a testimony to the nations, but the people of Israel were commanded to be witnesses and to declare God's glory, works, and judgment to the heathen.

The LORD said that he called and created and redeemed the nation of Israel (Isaiah 43:1). The LORD went on to say, "**This people have I formed for myself; they shall shew forth my praise**" (Isaiah 43:21). The LORD has also called and created and redeemed each member of his "**body the church**" (Colossians 1:18) for the same purpose. The Apostle Peter wrote in 1 Peter 2:9-12, "**But ye *are* a chosen generation, a royal priesthood, an holy nation, a peculiar people; that ye should shew forth the praises of him who hath called you out of darkness into his marvellous light**: Which in time past *were* not a people, but *are* now the people of God: which had not obtained mercy, but now have obtained mercy. Dearly beloved, I beseech *you* as strangers and pilgrims, abstain from fleshly lusts, which war against the soul; **Having your conversation honest among the Gentiles: that, whereas they speak against you as evildoers, they may by *your* good works, which they shall behold, glorify God in the day of visitation**."

The "day of visitation" is the day that God chooses to visit and call an individual by the gospel. My day of visitation was on a rainy day in June of 1979 as I was reading the New Testament in my house. The Holy Ghost reproved me for my sin of unbelief, gave me faith to believe his word, and saved me when I received and believed on the Lord Jesus Christ. God is now visiting the Gentiles "**to take out of them a people for his name**" (Acts 15:14).

After the church has been gathered to meet the Lord in the air (1 Thessalonians 4:16-18) the Lord will build again the nation of Israel, which is fallen down, and set it up: "**That the residue of men might seek after the Lord, and all the Gentiles, upon whom my name is called, saith the Lord, who doeth all these things. Known unto God are all his works from the beginning of the world**" (Acts 15:15-18). From the beginning it has always been God's purpose to save, love, and have a relationship with all men.

The Apostle Paul wrote to the church at Philippi, saying, "Wherefore, my beloved, as ye have always obeyed, not as in my presence only, but now much more in my absence, **work out your own salvation with fear and trembling**. For it is God which worketh in you both to will and to do of *his* good pleasure. Do all things without murmurings and disputings: That ye may be blameless and harmless, the sons of God, without rebuke, in the midst of a crooked and perverse nation, **among whom ye shine as lights in the world**; **Holding forth the word of life**; that I may rejoice in the day of Christ, that I have not run in vain, neither laboured in vain" (Philippians 2:12-16).

There are two main things to see in these verses. First, he commands the believers: "**work out your own salvation with fear and trembling**." This does not say that the believer is working FOR his own salvation or ON his own salvation, but that he is to work into his outward life and testimony that which the Spirit of God is working within him. "**For it is God which worketh in you both to will and to do of *his* good pleasure**" (Philippians 2:13).

We are to live in this world in obedience to our God, doing good works that the world can see. We are to "**shine as lights in the world**" (Philippians 2:15), that the world may "**see your good works, and glorify your Father which is in heaven**" (Matthew 5:16).

"**For we are his workmanship, created in Christ Jesus unto good works, which God hath before ordained that we should walk in them**" (Ephesians 2:10).

And not only should our lives demonstrate the power of God to become the sons of God in practice, but we are also to hold "**forth the word of life**." We are to proclaim the word of God to them by living the word of God; as well, we are to preach the gospel to them. We must do both! We must live right and speak right, speaking the truth in love. No one wants to listen to an obvious hypocrite. Who would be interested in a God who is powerless to deliver you from the bondage of sin?

ONLY THE TRUE GOD CAN SAVE

The Old Testament people were told in Isaiah 45:20-24, "Assemble yourselves and come; draw near together, ye *that are* escaped of the nations: they have no knowledge that set up the wood of their graven image, and pray unto a god *that* cannot save. Tell ye, and bring *them* near; yea, let them take counsel together: who hath declared this from ancient time? *who* hath told it from that time? *have* not I the LORD? and ***there is* no God else beside me; a just God and a Saviour; *there is* none beside me. Look unto me, and be ye saved, all the ends of the earth: for I *am* God, and *there is* none else. I have sworn by myself, the word is gone out of my mouth *in* righteousness, and shall not return, That unto me every knee shall bow, every tongue shall swear**. Surely, shall *one* say, in the LORD have I righteousness and strength: *even* to him shall *men* come; and all that are incensed against him shall be ashamed."

The New Testament identifies the "**just God and a Saviour**" spoken of by Isaiah (mentioned above in Isaiah 45:20-24) as "**Jesus**" (Philippians 2:10). The New Testament explains, "And being found in fashion as a man, he humbled himself, and became obedient unto death, even the death of the cross. **Wherefore God also hath highly exalted him, and given him a name which is above every name**: **That at the name of Jesus every knee should bow, of *things* in heaven, and *things* in earth, and *things* under the earth**; **And *that* every tongue should confess that Jesus Christ *is* Lord, to the glory of God the Father**" (Philippians 2:8-11).

The Father sent the Son into the world so that men might believe, so that men might confess and bow their knee to his "**Son Jesus Christ. This is the true God, and eternal life**" (1 John 5:20)! All believers should live for him and witness for him.

ISRAEL'S FAILURE

Do you remember Israel and God's purpose for them? Israel was to walk in the light of God's law "**in the sight of the nations**" (Deuteronomy 4:6), and they were to, "**Declare his glory among the heathen**" (Psalm 96:3). Israel failed to accomplish their duty because of spiritual pride. Do you remember Jonah's attitude toward the heathen in Nineveh? He ran from God in a vain attempt to avoid having to preach God's word to them! God desired their salvation. Jonah desired their damnation! When the people of Nineveh repented at the preaching of Jonah, "**it displeased Jonah exceedingly, and he was very angry**" (Jonah 4:1). Finally God said to Jonah, "**And should not I spare Nineveh, that great city, wherein are more than sixscore thousand persons that cannot discern between their right hand and their left hand; and *also* much cattle**?" (Jonah 4:11). "And Jonah prayed unto the LORD, and said, I pray thee, O LORD...I knew that thou *art* a gracious God, and merciful, slow to anger, and of great kindness, and repentest thee of the evil" (Jonah 4:2). Jonah knew God's plan and attempted to avert it; but God had the final say. I would encourage you to open up your Bible and read his pitiful story in the book of Jonah. There is much that you and can learn from his testimony.

At the time when Jesus walked in Israel, the Jews had rejected and ignored the Samaritans. When the Lord Jesus asked the Samaritan woman at the well for a drink of water, "Then saith the woman of Samaria unto him, How is it that thou, being a Jew, askest drink of me, which am a woman of Samaria? **for the Jews have no dealings with the Samaritans**" (John 4:9). When his disciples returned and saw that he spoke with the Samaritan woman they "**marvelled that he talked with the woman**" (John 4:27). In fact, the Jews had rejected all the nations of the Gentiles. Peter affirmed that truth to the household of Cornelius:

"And he [Peter] said unto them, **Ye know how that it is an unlawful thing for a man that is a Jew to keep company, or come unto one of another nation**; but God hath shewed me that I should not call any man common or unclean" (Acts 10:28).

Peter said that it was "unlawful" for the Jew to come to one of another nation! You will not find that in God's law! The Jews by their own traditions had made the law of God of none effect (Mark 7:9; Matthew 15:3-6). God wanted the called out nation of Israel to be a witness and a light to the Gentile nations! They failed!

THE CHURCH'S FAILURE

In Acts 1:8 Jesus declared, "*But ye shall receive power, after that the Holy Ghost is come upon you.*" The church needs the Spirit's power to be effective witnesses of Christ both in our local communities and also unto the uttermost parts of the earth. Praise God for the few Christian missionaries who are proclaiming the Gospel in every nation on earth. Nonetheless, the majority of the church is failing to reach the world with the gospel, because so many "Christians" have adopted the ways of the world. Many Christians fail to have the whole world in view with regard to evangelism. Some of the few who are engaged in evangelizing are concerned only with their local community. Even worse, many Christians love themselves too much! The lusts of other things, riches, pleasures, and cares of this life have taken away their zeal for God and their desire to reach the lost for the Lord Jesus Christ. We must never forget that we who are now saved were once "**dead in trespasses and sins**" (Ephesians 2:1) and on the broad way that leadeth to eternal destruction (Matthew 7:13-14). Somehow, God reached us with the gospel! Thank God! We were all dead, because Jesus Christ died for all. We should live unto Christ, who died for all. We should be about the business of reaching the lost for the one who died for them:

"**For the love of Christ constraineth us; because we thus judge, that if one died for all, then were all dead: And *that* he died for all, that they which live should not henceforth live unto themselves, but unto him which died for them, and rose again**" (2 Corinthians 5:14-15).

CONCLUSION

Fellow believer, it is only reasonable that we should offer our bodies on this earth as a living sacrifice (Romans 12:1-2) for the work of the ministry and for the glory of "**the great God and our Saviour Jesus Christ**" (Titus 2:13). If you are saved, I pray that you will walk in the light of God's word in fellowship with the Lord Jesus (1 John 1:7) and let men see your good works and hear your testimony of God's amazing grace through the outworking of God in your life.

If you are not saved, I pray that you will hear the gospel and believe on the Lord Jesus Christ and be saved (Acts 16:31) before you die in your sins. A good place to begin reading in the New Testament is *The Gospel According to St. John.* Read it and believe it, and trust the Lord Jesus Christ as your Saviour. Tomorrow may be too late! Jesus is coming for his church soon!

Chapter 28

A WORKING CHURCH

Our scriptural text of the day is 1 Thessalonians 1:5-10. The Bible states, "For our gospel came not unto you in word only, but also in power, and in the Holy Ghost, and in much assurance; as ye know what manner of men we were among you for your sake. And ye became followers of us, and of the Lord, having received the word in much affliction, with joy of the Holy Ghost: So that ye were ensamples to all that believe in Macedonia and Achaia. For from you sounded out the word of the Lord not only in Macedonia and Achaia, but also in every place your faith to God-ward is spread abroad; so that we need not to speak any thing. For they themselves shew of us what manner of entering in we had unto you, and how ye turned to God from idols to serve the living and true God; And to wait for his Son from heaven, whom he raised from the dead, *even* Jesus, which delivered us from the wrath to come."

THE WORD OF THE GOSPEL

The beginning part of 1 Thessalonians 1:5 says, "For our gospel came not unto you in word only."

What gospel? **"The gospel of the grace of God"** (Acts 20:24), "**how that Christ died for our sins according to the scriptures**; **And that he was**

buried, and that he rose again the third day according to the scriptures" (1 Corinthians 15:3-4). "**It is the power of God unto salvation to every one that believeth; to the Jew first, and also to the Greek**" (Romans 1:16; 1 Corinthians 1:18).

THE POWER OF THE GOSPEL

The next part of 1 Thessalonians 1:5 continues on with the thought and says, "...but also in power, and in the Holy Ghost..."

The Holy Ghost is given to all who believe in their heart that God raised Jesus Christ from the dead (Romans 10:9). Through the Holy Ghost, believers are empowered to be "**labourers together with God**" (1 Corinthians 3:9), and to witness and preach the same gospel, which saved them, to other people (John 1:12-13; Romans 15:18-19; 16:25-27; Acts 1:8; 4:33; 1 Corinthians 2:4-5; 1 Corinthians 4:19-20; Ephesians 3:7, 20; 6:10; Philippians 3:10; Colossians 1:9-11). This is what Paul had done when he preached the gospel with the power of God to the Thessalonians.

THE ASSURANCE OF THE GOSPEL

The third part of 1 Thessalonians 1:5 says, " ...and in much assurance..."

1. Assurance of understanding

Paul wrote to the Colossians that his desire was: "That their hearts might be comforted, being knit together in love, and unto all riches of the **full assurance of understanding**, to the acknowledgement of the mystery of God, and of the Father, and of Christ; In whom are hid all the treasures of wisdom and knowledge" (Colossians 2:2-3).

I have met many men who have some knowledge of the Bible, but they have no fear of God, nor wisdom, and no understanding. "**Full assurance of understanding**" (Colossians 2:2) comes as the result of obedience to God's word. *Understanding* is God's blessing upon the obedient. "**The fear of the LORD *is* the beginning of wisdom: and the knowledge of the holy *is* understanding**" (Proverbs 9:10): "*but* fools despise wisdom and instruction" (Proverbs 1:7). God said unto man: "**Behold, the fear of the Lord, that *is* wisdom; and to depart from evil *is* understanding**" (Job 28:28). The psalmist wrote: "The fear of the LORD *is* the beginning of wisdom: **a good understanding have all they that**

do *his commandments*: his praise endureth for ever" (Psalm 111:10). David also wrote: "**I have more understanding than all my teachers: for thy testimonies *are* my meditation. I understand more than the ancients, because I keep thy precepts**" (Psalm 119:99-100). The Lord Jesus said: "**If any man will do his will, he shall know of the doctrine, whether it be of God, or *whether* I speak of myself**" (John 7:17).

"**Full assurance of understanding**" (Colossians 2:2) is received by the believer as the result of spiritual exercise. The Lord Jesus said "to those Jews which believed on him, **If ye continue in my word, *then* are ye my disciples indeed; And ye shall know the truth, and the truth shall make you free**" (John 8:31-32). The scripture in 2 Peter 3:18 commands: "**But grow in grace, and *in* the knowledge of our Lord and Saviour Jesus Christ**." These scriptures do not mean that the believers should simply accumulate knowledge from God's word like a heartless, spiritless, and lifeless computer. Those who have been saved by grace through faith are God's "**workmanship, created in Christ Jesus unto good works, which God hath before ordained that we should walk in them**" (Ephesians 2:8-10). And the Lord commands: "**But be ye doers of the word**, and not hearers only, deceiving your own selves" (James 1:22).

EXERCISE

Paul wrote to Timothy: "But refuse profane and old wives' fables, and **exercise thyself *rather* unto godliness. For bodily exercise profiteth little: but godliness is profitable unto all things, having promise of the life that now is, and of that which is to come**" (1 Timothy 4:6-8). You could read all the best books on physical exercise and have the knowledge of how to build muscles and increase your endurance, but until you actually *do* the exercises, the information you have read will not profit your physical body! In the same way, if you have read the Bible from cover to cover, and you *think* you know all that it has to say, but you are not a "doer of the word," then you are deceiving yourself (James 1:22)! It has not profited you! If you are a doer of the word, then you will have your "**senses exercised to discern both good and evil**" (Hebrews 5:14). Paul was an obedient hearer who said: "**And herein do I exercise myself, to have always a conscience void of offence toward God, and *toward* men**" (Acts 24:16). In other words, Paul said that he was living his life in such a way so as not to be an offence toward God or man. The LORD said: "But let him that glorieth glory in this, that he understandeth and knoweth me, that I *am* the LORD **which exercise lovingkindness, judgment, and righteousness, in the earth**: for in these *things* I delight, saith the LORD" (Jeremiah 9:24). As God continues to conform the born again believer to the image of his Son (Romans 8:29), and as God works in him, the believer will also "exercise lovingkindness, judgment, and righteousness, in the earth."

2. Assurance of hope

Hebrews 6:10-11 tell us, "For God *is* not unrighteous to forget your work and labour of love, which ye have shewed toward his name, in that ye have ministered to the saints, and do minister. And we desire that every one of you do shew the same diligence to **the full assurance of hope** unto the end." Assurance of hope is given to those children of God who submit to God (James 4:7) and faithfully work "together with God" (1 Corinthians 3:9). By "hope" is meant to place **confidence** in; or to **trust** in with **confident** expectation of good (Noah Webster 1828 Dictionary). The Christian's *hope* is assured by God's infallible word, which will be fulfilled! This is not at all like the world's *hope*, which may or may not come to pass. The true believer's confidence is not in himself, but is in the Lord Jesus Christ and in all of his wonderful promises (Philippians 3:3). The Lord Jesus Christ *himself* is the Christian's great *hope*, both now and forever (1 Timothy 1:1; Titus 2:13; Joel 3:16; Jeremiah 17:7; 50:7; Hebrews 6:19; 7:19)! The born again believer has Christ in him, "**the hope of glory**" (Colossians 1:27)!

Is the Spirit of Christ in you? Since your salvation, have you continued in his word (John 8:31-32)? Are you purifying yourself, "even as he is pure" (1 John 3:3)? "**Now if any man have not the Spirit of Christ, he is none of his**" (Romans 8:9).

3. Assurance of faith

"Let us draw near with a true heart in full **assurance of faith**, having our hearts sprinkled from an evil conscience, and our bodies washed with pure water" (Hebrews 10:22). We obtain a **full assurance of faith** by believing and understanding God's word (Romans 10:17). True faith in God comes from understanding the word of God. Through Isaiah (Isaiah 6:9) and Jeremiah (Jeremiah 5:21), God was addressing people who heard his word with their ears, but they did not understand it. The people were *hearing* God's word, but it had no effect upon them, because they did not *understand* it. In the "parable of the sower" we read about those who *hear*, but do not *understand* (Matthews 13:19). Then we read about those who both hear and understand the word (Matthews 13:23). The Lord Jesus "called the multitude, and said unto them, **Hear, and understand**" (Matthew 15:10). The word of God not only brings faith, but gives wisdom and is able to build men up (2 Timothy 3:14-15; Acts 20:32). In Acts 20:32, "all them which are sanctified" refers to all the saved who were "sanctified by faith" (Acts 16:18) in the Lord Jesus Christ. The word of God is able to build up the saved child of God, so that he can serve the Lord in this life and receive an inheritance in God's eternal kingdom later (Acts 20:32).

The last part of 1 Thessalonians 1:5 says, "...as ye know what manner of men we were among you for your sake."

Paul, the apostle to the Gentiles, was set forth, "**for a pattern to them which should hereafter believe on him to life everlasting**" (1 Timothy 1:16). Because of this, Paul recounts many of the events of his ministry, so that we can know to expect trouble and persecution in the world when we live godly in the world (2 Corinthians 11:22-33). Paul wrote to Timothy: "**Yea, and all that will live godly in Christ Jesus shall suffer persecution**" (2 Timothy 3:12).

THE LORD SUFFERED FOR US

Do not be deceived by the "prosperity" and "feel good" preachers on television or radio who preach that you are not right with God if you are not financially rich or having "your best life now," like they are! Such men are hirelings who are deceiving the simple (Romans 16:17-18). If you want to know the absolute truth, then turn off the television and radio and read your Kings James Bible! The apostles made several statements regarding the *real* Christian life and its expectations. The following scriptures show how the Lord Jesus Christ suffered for our sakes: "**For Christ also hath once suffered for sins, the just for the unjust, that he might bring us to God, being put to death in the flesh, but quickened by the Spirit**" (1 Peter 3:18). "**That Christ should suffer, *and* that he should be the first that should rise from the dead, and should shew light unto the people, and to the Gentiles**" (Acts 26:23). "**But we see Jesus, who was made a little lower than the angels for the suffering of death, crowned with glory and honour; that he by the grace of God should taste death for every man**" (Hebrews 2:9).

CHRISTIANS ALSO SUFFER

The Lord Jesus is also an example for us to follow: "**For even hereunto were ye called: because Christ also suffered for us, leaving us an example, that ye should follow his steps**" (1 Peter 2:21). And if we follow the Lord's steps, by following the leadership of the Holy Ghost according to the word of

God, we will also suffer: "**For unto you it is given in the behalf of Christ, not only to believe on him, but also to suffer for his sake**" (Philippians 1:29). "**Forasmuch then as Christ hath suffered for us in the flesh, arm yourselves likewise with the same mind: for he that hath suffered in the flesh hath ceased from sin**" (1 Peter 4:1). See also 1 Peter 5:10, Colossians 1:24, and 2 Timothy 3:12.

BELIEVERS BECOME FOLLOWERS ...
... FOLLOWERS OF THE APOSTLE PAUL

The beginning of 1 Thessalonians 1:6 says, "And ye became followers of us..."

All believers should desire to be a good example to others. Because Paul was walking after the Spirit, therefore he could write to the church at Philippi: "**Brethren, be followers together of me, and mark them which walk so as ye have us for an ensample**" (Philippians 3:17); and to the church at Corinth he wrote: "**Be ye followers of me, even as I also *am* of Christ**" (1 Corinthians 11:1). In his second letter to the Thessalonians Paul commanded, "**that ye withdraw yourselves from every brother that walketh disorderly, and not after the tradition which he received of us. For yourselves know how ye ought to follow us: for we behaved not ourselves disorderly among you; Neither did we eat any man's bread for nought; but wrought with labour and travail night and day, that we might not be chargeable to any of you: Not because we have not power, but to make ourselves an ensample unto you to follow us**" (2 Thessalonians 3:6-9). Paul's very life was a good example for all to observe, for he lived a Spirit filled life in this world, and practiced what he preached. He worked for his food and other personal needs, in accordance with the inspired word of God. He wrote to them in his second letter, saying, "**For even when we were with you, this we commanded you, that if any would not work, neither should he eat**" (2 Thessalonians 3:10). Paul's *teaching* was also committed to faithful men, who are commanded to continue to teach and preach the truth for generations to come. Paul wrote to Timothy saying, "**And the things that thou hast heard of me among many witnesses, the same commit thou to faithful men, who shall be able to teach others also**" (2 Timothy 2:2).

FOLLOWERS OF THE LORD

The middle section of 1 Thessalonians 1:6 says, "...and of the Lord..."

These faithful men had also become followers of the Lord Jesus Christ, which is the calling of all born again believers. First Peter 2:21-24 describes the calling of all born again believers by saying: "**For even hereunto were ye called: because Christ also suffered for us, leaving us an example, that ye should follow his steps**: Who did no sin, neither was guile found in his mouth: Who, when he was reviled, reviled not again; when he suffered, he threatened not; but committed *himself* to him that judgeth righteously: **Who his own self bare our sins in his own body on the tree, that we, being dead to sins, should live unto righteousness: by whose stripes ye were healed**."

AFFLICTION WITH JOY

The last part of 1 Thessalonians 1:6 says, "...having received the word in much affliction, with joy of the Holy Ghost."

The Christian's life certainly includes affliction, but God also gives joy through the Holy Ghost in the midst of the affliction. After the Jews "raised persecution against Paul and Barnabas, and expelled them out of their coasts... they shook off the dust of their feet against them, and came unto Iconium. **And the disciples were filled with joy, and with the Holy Ghost**" (Acts 13:50-52). After having been beaten by the Jewish council and commanded that they should not speak in the name of Jesus, the apostles "**departed from the presence of the council, <u>rejoicing that they were counted worthy to suffer shame for his name</u>. And daily in the temple, and in every house, they ceased not to teach and preach Jesus Christ**" (Acts 5:41-42). Paul wrote to the Romans: "**Now the God of hope fill you with all joy and peace in believing, that ye may abound in hope, through the power of the Holy Ghost**" (Romans 15:13). After being beaten with many stripes, Paul and Silas were thrust into the inner prison, and their feet put in stocks. Then we read: "**And at midnight Paul and Silas prayed, and sang praises unto God: and the prisoners heard them**" (Acts 16:22-25). The result of the testimony of their joy and praise to God in the midst of their affliction was that the jailor and his family, and perhaps some other prisoners, were saved (Acts 16:26-34)! If you are a believer, may God bless you with the same "**joy and peace in believing**" (Romans 15:13).

BELIEVERS BECAME EXAMPLES

First Thessalonians 1:7 says, "So that ye were ensamples to all that believe in Macedonia and Achaia."

In other words, Paul was saying that God was working in these Thessalonians (Philippians 2:13), and making them an example of his grace among the other people in the area. In like manner, all Christians should be examples of God's grace to believers and unbelievers alike: "**Let no man despise thy youth; but <u>be thou an example of the believers, in word, in conversation, in charity, in spirit, in faith, in purity</u>**" (1 Timothy 4:12); "**In all things shewing thyself a pattern of good works: in doctrine *shewing* uncorruptness, gravity, sincerity, Sound speech, that cannot be condemned; that he that is of the contrary part may be ashamed, having no evil thing to say of you**" (Titus 2:7-8).

BELIEVERS BECAME PREACHERS

The beginning of 1 Thessalonians 1:8 says, "For from you sounded out the word of the Lord not only in Macedonia and Achaia, but also in every place your faith to God–ward is spread abroad..."

Under the law, the LORD told Moses to instruct the children of Israel: "...**in the day of atonement shall ye <u>make the trumpet sound throughout all your land</u>**" (Leviticus 25:9). In this case, the trumpet was to announce to all the people the day of atonement. Latter, the LORD told Isaiah: "**Cry aloud, spare not, <u>lift up thy voice like a trumpet</u>, and shew my people their transgression, and the house of Jacob their sins**" (Isaiah 58:1).

This church had been obedient to the commandment given to all of his disciples by the Lord Jesus, and they "sounded out the word." The Lord has commanded his church to preach the gospel to the whole world. After his resurrection from the dead, the Lord Jesus commanded his disciples: "**Go ye into all the world, and <u>preach the gospel to every creature</u>**" [(Mark 16:15) see also Matthew 28:19 and Acts 1:8]! About twenty-seven years later, the Apostle Paul wrote: "**So then faith *cometh* by hearing, and hearing by the word of God. But I say, Have they not heard? Yes verily, <u>their sound went into all the earth, and their words unto the ends of the world</u>**" (Romans 10:17-18). The believers at Thessalonica had entered into the ministry of preaching the gospel (1 Thessalonians 1:8), for God had sent them, according to his word: "**And how shall they preach, except they be sent? as it is written, How beautiful are the feet of them that preach the gospel of peace, and bring glad tidings of good things!**" (Romans 10:15).

The last part of 1 Thessalonians 1:8 says, "...so that we need not to speak any thing."

In other words, Paul was saying that wherever he went, he did not need to say anything about the Thessalonians turning to the Lord, for those things were sufficiently made known by people who had come to Paul from the Thessalonians, by those who had visited this church, and by this church's zeal in preaching the gospel. This church had a good testimony! This was not a dead church (James 2:17) like "the church of the Laodiceans" (Revelation 3:14-22), which typifies many churches today, who are so "carnal" and "worldly," and so void of the true gospel of the grace of God, that they are nothing more than hypocritical, man pleasing social clubs and entertainment centers! The church in Thessalonica had a living and active faith which brought forth good works (Ephesians 2:10). The Holy Spirit of God was working in them, "both to will and to do of his good pleasure" (Philippians 2:13). Paul likewise commended the church at Rome, saying, "**First, I thank my God through Jesus Christ for you all, that <u>your faith is spoken of throughout the whole world</u>**" (Romans 1:8). Are you part of such a church? Do you attend church regularly, when you are out on the street and able? Believers are commanded: "**And let us consider one another to provoke unto love and to good works: Not forsaking the assembling of ourselves together, as the manner of some *is*; but exhorting *one another*: and so much the more, as ye see the day approaching**" (Hebrews 10:24-25).

This church was doing the same work among others as the apostle had done among them! They were preaching the gospel to the people all around them. If you are saved, you should go and do the same. We should get the word of God out in some way, either by word of mouth or by the printed page. God said: "**my word…shall not return unto me void** [empty or vacant], **but it shall accomplish that which I** [the Lord] **please, and it shall prosper** [be successful] ***in the thing* whereto I sent it**" (Isaiah 55:11). "**For the word of God *is* quick** [alive; living], **and powerful, and sharper than any twoedged sword, piercing even to the dividing asunder of soul and spirit, and of the joints and marrow, and *is* a discerner of the thoughts and intents of the heart**" (Hebrews 4:12). And Paul said: "**For I am not ashamed of the gospel of Christ: for it is the power of God unto salvation to every one that believeth; to the Jew first, and also to the Greek**" (Romans 1:16). We would do well to follow the faith of the church in Thessalonica. Let's get the gospel of Jesus Christ out to as many as we are able, by the grace of God.

BELIEVERS REPENTED

First Thessalonians 1:9 says, "For they themselves shew of us what manner of entering in we had unto you, and how ye turned to God from idols to serve the living and true God."

The Macedonians and Achaians witnessed that the word of God had been very effectual among the Thessalonians' people. The gospel had come to them in word and power and with the Holy Ghost, and in much assurance (1 Thessalonians 1:5), and had been received of them in much affliction with the joy of the Holy Ghost (1 Thessalonians 1:6). The entrance of the apostle was not in vain (1 Thessalonians 2:1; 1 Corinthians 15:2), even though the gospel had been preached with much contention (1 Thessalonians 2:2). Nevertheless the gospel message had been received by them as "the word of God" (1 Thessalonians 2:13), which had worked effectually in them that believed (1 Thessalonians 2:13). The gospel had produced faith, and they had become followers of Christ (1 Thessalonians 1:9-10; 2:14). The fruitfulness of the believers in Thessalonica was proof that Paul's ministry to them had been true and effectual.

God had given them "**repentance to the acknowledging of the truth**" (2 Timothy 2:25), and they had repented of their unbelief and had believed "**the glorious gospel of Christ**" (2 Corinthians 4:4). After believing the gospel, and being "born of the Spirit" (John 3:6-8), these believers willfully and gratefully turned away from their dead idols to serve the living and true God. God hates and ridicules the absurd practice of idolatry (Psalm 115:4-8). God also says that the people who bow down to images *hate* him (Exodus 20:4-5)!

BELIEVERS ARE WAITING FOR THE LORD

The first part of 1 Thessalonians 1:10 says, "And to wait for his Son from heaven…"

Are you waiting and looking for the Lord Jesus Christ to come from heaven to take you to be with himself? I am "Looking for that blessed hope, and the glorious **appearing** of the great **God** and our **Saviour Jesus Christ**" (Titus 2:13)! When he comes, "**we** [born again believers] **shall all be changed…and the dead** [in Christ] **shall be raised incorruptible**" (1 Corinthians 15:51-53). He "**shall change our vile body, that it may be fashioned like unto his glorious body, according to the working whereby he is able even to subdue all things unto himself**" (Philippians 3:21)! Do you seek to be closer to the Lord each day? Are you purifying yourself, "even as he is pure" (1 John 3:2-3)? Do you continue in God's word (John 8:31-32)? Are you filled with the Holy Spirit (Ephesians 5:18)? Do you agree with the Apostle John's prayer, "**Even so, come, Lord Jesus**" (Revelation 22:20)?

The second part of 1 Thessalonians 1:10 says, "...**whom he raised from the dead, *even* Jesus**."

Belief in the physical resurrection of Jesus Christ from the dead is an essential part of the gospel of our salvation (1 Corinthians 15:3-4; Romans 6:9; 7:4; 2 Timothy 2:8). And one MUST believe the gospel before he can be saved (Ephesians 1:13). The scripture says, "That if thou shalt confess with thy mouth the Lord Jesus, and shalt **believe in thine heart** that God hath **raised** **him from the dead**, thou shalt be **saved**" (Romans 10:9)!

DELIVERED FROM WRATH

The last but not the least part of 1 Thessalonians 1:10 says, "...**which delivered us from the wrath to come**."

Believers will be delivered from the wrath to come when the Lord Jesus comes to get his church. The Lord will gather his saints to himself, when he descends from heaven with a shout (1 Thessalonians 4:16-18), "as a thief in the night" (1 Thessalonians 5:2). But only as a thief to those who are not waiting and looking for his appearing, the unbelievers. Then the "man of sin," "that Wicked," will be revealed (2 Thessalonians 2:7-8). "For God hath not appointed us [the church] to **wrath**, but to obtain **salvation** by our Lord Jesus Christ" [(1 Thessalonians 5:9) see also Romans 5:9; 1 Thessalonians 1:10, 5:9]! We, who are members of the body of Christ (Ephesians 5:29-30), will be delivered both from the "time of Jacob's trouble" (Jeremiah 30:7), called the "tribulation" (Matthew 24:29), and also from "**the lake which burneth with fire and brimstone: which is the second death**" (Revelation 21:8; 20:14-15)!

"**Believe on the Lord Jesus Christ, and thou shalt be saved**" (Acts 16:31).

Chapter 29

Commands for Believers

Our scriptural text for this sermon outline comes from 1 Thessalonians 5:11-22. The scriptures says, "Wherefore comfort yourselves together, and edify one another, even as also ye do. And we beseech you, brethren, to know them which labour among you, and are over you in the Lord, and admonish you. And to esteem them very highly in love for their work's sake. *And* be at peace among yourselves. Now we exhort you, brethren, warn them that are unruly, comfort the feebleminded, support the weak, be patient toward all *men*. See that none render evil for evil unto any *man*; but ever follow that which is good, both among yourselves, and to all *men*. Rejoice evermore. Pray without ceasing. In every thing give thanks: for this is the will of God in Christ Jesus concerning you. Quench not the Spirit. Despise not prophesyings. Prove all things; hold fast that which is good. Abstain from all appearance of evil."

In this short section of scripture, several very important commandments are given to believers. Let's look at the details of these commandments and apply them to our lives.

COMFORT

The Bible verse 1 Thessalonians 5:11 instructs believers to comfort themselves together. In other words, the Apostle Paul is saying that because of the things which he had written to them, they should comfort themselves when they meet together as a church (Hebrews 10:25). Paul had exhorted and comforted and charged them "as a father *doth* his children" (1 Thessalonians 2:11). He had also sent Timotheus to establish them, and to comfort them concerning their faith (1 Thessalonians 3:2). Specifically Paul had comforted them with his words concerning the "dead in Christ," and the promise of the coming of the Lord Jesus Christ for his church, after which event all born again believers shall "ever be with the Lord" (1 Thessalonians 4:13-17)! Then the apostle wrote: "**Wherefore comfort one another with these words**" (1 Thessalonians 4:18). It should be very comforting for every born again believer to realize that whatever he may be suffering in "this present evil world" (Galatians 1:4), one day all his troubles will be over! This alone is great cause to: "**Rejoice evermore**" (1 Thessalonians 5:16)!

COMFORT OF THE SCRIPTURES

All believers who continue in God's word (John 8:31-32) will receive much comfort: "**For whatsoever things were written aforetime were written for our learning, that we through patience and <u>comfort</u> of the scriptures might have hope**" (Romans 15:4). David wrote in Psalm 119:50-52 of how God's word comforted him: "**This *is* my comfort in my affliction**: for thy word hath quickened me. The proud have had me greatly in derision: *yet* have I not declined from thy law. **I remembered thy judgments of old, O LORD; and have comforted myself.**" David also wrote, "Yea, though I walk through the valley of the shadow of death, I will fear no evil: for thou *art* with me; **thy rod and thy staff they comfort me**" (Psalm 23:4).

GOD'S COMFORT

All born again believers have been given the Holy Ghost (John 14:18; 15:26; 16:17; Acts 9:31), who is called "**the Comforter**" (John 14:26), who abides with the believer for ever (John 14:16). Paul also wrote in 2 Thessalonians 2:16-17: "**Now our Lord Jesus Christ himself, and God, even our Father, which hath loved us, and hath given *us* everlasting consolation and good hope through grace, Comfort your hearts, and stablish you in every good word and work.**"

COMFORT OF OTHER BELIEVERS

Believers are also comforted by their mutual faith (Romans 1:12), and by the preaching and prophesying of God's word (1 Corinthians 14:3). Paul wrote that God comforted him and gave him the ability to comfort others with that same comfort. He wrote to the Corinthians: "**Blessed *be* God, even the Father of our Lord Jesus Christ, the Father of mercies, and the God of all comfort; Who comforteth us in all our tribulation, that we may be able to comfort them which are in any trouble, by the comfort wherewith we ourselves are comforted of God**" (Corinthians 1:3-4). Paul sent Tychicus to the Ephesians to tell them of his affairs and to comfort their hearts (Ephesians 6:22).

EDIFYING

Next, 1 Thessalonians 5:11 speaks that we are to, "edify one another, even as also ye do."

Similarly as his letter to the Thessalonians, Paul wrote to the Corinthian church that the Lord had given him authority as an apostle "**for edification, and not for your destruction**" (2 Corinthians 10:8). Again Paul wrote, "**but *we do* all things, dearly beloved, for your edifying**" (2 Corinthians 12:19). And again, in the same letter, Paul wrote: "Therefore I write these things being absent, lest being present I should use sharpness, **according to the power which the Lord hath given me to edification, and not to destruction**" (2 Corinthians 13:10).

To "edify" is to instruct and improve the mind in knowledge, particularly in moral and religious knowledge, and in faith and holiness. The body of Christ, the church, edifies itself in love (Ephesians 4:15-16). The act of charity edifies (1 Corinthians 8:1). All believers are to speak the truth in love, and "**follow after the things which make for peace, and things wherewith one may edify another**" (Romans 14:19). We are commanded to please our neighbour "**for *his* good to edification**" (Romans 15:2). Paul wrote to the believers in Corinth and said, "Even so ye, forasmuch as ye are zealous of spiritual *gifts*, **seek that ye may excel to the edifying of the church**" (1 Corinthians 14:12). According to Ephesians 4:11-13, God gave some of the early churches apostles and prophets, and today he has given the churches evangelists, and pastors and teachers, "For the perfecting of the saints, for the work of the ministry, **for the edifying of the body of Christ**: Till we all come in the unity of the faith, and of the knowledge of the Son of God, unto a perfect man, unto the measure of the stature of the fulness of Christ."

To forsake [leave, desert, or abandon] church is a sin. For the scripture commands: "**And let us consider one another to provoke** [excite, edify, encourage] **unto love and to good works: Not forsaking the assembling of ourselves together, as the manner of some *is*; but exhorting *one another*: and so much the more, as ye see the day approaching**" (Hebrews 10:24-25). In other words, as we get closer to the Lord's appearing, we should regularly attend a good Bible-preaching church, and be careful to "maintain good works" (Titus 3:8, 14).

The believers in Ephesus were commanded: "Let no corrupt communication proceed out of your mouth, **but that which is good to the use of edifying, that it may minister grace unto the hearers**" (Ephesians 4:29). In addition, Paul wrote to Timothy with instruction to, "**Neither give heed to fables and endless genealogies, which minister questions, rather than godly edifying which is in faith: *so do***" (1 Timothy 1:4). Believers are edified when the word is ministered to them in faith, and in love.

PASTORS

First Thessalonians 5:12-13 says, "And we beseech you, brethren, to know them which labour among you, and are over you in the Lord, and admonish you; And to esteem them very highly in love for their work's sake. *And* be at peace among yourselves."

Men who are over churches are designated as "bishops" (1 Timothy 3:1; Philippians 1:1), "elders" (1 Timothy 5:17-18), and "pastors" (Ephesians 4:11). The passage of 1 Timothy 3:1-7 gives the following qualifications of a bishop: "**This *is* a true saying, If a man desire the office of a bishop, he desireth a good work. A bishop then must be blameless, the husband of one wife, vigilant, sober, of good behaviour, given to hospitality, apt to teach; Not given to wine, no striker, not greedy of filthy lucre; but patient, not a brawler, not covetous; One that ruleth well his own house, having his children in subjection with all gravity; (For if a man know not how to rule his own house, how shall he take care of the church of God?) Not a novice, lest being lifted up with pride he fall into the condemnation of the devil. Moreover he must have a good report of them which are without; lest he fall into reproach and the snare of the devil.**" In addition, in Titus 1:7-9 Paul wrote the following to Titus: "**For a bishop must be blameless, as the steward of God; not selfwilled, not soon angry, not given to wine, no striker, not given to filthy lucre; But a lover of hospitality, a lover of good men, sober, just, holy, temperate; Holding fast**

the faithful word as he hath been taught, that he may be able by sound doctrine both to exhort and to convince the gainsayers."

Please notice that a bishop must be "**the husband of one wife**" (1 Timothy 3:2). Therefore, a woman is not qualified by scripture for the position of bishop, elder, or pastor. A bishop has the rule over the church, and this must be a man, for the scripture says: "**Let the woman learn in silence with all subjection. But I suffer not a woman to teach, nor to usurp authority over the man, but to be in silence**" (1 Timothy 2:11-12). To usurp authority is to seize and hold in possession by force or without right. Although there are women pastors, they have no scriptural right to be in that position.

Although women may not be a bishop, elder, or a pastor, Titus 2:4-5 instructs that women may teach children and other women. The aged women should be able to "teach the young women to be sober, to love their husbands, to love their children, [*t*]*o be* discreet, chaste, keepers at home, good, obedient to their own husbands, that the word of God be not blasphemed."

Regarding bishops, elders, or pastors, all believers are commanded:

1. "Salute all them that have the rule over you" (Hebrews 13:24).
2. "Let the elders that rule well be counted worthy of double honour, especially they who labour in the word and doctrine. For the scripture saith, Thou shalt not muzzle the ox that treadeth out the corn. And, The labourer *is* worthy of his reward" (1 Timothy 5:17-18).
3. "Remember them which have the rule over you, who have spoken unto you the word of God: whose faith follow, considering the end of *their* conversation" (Hebrews 13:7).
4. "Obey them that have the rule over you, and submit yourselves: for they watch for your souls, as they that must give account, that they may do it with joy, and not with grief: for that *is* unprofitable for you" (Hebrews 13:17).

WARN, COMFORT, SUPPORT, AND BE PATIENT!

The beginning of 1 Thessalonians 5:14 says, "Now we exhort you, brethren, warn them that are unruly…"

Paul warned the Ephesians' elders, saying: "Take heed therefore unto yourselves, and to all the flock, over the which the Holy Ghost hath made you overseers, to feed the church of God, which he hath purchased with his own blood. **For I know this, that after my departing shall grievous wolves enter in among you, not sparing the flock. Also of your own selves shall men arise, speaking perverse things, to draw away disciples after them. Therefore watch, and remember, that by the space of three years I ceased not to warn every one night and day with tears**" (Acts 20:28-31).

What believers should do with the *unruly*:

1. "Now I beseech you, brethren, mark them which cause divisions and offences contrary to the doctrine which ye have learned; and avoid them. For they that are such serve not our Lord Jesus Christ, but their own belly; and by good words and fair speeches deceive the hearts of the simple" (Romans 16:17-18).
2. "And if any man obey not our word by this epistle, note that man, and have no company with him, that he may be ashamed" (2 Thessalonians 3:14).
3. "But now I have written unto you not to keep company, if any man that is called a brother be a fornicator, or covetous, or an idolater, or a railer, or a drunkard, or an extortioner; with such an one no not to eat" (1 Corinthians 5:11).
4. "And have no fellowship with the unfruitful works of darkness, but rather reprove *them*" (Ephesians 5:11). See also Titus 1:12-14.

The second part of 1 Thessalonians 5:14 instructs us to, "...comfort the feebleminded, support the weak..."

In direct contrast and opposition to the ungodly lie of evolution, which teaches the "survival of the fittest," Christian doctrine teaches us to help the feebleminded and the weak:

1. "Strengthen ye the weak hands, and confirm the feeble knees. Say to them *that are* of a fearful heart, Be strong, fear not: behold, your God will come *with* vengeance, *even* God *with* a recompence; he will come and save you" (Isaiah 35:3-4)
2. "But I have prayed for thee, that thy faith fail not: and when thou art converted, strengthen thy brethren" (Luke 22:32).
3. "Him that is weak in the faith receive ye, *but* not to doubtful disputations" (Romans 14:1).
4. "We then that are strong ought to bear the infirmities of the weak, and not to please ourselves. Let every one of us please *his* neighbour for

his good to edification. For even Christ pleased not himself; but, as it is written, The reproaches of them that reproached thee fell on me" (Romans 15:1-3).

5. "Brethren, if a man be overtaken in a fault, ye which are spiritual, restore such an one in the spirit of meekness; considering thyself, lest thou also be tempted" (Galatians 6:1).
6. "I have shewed you all things, how that so labouring ye ought to support the weak, and to remember the words of the Lord Jesus, how he said, It is more blessed to give than to receive" (Acts 20:35).

The last section of 1 Thessalonians 5:14 says, "...be patient toward all *men*."

One who is patient has the quality of enduring evils without murmuring or fretfulness; of sustaining afflictions of body or mind with strength and firmness. He exhibits calmness and submission to the divine will. To suffer long, or to have longsuffering, demonstrates patience. "But the fruit of the Spirit is love, joy, peace, **longsuffering**, gentleness, goodness, faith" (Galatians 5:22). "And the servant of the Lord must not strive; but be gentle unto all *men*, apt to teach, **patient**, In meekness instructing those that oppose themselves; if God peradventure will give them repentance to the acknowledging of the truth" (2 Timothy 2:24-25). The longsuffering of God gives men space to repent and be saved by his grace.

Romans 2:4 says, "**Or despisest thou the riches of his goodness and forbearance and longsuffering; not knowing that the goodness of God leadeth thee to repentance**?"

Second Peter 3:9 says, "**The Lord is not slack concerning his promise, as some men count slackness; but is longsuffering to us–ward, not willing that any should perish, but that all should come to repentance**."

VENGEANCE BELONGS TO GOD

First Thessalonians 5:15 says, "See that none render evil for evil unto any *man*; but ever follow that which is good, both among yourselves, and to all *men*."

What a wonderful thing it would be if every one would leave the Lord's work in his hands. Men are way out of the will of God when they even *think* of taking vengeance on someone! Leave vengeance in God's hands. You should be very grateful for God's mercy toward you, and that he has not already given you the judgment that you deserve! The Apostle Paul wrote in Romans 12:19-21: "**Dearly beloved, avenge not yourselves, but *rather* give place unto wrath: for it is written, Vengeance *is* mine; I will repay, saith the Lord. Therefore if thine enemy hunger, feed him; if he thirst, give him drink: for in so doing thou shalt heap coals of fire on his head. Be not overcome of evil, but overcome evil with good.**"

Solomon warned even against *speaking* about taking vengeance on another. He wisely counseled, "**Say not thou, I will recompense evil; *but* wait on the LORD, and he shall save thee**" (Proverbs 20:22); and, "**Say not, I will do so to him as he hath done to me: I will render to the man according to his work**" (Proverbs 24:29).

The Lord Jesus Christ taught his disciples to love, bless, and pray for their enemies (Matthew 5:44-45). We know that God will take vengeance on a man who refuses his mercy and grace. For we read that, "**The wicked shall be turned into hell, *and* all the nations that forget God**" in Psalm 9:17. However God's work for all living believers is to somehow proclaim "**the glorious gospel of Christ**" (2 Corinthians 4:4). And that gospel is "**that Christ died for our sins according to the scriptures; And that he was buried, and that he rose again the third day according to the scriptures**" (1 Corinthians 15:3-4). We are to live our lives proclaiming his gospel so that all who believe might be saved! For we know that the Lord is "**not willing that any should perish, but that all should come to repentance**" (2 Peter 3:9).

UNSPEAKABLE JOY

First Thessalonians 5:16 exclaims for us to, "Rejoice evermore."

The Apostle Paul practiced, and was an example for what he preached! After describing the troubles and trials that he went through while in the service of the Lord (2 Corinthians 6:3-9), Paul described himself: "**<u>As sorrowful, yet alway rejoicing</u>; as poor, yet making many rich; as having nothing, and *yet* possessing all things**" (2 Corinthians 6:10). In the midst of seclusion from friends and family in a dark cold dungeon Paul also wrote to the Philippian church and said: "**Rejoice in the Lord alway: *and* again I say, Rejoice**" (Philippians 4:4). In addition, Peter, wrote to believers who had not yet seen the Lord Jesus Christ: "**Whom having not seen, ye love; in whom, though now**

ye see *him* not, yet believing, ye rejoice with joy unspeakable and full of glory" (1 Peter 1:8).

We born again believers are able to live our lives, "**Rejoicing in hope; patient in tribulation; continuing instant in prayer**," as Romans 12:12 says because as Titus 2:13-14 says, we are: "**Looking for that blessed hope, and the glorious appearing of the great God and our Saviour Jesus Christ; Who gave himself for us, that he might redeem us from all iniquity, and purify unto himself a peculiar people, zealous of good works.**" We can rejoice by faith in the words spoken by our Saviour, who said: "**Blessed are ye, when *men* shall revile you, and persecute *you*, and shall say all manner of evil against you falsely, for my sake. Rejoice, and be exceeding glad: for great *is* your reward in heaven: for so persecuted they the prophets which were before you**" (Matthew 5:11-12). And we can rejoice, because our names "**are written in heaven**" (Luke 10:20)!

Even evil men *rejoice* in their wickedness! They "**rejoice to do evil, *and* delight in the frowardness** [perverseness and disobedience] **of the wicked**" (Proverbs 2:14). But the fear of the wicked will come upon him. Then he will be no more on the earth. He will be in hell (Proverbs 10:24-25; Psalm 104:35)! Then God will not answer him when he cries out in his calamity (Proverbs 6:12-15; 1:24-32)! God will save you today, if you will believe on the Lord Jesus Christ, for the scripture says: "**behold, now *is* the accepted time; behold, now *is* the day of salvation**" (2 Corinthians 6:2).

UNCEASING PRAYER

First Thessalonians 5:17 instructs us to, "Pray without ceasing".

Obviously, this command includes prayer in all positions and situations. Paul was in a constant attitude of prayer, remembering that God was always his witness (1 Thessalonians 1:2-3; 2:13). Nehemiah prayed to God in his heart, and received an answer from God as he stood in front of the king. The king did not even know that Nehemiah was praying: "Then the king said unto me, For what dost thou make request? So I prayed to the God of heaven. And I said unto the king, If it please the king, and if thy servant have found favour in thy sight, that thou wouldest send me unto Judah, unto the city of my fathers' sepulchres, that I may build it" (Nehemiah 2:4-5).

A special designated time and place for scheduled prayer is also a great blessing, as depicted in Daniel 6:10.

CONTINUAL THANKSGIVING

First Thessalonians 5:18 says, "In every thing give thanks: for this is the will of God in Christ Jesus concerning you."

Not only are believers commanded to give thanks *in* every thing, but they are to be "**Giving thanks always <u>for</u> all things unto God and the Father in the name of our Lord Jesus Christ**" (Ephesians 5:20)!

1. We should thank God for victory and triumph in Christ (1 Corinthians 15:57; 2 Corinthians 2:14).
2. "**Thanks *be* unto God for his unspeakable gift**" (2 Corinthians 9:15).
3. We should give "**thanks unto the Father**, which hath made us meet to be partakers of the inheritance of the saints in light: Who hath delivered us from the power of darkness, and hath translated *us* into the kingdom of his dear Son" (Colossians 1:12-13).
4. We should "offer the sacrifice of praise to God continually, that is, the fruit of *our* lips **giving thanks to his name**" (Hebrews 13:15).
5. We should "Be careful for nothing; but in every thing by prayer and supplication **with thanksgiving** let your requests be made known unto God." (Philippians 4:6)

ADDITIONAL IMPORTANT COMMANDS

First Thessalonians 5:19 commands us not to, "Quench not the Spirit."

To quench means to extinguish, as to put out a flame (Mark 9:43; Hebrews 11:33-34). Whatever the believer might think or act to dampen or hinder the work of the Holy Ghost is a sin. Worldliness, pride, and selfish ambition can all quench the Spirit.

First Thessalonians 5:20 instructs us to, "Despise not prophesyings."

In Paul's day there may have still been men in the churches who had the gift of prophecy, for the Bible had not yet been completed. But today men can only speak prophecies which are written in the Holy Bible (1 Corinthians 13:8; Revelation 22:18-19). "**Beware of false prophets**" (Matthew 7:15; 2 Peter 2:1-3; 1 John 4:1-4). Mr. Harold Camping, the old man who announced that God's judgment day would be May 15, 2011, is a good example. Another good example would be the numerous failed predictions of the end of the world by

Jehovah Witnesses and their Watch Tower society in the years of 1914, 1918, 1925 and 1975.

First Thessalonians 5:21 tells us to, "Prove all things; hold fast that which is good."

All truth is proved by the word of God: "**Study to shew thyself approved unto God, a workman that needeth not to be ashamed, rightly dividing the word of truth**" (2 Timothy 2:15). There is no substitute! All spirits may successfully be proved and tried by the word of God: "**Beloved, believe not every spirit, but try** [test] **the spirits whether they are of God: because many false prophets are gone out into the world**" (1 John 4:1).

Last but not least, 1 Thessalonians 5:22 commands us to, "Abstain from all appearance of evil."

To abstain means to refrain from doing something. We are to be careful not to appear to be doing evil, even if we are not. I may not be doing an evil thing while alone in a house with a woman, but I would avoid such a circumstance for appearance sake. Do not stop to tie your shoe while in your neighbor's watermelon patch! Do not sit on the sidewalk drinking water out of a wine bottle! I'm sure you get the idea! And therefore a Christian is to be wise in his mannerisms and actions to be careful not to appear to be doing something unholy.

CONCLUSION

This entire sermon outline has been devoted to instructions and commands to born again believers. Only a man who has been "born of the Spirit" (John 3:8) has been given the power of God to keep these commandments (John 1:12-13). I was "born again" (John 3:3-7) while alone in my house reading the gospel of John. The purpose of John's gospel is to give faith to the reader. Concerning his gospel, John wrote: "**But these are written, that ye might believe that Jesus is the Christ, the Son of God; and that believing ye might have life through his name**" (John 20:31). You can be saved in any location when you confess with your mouth the Lord Jesus, and believe in your heart that God raised him from the dead (Romans 10:9)!

"**Believe on the Lord Jesus Christ, and thou shalt be saved**" (Acts 16:31).

Chapter 30

PRIDE GOETH BEFORE DESTRUCTION

God loves and cares for you and me very much. Because of his great love for us, he gives us a warning that we ought to consider and take great heed to. In the inspired holy scriptures of God, God says in Proverbs 16:18 that "**Pride *goeth* before destruction, and an haughty spirit before a fall**."

PRIDE is defined by Noah Webster in his 1828 American Dictionary of the English Language as "Inordinate [irregular; disorderly; excessive; immoderate] self-esteem; an unreasonable conceit of one's own superiority in talents, beauty, wealth, accomplishments, rank or elevation in office, which manifests itself in lofty airs, distance, reserve, and often in contempt of others." Pride is that spirit that demands to have control of self in direct rebellion against the holy commandment to submit to God (James 4:7; Psalm 119:21; Psalm 12:3-4).

"Thou [God] **hast rebuked the proud that are cursed, which do err from thy commandments"** (Psalm 119:21).

"The LORD shall cut off all flattering lips, and the tongue that speaketh proud things: **Who have said, With our tongue will we prevail; our lips are our own: who is lord over us**?" (Psalm 12:3-4).

THE ORIGIN OF PRIDE

God created all things (Colossians 1:16). One created being that he made, which was the most powerful, beautiful, and wise creature of all beings, was the cherub named Lucifer. He was the anointed cherub that was very close to the very throne of God (Ezekiel 28:14). He was perfect in all his ways until iniquity was found in him (Ezekiel 28:15). His heart was lifted up because of his beauty (Ezekiel 28:17). In 1 Timothy 3:6 the Apostle Paul gives one of the qualifications of a bishop, that he be "**Not a novice, lest being lifted up with pride he fall into the condemnation of the devil**." The devil (whose name is Lucifer) was **lifted up with pride**. Pride brought Lucifer's condemnation. Among other things, Lucifer said in his heart, "**I will be like the most High**" (Isaiah 14:14). What arrogant pride! The creature rebelling against his Creator!

THE KING OVER ALL THE CHILDREN OF PRIDE

In Job chapter 41 God describes a fire breathing dragon, leviathan, as a picture or type of the devil. He closes his remarks by saying, "**Upon earth there is not his like, who is made without fear. He beholdeth all high things: he is a king over all the children of pride**" (Job 41:33-34).

We read in Proverbs 16:18, "**Pride goeth before destruction, and an haughty spirit before a fall**." Because of his pride Lucifer fell from his original position in heaven (Isaiah 14:12). His name has been changed to Satan, which means adversary. He now is **the god of this world** (2 Corinthians 4:4), who is blinding men's minds **lest the light of the glorious gospel of Christ, who is the image of God, should shine unto them** (2 Corinthians 4:3-4). He is **the accuser of our brethren** (Revelation 12:10). He walketh to and fro throughout the earth as a roaring lion **seeking whom he may devour** (1 Peter 5:8). He still has access to the throne of God where he accuses the saints before God (Job 1:6-12; Zechariah 3:1).

During the tribulation period, Satan and his angels will finally and permanently be cast out of heaven. After he and his angels fight with Michael and his angels, there will be no more place for him in heaven (Revelation 12:7-11). At the second coming of Christ, Satan will be bound and cast into the bottomless pit for a thousand years (Revelation 20:1-3). After the thousand years, Satan will be loosed out of his prison to lead the remaining children of pride to surround Jerusalem where God will send fire from heaven and devour them (Revelation 20:7-9). Then Satan will be **cast into the lake of fire and brimstone, where**

the beast and the false prophet are, and shall be tormented day and night for ever and ever (Revelation 20:10). Therefore, Satan, the king over all the children of pride, because of his proud and haughty spirit, will suffer eternal torments and destruction in the lake of fire and brimstone. And so we see in Satan the fulfillment of God's promise, that, "**Pride *goeth* before destruction, and an haughty spirit before a fall**" (Proverbs 16:18). Satan's pride caused him to sin in the beginning (John 8:44), and at the end of the world God will bring Satan's destruction (Revelation 20:10).

Satan's case shows that the punishment for pride can come many years later. Because they see no immediate judgment, proud men think they are getting away with their rebellion against God. Nevertheless, in the end they will face the same consequences that Satan did, unless they repent and receive Jesus Christ as their Saviour and Lord.

"**Because sentence against an evil work is not executed speedily, therefore the heart of the sons of men is fully set in them to do evil**" (Ecclesiastes 8:11).

MAN'S FIRST SIN

Adam and Eve were submissive to God in the beginning. They were humble, happy, and walking with joy and fellowship with the Lord in the beautiful garden of Eden. However, when Eve was deceived by the devil, both she and her husband rebelled against God's commandment. On the very day Adam and Eve ate from the forbidden tree of the knowledge of good and evil they were spiritually separated from God and became **dead in trespasses and sins** (Ephesians 2:1; Genesis 2:17). Because they believed the devil and ate of the tree, they submitted to Satan as their king. At that time, the disobedient prideful spirit of Satan entered into Adam and Eve.

As a result of their disobedience to God, the entire human race after them are also born into the world infected by the same spirit of disobedience working in them (Ephesians 2:2). Satan is the spiritual father of all natural born men (John 8:44). All men's hearts are corrupted by sin and are **deceitful above all things, and desperately wicked** (Jeremiah 17:9). If you have not been born again, at which time the believer who submits to God receives a new heart from God (Ezekiel 36:26), then you are still cursed with a wicked heart which you inherited from Adam. This wicked heart is the fountainhead of all men's wickedness, including **pride**. Out of this wicked heart **proceed evil thoughts, adulteries, fornications, murders, [t]hefts, covetousness, wickedness, deceit,**

lasciviousness, an evil eye, blasphemy, pride, foolishness: All these evil things come from within, and defile the man (Mark 7:21-23). If you have not been born again (John 3:3-7), then your refusal to submit to God is the result of pride. If you insist on your rebellion to save [prolong and keep] the wicked life you are living, then you will eventually lose it (Mark 8:35). Not only will you lose your life to death, but you will then lose your soul to eternal death (Mark 8:36). You will go to hell where Satan, your spiritual father will be, and also you will suffer the torments of the damned for ever (Luke 16:23; Revelation 14:11; 20:14-15). But if you will turn from your wicked ways (Isaiah 55:6-7) and submit to God through **repentance toward God and faith toward our Lord Jesus Christ** (Acts 20:21), then your life and soul will be saved (Mark 8:35).

GOD FOREWARNS THE PROUD

There are many warnings from God in the Bible against proud men. God warns them of their final destruction and eternal misery many times. A few of these verses are listed below:

"And I [God] will punish the world for *their* evil, and the wicked for their iniquity; and **I will cause the arrogancy of the proud to cease, and will lay low the haughtiness of the terrible**" (Isaiah 13:11).

"**The LORD shall cut off all flattering lips, *and* the tongue that speaketh proud things**: Who have said, With our tongue will we prevail; our lips *are* our own: who *is* lord over us?" (Psalm 12:3-4).

"The LORD will destroy the house of the proud: but he will establish the border of the widow" (Proverbs 15:25).

Every one *that is* proud in heart *is* an abomination [a thing extremely hated and detested] **to the LORD: *though* hand *join* in hand, he shall not be unpunished**" (Proverbs 16:5).

DAVID FOOLISHLY ENVIED THE WICKED

In Psalm 73 king David admitted that he had envied the foolish when he **saw the prosperity of the wicked** (Psalm 73:3). He noted that these rich, yet foolish, men **are not in trouble as other men** (Psalm 73:5). David went on to say, "**Their eyes stand out with fatness: they have more than heart could wish. They are corrupt, and speak wickedly concerning oppression: they**

speak loftily. They set their mouth against the heavens, and their tongue walketh through the earth. Therefore his people return hither: and waters of a full cup are wrung out to them. And they say, How doth God know? and is there knowledge in the most High? Behold, these are the ungodly, who prosper in the world; they increase in riches" (Psalm 73:7-12). He went on to say that even though these foolish wicked men of the world are not **plagued like other men**, yet, **pride compasseth them about as a chain** (Psalm 73:5-6). They are slaves to their pride without realizing their condition of slavery. For this reason they are foolish!

Further in Psalm 73 we then read how that David went into the house of the LORD and learned the truth about these foolish, wicked proud men. David learned that God has set these men **in slippery places**, and that he casts **them down into destruction** [hell]. God brings them **into desolation, as in a moment! They are utterly consumed with terrors** (Psalm 73:18-19). In other words, wicked proud men, while in the kingdom of their father the devil [Satan is the god of this world (2 Corinthians 4:3-4)] live a prideful and arrogant life. Pride, as a chain, has them surrounded (Psalm 73:6). But at their death, in a moment, this chain will have them bound forever in the damnation of hell. At their death they will lift up their eyes in hell (Luke 16:22-23), where they will be utterly consumed with desolation and terrors! The Lord despises their image.

GOD HATES AND JUDGES PRIDE

The first mention of the word **pride** is found in Leviticus 26:1-20, which has to do with Israel's obedience to God's commandments. The LORD warns Israel what he will do if they rebel against his commandments, saying, "**And I will break the pride of your power; and I will make your heaven as iron, and your earth as brass: And your strength shall be spent in vain: for your land shall not yield her increase, neither shall the trees of the land yield their fruits**" (Leviticus 26:19-20).

The LORD has purposed **to stain the pride of all glory, and to bring into contempt all the honourable of the earth** (Isaiah 23:9). This means that every proud man who exalts himself against God will be brought low.

"**For the day of the LORD of hosts *shall be* upon every *one that is* proud and lofty, and upon every *one that is* lifted up; and he shall be brought low**" (Isaiah 2:12).

"**A man's pride shall bring him low: but honour shall uphold the humble in spirit**" (Proverbs 29:23).

Speaking of the day of the LORD, when the Lord Jesus Christ will come back to earth **with his mighty angels, in flaming fire taking vengeance on them that know not God, and that obey not the gospel of our Lord Jesus Christ** (2 Thessalonians 1:7-8), the prophet Malachi wrote in Malachi 4:1, "**For, behold, the day cometh, that shall burn as an oven; and all the proud, yea, and all that do wickedly, shall be stubble: and the day that cometh shall burn them up, saith the LORD of hosts, that it shall leave them neither root nor branch.**"

The Christian is commanded not to love **the things that are in the world. For all that is in the world, the lust of the flesh, and the lust of the eyes, and the pride of life, is not of the Father, but is of the world**, according to 1 John 2:15-16. The LORD hates **pride** (Proverbs 8:13) and **a proud look** (Proverbs 6:17). **Every one that is proud in heart is an abomination to the LORD** (Proverbs 16:5). This means that God has extreme hatred for them. The unrepentant proud are among the **abominable**, who will suffer torments in the lake of fire for ever (Revelation 21:8).

EXAMPLES OF PROUD MEN

CAIN

Cain rebelled against God's clear commandment of what to bring for an offering unto the LORD (Hebrews 11:4). Cain being proud and lacking faith brought an unacceptable offering (Genesis 4:5). Cain thought that the fruit which he had grown would do just as well. God had not respect for Cain's offering and therefore would not accept it, but told him that if he would bring the right offering that he would be accepted. Instead Cain rose up and killed his brother Abel. Cain **was of that wicked one** (1 John 3:12). This means that even though Cain's natural father was Adam (Genesis 4:1), nevertheless his spiritual father was the devil. Every one of us came into this world with the devil as our father (John 8:44)! No wonder the unsaved world walks in such darkness!

MEN OF SODOM

The Bible tell us in Genesis 13:13 that **the men of Sodom were wicked and sinners before the LORD exceedingly**. Pride was the chief sin of Sodom

(Ezekiel 16:49-50). Their wickedness was so great that God thought it good to take them away and put them into hell, where they are still **suffering the vengeance of eternal fire** (Jude 7). What prideful arrogance for men and women today to parade down our city streets on "Gay Pride Day" and boast of the same sin for which God destroyed the men of Sodom! **Except ye repent, ye shall all likewise perish** (Luke 13:3, 5)!

PHARAOH

Pharaoh was the prideful, hardened, rebellious king of Egypt, whose pride blinded him to the truth. Pharaoh's men finally said to him, "**knowest thou not yet that Egypt is destroyed**?" (Exodus 10:7). Pharaoh resisted the LORD over and over again, but finally the LORD brought Pharaoh and his army to complete destruction (Exodus 14:23-31; Proverbs 16:18).

NABAL

Nabal's wife Abigail called her husband a **man of Belial** (1 Samuel 25:25). According to the Strong's Exhaustive Concordance of the Bible, this means that Nabal was a "worthless, good for nothing, unprofitable, base fellow."[13] David and his men had befriended and protected Nabal's shepherds and flocks. Sometime later when David and his men needed some food and supplies, Nabal refused David's request for supplies when David asked for help. Nabal was a selfish, arrogant, and proud man who was headed for destruction. After turning David's servants away, Nabal held a drunken feast. But ten days later, **the LORD smote Nabal, and he died** (1 Samuel 25:38; Proverbs 16:18).

HAMAN

Haman was promoted by king Ahasuerus of Persia to be the chief prince in his kingdom. His position caused Haman to be lifted up in pride (Esther 3; 1 Timothy 3:6). Haman loved to have the preeminence and high respect among men. He loved to see men bowing down to him. When Haman heard that a Jew named Mordecai did not bow down to him, **then Haman was full of wrath** (Esther 3:5). Haman sought to destroy all the Jews in the kingdom (Esther 3:6)! He even built a gallows on which to hang Mordecai and deviously persuaded the king to sign a decree for all the Jews to be killed. You should read the rest of the story in Esther chapters 3 thru 10. As things turned out, Haman himself was hung on the gallows he had built for Mordecai, and Mordecai was promoted by the king!

God warns us in Galatians 6:7, "**Be not deceived; God is not mocked: for whatsoever a man soweth, that shall he also reap**."

Second Samuel 22:26-28 says, "With the merciful thou wilt shew thyself merciful, *and* with the upright man thou wilt shew thyself upright. With the pure thou wilt shew thyself pure; and **with the froward** [perverse, ungovernable, disobedient] **thou wilt shew thyself unsavoury** [unpleasing, disgusting]. And the afflicted people thou wilt save: but **thine eyes *are* upon the haughty** [Proud and disdainful; having a high opinion of one's self, with some contempt for others; lofty and arrogant]**, *that* thou mayest bring *them* down**."

God repeats himself in Psalm 18:25-27, saying, "With the merciful thou wilt shew thyself merciful; with an upright man thou wilt shew thyself upright; With the pure thou wilt shew thyself pure; and with the froward thou wilt shew thyself froward. For thou wilt save the afflicted people; **but wilt bring down high looks** [an high look is sin (Proverbs 21:4)]."

NEBUCHADNEZZAR

God was merciful to this proud king of Babylon, who boasted about the great city of Babylon that he had built (Daniel 4:29-30). Instead of destroying him, God put him out to pasture and made him to eat grass like an ox for seven years (Daniel 4:31-33)! At the end of this time Nebuchadnezzar humbled himself and praised God (Daniel 4:34-37). Sinner, God will also save you if you will humble yourself as a little child (Luke 18:17) and repent and acknowledge the truth (2 Timothy 2:24-26) and receive the Lord Jesus Christ by faith as your personal Saviour (John 1:12-13). Do it now before it is too late!

Second Peter 3:9 informs us that, "The Lord is **longsuffering to us-ward, not willing that any should perish, but that all should come to repentance**."

BELTASHAZZAR

God destroyed this proud king, because he did not learn from Nebuchadnezzar's mistake (Daniel 5).

HEROD

King Herod was lifted up in pride when the people who heard him speak **gave a shout, *saying, It is* the voice of a god, and not of a man. And immediately**

the angel of the Lord smote him, because he gave not God the glory: and he was eaten of worms, and gave up the ghost (Acts 12:22-23).

MYSTERY BABYLON

This is the great whorish religion of Satan (Revelation 17), which has deceived a great number of people. Of this false and proud religion, the Bible then says in the next chapter, "**How much she hath glorified herself, and lived deliciously, so much torment and sorrow give her: for she saith in her heart, I sit a queen, and am no widow, and shall see no sorrow. Therefore shall her plagues come in one day, death, and mourning, and famine; and she shall be utterly burned with fire: for strong *is* the Lord God who judgeth her**" (Revelation 18:7-8).

DIOTROPHES

This was a man in the church who loved to have the preeminence. In his pride, he wanted others in the church to think he was some great man. He was so proud that he refused to allow John the apostle to come to his church (3 John 1:9-10)!

ANTICHRIST

The antichrist is also called, **the man of sin** and **the son of perdition** in 2 Thessalonians 2:3. He will be revealed after the church has been gathered out to meet the Lord in the air (1 Thessalonians 4:16-18). This man will be empowered by Satan, the king of the children of pride. In the middle of the seven-year tribulation period he will, with boastful pride, claim to be God and demand to be worshipped! It is he who 2 Thessalonians 2:4 warns about: "**Who opposeth and exalteth himself above all that is called God, or that is worshipped; so that he as God sitteth in the temple of God, shewing himself that he is God**." Revelation 13:8 further gives details, "**And all that dwell upon the earth shall worship him, whose names are not written in the book of life of the Lamb slain from the foundation of the world**."

This "beast," as God calls the antichrist, will be **cast alive into a lake of fire and brimstone** (Revelation 19:20). Later after the millennial reign of Christ, Satan himself will be cast into the same lake of fire (Revelation 20:10), just as God promised him long ago (Isaiah 14:12-15). In the end, Satan, the **king over all the children of pride** (Job 41:34), and all of his unrepentant children (unbelievers) will be permanently assigned to eternal torments in the same lake of fire (Revelation 20:11-15). It is there that **the smoke of their torment** [will ascend] **up forever and ever** (Revelation 14:11).

Proud man, except you repent and receive Jesus Christ, you will remain on the broad way that leads to destruction (Proverbs 16:18)! A proud man will not seek after God (Psalm 10:4); but our merciful God is himself seeking the lost, convicting them of their sin, and drawing them to Jesus Christ. God wants to show mercy to all men, for Christ on the cross did **taste death for every man** (Hebrews 2:9). God calls and invites all men to salvation through the gospel (2 Thessalonians 2:13-14), "**how that Christ died for our sins according to the scriptures; And that he was buried, and that he rose again the third day according to the scriptures**" (1 Corinthians 15:3-4).

"**And the Spirit and the bride say, Come. And let him that heareth say, Come. And let him that is athirst come. And whosoever will, let him take the water of life freely**" (Revelation 22:17).

I strongly encourage you to read the gospel of John, for **faith cometh by hearing, and hearing by the word of God** (Romans 10:17). God has made salvation **of faith, that it *might* be by grace** (Romans 4:16; Ephesians 2:8-9) that you may have the gift of eternal life.

"And they said, **Believe on the Lord Jesus Christ, and thou shalt be saved, and thy house**" (Acts 16:31).

Chapter 31

Dead or Alive?

INTRODUCTION

We read in Ephesians 5:29-32 that all born again believers in Jesus Christ are joined unto Christ in one body called the church. Whether or not we can understand or explain this mystery, has no bearing whatsoever on its truth. If you are a Bible believer, you will believe many things that you have not seen and many things that you cannot explain or understand, "**For we walk by faith, not by sight**" (2 Corinthians 5:7). Nevertheless the word of God works effectually in you, because you receive it by faith (1 Thessalonians 2:13). You believe "**the mysteries of God**" (1 Corinthians 4:1) simply because God's word declares them to be true (Romans 10:17).

In this sermon we are going to use Paul's illustration of marriage under the law in Romans 7:1-6 to study some other passages that relate to this Christian mystery at hand. We will discover that no one can be joined unto Christ until a particular death has taken place!

MARRIAGE UNDER THE LAW

Before you further read this sermon, first, I strongly encourage you to open your Bible and read Romans 7:1-6. The following is an *illustration* of the mystery that takes place when a sinner is converted and saved by faith in Jesus Christ.

Romans 7:1 says, "Know ye not, brethren, (for I speak to them that know the law,) how that the law hath dominion over a man as long as he liveth?" The nature of all laws pertaining to mankind is that once a man is dead he is outside of their jurisdictions. Romans 7:2-3 says, "For the woman which hath an husband is bound by the law to *her* husband so long as he liveth; but if the husband be dead, she is loosed from the law of *her* husband. So then if, while *her* husband liveth, she be married to another man, she shall be called an adulteress: but if her husband be dead, she is free from that law; so that she is no adulteress, though she be married to another man."

Because of the death of her original husband the woman is freed from the law that prevented her from marrying another man. The law did not die! Her old husband died! Now she is free under the same law to be married to another man. When she marries another man she is no adulteress, because she has met the demands and restrictions of the law. Under the law she had to wait until her old husband was dead before she could marry another man.

Paul uses the law of marriage as an *illustration* [or allegory] to teach what happened to the sinner when he was born again. We MUST understand the elements of this allegory before we can get the right understanding of this very important doctrine.

1. "**The woman**" (Romans 7:2) refers to "**ye**," that is to your self, or to your soul (Romans 7:4; compare also Matthew 16:26 with Luke 9:25 to see that your "self" is your "soul").
2. "**an husband**" (Romans 7:2) refers to "**our old man**" (Romans 6:1-11).
3. "**the law**" (Romans 7:1) refers to "**the law**" (Romans 7:4).
4. "**another man**" (Romans 7:4) refers to "**him who is raised from the dead**" (Romans 7:4).

THE OLD MAN IS DEAD!

In this illustration or allegory, Paul likens our soul to a woman, and he likens our sinful flesh, our "**old man**," to a husband. As the woman was married to her husband and bound to him under the law until his death, so we [our souls] were married and bound to our flesh; we were married and bound to our "**old man**," before he was crucified with Christ and died (Romans 6:6;

Galatians 2:20). After the death of "**our old man**" (Romans 6:6) we were free to marry another—*even Christ*. That our "**old man**" has already been crucified is the clear and unmistakable statement of the scripture. You will notice that I have some of the scriptures written in capital letters; this is to show emphasis for you:

"KNOWING THIS, THAT OUR OLD MAN IS CRUCIFIED WITH *HIM*, **that the body of sin might be destroyed, that henceforth we should not serve sin**" (Romans 6:6).

"I AM CRUCIFIED WITH CHRIST: **nevertheless I live; yet not I, but Christ liveth in me: and the life which I now live in the flesh I live by the faith of the Son of God, who loved me, and gave himself for me**" (Galatians 2:20).

"**And if Christ *be* in you,** THE BODY *IS* DEAD BECAUSE OF SIN ["our old man" (Romans 6:6)]**; but the Spirit *is* life because of righteousness**. **But if the Spirit of him that raised up Jesus from the dead dwell in you, he that raised up Christ from the dead shall also quicken your mortal bodies by his Spirit that dwelleth in you** [the quickened mortal body of the believer is made a member of the body of Christ (Ephesians 5:30), who is "**alive for evermore**" (Revelation 1:18)!]" (Romans 8:10-11).

Next in our sermon, the beginning of Romans 7:4 says, "Wherefore, my brethren, ye also are become dead to the law by the body of Christ…"

In the illustration, as the woman was "**loosed from the law of her husband**" (Romans 7:2), and made "**free from that law**" (Romans 7:3), because her husband died; so the born again believer has become "**dead to the law by the body of Christ**," because "**the old man**" died when he was "**crucified with Christ**" (Romans 6:6; Galatians 2:20). Therefore we are become dead to the law by our crucifixion with Christ at which time our "**body of sin**" (Romans 6:6) was destroyed!

The law of marriage, which prevents all sinners from being joined unto Christ, as long as they are married to "**the old man**," cannot prevent their marriage to Christ once "**the old man is crucified with him**" (Romans 6:6). The marriage union between the born again believer and Christ may now take place according to same the law! This wonderful and miraculous "**operation of God**" is also described as "**the circumcision made without hands, in putting off** THE BODY OF THE SINS OF THE FLESH **by the circumcision of Christ**" (Colossians 2:11-12).

The "**BODY OF THE SINS OF THE FLESH**" has been "**put off**" by the "**operation of God**!" The old wretched sinful man is DEAD INDEED (Romans 6:11). He is "**put off**." He is dead!

Colossians 3:8-11 says, "But now ye also put off all these; anger, wrath, malice, blasphemy, filthy communication out of your mouth. Lie not one to another, **seeing that YE HAVE PUT OFF THE OLD MAN WITH HIS DEEDS**; **AND HAVE PUT ON THE NEW *MAN*, which is renewed in knowledge after the image of him that created him**: **Where there is neither Greek nor Jew, circumcision nor uncircumcision, Barbarian, Scythian, bond *nor* free: but Christ *is* all, and in all**."

The word of God, which is the "**sword of the Spirit**" (Ephesians 6:17) actually divided the "**soul and spirit**" from the "**joints and marrow**"—the flesh (Hebrews 4:12). The "**old man**" was then crucified with Christ (Romans 6:6), the soul was redeemed (Psalms 34:22; 49:15), and the spirit was born again (John 3:3-7; 1 Peter 1:23).

THE MYSTERY OF CHRIST AND THE CHURCH

The middle section of Romans 7:4 continues to say, "…that ye should be married to another, even to him who is raised from the dead…"

Before being born of the Spirit all were married to "**the old man**," "**the body of the sins of the flesh**" (Colossians 2:12). Now that the "**old man**" is dead and put off, we have been made free to marry another, even the Lord Jesus Christ, who is raised from the dead. We who have been born of the Spirit (John 3:3-7) have been joined to Christ. If we had been joined unto Christ before our old man was dead, then both Christ and the believer would be committing adultery under the law!

"**For no man ever yet hated his own flesh; but nourisheth and cherisheth it, even as the Lord the church**: **FOR WE ARE MEMBERS OF HIS BODY, OF HIS FLESH, AND OF HIS BONES. For this cause shall a man leave his father and mother, and shall be joined unto his wife, and they two shall be one flesh. This is a great mystery: but I speak concerning Christ and the church**" (Ephesians 5:29-32).

Believers are baptized into Christ by the Holy Spirit. "**For by one Spirit are we all baptized into one body, whether *we be* Jews or Gentiles, whether**

***we be* bond or free; and have been all made to drink into one Spirit**" (1 Corinthians 12:13).

"For ye are all the children of God by faith in Christ Jesus. **For as many of you as have been baptized into Christ have put on Christ**. There is neither Jew nor Greek, there is neither bond nor free, there is neither male nor female: **for ye** [Jew and Greek] **are all one in Christ Jesus**. And if ye *be* Christ's, then are ye Abraham's seed, and heirs according to the promise" (Galatians 3:26-29).

Believers become "one spirit" and "one body" with the Lord. For 1 Corinthians 6:15-17 says, "**Know ye not that your bodies are the members of Christ?** [S]hall I then take the members of Christ, and make *them* the members of an harlot? God forbid. What? know ye not that he which is joined to an harlot is one body? for two, saith he, shall be one flesh. **But he that is joined unto the Lord is one spirit**." Also, I would encourage you to read 1 Corinthians 12:12-14, 27 and Colossians 1:18, 24.

This truth is also contained in 2 Corinthians 5:17, which reads: "**Therefore if any man *be* in Christ, *he is* a new creature: old things are** [present tense] **passed away; behold, all things are become new**" (2 Corinthians 5:17). Our spirit has been born again (John 3:6). Our soul has been redeemed (Psalm 34:22; James 1:21). And "**our old man is crucified with him**" (Romans 6:6) and we have been made "**members of his body, of his flesh and of his bones**" (Ephesians 5:30)!

Other scriptures speak of Christ as the bridegroom and the church as the bride or the Lamb's wife (Isaiah 61:10; 62:5; John 3:29; Revelation 21:9-10).

The end of Romans 7:4 says, "...that we should bring forth fruit unto God."

There can be no genuine fruit of righteousness (Philippians 1:9-11; Romans 6:22) or fruit of the Spirit (Galatians 5:22-23; Colossians 1:3-11) unless the Spirit of Christ indwells the person. Romans 8:8-9 tells us, "**So then they that are in the flesh cannot please God. But ye are not in the flesh, but in the Spirit, if so be that the Spirit of God dwell in you. Now if any man have not the Spirit of Christ, he is none of his.**"

As the law has dominion over a man as long as he lives, sin also has dominion over a man as long as he is under the law (Romans 6:1-11). But NOW we [who have been saved by God's grace through faith in Jesus Christ (Ephesians 2:8-9)] have been "**made free from sin**" (Romans 6:22), because we who are saved are "**dead with Christ**" (Romans 6:8). As a result, we are not subject to sin—we are not under sin's dominion—because, "**he that is dead is freed from sin**" (Romans 6:7), and we are not subject to the law, because we "**are not under the law, but under grace**" (Romans 6:14). We are to reckon [to reason and conclude from the scriptures] that these things are true: "**Likewise reckon ye also yourselves to be dead indeed unto sin, but alive unto God through Jesus Christ our Lord**" (Romans 6:11).

These things are so. They are true according to the word of God. Whether or not you experience them or feel them or see them or can understand and explain them, nevertheless they are true. They are "**a great mystery**" (Ephesians 5:32)!

Continuing with our sermon, Romans 7:5 says, "For **WHEN WE WERE IN THE FLESH** [before salvation], the motions of sins, which were by the law, did work in our members to bring forth fruit unto death." The Bible says we WERE "**in the flesh**," that is, we were married to the flesh, the old man, before we were born again. A man is either "**in the flesh**" or "**in the Spirit**" (Romans 8:6-10). He is either lost or saved. The "**flesh**" is "**carnal, sold under sin**" (Romans 7:14). In the flesh of the "**old man**" "**dwelleth no good thing**" (Romans 7:18). The "**old man**" is called, a "**wretched man**" (Romans 7:24). The "**flesh**" is called "**the body of this death**" (Romans 7:24). "**So then they that are in the flesh cannot please God**" (Romans 8:8). However, thank God we read in the following verse, "**But YE ARE NOT IN THE FLESH, BUT IN THE SPIRIT, IF SO BE THAT THE SPIRIT OF GOD DWELL IN YOU…**" (Romans 8:9).

In the fleshly members [arms, legs, hands, sexual organs, etc.] of the "**old man**" dwelt "**the law of sin**" (Romans 7:23). This law of sin kept the unregenerated (not renewed in heart before God) sinner under "**captivity**," so that he could not do the good that he wanted to do, and caused him to do the evil that he did not want to do (read Romans 7:15-23)!

After being born again we are not "**in the flesh**" (Ephesians 2:11-17), that is, our SOUL is no longer joined [married] to the flesh (Romans 8:8-9). Our soul is joined [married] to Christ. You are either lost and "**in the flesh**" (Romans 7:5; Ephesians 2:11) or you are saved and "**in Christ**" (Ephesians 2:12). The fact is that if you are saved, then "**the law of the Spirit of life in Christ Jesus**" has made you "**free from the law of sin and death**" (Romans 8:2) that dwelt in the fleshly members of "**the old man**."

Practically, we are still living geographically "in the flesh" (2 Corinthians 10:3; Galatians 2:20). We are still human beings in a physical body. Nevertheless, the great mystery is that it is NO LONGER the flesh of the "**old man**"! We now live in the flesh of the new man, Christ Jesus (Ephesians 5:29-30)! The "**old man**" was crucified with him (Romans 6:6). The "**new man**" has been quickened [made alive] together with him (Colossians 2:13; Ephesians 2:5), and we now live "**in the likeness of his resurrection**" (Romans 6:5).

THAT OLD MAN IS DEAD!

Romans 7:6 starts by stating, "But now we are delivered from the law, <u>THAT</u> being dead wherein we were held…" It was not the law that died! "**The law is holy, and the commandment holy, and just, and good**" (Romans 7:12). The Lord Jesus Christ came not to destroy but to fulfill the law (Matthew 5:17-18). Furthermore, the righteousness of the law is fulfilled in born again believers "**who walk not after the flesh, but after the Spirit**" (Romans 8:4). For a further study, I would encourage you to read 1 Timothy 1:8-11 to see the proper purpose and use of the law.

Before our salvation, we were held in bondage to "**the old man**." But after we became "**the children of God by faith in Christ Jesus**" (Galatians 3:26) "**we are delivered from the law**" that bound us to "**the old man**," because "**our old man is crucified with him**" at the very moment that we "**passed from death unto life**" (John 5:24)! At this same moment we were delivered from our bondage to the "**body of this death**" (Romans 7:24) and we were "**baptized into one body**" by "**one Spirit**" (1 Corinthians 12:13) and made "**members of his** [Jesus Christ's] **body, of his flesh, and of his bones**" (Ephesians 5:30)!

God delivers poor helpless and hopeless sinners from the bondage and penalty of sin (Psalms 56:13; 86:13; Isaiah 38:17; Colossians 1:13). It is God, "**Who hath delivered us from the power of darkness, and hath translated *us* into the kingdom of his dear Son**" (Colossians 1:13)! Hallelujah!

Therefore, when Romans 7:6 says "***<u>THAT</u>*** **being dead wherein we were held**" speaks of "**the old man**," who has been crucified with Christ (Romans 6:6). Before being born again we were held by the cords of our sins in bondage to and under the curse of the law, which condemned us, but "**Christ hath redeemed us from the curse of the law, being made a curse for us: for it is written, Cursed *is* every one that hangeth on a tree: That the blessing of Abraham might come on the Gentiles through Jesus Christ; that we might receive the promise of the Spirit through faith**" (Galatians 3:13-14). You may also read the following scriptures for a more extensive understanding: John 8:30-36; Proverbs

5:22-23; Psalm 107:10-15; Isaiah 61:1; Romans 8:6, 21; 7:24; Colossians 2:11; and 2 Peter 1:4.

The law is not dead. It is the "**old man**," who was crucified with Christ, who is dead! It is only because Christ died under the law for our sins and crucified our "**old man**" with him, that we are now "**delivered from the law**."

Romans 7:6 continues with the thought, saying, "…**that we should serve in newness of spirit, and not in the oldness of the letter**." This is made possible because the redeemed of the Lord have entered, "**by the blood of Jesus, [b]y a new and living way, which he hath consecrated for us, through the veil, that is to say, his flesh**" (Hebrews 10:19-22). The letter of the law killeth, but "**the spirit giveth life**" (2 Corinthians 3:5-17). The liberty given by the Spirit of the Lord is not liberty to do what one pleases, but freedom from the bondage and dominion of sin so that we might, through the power of the Spirit of God do what is right (Romans 6:18, 22; 8:2; Galatians 5:1, 13; 1 Peter 2:16) and glorify "**the great God and our Saviour Jesus Christ**" (Titus 2:13)!

CLARIFICATION

We are not teaching sinless perfection, even for those who are "**in Christ Jesus**" (Romans 8:1-2)! If we believers say that we have no sin or that we have not sinned, then we are deceived and we make God a liar! Read 1 John 1:6-10. What we are teaching, according to the scriptures, is that "**our old man is crucified with him**" (Romans 6:6). Therefore, "**the law of sin**" (Romans 7:23) which worked in the members of the "**old man**" no longer works in us, who are now members of the body of Christ Jesus (Ephesians 5:30).

In the light of this doctrine, believers have no more excuse for sin! Many times men have blamed their sins on the law of sin, which works in the members of the old man, using Romans chapter 7 to back up their excuse, whether if they realize it or not. There can be no more such excuse for sin, because clearly we are no longer under the dominion of sin (Romans 6:14). So when we [born again believers] choose to sin by walking "**after the flesh**" (Romans 8:13) we are making a free will choice. We are sinning willfully (Hebrews 10:26-31)! We can no longer blame our sin on the "**law of sin**," because we were freed from that law when "**our old man**" was crucified with Christ! As a born again believer you still have the choice to yield yourself to the flesh or to the Spirit (Romans 6:13-16), which are contrary one to the other (Galatians 5:16-17). God has not taken away your free will. God does not force you to do his will like some mindless robot, even though you are one of his blood bought sons! If you love the Lord you will keep his commandments by the power of the Spirit of Christ which is in you (John 14:15; 1:12-13; Colossians 1:27)!

The believers who love God strive to keep his commandments, even though none of them does so perfectly. If you desire to see other men saved by the grace of God, then you must sow to the Spirit to reap [bring in] this kind of treasure. If you sow to the flesh, all you will reap is corruption! This is your free will choice. Only "**the love of Christ constraineth** [compels] **us**" (2 Corinthians 5:13) not to live henceforth to ourselves, but to live "**unto him which died for them** [us], **and rose again**" (2 Corinthians 5:13-15).

"**Be not deceived; God is not mocked: for whatsoever a man soweth, that shall he also reap. For he that soweth to his flesh shall of the flesh reap corruption; but he that soweth to the Spirit shall of the Spirit reap life everlasting**" (Galatians 6:7-8).

ONE NEW MAN: JESUS CHRIST AND HIS BODY THE CHURCH

Paul told the Gentile believers to remember that in the past, that is, before the day of their salvation, they were "**in the flesh,**" "**without Christ…having no hope, and without God in the world**" (Ephesians 2:11-12). Then he continues: "**But now in Christ Jesus ye who sometimes were far off are made nigh by the blood of Christ. For he is our peace, who hath made both** [Jew and Gentile] **one, and hath broken down the middle wall of partition *between us*; Having abolished in his flesh the enmity, *even* the law of commandments *contained* in ordinances; for to make in himself of twain one new man, *so* making peace; And that he might reconcile both** [Jew and Gentile] **unto God in one body by the cross, having slain the enmity thereby**: And came and preached peace to you which were afar off, and to them that were nigh. **For through him we both have access by one Spirit unto the Father**" (Ephesians 2:13-18).

ONE ACCESS TO THE FATHER

Ephesians 2:18 says, "For through him [Jesus Christ] we both have access by one Spirit unto the Father." The Lord Jesus Christ declared, "**I am the way, the truth, and the life: no man cometh unto the Father, but by me**" (John 14:6)! He is the "**one mediator** [the only one who can bring reconciliation] **between God and men**" (1 Timothy 2:5-6).

You must come to Jesus Christ by faith believing the gospel, "**how that Christ died for our sins according to the scriptures; And that he was buried, and that he rose again the third day according to the scriptures**" (1 Corinthians 15:3-4). If you try to climb up to God some other way, you are "**a thief and a robber**" (John 10:1)!

There is a great multitude of religions today that preach false gospels for which they are accursed (Galatians 1:8-9). These false religions preach you must do some type of works as in some kind of humanistic efforts, or toil and exert yourself in order to try to attain mercy before God. These are liars and they make their followers two fold more the children of hell than themselves (Matthew 23:15)! They are "**denying the Lord that bought them, and bring upon themselves swift destruction**" (2 Peter 2:1)! They are all going against the Lord who is "**not willing that any should perish, but that all should come to repentance**" (2 Peter 3:9).

Sinner, why don't you repent of your wicked unbelief and come to Jesus Christ NOW? The Lord promised, "**him that cometh to me I will in no wise cast out**" (John 6:37). If you will receive the Lord Jesus by faith he will save you (John 1:12-13)! For the Bible says in John 1:12, "**But as many as received him, to them gave he power to become the sons of God, *even* to them that believe on his name**." God gives the assurance of this promise, saying, "**Believe on the Lord Jesus Christ, and thou shalt be saved**" (Acts 16:31).

Chapter 32

DEATH

WHY *DEATH*?

A question that I hear often is how did death enter into the world? Let us discover the answer to this question from God's word, the Holy Bible.

When a man's dead body is discovered, an autopsy would need to be performed to determine the actual cause of death. The man may have died as a result of heart failure, kidney failure, cancer, a drug overdose, a gunshot wound, stabbing, drowning, or any other of a great number of possible causes. Nonetheless, the truth of the matter is that the root cause of all deaths is "sin." Before Adam and Eve sinned in the garden of Eden there was no death in the world! But after Adam was formed from the dust of the ground, God promised death to Adam if he ate of the forbidden fruit on one tree, saying, "**But of the tree of the knowledge of good and evil, thou shalt not eat of it: for in the day that thou eatest thereof thou shalt surely die**" (Genesis 2:17).

ADAM PASSED FROM LIFE TO DEATH

When Adam and Eve ate of the fruit of the tree of good and evil, against the simple commandment of God, they passed from the life of God unto the death which is the result of sin (James 1:13-15). For the scripture says, "Let no man say when he is tempted, I am tempted of God: for God cannot be tempted with evil, neither tempteth he any man: But every man is tempted, when he is drawn away of his own lust, and enticed. Then when lust hath conceived, it bringeth forth sin: **and sin, when it is finished, bringeth forth death**" (James 1:13-15).

Physical death passed upon all men because of Adam's sin back in the garden of Eden. Romans 5:12 tells explains to us, "**Wherefore, as by one man sin entered into the world, and death by sin; and so death passed upon all men, for that all have sinned**."

God gave Adam one simple commandment, Adam broke that commandment and therefore received God's promised curse as the result of his sin, which was death (Genesis 2:17). "**Sin is the transgression of the law**" (1 John 3:4), and "**the wages of sin *is* death**" (Romans 6:23).

YOUR APPOINTMENT WITH DEATH

As a result of Adam's sin, "**it is appointed unto men once to die, but after this the judgment**" (Hebrews 9:27). The exception to this rule of physical death to all men is that all of the born again children of God in Christ, who remain alive on earth until the coming of the Lord Jesus in the rapture (compared as a thief in the night) will escape physical death. At that time the Lord "**shall change our vile body, that it may be fashioned like unto his glorious body, according to the working whereby he is able even to subdue all things unto himself**" (Philippians 3:21). Then all those who are "**in Christ**" will be caught up to meet the Lord in the air (1 Thessalonians 4:16-18).

GOD'S MERCY

The Bible tells us in Genesis 1:27 and 9:6 that God formed Adam "**in the image of God**." After disobeying God and receiving the sinful curse, Adam would have lived in his created condition forever if afterwards he would have eaten of the fruit of the tree of life (Genesis 3:22)! Nevertheless, after Adam and Eve sinned, God showed great mercy to drive them out from the garden of Eden, so that they could not eat of the tree of life and live forever in a sin cursed world. Had they eaten of the tree of life after they sinned against God, they would have been cursed to live forever in sorrow and hard labour and pain in "**this present evil world**" (Galatians 1:4)! That would have been an unthinkable tragedy!

GOD'S PLAN OF REDEMPTION

I thank God that he "**foreordained before the foundation of the world**" (1 Peter 1:20) a plan to redeem Adam and Eve and all of their offspring from the condemnation of eternal death in the lake of fire (Revelation 20:14-15; 1 Peter 1:18-21)! This he would do by offering his "**only begotten Son**" as a sacrifice for all sinful men. The gospel, or good news, that the whole world needs to hear is, "**how that Christ died for our sins according to the scriptures; And that he was buried, and that he rose again the third day according to the scriptures**" (1 Corinthians 15:3-4). God made his Son "***to be* sin for us, who knew no sin; that we might be made the righteousness of God in him**" (2 Corinthians 5:21).

After his bodily resurrection the Lord Jesus exclaimed to John the apostle, "I *am* he that liveth, and was dead; and, behold, **I am alive for evermore**, Amen; and have the keys of hell and of death" (Revelation 1:18). We read in Romans, "**Knowing that Christ being raised from the dead dieth no more; death hath no more dominion over him**" (Romans 6:9). God's Son Jesus Christ conquered death, hell, and the grave! Moreover, all of us who are "**in Christ**" are "**more than conquerors through him that loved us**" (Romans 8:37)!

When you believe on the Lord Jesus Christ alone for salvation—not trusting in any work of righteousness you have done (Titus 3:5-7) or in any religious work or observance you might do—God will save you and give you everlasting life (John 3:16; 6:40, 47). We read in the gospel of John, "**He that believeth on the Son hath everlasting life: and he that believeth not the Son shall not see life; but the wrath of God abideth on him**" (John 3:36).

THE PASSAGE FROM DEATH TO LIFE

God made reconciliation to himself possible to all men "**by the death of his Son**" (Romans 5:10), who did "**taste death for every man**" (Hebrews 2:9). The Lord Jesus Christ "**is our peace,**" who came "**that he might reconcile both** [Jew and Gentile] **unto God in one body by the cross**" (Ephesians 2:14-16). Through Jesus Christ, the "**one mediator between God and men**" (1 Timothy 2:5), all men may "**have access by one Spirit unto the Father**" (Ephesians 2:18). None of mankind has access to God except through Jesus Christ, who made this very clear when he said, "**I am the way, the truth, and the life: no man cometh unto the Father, but by me**" (John 14:6). No religion in the world can give anyone access to God by any other means!

In the very moment God gives a lost man "**repentance to the acknowledging of the truth**" (2 Timothy 2:25), and the man—of his own free will—receives and believes on the Lord Jesus Christ, he is "**born of God**" (John 1:12-13). He is "**born again**" by the Spirit of God (John 3:3-7). He becomes one of "**the children of God by faith in Christ Jesus**" (Galatians 3:26). At that moment the believer "**hath everlasting life, and shall not come into condemnation; but is passed from death unto life**" (John 5:24)! Furthermore, the Lord Jesus Christ said, "**I am the resurrection, and the life: he that believeth in me, though he were dead, yet shall he live: And whosoever liveth and believeth in me shall never die. Believest thou this?**" (John 11:25-26).

"**We know that we have passed from death unto life, because we love the brethren. He that loveth not *his* brother abideth in death**" (1 John 3:14).

Of course, when the Lord said that the believer would "**never die**," he is not referring to the death of the body, but to the soul and spirit of the man. Your body is nothing more than a temporary vessel to house your soul and spirit while living on the earth. Your body is expendable and temporary, but your soul and spirit are eternal.

PHYSICAL DEATH OF THE RIGHTEOUS

"The righteous" are all those who have been born again. They have received eternal life through "**the righteousness of God *which* is by faith of Jesus Christ**" (Romans 3:22; Philippians 3:9). According to the word of God, they know that they have eternal life (1 John 5:13), and they know that their physical bodies are only temporary: "**For which cause we faint not; but though our outward man perish, yet the inward *man* is renewed day by day. For our light affliction, which is but for a moment, worketh for us a far more exceeding *and* eternal weight of glory; While we look not at the things which are seen, but at the things which are not seen: for the things which are seen *are* temporal; but the things which are not seen *are* eternal**" (2 Corinthians 4:16-18).

Although our bodies are appointed to die and are only temporary, I believe that a born again Christian should do all that is in his power to keep himself in the very best of health, that he might glorify God and serve God in this earth with a long life and to the very best of his ability (3 John 1:2): "**What? know ye not that your body is the temple of the Holy Ghost *which is* in you, which ye have of God, and ye are not your own? For ye are bought with**

a price: therefore glorify God in your body, and in your spirit, which are God's" (1 Corinthians 6:19-20).

If a believer drinks alcohol, he may develop cirrhosis of the liver just as easily as a lost man. If a believer smokes tobacco, he may develop lung or throat cancer just as easily as a lost man. If a believer eats junk food and does not exercise his body, he is just as liable to cancer and diseases as anyone else is! A believer should avoid everything that defiles his body: "**Know ye not that ye are the temple of God, and *that* the Spirit of God dwelleth in you? If any man defile the temple of God, him shall God destroy; for the temple of God is holy, which *temple* ye are**" (1 Corinthians 3:16-17).

DEATH IS A BLESSING TO THE BELIEVER!

Ecclesiastics 7:1 says, "**A good name *is* better than precious ointment; and the day of death than the day of one's birth**."

The scriptures are very clear about what happens to the soul and spirit of the believer when his physical body dies. Let's take a look at the outstanding ones. At the death of his physical body, the believer's soul and spirit leave his body and go to be with the Lord in heaven: "**Therefore *we are* always confident, knowing that, whilst we are at home in the body, we are absent from the Lord**: **(For we walk by faith, not by sight:) We are confident, *I say*, and willing rather to be absent from the body, and to be present with the Lord**" (2 Corinthians 5:6-8).

I do not know how much plainer this could be! In other words, as long as we are residing in our physical bodies on earth we are absent from the presence of the Lord who is in heaven. When our bodies die on earth we will depart and be absent from our bodies and present with the Lord in heaven.

In the following verses the Apostle Paul says, "**to die is gain**" (Philippians 1:21). In other words, death is a blessing for a believer! Why? Because he gets to leave this old, sin cursed world and go to heaven to be with his Lord and Saviour Jesus Christ! Paul said that he desired to die and go to be with Christ, which would be far better than to stay on earth in the flesh! "**For to me to live *is* Christ, and to die *is* gain**. **But if I live in the flesh, this *is* the fruit of my labour: yet what I shall choose I wot not**. **For I am in a strait betwixt two, having a desire to depart, and to be with Christ; which is far better**: **Nevertheless to abide in the flesh *is* more needful for you**" (Philippians 1:21-24).

What does it mean to "**sleep in Jesus**" (1 Thessalonians 4:14)? When the saint dies, his body goes to sleep and is normally put to bed in the dust with a shovel. Daniel spoke of the resurrection from the dead, saying, "**And many of them that <u>sleep in the dust of the earth</u> shall awake, some to everlasting life, and some to shame *and* everlasting contempt**" (Daniel 12:2).

When the Lord Jesus comes as a thief in the night to gather his church together to meet him in the air, "**them also which sleep in Jesus will God bring with him**" (1 Thessalonians 4:14). The Lord could not bring these saints "**with him**" unless they were already with him! These saints are absent from their bodies and present with the Lord at the time of his coming. At this resurrection of the just their new and glorified bodies will rise from the dust and clothe them, then we which are alive and remain will be changed (1 Corinthians 15:51-53) and "**shall be caught up together with them in the clouds, to meet the Lord in the air: and so shall we ever be with the Lord**" (1 Thessalonians 4:16).

Paul was stoned and dragged out of the city of Lystra supposing that he had been dead (Acts 14:19). Paul probably was dead temporarily, then God raised him up again. This was probably the occasion spoken of by Paul when he wrote: "**I knew a man in Christ above fourteen years ago, (whether in the body, I cannot tell; or whether out of the body, I cannot tell: God knoweth;) such an one caught up to the third heaven. And I knew such a man, (whether in the body, or out of the body, I cannot tell: God knoweth;) How that he was caught up into paradise, and heard unspeakable words, which it is not lawful for a man to utter. Of such an one will I glory: yet of myself I will not glory, but in mine infirmities**" (2 Corinthians 12:2-5).

Paul did not know whether he was "**in the body**" or "**out of the body**." This indicates that there is little difference between the appearance of the soul and the body. During the tribulation period John said, "**I saw under the altar the souls of them that were slain for the word of God, and for the testimony which they held**" (Revelation 6:9). Their bodies had been slain on the earth and were sleeping in the dust of the earth, but their souls were under the altar in heaven speaking to God, and John could SEE them! Their souls evidently had bodily shapes, for "**white robes were given unto every one of them; and it was said unto them, that they should rest yet for a little season, until their fellowservants also and their brethren, that should be killed as they *were*, should be fulfilled**" (Revelation 6:11).

Now that we have seen that all believers go to be with the Lord at the occasion of their physical deaths, we can understand the following scriptures: "**Precious in the sight of the LORD *is* the death of his saints**" (Psalm 116:15). "**He shall redeem their soul from deceit and violence: and precious shall their blood be in his sight**" (Psalm 72:14). "**For whether we live, we live unto the Lord; and whether we die, we die unto the Lord: whether we live therefore, or die, we are the Lord's**" (Romans 14:8).

Precious in the sight of the Lord also must be the Christ honoring deaths of the many martyrs of Jesus who brought glory to him by his grace as they faced their murderers and tormentors.

The Lord takes his children home to heaven through death, sometimes even as young men, or as little children, in order that they may escape "**the evil to come**." Isaiah 57:1 tells us this: "**The righteous perisheth, and no man layeth *it* to heart: and merciful men *are* taken away, none considering that the righteous is taken away from the evil *to come*.**"

The Lord was ready to take king Hezekiah home and deliver him from the trouble ahead, but Hezekiah begged the Lord for more years. It would have been better if Hezekiah would have left this earthly life at the Lord's appointed time, for in the fifteen years granted to him Hezekiah had a son born unto him named Manasseh, who committed great evil before the Lord as king of Judah (2 Kings 21).

Men who have been a great blessing to others in this life are sometimes taken away suddenly without warning and with no apparent reason. They may be taken to be with the Lord in order to escape the evil that is coming on the earth. Thank God for the blessed hope of our Lord Jesus Christ, who is coming soon to deliver his church from "**this present evil world**" (Galatians 1:4) and from "**the wrath to come**" (1 Thessalonians 1:10)!

PHYSICAL DEATH OF THE WICKED—IT IS A LIVING DEATH!

It is very important for you to know that man is composed of three parts that make up the whole: "**spirit and soul and body**" (1 Thessalonians 5:23). At physical death the spirit and soul of man, the eternal part of man, "**himself**" (compare Luke 9:25 with Matthew 16:26), depart his dead body and go either to heaven or to hell. The Lord Jesus asked, "**For what is a man profited, if he shall gain the whole world** [while he is alive in his body], **and lose his own**

soul [when his soul goes to hell]**? or what shall a man give in exchange for his soul?**" (Matthew 16:26). There is nothing you can give in exchange for your soul! God gave his Son to die for you on the cross that your soul might be saved from hell! Jesus Christ is the only possible escape from eternal torments for every man!

The wicked are all those who are physically alive but have not been born of the Spirit. They are said to be "**dead in trespasses and sins**" (Ephesians 2:1). This means that their spirit and soul are separated from God because of sin. They are said to be "**in the congregation of the dead**" (Proverbs 21:16), and except they be "**born again**" they will go to the torments of hell for ever!

"**But she that liveth in pleasure is dead while she liveth**" (1 Timothy 5:6).

God has "**no pleasure in the death of the wicked; but that the wicked turn from his way and live**" (Ezekiel 33:11), for at their death, "**The wicked shall be turned into hell, *and* all the nations that forget God**" (Psalm 9:17).

Normally physical death is not a pleasant thing for the lost or for the saved, even though some do seem to die peacefully in their sleep. Most people die by means of a terminal illness, sickness, hospital beds and nursing home beds, or by violent means. Solomon wrote of the last days of a man's life saying that they will be evil days, because there is sorrow and pain associated with old age. Old people tremble and are bowed down, they loose their teeth, their eyes grow dim with sight, their hearing diminishes, they become fearful of heights and other things until their body dies and returns to the dust of the earth, then their "spirit shall return to God who gave it" (see Ecclesiastics 12:1-7).

"**For all flesh *is* as grass, and all the glory of man as the flower of grass. The grass withereth, and the flower thereof falleth away: But the word of the Lord endureth for ever. And this is the word which by the gospel is preached unto you**" (1 Peter 1:24-25). "**Man *that is* born of a woman *is* of few days, and full of trouble" He cometh forth like a flower, and is cut down: he fleeth also as a shadow, and continueth not. Seeing his days *are* determined, the number of his months *are* with thee** [God]**, thou hast appointed his bounds that he cannot pass**" (Job 14:1,2,5). "**Whereas ye know not what *shall be* on the morrow. For what *is* your life? It is even a vapour, that appeareth for a little time, and then vanisheth away**" (James 4:14).

The Lord told of a rich man who boasted of all his goods, who built new barns to store up all his fruits and goods. The scriptures say then he boasted: "**And I will say to my soul, Soul, thou hast much goods laid up for many years; take thine ease, eat, drink, *and* be merry. But God said unto him, *Thou* fool, this night thy soul shall be required of thee: then whose shall those things be, which thou hast provided?**" (Luke 12:19-20). Therefore, we should take heed and do as Proverbs 27:1 warns about: "**Boast not thyself of to morrow; for thou knowest not what a day may bring forth.**"

Sinner friend, you do not know when you will die. You do not know when the church will be caught up out of this world by the Lord and leave you behind to face the worst time this old world will ever see. God is commanding all men everywhere to repent of their unbelief and to believe on his Son Jesus Christ (Acts 17:30; 1 John 3:23). Come to the Lord Jesus Christ today and receive the gift of God (Romans 6:23) and "**take the water of life freely**" (Revelation 22:17). The pleasures of sin are for a season (Hebrews 11:24-26) in this brief physical life and are not worth an eternity of suffering in the lake which burneth with fire and brimstone, which is the second death (Revelation 20:14-15)!

Jesus gave the account of the deaths of the rich man, who was wicked, and Lazarus, who was righteous, saying: "**And it came to pass, that the beggar died, and was carried by the angels into Abraham's bosom** [another name for paradise (Luke 23:43)]**: the rich man also died, and was buried; And in hell he lift up his eyes, being in torments, and seeth Abraham afar off, and Lazarus in his bosom**" (Luke 16:22-23).

The wicked people of Sodom and Gomorrha are given for an example to show the terrible end of those who die outside of Jesus Christ. Jude 1:7 says, "**Even as Sodom and Gomorrha, and the cities about them in like manner, giving themselves over to fornication, and going after strange flesh, are set forth for an example, suffering the vengeance of eternal fire.**"

THE DEATH OF JESUS CHRIST

"**For God sent not his Son into the world to condemn the world; but that the world through him might be saved**" (John 3:17). "**This *is* a faithful saying, and worthy of all acceptation, that Christ Jesus came into the world to save sinners; of whom I am chief**" (1 Timothy 1:15).

Jesus Christ came into the world to suffer the death penalty for your sins! God made Jesus Christ "***to be* sin for us, who knew no sin; that we might be made the righteousness of God in him**" (2 Corinthians 5:21). Jesus died and did "**taste death for every man**" (Hebrews 2:9). He is the propitiation [the only sacrifice that is pleasing and acceptable to God to pay for your sins] "**for *the sins of* the whole world**" (1 John 2:2; Romans 3:25; 1 John 4:10). God, by means of the hands of wicked men (Psalm 17:13-14), crucified his only begotten Son for our sins! The Holy Bible says, "**Yet it pleased the LORD to bruise him; he hath put *him* to grief: when thou shalt make his soul an offering for sin, he shall see *his* seed, he shall prolong *his* days, and the pleasure of the LORD shall prosper in his hand**" (Isaiah 53:10). The Lord Jesus Christ was, "**despised and rejected of men; a man of sorrows, and acquainted with grief**" (Isaiah 53:3).

For further detailed descriptions of all the pains and agonies the Lord Jesus suffered for your sins read Isaiah chapter 53 and Psalm chapter 22. The Lord Jesus Christ suffered beyond our ability to comprehend it. His death was very painful and cruel. We read, "**He was oppressed, and he was afflicted, yet he opened not his mouth: he is brought as a lamb to the slaughter, and as a sheep before her shearers is dumb, so he openeth not his mouth. He was taken from prison and from judgment: and who shall declare his generation? for he was cut off out of the land of the living: for the transgression of my people was he stricken**" (Isaiah 53:7-8).

Jesus Christ died a horrible and shameful death so that he could redeem sinners from eternal suffering in a lake of fire and bring "**many sons unto glory**" (Hebrews 2:10). He "**endured the cross, despising the shame**," because of "**the joy that was set before him**" (Hebrews 12:2): the joy of having an everlasting kingdom of men who would be eternally redeemed by his blood (Hebrews 9:12)! In his eternal kingdom "**there shall be no more death**, neither sorrow, nor crying, neither shall there be any more pain: for the former things are passed away" (Revelation 21:4).

SECOND DEATH

Will you willfully remain in the congregation of Adam's rebellious offspring and suffer physical death only to be cast into hell where you will begin the eternal torments of the "**second death**" (Revelation 20:14), or will you repent of your wicked rebellion against your Creator and believe on the Lord Jesus Christ and be saved? Will you remain spiritually dead in Adam, or will you be made spiritually alive in Christ?

"**But now is Christ risen from the dead, *and* become the firstfruits of them that slept. For since by man** [Adam] ***came*** **death, by man** [Jesus Christ] ***came*** **also the resurrection of the dead. For as in Adam all die, even so in Christ shall all be made alive**" (1 Corinthians 15:20-22). "And they said, **Believe on the Lord Jesus Christ, and thou shalt be saved**, and thy house" (Acts 16:31).

Chapter 33

JUDGMENT SEAT OF CHRIST

After death all men will stand before the Lord Jesus Christ their Creator and give account to him (Matthew 12:36; Romans 14:12; 1 Peter 4:3-5) of their lives. The Bible says in Hebrews 9:27-28, "And as it is appointed unto men once to die, but **after this the judgment**: So Christ was once offered to bear the sins of many; and unto them that look for him shall he appear the second time without sin unto salvation." All shall be judged, whether a person is "righteous" or "wicked."

The "righteous" will "all stand before the judgment seat of Christ" (Romans 14:10) after the "resurrection of the just" (Luke 14:14), when the Lord Jesus gathers the church to meet him in the air (1 Thessalonians 4:16-18). "**For the Son of man shall come in the glory of his Father with his angels; and then he shall reward every man according to his works**" (Matthew 16:27). "**He shall call to the heavens from above, and to the earth, that he may judge his people**" (Psalm 50:4). "For we know him that hath said, Vengeance *belongeth* unto me, I will recompense, saith the Lord. And again, **The Lord shall judge his people**." (Hebrews 10:30)

The "wicked" will not be judged until a thousand years later after the resurrection of the unjust (Acts 24:15) at the "great white throne" (Revelation 20:11).

It is the Lord Jesus Christ who will judge his own blood-bought children at the first resurrection and the devil's children (John 8:44) at the second resurrection (Acts 17:30). "**For the Father judgeth no man, but hath committed all judgment unto the Son**" (John 5:22). "And **he commanded us to preach unto the people, and to testify that it is he** [the Lord Jesus Christ] **which was ordained of God *to be* the Judge of quick** [the living children of God who have been born of the Spirit (John 3:6-8)] **and dead**" (Acts 10:42).

For a Christian, knowledge about the "judgment seat of Christ" will encourage faithfulness to God in his daily walk and a desire to work together with God (1 Corinthians 3:9) to accomplish "good works" (Ephesians 2:10) in his life.

I. THE PEOPLE OF THE JUDGMENT SEAT (Romans 14:10)

Romans 14:10 says, "But why dost thou judge thy brother? or why dost thou set at nought thy brother? **for we** [born again believers] **shall all stand before the judgment seat of Christ**."

The book of Romans is a letter written by the Apostle Paul to the "saints" [born again believers] in Rome: "To all that be in Rome, beloved of God, called *to be* **saints**: Grace to you and peace from God our Father, and the Lord Jesus Christ." (Romans 1:7)

Paul is not saying that everyone who reads Romans 14:10 will stand before the judgment seat of Christ, but that **all** of those who have received God's righteousness through faith in Jesus Christ (Romans 3:22) will stand there to be judged. The ungodly "dead" will not stand at the judgment seat of Christ, but will wait in hell to be brought up from the dead a thousand years later to face God at the "great white throne" (Revelation 20:11) judgment.

"Therefore the **ungodly shall not stand in the judgment** [the judgment seat of Christ], nor sinners in **the congregation of the righteous** [when the Lord gathers all his people together, the ungodly will not be among them!]" (Psalm 1:5). "And I saw the **dead** [these are sinners who were never born again, so they are said to be "dead in trespasses and sins" (Ephesians 2:1)], small and great, stand before God; and the books were opened: and another book was opened, which is *the book* of life: and the **dead** were judged out of those things which were written in the books, according to their works." (Revelation 20:12)

II. THE PURPOSE OF THE JUDGMENT SEAT (2 Corinthians 5:10)

"For **we must all appear** before the judgment seat of Christ; **that every one may receive the things *done* in *his* body, according to that he hath done, whether *it be* good or bad**" (2 Corinthians 5:10).

Here Paul is writing, "...**unto the church of God which is at Corinth, with all the saints which are in all Achaia**" (2 Corinthians 1:1). Therefore, "we" in this verse refers to all of God's blood bought people and NOT to the ungodly.

The purpose of the judgment seat is clearly stated in 2 Corinthians 5:10. In other words, every child of God must stand before the Lord Jesus Christ and receive his righteous judgment for the things that he did in his body since he was saved by the grace of God, whether his works were good or bad! Ecclesiastics 12:13-14 says, "Let us hear the conclusion of the whole matter: Fear God, and keep his commandments: for this *is* the whole *duty* of man. **For God shall bring <u>every work</u> into judgment, with every secret thing, whether *it be* <u>good</u>, or whether *it be* <u>evil</u>.**"

"And whatsoever ye do, do *it* heartily, as to the Lord, and not unto men; Knowing that of the Lord ye shall receive **the reward of the inheritance**: for ye serve the Lord Christ. But he that doeth **wrong** shall receive for the **wrong** which he hath done: and there is no respect of persons" (Colossians 3:23-25). Therefore, "If thou sayest, Behold, we knew it not; doth not he that pondereth the heart consider *it*? and he that keepeth thy soul, doth *not* he know *it*? and **shall *not* he render to *every* man according to his works**" (Proverbs 24:12)?

There can be no doubt from the above scriptures that God will judge every work, even "every idle word" (Matthew 12:36)! It is very important to understand that this is a judgment of "works." Works has never saved anyone! We are not saved by what we do, but by what the Lord Jesus Christ did FOR US: "For I delivered unto you first of all that which I also received, how that **Christ died for our sins according to the scriptures; And that he was buried, and that he rose again the third day according to the scriptures**" (1 Corinthians 15:3-4).

Neither can "bad works" cause a child of God to "lose salvation"! We are saved by grace and not by works (Ephesians 2:8-9; Titus 3:5). "**For by grace are ye saved through faith; and that not of yourselves: *it is* the gift of God: Not of works, lest any man should boast**" (Ephesians 2:8-9). Titus 3:5 reiterates, "**Not by works of righteousness which we have done, but**

according to his mercy he saved us, by the washing of regeneration, and renewing of the Holy Ghost."

Furthermore the born again believer is not kept by works, but by God through faith: "Blessed *be* the God and Father of our Lord Jesus Christ, which **according to his abundant mercy hath begotten us again unto a lively hope by the resurrection of Jesus Christ from the dead, [t]o an inheritance incorruptible, and undefiled, and that fadeth not away, reserved in heaven for you, [w]ho are kept by the power of God through <u>faith</u> unto salvation ready to be revealed in the last time**" (1 Peter 1:3-5). The "inheritance incorruptible, and that fadeth not away, reserved in heaven for you" (1 Peter 3:4) is eternal life, "which God, that cannot lie, promised before the world began..." (Titus 1:2).

God made eternal life a promise to all the children who put their trust in the Lord Jesus Christ. He saved them by faith and he keeps them safe in Christ. We can say without doubt that a born again child of God can NEVER lose eternal life, which is a gift from God. However, a born again child of God can lose his joy, peace, happiness, health, riches, family, friends, freedom, job, and also his physical life as a result of "bad works," or "the works of the flesh" (Galatians 5:19). As we will see, he can also lose rewards in the kingdom of Christ because of his bad works. That is, he can lose his "reward of the inheritance" (Colossians 3:24) and the privilege to reign with Christ on the earth for a thousand years. He can lose these things because he denied the Lord the sacrifice of his body to be used by God for "good works" (Ephesians 2:10) in this life (Romans 12:1-2). Therefore the Lord will deny him the honors and privileges due only to his faithful servants, who will reign together with Christ over all the earth for a thousand years after his second coming (2 Timothy 2:11-12).

BAD WORKS are "the works of the flesh." Galatians 5:19-21 tells us, "Now the works of the flesh are manifest, which are *these*; Adultery [fornication with a married person], fornication [any sexual activity outside of marriage], uncleanness [indecency, obscene, filthiness], lasciviousness [looseness, irregular indulgence of animal desires, lustfulness], Idolatry [giving honour to images, statues, or representations of anything made with hands], witchcraft [sorcery, drug use, enchantments, intercourse with the devil], hatred, variance [a difference that causes controversy], emulations [rivalry accompanied with the desire of depressing another], wrath [anger], strife [arguments], seditions [violent or irregular opposition to law], heresies [false teachings against the scriptures],

Envyings, murders, drunkenness, revellings [partying and noisy feasting], and such like: of the which I tell you before, as I have also told *you* in time past, that **they which do such things shall not inherit the kingdom of God**."

As you can see a carnal believer, who walks after the flesh, "shall not inherit the kingdom of God" (Galatians 5:19-21). But this cannot possibly mean that a born again believer will not inherit eternal life, which is by grace (Titus 3:7). He received eternal life when he received and believed on the Lord Jesus Christ (John 5:24; 6:47; 1 John 5:12). For the scriptures say, "That **being justified by his grace, we should be made heirs** [those that receive an inheritance] **according to the hope of eternal life**" (Titus 3:7). "**Verily, verily, I say unto you, He that heareth my word, and believeth on him that sent me, hath everlasting life, and shall not come into condemnation; but is passed from death unto life**" (John 5:24).

If God's children submit themselves to God then they will also inherit other blessings. Good works are not possible until a man is saved by God's grace (Ephesians 2:8-9; Titus 2:11). Then grace teaches (Titus 2:12-14) and begins to work in that man (1 Corinthians 15:10; Ephesians 2:10; Philippians 2:13).

"Inherit" can mean either to possess the inheritance, or to enjoy the inheritance. Since "**the kingdom of God is not meat and drink; but righteousness, and peace, and joy in the Holy Ghost**" (Romans 14:17), it stands to reason that the believer who walks "after the flesh" (Romans 8:13) is not only pursuing evil "to his own death" (Proverbs 11:19), but is not walking in righteousness and therefore cannot **enjoy** [inherit] the peace and joy of the kingdom of God in his present life.

The Bible mentions two kinds of inheritances:

HEIRS OF ETERNAL LIFE BY GRACE

"And if children, then heirs; heirs of God [**heirs of eternal life**], and joint–heirs with Christ [**heirs of the rewards of the inheritance, which are conditioned by our works**]; if so be that we suffer with *him*, that we may be also glorified together." (Romans 8:17)

HEIRS OF REWARDS AND BLESSINGS BY WORKS

"**Blessed *are* the meek: for they shall inherit the earth**." (Matthew 5:5)

"For God *is* not unrighteous to forget **your work and labour of love**, which ye have shewed toward his name, in that **ye have ministered to the saints, and do minister**. And we desire that every one of you do shew the same diligence to the full assurance of hope unto the end: That ye be not slothful, but followers of them **who through faith and patience inherit the promises**." (Hebrews 6:10-12)

"Finally, *be ye* all of one mind, having compassion one of another, love as brethren, *be* pitiful, *be* courteous: Not rendering evil for evil, or railing for railing: but contrariwise blessing; knowing that ye are thereunto called, **that ye should inherit a blessing**." (1 Peter 3:8-9)

One aspect of the inheritance is that there also will be crowns received for good works at the judgment seat of Christ. There are five crowns which all believers can work for today to obtain at the judgment seat of Christ. They are as follows:

1. **Crown of rejoicing**, the soul winners crown:
   "For what *is* our hope, or joy, or **crown of rejoicing**? *Are* not even ye in the presence of our Lord Jesus Christ at his coming? For ye are our glory and joy." (1 Thessalonians 2:19-20)
2. **Crown of glory**, for the faithful minister:
   "And when the chief Shepherd shall appear, ye shall receive a **crown of glory** that fadeth not away." (1 Peter 5:4)
3. **Crown of life**, for the one who endures temptation:
   "Blessed *is* the man that endureth temptation: for when he is tried, he shall receive the **crown of life**, which the Lord hath promised to them that love him." (James 1:12)
4. **Incorruptible crown**, for clean living:
   "And every man that striveth for the mastery is temperate in all things. Now they *do it* to obtain a **corruptible crown**; but we an incorruptible." (1 Corinthians 9:25)
5. **Crown of righteousness**, to them who look forward to the coming of the Lord:
   "I have fought a good fight, I have finished *my* course, I have kept the faith: Henceforth there is laid up for me a **crown of righteousness**, which the Lord, the righteous judge, shall give me at that day: and not to me only, but unto all **them also that love his appearing**." (2 Timothy 4:7-8)

The crowns that believer will receive as a result of our working "together with God" (1 Corinthians 3:9) and allowing God to work in us, "both to will and to do of his good pleasure" (Philippians 2:13) will then gladly be given to the Lord Jesus Christ, who alone is worthy "**to receive power, and riches, and wisdom, and strength, and honour, and glory, and blessing**." (Revelation 5:12)

Now that we know that God is going to give rewards and crowns to his faithful children, and that ALL of his children must stand before the judgment seat of Christ, let's find out exactly what is going to happen to the child of God who loves this life more than he loves God. This is he who does not submit himself to God's righteous commandments, but rather walks after the flesh. We already KNOW that he will not be left behind at the gathering together of the church to meet the Lord in the air, for "WE MUST ALL APPEAR..." (2 Corinthians 5:10). Now let's look at our last major scripture on the judgment seat of Christ.

III. THE PRODUCT OF THE JUDGMENT SEAT (1 Corinthians 3:11-15)

Jesus Christ is the "ROCK" (1 Corinthians 10:4) and the "foundation" (1 Corinthians 3:11) upon which he is building his church. We who are saved are called "lively stones" (1 Peter 2:5), and, "his workmanship, created in Christ Jesus unto good works..." (Ephesians 2:10). Our work in this life is to serve God (Matthew 4:10), obey his commandments (Acts 5:29), and preach the gospel to every creature (Mark 16:15), because we know that God is "not willing that any should perish, but that all should come to repentance" (2 Peter 3:9); and because the gospel is "the power of God unto salvation to every one that believeth" (Romans 1:16).

At the "judgment seat of Christ" Jesus Christ will judge the **work** of all Christians "whether it be good or bad" (2 Corinthians 5:10). The judgment is said to be like passing materials through a fire to test their properties (1 Corinthians 3:12-13). The gold, silver, and precious stones represent "good works," while the "wood, hay, and stubble" represent "bad works." The materials representing "good works" will pass through the fire unharmed, but the materials representing "bad works" will be burned up. These may be things that appeared good to men, but which will fail the fiery trial at the judgment seat of Christ, for he said: "**I the LORD search the heart, *I* try the reins, even to give every man according to his ways, *and* according to the fruit of his doings**" (Jeremiah 17:10).

There are many who do things for the praise of men and not for the glory of God. They will have their reward in this life from men, but lose their reward from God in heaven (Matthew 6:2, 5, 16). What about the believer who submits to God and whose works pass through the fire: "**If any man's work abide which he hath built thereupon, he shall receive a reward**" (1 Corinthians 3:14).

What about the child of God who lived a carnal life and did not bring glory to God in his life? We already know that he must stand before the judgment seat of Christ (Romans 14:10; 2 Corinthians 5:10). However, what will happen to the backslider who wasted his life on the "flesh" and did not work together with God after he was saved? There are many who teach that such a man will be cast out of God's family and assigned to hell! "Nevertheless what saith the scripture" (Galatians 4:30)? The scriptures teach: "**If any man's work shall be burned, he shall suffer loss: but <u>he himself shall be saved</u>; yet so as by fire**" (1 Corinthians 3:15). He will be saved, because Jesus Christ is his Saviour! No one ever received eternal life from God because of works, neither could any man keep eternal life by works! Yet even though he has eternal life, he will stand ashamed before the Lord at his coming (1 John 2:28) and will lose rewards from the Lord that he could have earned by walking with and serving his Saviour in this life.

Therefore, "**Look to yourselves, that we lose not those things which we have wrought, but that we receive a full reward**" (2 John 1:8). He is coming with a reward to distribute among his faithful believers, because Jesus Christ said, "And, behold, I come quickly; and **my reward *is* with me, to give every man according as his work shall be**" (Revelation 22:12). "**Knowing therefore the terror of the Lord, we persuade men**; but we are made manifest unto God; and I trust also are made manifest in your consciences" (2 Corinthians 5:11).

Speaking to believers who "sin wilfully" after they get saved, the Bible says that they are worthy of punishment worse than being stoned to death, because they have acted with angry hatred and contempt and malice and defiance against the Holy Spirit of grace (Hebrews 10:26-31).

Speaking of those who have believed in vain and were never saved in the first place, those who say, "Let us do evil, that good may come," the Bible says that their "damnation is just" (Romans 3:8)!

Therefore, the PRODUCT of the judgment seat of Christ will be that all of God's children will have received their rewards from the hand of Jesus Christ, the righteous Judge of all the earth (Isaiah 53:12). Some will walk away empty handed, and counted as "least in the kingdom of heaven" (Matthew 5:19), while others will reign with Christ as "kings and priests" (Revelation 1:6; 5:10) in the "kingdom of heaven" (2 Timothy 2:12; Revelation 20:6). If we deny the Lord the sacrifice of our lives in this present life, then he will also deny us the privilege to reign with him during his thousand year reign on this earth (2 Timothy 2:11-12).

The "reward" (Obadiah 1:15) of the wicked will be eternal suffering in the everlasting burnings of the lake of fire. Likewise, Isaiah 33:14 asks a good question: "**The sinners in Zion are afraid; fearfulness hath surprised the hypocrites. Who among us shall dwell with the devouring fire? who among us shall dwell with everlasting burnings?**" Psalm 9:17 explains the answer, saying, "**The wicked shall be turned into hell, *and* all the nations that forget God**."

If you have not received Jesus Christ as your personal Saviour, I urge you to do it now (2 Corinthians 6:2); for you do not know what tomorrow may bring (Proverbs 27:1).

"And they said, **Believe on the Lord Jesus Christ, and thou shalt be saved**, and thy house." (Acts 16:31)

Chapter 34

THE LAST DAYS

TIME IS RUNNING OUT!

During the past two hundred years many things have accelerated exponentially. When something grows exponentially, that means its RATE of increase increases with time. For instance, let's take a certain bacterium which doubles itself every minute. If we place one of these bacteria in a jar and begin timing, then after the first minute there will be two bacteria in the jar. At the end of two minutes there will be four bacteria, and at the end of three minutes there will be eight bacteria, and so forth. If it takes sixty minutes for the bacteria to multiply and fill the jar, then at what time will the jar be exactly half-full? Think before you answer. The jar will be exactly half-full at fifty-nine minutes! It would take the bacteria fifty-nine minutes to reach the half way mark and only one more minute to completely fill the jar! This is the kind of thing we see happening in the world with respect to many different things.

SIGNS OF THE LAST DAYS

Writing to the children of God in about AD 90, John the apostle wrote, "Little children, **it is the last time**: and as ye have heard that antichrist shall come, even now are there many antichrists; whereby we know that **it is the last time**" (1 John 2:18). John referred to his days as "**the last time**."

The Apostle Peter wrote, "…**that there shall come in the last days scoffers**, walking after their own lusts, [a]nd saying, Where is the promise of his coming? [F]or since the fathers fell asleep, all things continue as *they were* from the beginning of the creation" (2 Peter 3:3-4). For example, the scoffers mentioned here do not believe the biblical account of the earth-changing catastrophe of Noah's flood. They try to explain away many scientific facts which support the catastrophe of the world wide flood in Noah's day. One of these evidences is the millions of fossils found in sedimentary rock layers all over the earth. They also scoff at the preaching of the second coming of Jesus Christ. Jude also reminds us of "**mockers in the last time, who should walk after their own ungodly lusts**" (Jude 1:17-18). The Apostle Paul's warning of perilous times reads like a daily newspaper in our days. He wrote, "**This know also, that in the last days perilous times shall come**. For men shall be lovers of their own selves, covetous, boasters, proud, blasphemers, disobedient to parents, unthankful, unholy, [w]ithout natural affection, trucebreakers, false accusers, incontinent, fierce, despisers of those that are good, [t]raitors, heady, highminded, lovers of pleasures more than lovers of God; Having a form of godliness, but denying the power thereof: from such turn away" (2 Timothy 3:1-5).

The Lord Jesus Christ warned of how the world would be before his second coming, saying that it would be "**...as it was in the days of Noe** [Noah]," and "...**also as it was in the days of Lot**" (Luke 17:26-30). In the days of Noah, we read, "And GOD saw that **the wickedness of man *was* great in the earth, and *that* every imagination of the thoughts of his heart *was* only evil continually**" (Genesis 6:5). Further, saying, "**The earth also was corrupt before God, and the earth was filled with violence**" (Genesis 6:11). Do we not see wickedness and violence abounding in our day?

In the days of Lot, "**the men of Sodom *were* wicked and sinners before the LORD exceedingly**" (Genesis 13:13). Lot invited the two angels into his house and fed them a meal. And the scripture says, "But before they lay down**, the men of the city, *even* the men of Sodom**, compassed [surrounded] the house round, both old and young, all the people from every quarter: And they called unto Lot, and said unto him, Where *are* the men which came in to thee this night? **bring them out unto us, that we may know them** [have sexual commerce with them (Genesis 4:1; Matthew 1:25)]" (Genesis 19:4-5). These were men who, "**leaving the natural use of the woman, burned in their lust one toward another; men**

with men working that which is unseemly [indecent]" (Romans 1:27). Jude says of them, "Even as Sodom and Gomorrha, and the cities about them in like manner, **giving themselves over to fornication, and going after strange flesh**, are set forth for an example, suffering the vengeance of eternal fire" (Jude 1:7). The proliferation of fornication and pornography in the secular world today is a sign that we are nearing the day of Christ.

INCREASE WAS PROPHESIED

The LORD gave two major signs of the last days to the prophet Daniel when he said, "But thou, O Daniel, shut up the words, and seal the book, *even* to **the time of the end**: **many shall run to and fro, and knowledge shall be increased**" (Daniel 12:4).

1. Increase in the speed and extent of travel—"many shall run to and fro..."

At the time of man's earliest history, a camel caravan, moving along at about eight miles per hour, was the fastest mode of transportation. Around 1600 BC, with the invention of the horse-drawn chariot, the maximum speed was about twenty miles per hour. Even the first steam locomotive, which had a top speed of about fifteen miles per hour, could not exceed the speed of the chariot. The chariot's speed was not exceeded until the late 1880s when steam locomotives began to reach speeds of one hundred miles per hour. It took the human race six thousand years to reach that speed. However, in just sixty more years, military aircraft were moving along at four hundred miles per hour. The time gap was closed when, in a mere twenty more years, aircraft were moving at four thousand miles per hour and men in space capsules were circling the earth at eighteen thousand miles per hour. If this were put on a graph that represented progress in the speed of travel, the line would leap vertically off the sheet of paper.[14]

2. Increase in knowledge—"and knowledge shall be increased."

From the time of Noah's flood to about 1800 AD, knowledge doubled but once. In other words, at the end of a five thousand-year period people knew only about twice as much as they did at the beginning of that period. In the next hundred years, however, it doubled a second time. Then in half that time—just the next fifty years—it doubled a third time. It has been estimated that by the 1990s man's knowledge was doubling every eighteen months.

For example, technology grows out of knowledge. Scientists who are able to harness the forces of nature, and to unleash those forces, contribute to knowledge and technology. Because of the rapid increase in knowledge, ninety percent of all scientists who have ever lived are living today.[15]

For centuries medical knowledge and medical research was at a standstill. A thousand years ago people were still dealing with broken bones the way they dealt with the problem four thousand years before that. But that has changed. While it is true that ninety percent of all the scientists who have ever lived are alive today, it is also true that ninety percent of all medicines and drugs used at the present time were unknown ten years ago. Amazing, isn't it? Just as amazing is the fact that seventy-five percent of all workers who will be employed in industry in the next ten years will be producing goods that have not yet been invented.[16]

The scientific breakthroughs of the twentieth century were staggering. "In 1900," writes Barbara Palmer, Science Notebook editor of the *Daily Oklahoman,* "Gregor Mendel's 19th century work on heredity was just being dusted off by scientists; by 1997, the world's first artificial chromosome was created. The Wright brothers made the first flight of a powered aircraft in 1903—in 1999 some of us were putting down deposits for the first commercial sub-orbital space flights." Almost all science was developed within the last one hundred years, and the pace of development is growing exponentially.

The first abdominal surgery was performed in 1809. Today surgeons are transplanting hearts, kidneys, and other vital organs effortlessly every single day. The first successful steamboat journey was made in 1807; the first automobiles were produced in America in 1892; the first powered flight was in 1903, and in 1969, the first man walked on the moon. The first printing press was developed in 1450; the first electric battery in 1800; the first electric motor in 1821; the first telegraph machine in 1844; the first telephone in 1876; the first light bulb in 1879; the first general radio broadcasts in 1920; the first television in 1930s; the first commercial computers in 1940s; and the first communications satellite in 1962. Most of these developments have occurred in the last 200 years. Before that, for about 5800 years the fastest means of transportation was a man riding a horse, and communication was limited either to that written on parchment or paper or to people speaking face to face. Today men who are flying at speeds exceeding the speed of sound may talk to one another anywhere on the earth or even in outer space via the wireless internet technologies! Certainly, we are living in the time of the end, when men are running to and fro, and knowledge is increased.

ADVANCES IN TECHNOLOGY

Satellite television. During the tribulation period God's two witnesses [Moses and Elijah] will be killed by the antichrist, and their dead bodies will lie in the street of Jerusalem. And we read, "**And they of the people and kindreds and tongues and nations shall see their dead bodies three days and an half**, and shall not suffer their dead bodies to be put in graves" (Revelation 11:9). How, before the advent of satellite television, would the people of the nations be able to view this event? The technology, which has been developed within the last seventy years, enables this prophecy to be fulfilled.

Microchip implant. During the reign of the Antichrist (a world dictator) he will be able to control the buying and selling of goods through some advanced technological system. Perhaps part of this system could incorporate the use of an implanted "microchip." The technology for such a system is available at the present time. I do not believe the implanted microchip itself is the "mark of the beast," but it may be used by him to control the economy of the world. The "mark of the beast" will be a MARK in the right hand or upon the forehead (Revelation 13:16; 20:4) of those people who turn from the true and living God to **worship** the antichrist (Revelation 14:9-11; 16:2; 19:20; 20:4). This mark will be an outward sign of allegiance and dependency toward man and government for survival rather than dependence toward God. The antichrist is also called "the man of sin, the son of perdition," "the beast," and "that Wicked."

AGE OF THE EARTH

The true age of the earth, according to the scriptures, is about 6000 years: not 4.5 billion years, as taught by false science! The first week of seven normal twenty-four hour days, during which God created all things, typifies [represents] seven thousand years, with one day representing a thousand years. While speaking about the second coming of Jesus Christ, the Apostle Peter wrote, "But, beloved, be not ignorant of this one thing, that **one day *is* with the Lord as a thousand years**, and a thousand years as one day" (2 Peter 3:8). Then in verse 10 he writes, "But **the day of the Lord** will come as a thief in the night; in the which the heavens shall pass away with a great noise, and the elements shall melt with fervent heat, the earth also and the works that are therein shall be burned up" (2 Peter 3:10).

The day of the Lord [the final thousand years of earth's history] will begin seven years after the sudden and unannounced rapture [catching away] of the born again believers [the church] to meet the Lord in the air (1 Thessalonians 4:16-18; 1 Corinthians 15:51-53). Then after those days of the great tribulation, the heaven shall be opened and the LORD, he who is Faithful and True, with the armies of heaven shall return to this earth on white horses. Out of the LORD's mouth goeth a sharp sword, that with it he should smite the antichrist, the kings and their armies and loyal followers who gather themselves together to make war against Christ (Revelation 19:11-21). With the conclusion of this war, then Christ shall set up his Kingdom and rule the nations.

The day of the Lord will last for a thousand years (Revelation 20:4), during which time the whole earth will be at **rest** (Isaiah 14:7). God rested on the seventh day, and the seventh and last thousand-year period on earth, called "**the day of the Lord**," will be a period of rest for the earth. This is the time when the Lord Jesus Christ will reign as King over the whole earth. Of this time the scripture says, "And in that day there shall be a root of Jesse [Jesus Christ], which shall stand for an ensign of the people; to it shall the Gentiles seek: and **his rest shall be glorious**" (Isaiah 11:10).

And when the thousand years [the day of the Lord] are expired, Satan shall be loosed out of his prison, and shall go out to deceive the nations once more to gather them together to make war against the saints and the beloved city. Then fire shall come down from God out of heaven, and devour them. And the devil that deceived them shall be cast into the lake of fire. Then God shall cast out all those wicked unbelievers whose names are not in the book of life, who over the generations have rejected the grace offered to them through the gospel of Jesus Christ. These shall be given their eternal retribution due unto them when Christ shall say unto them, "Depart from me, ye cursed, into everlasting fire, prepared for the devil and his angels" (Matthew 25:41); the eternal death. Then death and hell also shall be cast into the lake of fire. This is the second death. (Revelation 19:11-Revelation 20:15).

Afterwards, a new heaven and a new earth shall be seen: for the first heaven and the first earth shall pass away. And the tabernacle of God shall be with men, and he will dwell with them, and they shall be his people, and God himself shall be with them, *and be* their God. For the former things shall pass away and God shall make all things new (Revelation 21:1-5).

WE LIVE IN THE LAST DAYS

In the first chapter of Genesis we find that after the fourth day, on the fifth day of creation, God created the first living creatures. This is a figure [picture] of what God would do after the first four thousand years. After four thousand years from the beginning of the world, we read, "But when the fulness of the time was come, God sent forth his Son, made of a woman, made under the law, [t]o redeem them that were under the law, that we might receive the adoption of sons" (Galatians 4:4-5). Jesus Christ came into this present evil world of darkness and sin as the light and the life of the world (John 1:4; 14:6).

Many men have studied out the chronology given in the Bible and have all arrived at around four thousand years from the first Adam until the last Adam [Jesus Christ] (1 Corinthians 15:45). If the first week, during which God created all things, is representative of seven thousand years, with one day representing a thousand years (2 Peter 3:8), then the remaining time until the end of the world, after Jesus Christ came into the world, would be three thousand years, or three prophetic days. In 780 BC, Hosea the prophet wrote what the Jews would say some time after God would send the Romans to destroy their temple and their city in AD 70. Hosea wrote they would say, "Come, and let us return unto the LORD: for he hath torn [the veil of the temple was rent in two from the top to the bottom at the crucifixion of Christ (Matthew 27:51)], and he will heal us; he hath smitten [God smote the city of Jerusalem by Titus the son of the Roman governor in AD 70 (Daniel 9:26; Mark 13:2)], and he will bind us up. **After two days** [two thousand years] will he revive us: **in the third day** [last thousand years of this world] he will raise us up [Isaiah 66:8; Ezekiel 37:1-14], and we shall live in his sight [Revelation 20:4]" (Hosea 6:1-2).

"After two days" [after the two thousand year church age, of which we are nearing the end], and during the tribulation period, the Lord will meet Israel in the wilderness (Ezekiel 20:33-35; Zechariah 13:6-9; Revelation 12:14). At the end of the tribulation, the nation of Israel will be raised up (Ezekiel 37:1-14; Isaiah 66:8) to live in the sight of the Lord during the third day [third thousand year period] after the resurrection of Christ. This will be the last thousand years of this earth's history and the seventh day from the creation of the world.

We believe that "the last days" is a reference to the time-period which began at the birth of the Lord Jesus Christ about two thousand years ago. Jesus Christ came into the world to save sinners and to establish a new testament. "God, who at sundry times and in divers manners spake in time past unto the fathers by the prophets, **Hath in these last days spoken unto us by *his* Son**, whom he hath appointed heir of all things, by whom also he made the worlds" (Hebrews 1:1-2). Therefore, "the last days" are the three final days of world history which signify the final three thousand years. Today we must be very close to the end of the church age [the present "two days"]. The "last days" began at the birth of Christ and have continued for almost two thousand years now. We who are saved are "Looking for that blessed hope, and the glorious appearing of the great God and our Saviour Jesus Christ" (Titus 2:13).

THE END OF THE CHURCH AGE

The Apostle Paul, speaking of the sudden rapture [catching away] of the church from the earth to meet the Lord in the air (1 Thessalonians 4:16-18), wrote to the church of the Thessalonians, "But of the times and the seasons, brethren, ye have no need that I write unto you. **For yourselves know perfectly that the day of the Lord so cometh as a thief in the night. For when they shall say, Peace and safety; then sudden destruction cometh upon them, as travail upon a woman with child; and they shall not escape. But ye, brethren, are not in darkness, that that day should overtake you as a thief**" (1 Thessalonians 5:1-4). Men are writing entire books today listing all the signs of the times in which we now live. We who know the Lord as our Saviour and believe the Holy Bible is his infallible word believe that our Saviour Jesus Christ is coming very soon. We are praying, "Even so, come, Lord Jesus" (Revelation 22:20).

According to the scriptures, the "day of Christ [same as the "day of the Lord"]" (2 Thessalonians 2:2) will not come, "except there come a falling away first, and that man of sin be revealed, the son of perdition" (2 Thessalonians 2:3). The "falling away" from the faith has been increasing exponentially in the last two hundred years. More and more "churches" are forming congregations that do not believe even the fundamental doctrines of the Bible.

Of course the man of sin [the antichrist], cannot be revealed until the Holy Ghost, whose temple is the living church on earth [all born again believers] is "taken out of the way. And then shall that Wicked [the antichrist] be revealed" (2 Thessalonians 2:8-9). The antichrist is the one "whose coming is after the working of Satan with all power and signs and lying wonders, [a]nd with all deceivableness of unrighteousness in them that perish; because they received not the love of the truth, that they might be saved. And for this cause God shall send them strong delusion, that they should believe a lie: That they all might be damned who believed not the truth, but had pleasure in unrighteousness" (2 Thessalonians 2:9-12).

If the Holy Ghost is convicting you to repent and is drawing you to come to Jesus Christ so that you might be saved, then you need to come to him today (1 Corinthians 6:1-2)! In other words, when Jesus Christ comes down into earth's atmosphere into the clouds, he will call all his people up to meet him in the air (1 Thessalonians 4:16-18). Only then will the antichrist, that Wicked, be revealed. Then shall come the "the day of Christ" (2 Thessalonians 2:2; Phil. 1:10; 2:16). The day of Christ is also called "the day of the Lord Jesus" (1 Corinthians 5:5; 2 Corinthians 1:14) and "the day of the Lord" (1 Thessalonians 5:2; 2 Peter 3:10).

CONCLUSION

The entire history of the world, from its creation (Genesis 1:1) to its complete destruction by fire (2 Peter 3:9), is revealed through the history and the prophecies in the Holy Bible. "For thus saith the LORD that created the heavens; God himself that formed the earth and made it; he hath established it, he created it not in vain, he formed it to be inhabited: I *am* the LORD; and *there is* none else" (Isaiah 45:18). God created the earth and man on the earth to work out his great plan of redemption and salvation so that he might have an eternal kingdom of men to enjoy his presence and pleasures forevermore (Psalm 16:11). However, most men will waste their lives enjoying "the pleasures of sin for a season" (Hebrews 11:25) and end up in "outer darkness" (Matthew 8:12; 22:13; 25:30; Jude 1:13) suffering "the vengeance of eternal fire" (Jude 1:7))! They chose the broad way "that leadeth to destruction" rather than the narrow way, "which leadeth unto life" (Matthew 7:13-14). This is certainly not God's will for you (2 Peter 3:9)!

At this present time God is calling men to be saved through obedience to the gospel (Romans 10:16; 2 Thessalonians 2:14). God is now visiting the Gentiles, "to take out of them a people for his name" (Acts 15:14). Tragically, the vast majority of men have been blinded to "the light of the glorious gospel of Christ, who is the image of God" (2 Corinthians 4:3-4). Satan, through his spiritually blinded children—we were all born spiritually blind—uses false religious philosophy (Colossians 2:8) and science (1 Timothy 6:20) to blind "the minds of them which believe not, lest the light of the glorious gospel of Christ, who is the image of God, should shine unto them" (2 Corinthians 4:4). Instead of finding the truth, they choose to be "turned unto fables" (2 Timothy 4:4). Instead of believing the absolute, unchanging truth of the Holy Bible, men are trusting the relative truths [lies] of other men [Darwin's false theory of evolution, for example]. The Bible warns, "But evil men and seducers shall wax worse and worse, deceiving, and being deceived" (2 Timothy 3:13). These are the blind leading the blind, who will both fall into the horrible pit of hell (Luke 6:39) if they die without Jesus Christ.

Sinner, you can be assured that the Lord, who made all things for his pleasure (Revelation 4:11), has "no pleasure in the death of the wicked; but that the wicked turn from his way and live" (Ezekiel 33:11). The Lord is "not willing that any should perish, but that all should come to repentance" (2 Peter 3:9). Therefore God "now commandeth all men every where to repent" (Acts 17:30), and "That we should believe on the name of his Son Jesus Christ, and love one another, as he gave us commandment" (1 John 3:23). God has given every man a free will to choose what he will do with his only begotten Son, the Lord Jesus Christ. Men will either receive him and be saved (John 1:12-13), or they will reject him, and then be condemned by the word of God (John 12:48) at the great white throne judgment, where they will be cast into the lake of fire, which is the second death (Revelation 14:11; 20:11-15).

We are no doubt living in "the last days." More specifically, we are living at the end of the two day [two thousand year] period we call the "church age." The third and final day [thousand year period] is about to begin. Very soon [no man knows the day nor the hour (Matthew 25:13)], like a thief in the night, the Lord Jesus Christ will come, the church age will be over, and the tribulation period will begin with a false peace (Daniel 8:25). The world will then enter the worst time that it has ever or will ever see (Mark 13:19)!

After the rapture, God will seal the damnation of the men who resisted the call of the Holy Ghost by the gospel (1 Corinthians 15:3-4). They will be damned because they refused to repent (2 Thessalonians 2:9-12). Even after they see the terrible events during the tribulation, we can read about them in the book of Revelation. "And the rest of the men which were not killed by these plagues yet repented not of the works of their hands, that they should not worship devils, and idols of gold, and silver, and brass, and stone, and of wood: which neither can see, nor hear, nor walk: **Neither repented they of their murders, nor of their sorceries, nor of their fornication, nor of their thefts**" (Revelation 9:20-21).

If you do not repent when God calls you by his word and Spirit, then, after the rapture, you will not be able to repent. It may be now or never for some of you reading this sermon. I hope and pray that you will be saved from the everlasting torments of the damned in hell. Repent before you pass the deadline.

The best book in the Holy Bible to read for salvation is the gospel of John. It is absolutely true. If you will seek God with all your heart, he will be found of you (Jeremiah 29:13)!

Endnotes

[1] Lloyd-Jones, David M. *Romans: Exposition of Chapter 6 : The New Man (Romans Series) (Romans (Banner of Truth))*. Grand Rapid Michaigan, USA: Zondevan House, August, 1981. Print. Pages 208-209.

[2] Fox, E. "Homosexual Lifespan." *Homosexual Lifespan*. N.p., n.d. Web. 10 Sept. 2012. <http://theroadtoemmaus.org/RdLb/22SxSo/PnSx/HSx/hosx_lifspn.htm>.

[3] Mason, Colin, and Steven Mosher. "Earth Day: Abortion Has Killed 1-2Billion Worldwide in 50 Years." *Earth Day: Abortion Has Killed 1-2 Billion Worldwide in 50 Years*. Www.LifeNews.com, 21 Apr. 2011. Web. 17 Sept. 2012. <http://www.lifenews.com/2011/04/21/earth-day-abortion-has-killed-1-2-billion-worldwide-in-50-years/>.

[4] "Dawkins Interview By Gordy Slack 2005 Sec Pdf Free Ebook Download from Www.godslasteraar.org." *EbookBrowse.com*. N.p., 2010. Web. 10 Sept. 2012. <http://ebookbrowse.com/dawkins-interview-by-gordy-slack-2005-sec-pdf-d340662858>.

[5] Ibid

[6] Ibid

[7] Ibid

[8] Ibid

[9] Jones, Bob. *Chapel Sayings of Dr. Bob Jones Sr*. Greenville, South Carolina: Bob Jones University. ISBN # 2800840052621. Print.

[10] Henry, Matthew. "Acts 13:22." *SwordSearcher*. Computer software. Vers. 6.0.2.5. 1995-2010 StudyLamp Software LLC. Web. 11 Sept. 2012.

[11] Doherty, Shawn. "Rates of STDs among Teens Reach Epidemic Levels." *Madison.com*. The Capital Times, 06 Jan. 2010. Web. 10 Sept. 2012. <http://host.madison.com/ct/news/local/health_med_fit/article_96d0ee57-e3dc-59d7-a5ec-e5cbc5b71ffc.html>.

[12] Sekulow, Jay. "Jay Sekulow: 39 Years, 54 Million Babies â€“ The March Against Roe v. Wade - Faith & Justice." *Faith & Justice*. N.p., 28 Aug. 2012. Web. 10 Sept. 2012. <http://blog.beliefnet.com/faithandjustice/2012/01/jay-sekulow-39-years-54-million-babies-the-march-against-roe-v-wade.html>.

[13] "Belial." *The New Strong's Exhaustive Concordance of the Holy Bible*. Nashville, Camden, Kansas City.

USA.: Thomas Nelson Publishers, 1984. Print. Page 122.

[14] Toffler, Alvin. *Future Shock.* Toronto: Bantam, 1971. Print. Page 26.

[15] Toffler, Alvin. *Future Shock.* Toronto: Bantam, 1971. Print. Page 27.

[16] Beshore, F. Kenton. *The Millennium, the Apocalypse, and Armageddon.* Springfield, Missouri: 21st Century Press, 2001. Print. Page 433.

If you have any questions, concerns, if you notice any mistakes inside this book, or if you desire to inquire about additional resources by *Go Soulwinning Ministries*, please visit:

www.GoSoulwinning.com
or
www.GoSoulwinningPublishing.com

www.ingramcontent.com/pod-product-compliance
Lightning Source LLC
Chambersburg PA
CBHW070118100426
42744CB00010B/1855

* 9 7 8 0 6 1 5 7 9 6 9 2 5 *